HUMAN RESOURCE DEVELOPMENT REVIEW

HUMAN RESOURCE DEVELOPMENT REVIEW

Research and Implications

Darlene Russ-Eft
Hallie Preskill
Catherine Sleezer

SAGE Publications
International Educational and Professional Publisher
Thousand Oaks London New Delhi

For information address:

SAGE Publications, Inc.
2455 Teller Road
Thousand Oaks, California 91320
E-mail: order@sagepub.com

SAGE Publications Ltd.
6 Bonhill Street
London EC2A 4PU
United Kingdom

SAGE Publications India Pvt. Ltd.
M-32 Market
Greater Kailash I
New Delhi 110 048 India

Printed in the United States of America

Library of Congress Cataloging-in-Publication Data

Main entry under title:

Human resource development review: Research and implications /
   authors, Darlene Russ-Eft, Hallie Preskill, and Catherine Sleezer.
       p.   cm.
   Includes bibliographical references and index.
   ISBN 0-7619-0560-X (cloth: acid-free paper). — ISBN
0-7619-0561-8 (pbk. : acid-free paper)
       1. Organizational learning—Research—United States.
   2. Organizational effectiveness—Research—United States.
   3. Manpower policy—Research—United States. I. Russ-Eft, Darlene F.
   II. Preskill, Hallie S. III. Sleezer, Catherine.
   HD58.H86   1996
   658.3′124—dc20   96-25363

97 98 99 00 01 02 03 10 9 8 7 6 5 4 3 2 1

Acquiring Editor:	C. Deborah Laughton
Editorial Assistant:	Eileen Carr
Production Editor:	Astrid Virding
Production Assistant:	Karen Wiley
Typesetter/Designer:	Christina Hill
Indexer:	Teri Greenberg
Cover Designer:	Lesa Valdez
Print Buyer:	Anna Chin

CONTENTS

Conclusion   **391**

Author Index   **399**

Subject Index   **409**

About the Authors   **423**

List of Contributors   **425**

ACKNOWLEDGMENTS

Writing this book was both a learning and performance effort—and it involved individual, team, and organizational contributions. We would like to express our appreciation to those who assisted in this effort. First, we thank Ed Schroer and Laurie Bassi of the American Society for Training and Development (ASTD) and the current and past members of the ASTD Research Committee for their continuing support: Doris Adams, Theodore Bloomer, Nancy Dixon, John Gumpert, Gary McLean, Victoria Marsick, Joseph Martocchio, Karen Medsker, Jack Phillips, William Rothwell, Richard Swanson, Jon Werner, and Meena Wilson. Second, we thank C. Deborah Laughton of Sage for her support, encouragement, and suggestions. We also appreciate the support from our respective institutions: Zenger Miller, University of New Mexico, and Oklahoma State University.

Various individuals made significant contributions to this book. Lilanthi Ravishankar of Zenger Miller reviewed and commented on the section written by Darlene Russ-Eft. Michael Kroth of the University of New Mexico provided research, editing, and administrative support to Hallie Preskill. Wilda Reedy provided typing support, and Jill Hough, a doctoral student at Oklahoma State University and an independent HRD consultant, provided research, editing, and administrative support to Catherine Sleezer. Jan Stiles reviewed the book for continuity and structure and provided editorial revision.

Karen Kelley from Zenger Miller deserves special thanks. She persevered in contacting editors and authors for permissions and provided overall administrative support for the entire project.

Also, we would like to thank each of the publishers and authors of the research articles. The publishers granted us permission to reprint the articles that have appeared in their entirety, with only minor adjustments to style made for consistency. The researchers completed and published the various studies and have been kind enough to allow their work to be reprinted. Without them this book would not have been possible.

Finally, we acknowledge important support and encouragement from our families, friends, and work colleagues.

INTRODUCTION

Rationale and Standards

This book is the first step in an effort initiated by the Research Committee of the American Society of Training and Development to begin a thorough review of the research in human resource development. Our purpose in writing this particular book is to inform, stimulate, and influence research and practice in human resource development (HRD). To do that, we will present and review exemplary studies, discuss the practical implications of this research, and identify themes for future practice and research.

Specifically, our goals for the book are:

♦ To identify major areas of research and assemble exemplary research conducted within each selected area during the five years from 1990 to 1995

♦ To encourage research into issues related to HRD by stimulating wider dissemination of research findings

♦ To promote a broader understanding of research design and methodology

♦ To stimulate new thinking regarding research approaches

♦ To encourage practitioners to make decisions informed by research findings that involve exemplary content and instructional methodology

Journals and Databases Reviewed

Reviewing the literature on HRD research or on any field is a daunting task. To make the task more manageable for both reviewers and readers, we segmented the field into categories that reflect central areas or issues and allow readers to more easily select topics and issues of interest to them.

Two major methods provide a basis for such segmentation:

1. Inductive: What literature exists? How can it be classified?
2. Deductive: What topics do experts and potential users believe are important?

Although each method promises certain advantages, we combined the two to realize the following benefits:

- Each article covers the available literature
- Each article covers topics that experts consider important
- The articles contribute to both HRD practice and research

Table 1 presents the HRD topic areas used in selecting research articles for this book. We identified these topics through a search of recent literature and with recommendations from the following groups:

- American Educational Research Association: Special Interest Group in Training in Business and Industry
- American Society for Training and Development: Professor's Network
- American Society for Training and Development: Research Committee
- *Human Resource Development Quarterly:* Editorial Board

HRD Areas for Selecting Research Articles

Here are the sources that we used to identify the research articles. The first source of information was the available literature. The following journals (listed in alphabetical order) were reviewed.

Academy of Management Journal
Adult Education Quarterly
American Psychologist
Educational Evaluation and Policy Analysis

TABLE 0.1 Learning and Performance

Individual Learning and Performance	Team Learning and Performance	Organizational Learning and Performance
Learning theories	Team learning	Organizational learning
Instructional and delivery methods	Team performance	The learning organization
Role of technology	Team building	Workplace learning
Mental models	Team development	Organizational culture
Competencies Expertise		Change management

Evaluation Practice
Evaluation and Program Planning
Evaluation Review
Group and Organization Studies
Human Resource Development Quarterly
Journal of Applied Psychology
Journal for Applied Behavioral Science
Journal of Management Education
Journal of Management Studies
Management Communication Quarterly
Management Learning
Organization Science
Performance Improvement Quarterly
Psychological Science

Relevant conferences provided the second source of information on potential articles. We reviewed the agendas of the annual meetings for the following organizations (listed alphabetically):

Academy of Human Resource Development

American Educational Research Association (specifically, Special Interest Group in Training in Business and Industry)

American Psychological Association (specifically, Industrial and Organizational Psychology)

American Psychological Society (specifically, Industrial and Organizational Psychology)

American Society for Training and Development

National Association for Performance and Instruction

Database and literature review sources made up the third source of information. These included:

ABI Inform
ASTD Index of Literature
Business Periodical Index
Education Research Information Center (ERIC)
Human Resources Yearbook (published by Prentice Hall)
Organizational Development Network
PsychoInfo

The final source of information on potential articles was the various user or contributor groups that have already been mentioned. By contacting these groups, we verified that the topics and articles selected addressed the needs and interests of HRD practitioners and scholars.

Approach

Our approach to this book was comprehensive in that as we covered the research areas related to HRD theory and practice on individual, team, and organizational learning and performance. At the same time, it was detailed insofar as we selected examples of exemplary research.

We began by dividing the topics among the three authors: individual learning and performance to Darlene Russ-Eft, team learning and performance to Catherine Sleezer, and organizational learning and performance to Hallie Preskill. Each author identified 7 to 10 articles for possible inclusion.

The articles we have selected represent a broad range of issues confronting HRD practitioners and researchers in the study of learning and performance at the individual, team, and organizational levels. Further, the articles also represent a broad range of research methods available with which to address HRD issues and questions. We have selected articles that display the following characteristics:

- A well-grounded theoretical framework
- An appropriate mode of inquiry
- A systematic approach to research
- A well-executed methodology
- A well-grounded analysis and interpretation
- An original contribution to the field
- A clear and well-organized written presentation

♦ An appeal to a large audience

The articles selected by each author were shared, discussed, and often debated with the other authors. We focused on the importance and range of the issues raised in the articles and on the variety of research methods displayed. We tried to highlight articles from a variety of journals and researchers. Articles written by any of the three authors of this book were eliminated. In addition, we restricted the inclusion of any researcher to one article for the entire book.

We confined our final selection to articles published in the years 1990 to 1995, choosing five articles for each part, each article in a separate chapter. Limiting the number of articles ensured that the resulting compilation and review would be of reasonable length. Focusing on the last 5 years meant that readers would get an overview of the most recent research literature. To recognize important research that precedes the past 5 years and other timely studies, we listed additional resources. By limiting what we included in each part of the book, we ensured that each category would receive approximately the same level of coverage and acknowledged the challenge of not being able to include all of the quality studies on these topics.

At the beginning of each part, we define the type of learning under discussion, introduce the research, and provide background information on how this research contributes to the field. Each introduction provides an overview of issues raised by the studies and outlines the methods used in the research. The sections that follow each article review the implications for HRD practice, research design, and future inquiry. As you read each study, we encourage you to identify implications and then compare your thoughts with ours.

How Practitioners Can Use This Book

As a practitioner, you might begin by reviewing the introduction to each section of this book and the passages detailing HRD implications. This will help you identify the chapters of greatest interest to you.

When you read any chapter, we recommend that you use two specific tools to facilitate understanding and evaluation: the criteria listed on pages xvi and xvii and the practical questions listed on page 55. Both of these tools will help you determine if there are any design flaws and indicate whether the research is of practical significance to you.

We also recommend that as an HRD practitioner you consider your practices in light of the research results. For example, the consistent message about the disconnects between (a) employee satisfaction with training, (b) self-assessments of performance, and (c) actual output should raise a red flag for practitioners who are funding efforts using only the first two measures.

After reviewing one or more of these chapters, you can benefit by saving the chapters and the two tools just mentioned. The tools can be used for critically reviewing research articles in the future. The chapters themselves can provide models for that review.

Finally, for practitioners who want to stay on the leading edge of research, we recommend reviewing the sections labeled *Suggestions for Future Inquiry*. Every month or every quarter, a quick scan of the research journals will provide information on studies that address some of the issues raised here.

How Researchers Can Use This Book

As part of your research, you will benefit from a review of all the chapters and subsequent sections of this book that focus on the implications for research design and methods. As a researcher, you can build on the content of these studies. Furthermore, the methodological limitations provide opportunities for future research.

The sections titled *Suggestions for Future Inquiry* also identify some of our thinking about the next steps that are needed. Issues pointed out in these sections are of current concern and can be addressed in planned research studies.

The field of HRD research can benefit from the systematic application of standards for good research. We recommend the criteria listed on page xvi and the questions appearing on page xiv as a beginning for the development of such standards.

Finally, we encourage you to use the model shown in Figure 16.3 as a guide to investigating the complex relationships existing in HRD research. You may want to test this model or use it to evaluate HRD interventions in the future.

P AR T

INDIVIDUAL
LEARNING AND
PERFORMANCE

This part focuses on individual learning and performance, which forms the basic starting point for all learning and performance within organizations, whether that learning is applicable to individuals, teams, or the organization itself. When teams and organizations disband or disappear, any learning that has occurred can still remain with the individuals who were members of those teams or organizations.

This introduction begins with a definition of individual learning. This definition will provide a context for the discussion of the chapters that follow.

Definition of Individual Learning

Hilgard and Bower (1966) proposed the following definition:

> Learning is the process by which an activity originates or is changed through reacting to an encountered situation, provided that the characteristics of the change in activity cannot be explained on the basis of native response tendencies, maturation, or temporary states of the organism (e.g., fatigue, drugs, etc.). (p. 2)

1

This definition implies that the outcomes of the learning process can be observed but that the process itself is unobservable. McGeoch (1946) stated,

> Learning, as we measure it, is a change in performance as a function of practice. In most cases, if not in all, this change has a direction which satisfies the current motivating conditions of the individual. (pp. 3-4)

Learning and performance do not form a single unified process but involve multiple processes. "A skilled response . . . means one in which receptor-effector feedback processes are highly organized, both spatially and temporally. The central problem for the study of skill learning is how such organizations or patterning comes about" (Fitts, 1964, p. 244).

Even Ebbinghaus (1885/1964) noted that multiple processes were involved, " . . . including Learning, Retention, Association and Reproduction" (p. xiii).

Individual Learning Processes as a Focus for the Articles

The articles in the following five chapters highlight certain processes that are important for individual learning. When stimuli are presented, they are perceived by individuals, as they in turn respond or react. Such stimuli include the content of training and development efforts. The responses may be specific performance. These stimuli and responses are encoded by the individual; we can view such encoding as some form of recording of the stimuli and responses. With repetition and reinforcement, such encoding becomes more stable and connections are made with previous learning and experience. The encoding and the associated connections may yield a mental model or a neural net of the situation. (Some theories propose that memory consists of sets of nodes with links connecting those nodes.) Reproduction and generalization, which result in performance, call on those encoded connections, mental models, or neural nets to yield an appropriate response. Furthermore, with repeated reproduction and generalization, the individual develops new and different neural nets or mental models that can result in improved performance.

The articles included in this part highlight certain important processes involved in learning and skilled performance. The Baldwin article (Chapter 1) focuses on behavior modeling training and emphasizes the importance of variety in behavioral models to improve encoding and retrieval processes. Presumably, variety in these behavioral

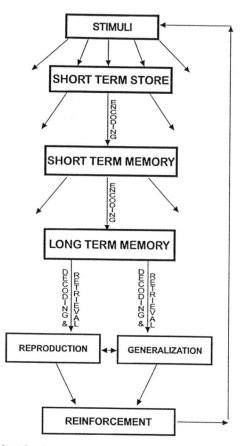

Figure I.a. Individual Learning Process

models facilitates the development of richer and more elaborate mental models. The individual can better retrieve and use this mental model when more paths exist to reach the model. The goal of accelerated learning methods, as described by Swets and Bjork (Chapter 2), is also to aid learners in the encoding and retrieving of information. Bretz and Thompsett (Chapter 3) test whether such aids lead to performance differences. The Rowe and Cooke article (Chapter 4) points toward the importance of mental models in developing expertise. The development of such mental models comes through behavioral reproduction and generalization, leading to reinforcement. Finally, Sternberg, Wagner, Williams, and Horvath (Chapter 5) discuss the development of tacit knowledge in contrast to formal academic knowledge. This last article leaves us with questions about the development of expertise and high performance.

Overview of the Articles

The Baldwin article (Chapter 1) examines the effectiveness of alternative methods for presenting behavior modeling training. Behavior modeling involves the use of models, in person or on video, that demonstrate the behaviors to be learned. Processes that facilitate the learning include attention, retention, motor reproduction, and motivation (Bandura, 1977). According to social learning theory, the learner must first pay attention to the behavior of the model. Next, the learner must use retention processes to encode and store the behavioral information. Then the learner must perform the behavior (motor reproduction). Finally, reinforcement or other motivational processes must occur for the learner to continue using the behavior.

Baldwin questioned whether variability of the behavioral model would enhance or reduce individual learning. Variability was introduced through the use of multiple models and through the use of positive and negative models. Controversy surrounds the use of negative or nonexemplary models because negative models might provide less information than positive models and might hinder learning by distracting the learner from what is important. On the other hand, a combination of positive and negative models might enhance learning and generalization by enabling observers to tests hypotheses about a concept (Bruner, Goodnow, & Austin, 1956) or by facilitating the unlearning of previously existing behavior (Lewin, 1951; Russell, Wexley, & Hunter, 1984).

The author also examined the outcomes of training using multiple methods: reaction, learning, retention, reproduction, and generalization. This study showed that various manipulations and conditions have different effects on different outcomes. Human resource development professionals may want to take heed. What seems to have no effect on trainee reactions, for example, may yield important outcomes in generalization.

An important part of the Baldwin study involved the research method. The study used an experimental design that crossed model variability (one versus two scenarios) with model competence variability (a positive model only versus a positive and negative model). Note that the researcher maintained the same number of trainees in each condition (with 18 trainees in each), controlled for the number of video models displayed (with all groups viewing four models), matched the time of the video to ensure equal exposure across conditions, and kept the focal model constant across the scenarios. Although the trainees were business students, they were receiving training in a management skill, assertive communication, which was perceived as important for future employment.

In terms of training outcomes, Baldwin examined not only trainee reactions, but also learning (as measured by a 12-item test on the six learning points), retention (using the same 12-item test administered four weeks later), and behavioral reproduction (using role play). The most creative measure, however, focused on behavioral generalization. Following the retention testing, trainees faced a situation in which they could apply their assertiveness communication skills (in this case, another student trying to raise money through the sale of expensive business publications). Given the experimental design, Baldwin employed multiple analysis of variance to test for overall effects. This was followed by separate univariate analyses of variance and mean comparisons to test differences among the groups on specific outcome measures.

An experimental design, such as that used by Baldwin, helps to define learning and performance outcomes yielded within a controlled environment. The Swets and Bjork article, which appears next, points toward the usefulness of experimental research for making practical decisions regarding training.

Focused on enhancing human performance, the Swets and Bjork article (Chapter 2) presents an overview of work done by a committee from the National Research Council. This research was undertaken on behalf of the United States Army because of its critical need to effectively train individual soldiers. The committee reviewed various "New Age" techniques used for training and self-help. These techniques included sleep learning, accelerated learning, methods for improving motor skills, altered mental states, stress management, influence strategies, group cohesion, and parapsychology. In most cases, the committee found little scientific evidence that such techniques led to enhanced performance.

For example, one such method, sleep learning, was described as the auditory presentation of verbal materials during sleep. "Scientific" evidence indicated no benefit from learning occurring during verified sleep (as confirmed by electrical recordings of brain activity). More recent evidence from studies of "implicit memory" or "learning without awareness" has shown that the testing procedures for sleep learning may have been insensitive to the effects of "learning without awareness." More important, from a cost-benefit perspective, shortened training from the use of sleep learning methods could outweigh the costs of disrupted sleep, especially when one must train military troops within a short period of time. As a consequence, the National Research Council recommended that there be further investigation into sleep learning.

Another example from this study is that of accelerated learning, or Suggestive Accelerative Learning and Teaching Techniques (SALTT). This technique uses a combination of physical and mental relaxation, guided imagery, presentation phases, and active and passive reviews (generally accompanied by music). The committee concluded that claims for enhanced learning and performance were unwarranted. Nevertheless, it recommended that research examine alternative training methods to determine the specific components that may be effective.

The committee demonstrated the importance of examining all of the evidence concerning purported training methods. This evidence was not simply limited to testimonials but also included rigorous scientific studies. In addition, the committee considered cost-benefit implications.

In this case, however, committee members did not undertake primary research on all the methods. Instead, they reviewed previous research to identify which "New Age" training methods seemed promising enough to warrant use by the military. These researchers considered scientific justification from both basic research studies and field tests to assess operational potential and likely cost-effectiveness. In addition, they examined the relationship between proposed methods and existing theory to determine if certain aspects of a method might prove useful.

The Bretz and Thompsett article (Chapter 3) follows up the presentation by Swets and Bjork. Bretz and Thompsett focused on what they termed *integrative learning* (which Swets and Bjork termed *accelerated learning*). The study compared two methods for training in manufacturing resource planning: (a) the traditional method and (b) an integrative learning method. The traditional method used a lecture-based delivery but incorporated examples and allowed trainees to ask questions at any time. The integrative learning method employed relaxation; presentation; an advanced method of organization that provided a framework for the material; reinforcement through discussions, games, stories, and poetry; student presentation of material; and review using a story accompanied by baroque music.

The researchers raised issues concerning the adoption of certain training methods within organizations. Indeed, they cited Goldstein (1986, 1991) in claiming that training methods are seen as fads and that rigorous evaluation of training programs is almost nonexistent. In many cases, organizations argue that evaluating training is "too expensive." As a result, many organizations adopt certain training methods— the integrative learning method is one example—based on faith and the fact that other organizations also use them. The results of the study showed that the use of the integrative method yielded the same *learning* results as did the traditional lecture method. If an organization is worried about cost-effectiveness, then such results argue against using the integrative method because it requires small class sizes and more instructor intervention.

Another argument for the use of certain training methods is based on the favorable reactions of participants. If we follow the logic set forth by Kirkpatrick (1959a, b; 1960a, b), favorable reactions are a precursor to learning, generalization, and transfer. Note that in the Bretz and Thompsett study, the correlation between reaction and learning was small and nonsignificant. This means that favorable reactions led to both high and low levels of learning and that unfavorable reactions led to both high and low levels of learning. Such findings contradict Kirkpatrick's assertion but confirm Dixon's findings (1990). This means that rigorous evaluation cannot depend solely on reactions to training, unless that is viewed as the only desired outcome of training.

The research method used by Bretz and Thomsett is somewhat similar to that used by Baldwin in that a rigorous research design was applied. The Solomon four-group design enabled the researchers to (a) test the effects of the training method (traditional versus integrative), (b) ensure that few differences existed between groups at the time of pretesting, and (c) determine if the pretest had any effect on reaction or learning. The Baldwin study, in contrast, failed to control for any pretest differences among the groups. Although the Bretz and Thompsett study was undertaken within an organizational setting, the researchers were able to assign trainees randomly to the various conditions, with the exception of a no-training control group. Note that unequal group sizes resulted because of differing class size requirements for the two methods, differences in the physical sizes of classrooms, and some scheduling changes. In contrast, in the Baldwin study the researcher ensured equal group sizes.

Bretz and Thomsett did, however, gather information to control for pretraining differences in (a) general cognitive ability, using the Wonderlic Personnel Test (Wonderlic, 1983); (b) individual preferences for types of learning, using the Productivity Environmental Preference Survey (Price, Dunn, & Dunn, 1991); (c) affective state during training, using the Watson, Clark, and Tellegren (1988) Positive and Negative Affectivity Scale; and (d) subjective well-being, using the G.M. Faces scale (Kunin, 1955). In terms of outcomes, the researchers measured reaction to the training (using a modified G.M. Faces scale) and learning (using a knowledge test focused on the knowledge addressed in the training program). After creating this knowledge test, researchers administered it to experts and novices to determine if the test actually discriminated between these groups. Then the researchers examined learning and reaction outcomes by testing gain scores and by examining the results of regression analyses (to determine the best predictors of learning and reaction).

The rigorous experimental designs employed in some studies are useful for answering certain research questions. Such questions typically seek predictions of cause-and-effect relationships or significant differences between treatment groups. In some cases, however, a mixed method combining qualitative and quantitative approaches provides the greatest insights.

The Rowe and Cooke article (Chapter 4) is an example of research using a mixed method. This study addresses issues related to the use of mental models in training. Learning theory proposes that humans interacting with equipment, systems, or processes create mental models or internal mental representations. Such mental models contain knowledge of the basic components, the possible states of those components, and the relationships among those components (Hegarty, 1991). The Rowe and Cooke study showed that the concept of mental models could be measured. Further, the researchers clearly distinguished between experts and novices in the types of mental models people used. Finally, the researchers compared different approaches to measuring mental models in terms of their ability to predict troubleshooting performance.

Rowe and Cooke used a case study approach, combining qualitative and quantitative methods to examine whether mental models are predictive of behavior. The subjects for this particular study were selected because of their previous training and experience in an airborne electronic troubleshooting career with the U.S. Air Force. They were also selected to represent a wide range of experience, with some having only 2 months of experience and others having more than 10 years of experience.

The measurement of troubleshooting performance was obtained from protocols verbalized by subjects, along with statements as to the results of these actions. As with the Baldwin study and the Bretz and Thompsett study, experts assigned scores to these protocols and the researchers determined the interrater reliability of these scores. Four technicians were identified as being experts; these high performers obtained performance scores that were at least one standard deviation above the mean of all technicians. The researchers then examined four different procedures for measuring mental models: (a) the laddering interview, (b) relatedness ratings, (c) diagramming, and (d) think-aloud and verbal troubleshooting. Correlations were then used to examine the level of agreement among the four experts using each mental measurement method. In addition, correlations indicated whether a relationship existed between the mental models and the troubleshooting performance.

Mental models are internal representations of some external relationships that are used in solving practical problems. The Sternberg, Wagner, Williams, and Horvath article (Chapter 5) used this theory to distinguish between (a) academic knowledge, learning, and performance and (b) practical intelligence, knowledge, learning, and performance. Formal academic knowledge (also considered fluid ability) requires an ability to deal with testing situations, intelligence tests, and aptitude tests. In contrast, tacit knowledge (or practical learning and performance) is (a) procedural and related to some action, (b) tends to be acquired without direct help from others, and (c) allows people to attain goals that they value.

The Sternberg et al. article raises several issues with regard to training. The researchers claimed that tacit knowledge is acquired without "environmental support" (without training). Does this mean that training is not needed? Perhaps training is not needed if organizations simply want people to use trial-and-error methods to develop knowledge. However, Jacobs, Jones, and Neil (1992) showed the advantages of structured versus unstructured on-the-job training.

Another issue concerning training that is raised by this chapter is the proposition that tacit or practical knowledge, which remains implicit, allows for individual differences. According to Sternberg et al., those who acquire that knowledge gain a competitive advantage over those who fail to acquire that knowledge. We could argue that by making such tacit knowledge available through training, individual differences would disappear. This means that whatever is not trained and developed in individuals could become the criterion on which high and low performance are distinguished.

Sternberg et al. began by developing a theoretical model contrasting formal, academic knowledge and practical, tacit knowledge. They fitted their concepts within the context of previous work, such as that by Horn and Cattell (1966). They provided some examples of the concept of tacit knowledge and then described studies undertaken to operationalize the concept through testing methods. For example, they described the development of a general and a level-specific measure of managerial knowledge. They examined certain issues, such as whether tacit knowledge is domain-specific or possesses some generality and whether tacit knowledge is or is not some version of general intelligence. Finally, they presented the results of studies to determine the relationships between tacit knowledge measures, other aptitude and ability tests, and job performance ratings. The researchers also described regression analyses, examining various tests and demographic variables to determine the best predictors of job performance. All of this information and examination provided a framework for supporting the case for the usefulness of measuring tacit knowledge.

References

Bandura, A. (1977). *Social learning theory.* Englewood Cliffs, NJ: Prentice Hall.

Bruner, J. S., Goodnow, J. J., & Austin, G. A. (1956). *A study of thinking.* New York: Wiley.

Dixon, N. D. (1990). The relationship between trainee responses on participant reaction forms and posttest scores. *Human Resource Development Quarterly, 1,* 129-137.

Ebbinghaus, H. (1964). *Memory.* (H. A. Ruger & C. E. Bussenius, Trans.). New York: Dover. (Original work published 1885)

Fitts, P. M. (1964). Perceptual-motor skill learning. In A. W. Melton (Ed.), *Categories of human learning.* New York: Academic Press.

Goldstein, I. L. (1986). *Training in organizations* (2nd ed.). Pacific Grove, CA: Brooks/Cole.

Goldstein, I. L. (1991). Training in work organizations. In M. D. Dunnette & L. M. Hough (Eds.), *Handbook of industrial and organizational psychology* (Vol. 2, pp. 507-620). Palo Alto, CA: Consulting Psychologists Press.

Hegarty, M. (1991). Knowledge and process in mechanical problem solving. In R. J. Sternberg & P. A. Frensch (Eds.), *Complex problem solving: Principles and mechanisms* (pp. 253-285). Hillsdale, NJ: Lawrence Erlbaum.

Hilgard, E. R., & Bower, G. H. (1966). *Theories of learning* (3rd ed.). New York: Appleton-Century-Crofts.

Horn, J. L., & Cattell, R. B. (1966). Refinement and test of the theory of fluid and crystallized intelligence. *Journal of Educational Psychology, 57,* 253-270.

Jacobs, R. J., Jones, M. J., & Neil, S. (1992, Summer). A case study in forecasting the financial benefits of unstructured and structured on-the-job training. *Human Resource Development Quarterly, 3,* 133-139.

Kirkpatrick, D. L. (1959a, Nov.). Techniques for evaluating training programs. *Journal of the American Society of Training Directors, 13,* 3-9.

Kirkpatrick, D. L. (1959b, Dec.). Techniques for evaluating training programs—Part 2: Learning. *Journal of the American Society of Training Directors, 13,* 21-26.

Kirkpatrick, D. L. (1960a, Jan.). Techniques for evaluating training programs—Part 3: Behavior. *Journal of the American Society of Training Directors, 14,* 13-18.

Kirkpatrick, D. L. (1960b, Jan.). Techniques for evaluating training programs—Part 4: Results. *Journal of the American Society of Training Directors, 14,* 28-32.

Kunin, T. (1955). The construction of a new type of attitude measure. *Personnel Psychology, 8,* 65-78.

Lewin, K. (1951). *Field theory in social science.* New York: Harper-Row.

McGeoch, J. A. (1946). *The psychology of learning: An introduction.* New York: Longmans, Green.

Price, G. E., Dunn, R., & Dunn, K. (1991). *Productivity environmental preference survey manual.* Lawrence, KS: Price Systems.

Russell, J. S., Wexley, K. N., & Hunter, J. E. (1984). Questioning the effectiveness of behavior modeling training in an industrial setting. *Personnel Psychology, 37,* 465-481.

Watson, D., Clark, L. A., & Tellegren, A. (1988). Development and validation of brief measures of positive and negative affective: The PANAS scales. *Journal of Personality and Social Psychology, 54,* 1063-1070.

Wonderlic, E. F. (1983). *Wonderlic personnel test manual.* Northfield, IL: E. F. Wonderlic & Associates.

Effects of Alternative Modeling Strategies on Outcomes of Interpersonal-Skills Training

Timothy T. Baldwin
Indiana University

THE EFFECTS OF TWO ALTERNATIVE MODELING STRATEGIES—USING MULTIPLE scenarios and combining negative and positive model displays—on outcomes of a behavior modeling training program were explored. Trainees (N = 72) participated in a program on assertive communication structured to allow for a controlled experimental design that crossed scenario variability (one vs. multiple scenarios) with model display variability (positive model displays vs. positive and negative model displays). Outcomes assessed included trainee reactions, learning, and retention and behavioral measures of reproduction and generalization. The effects of multiple scenarios were negligible, but the positive and negative combination of model displays had a significant positive effect on trainee generalization and a significant negative effect on reproduction. Implications for future modeling research and practice are discussed.

In recent years, behavior modeling training (A. P. Goldstein & Sorcher, 1974) has emerged as the most popular approach for teaching interpersonal and supervisory skills (Decker & Nathan, 1985). Based on

Source: Baldwin, T. (1992). Effects of alternative modeling strategies on outcomes of interpersonal-skills training. *Journal of Applied Psychology, 77*(2), 147-154. Used by permission.

Author's Note: I gratefully acknowledge the assistance of Kenneth Wexley, J. Kevin Ford, John Hollenbeck, Scott Snell, and Richard Cosier.

Bandura's (1977) theory of observational learning, modeling training is governed by four component processes: attention, retention, motor reproduction, and motivation. Stated simply, the objective is to have people observe a model, remember what the model did, do what the model did, and, finally, use what they have learned on the job (Decker & Nathan, 1985).

Much research has demonstrated that behavior modeling can be a successful training technique (Burke & Day, 1986; Kraut, 1976; Latham & Saari, 1979; Meyer & Raich, 1983). However, recent researchers have noted that there remain enough inconclusive results and untested assumptions, particularly with respect to trainees' ability to generalize modeled skills to settings outside the training context, to make complacency with the existing process ill-advised (Parry & Reich, 1984; Robinson, 1980). For example, in a review and meta-analysis, Russell and Mayer (1985) found that the majority of empirical studies evaluating behavior modeling relied solely on trainee reactions and paper-and-pencil learning criteria and did not assess behavioral outcomes. Furthermore, when behavioral outcomes have been assessed, the results have not been unequivocal (cf. McGehee & Tullar, 1978; Russell, Wexley, & Hunter, 1984).

Unfortunately, despite the explosive increase in industrial applications of modeling training and some recent critiques of the existing process, empirical research on the technique has seriously waned in the last decade. In fact, with the exception of the work of Decker and colleagues on variations in the presentation of learning points (Decker, 1980, 1982; Hogan, Hakel, & Decker, 1986; Mann & Decker, 1984), little in the recent scientific literature has been reported on attempts to improve or enhance the behavior modeling components. Although the fundamental precepts of the method are sound, there is clearly a need for research that explores the effects of refinements, particularly on outcomes such as trainee generalization and transfer (Decker & Nathan, 1985).

Several studies conducted outside of an industrial training context have indicated that conventional model displays may be the weakest component of the process (McFall & Twentyman, 1973; Stone & Vance, 1976). More specifically, it has been suggested that existing model displays too often consist of simple, redundant, and unrealistic video models (Parry & Reich, 1984). That is, in the terms of learning theories, existing modeling programs could be characterized as having a relatively low degree of variability in the learning stimuli presented to trainees (Ellis, 1965).

Of course, this lack of variability is appropriate and even optimal for the training of many skills. For example, much of the conduct being modeled in motor skills is exactly prescribed, and hence it is desirable for trainees to adopt the modeled behaviors in essentially the same form as they are portrayed (Bandura, 1977). That is, there is little leeway permitted in the proper way to safely operate a power tool or perform a mechanical operation. Consequently, the objective is to have trainees mimic behavior as closely as possible, and a low degree of variability in the training stimulus has been found to be well-suited to that end (Bandura, 1977; Ellis, 1965).

On the other hand, the ultimate objective of most interpersonal and supervisory-skills training is not simply to enable the trainee to be able to reproduce just those behaviors specifically modeled. Rather, the goal is more to inculcate generalizable rules or concepts, specifying a class of behaviors to be used when certain stimuli are present (Decker & Nathan, 1985). The notion is that observers will extract the common attributes exemplified in modeled responses and formulate the rules for generating behavior with similar structural characteristics. Given that basic research on learning has frequently demonstrated a relationship between stimulus variability and learner generalization (Ellis, 1965; Stokes & Baer, 1977), the lack of variability in model displays may be suboptimal for much interpersonal skills training.

One alternative for increasing variability in modeling design is to use multiple scenarios. In fact, several studies in the social and counseling literature suggest that multiple scenarios can enhance training outcomes (Bandura & Menlove, 1968; Cominsky, 1982; Lumsdaine, Sulzer, & Kopstein, 1961). For example, Bandura and Menlove (1968) found that children who observed filmed models interacting with several dogs tended to show less fear than children who viewed a model with a single dog. Other studies have shown the superiority of multiple scenarios for teaching counseling skills (Cominsky, 1982) and reducing errors in the reading of a micrometer (Lumsdaine et al., 1961).

A more provocative alternative for increasing variability in the modeling process involves modifying conventional model displays to include negative or nonexemplary examples. Positive models have been traditionally preferred in a learning context because they make desired points or behaviors directly perceptible (A. P. Goldstein & Sorcher, 1974; Skinner, 1938). Negative models, on the other hand, do not put the desired knowledge or behaviors in direct view but simply present what is not correct. It has been further argued that positive instances somehow provide more information and are easier to assimilate than negative examples. In the worst case, negative examples might even detract from positive learning and generalization by creating noise (Berliner, 1969).

The arguments above are compelling, but only with respect to using negative models alone. That is, despite the traditional preference for positive models, there is conceptual and empirical evidence to suggest that negative examples, used in combination with positive examples, may be beneficial in a training context. For example, in a summary of research on learning and generalizing new concepts, Bruner, Goodnow, and Austin (1956) proposed that in the course of trying to learn a new concept, one could conceivably be exposed to instances of three types: (a) positive, whereby the instance exhibits the characteristics consistent with the concept; (b) negative, whereby the instance does not exemplify the concept being sought; and (c) irrelevant, whereby the instance does not relate to the concept at hand. Bruner et al. theorized that both positive and negative instances can be informational in that each allows the observer to either confirm or refute a hypothesis tentatively developed about the desired concept. A combination of positive and negative examples was concluded to be the optimal instructional approach for enhancing generalization, and this conclusion has been conceptually supported elsewhere as well (Becker & Engelmann, 1977).

In addition, there is evidence from the educational literature that suggests that the rate of incorrect trainee behavior may actually be independent of the rate of correct behavior (Calkin, 1979). That is, contrary to the conventional training assumption, teaching trainees to perform correctly does not necessarily mean that there will be a simultaneous decrease in their ineffective behavior. This calls attention to the importance of unfreezing (Lewin, 1951) or what training researchers have more specifically labeled unlearning (Russell et al., 1984).

The concept of unlearning is relevant in situations in which trainees enter a training program with a preconceived understanding or behavioral history that is inconsistent with the desired principles. In fact, some researchers have even argued that it is probably the rule, rather than the exception, that adult trainees enter interpersonal-skills training programs with at least some misconceptions of what constitutes effective behavior (Russell et al., 1984). Therefore, to be successful in inculcating trainees with desired learning, the task is not simply to teach and strengthen new, effective behavior strategies. The objective is also to extinguish old, ineffective ways of coping with situations.

To maximize such unlearning, a trainee must be made aware of and accept that existing behavior patterns are ineffective and be provided with alternative effective behaviors to model. Trainees exposed to both effective and ineffective model examples might plausibly be better equipped to do this via a sort of inoculation effect (McGuire, 1964). That is, the exposure to incorrect ways of performing a skill, possibly parallel to the trainee's existing behavior, may induce the trainee to avoid established patterns and to attend to the new correct illustrations of desired behavior.

With respect to empirical evidence, some research outside of industrial training contexts demonstrates the potential utility of the inclusion of negative models in the behavior modeling process (Bourne & Guy,

1968; Newman & Fuqua, 1988; Trimble, Nathan, & Decker, 1991). For example, in the case of learning the rules for accurate mathematical problem solving, researchers have found that subjects performed best on generalizing rules when the greatest variety of instances (mixture of positive and negative) were presented (Bourne & Guy, 1968). Other recent studies have concluded that negative models do not interfere with desirable learning and can produce outcomes similar to those achieved by positive models (Newman & Fuqua, 1988; Trimble et al., 1991).

On the other hand, a study in the counseling literature on the training of questioning skills compared mixed competence models with purely positive models and concluded that using the purely positive model was the most effective strategy (Alssid & Hutchison, 1977). However, two points regarding that study should be noted. First, the research did not control for amount or time of video exposure, and hence the results are confounded by the amount of information presented to trainees in each condition. Specifically, trainees in the pure-positive group were exposed to more task relevant information than trainees in the mixed condition. Second, the evaluation criteria consisted solely of a behavioral reproduction measure and did not assess generalization, the outcome most likely to be enhanced with variable stimuli (Stokes & Baer, 1977). Nonetheless, the existence of equivocal results confirms the need for more controlled experimentation in this area.

The purpose of the present study, then, was to explore the effects of two alternative modeling strategies: (a) using multiple scenarios and (b) combining positive and negative model displays. Both manipulations were incorporated into a behavior modeling program, and five out-comes—reaction, learning, retention, reproduction, and generalization—were assessed. On the basis of the conceptual and empirical evidence already discussed, it was expected that a modeling strategy that used multiple scenarios and allowed trainees to see both correct and incorrect models in juxtaposition would increase trainees' proficiency at general-izing learning to a different context.

Method

Sample

In response to the increasing demand from business employers for job applicants with stronger interpersonal competencies, a practical, skills-based training program on assertive communication (Smith, 1975) was created at a major university in the midwestern United States and served as the setting for this research. The program was presented as a unique opportunity for business students to receive training in an important management skill in a professional seminar context. A total of 72 trainees ultimately completed the program; 30 were men and 42 were women.

Experimental Conditions

To isolate the specific effects of nonexemplary model displays, apart from what might be attributed solely to the inclusion of multiple scenarios, an experimental design was created that crossed scenario variability (one vs. two scenarios) with model competence variability (positive model display vs. positive and negative model display). Therefore, each trainee was randomly assigned to one of four conditions, which included exposure to either (a) one scenario demonstrated with a positive model display (Condition 1), (b) two scenarios demonstrated with two positive model displays (Condition 2), (c) one scenario demonstrated with both a positive and a negative model display (Condition 3), or (d) two scenarios, each demonstrated with a positive and a negative model display (Condition 4). The decision to use two scenarios was based on research by Duncan (1958), who found that differences in learner outcomes were most marked in going from only one to two different stimuli. That is, increasing the number of stimuli above two had a rapidly decreasing effect. Furthermore, because Bandura (1977) suggested that at least two showings of a scenario is superior to a single showing, equalizing time exposure in this study meant that a trainee in any of the four conditions actually saw a total of four video showings in the course of his or her program.

Training Program and Procedure

Training content. The topic of the training program, assertive communication, has been used in previous training research (Decker, 1980, 1982) and is among the most prevalent topics for interpersonal-skills training in industrial contexts (Whetten & Cameron, 1984). The training program in the present study was based on the model of assertiveness developed by Smith (1975), who defined assertive communication as direct expression of one's feelings, preferences, needs, and opinions in a way that is neither threatening nor punishing to another person and that does not involve undue amounts of anxiety or fear for the person exhibiting the assertive behavior.

The six learning points of the program were also adapted from Smith (1975); they were (a) speak clearly and to the point with no dramatic changes in voice tone; (b) be honest about your feelings and needs and accept responsibility for them; (c) be persistent in a request or answer with calm repetition; (d) accept manipulative or sidetracking statements by calmly acknowledging the probability that there may be some truth in the statement; (e) acknowledge and accept your feelings and faults without apologizing for them; and (f) check for closure and two-way understanding of outcomes or compromise.

Therefore, using the categories proposed by Decker and Nathan (1985), the learning points in the program were of the rule-oriented type. That is, they specified rules underlying sets of behavior that could be used in different situations. Decker and Nathan (1985) suggested that such rule-oriented learning points are most appropriate for complex social skills and also lend themselves well to generalizing learning content to different stimuli in the transfer context.

Training procedure. The training program was 2.5 hours long and was conducted following the conventional procedure for a behavior modeling program (Decker & Nathan, 1985). The session began with an introduction of the trainer (operating from a prepared script) and a general overview of the topic of assertive communication. All trainees were given a copy of the learning points and asked to read them over carefully, write them down, think about them, and ask for clarification on any points that were unclear. Presentation of the learning points was followed by the showing of the modeling displays, which differed depending on the training strategy employed.

Modeling scenarios. The modeling displays in this study were video-taped sequences of persons using assertive communication skills. A pilot study of 25 trainees, similar in age and background to the subsequent sample, was used to facilitate the development of appropriate model displays. First, each subject in the pilot group was asked to select, from a list of potential assertive situations derived from Smith (1975), the two assertive scenarios he or she felt most likely to encounter. Results were calculated, and the two highest-rated scenarios were then filmed in both a positive and negative format. Care was taken in the filming of the scenarios to avoid introducing potential confounds that have plagued modeling research in the past. For example, the focal model character was kept constant through all scenarios, and the time of the videos was matched to ensure equal video exposure across conditions.

With respect to the two negative scenarios, there are, of course, an infinite number of ways in which a focal character might not demonstrate the points correctly. However, the objective in designing the negative scenarios was to create distinctive yet realistic portrayals of a person failing to use appropriately the specific assertive skills depicted in the positive scenarios. For example, the focal character in the negative model often varied his voice tone, tried to come up with more persuasive responses, got sidetracked by some responses, did not check for under-standing or closure, and so on.

The pilot group was shown each of the four videos and asked to provide a rating to ensure that the modeling stimuli included all atten-tional processes outlined by Bandura (1977) and A. P. Goldstein and Sorcher (1974). Results of those ratings were consistent with previous tests of video scenarios used in assertiveness training (Decker, 1980, 1982) and showed that pilot subjects perceived the models as believable and similar to themselves, the situations as relevant, the displays as clear and free of extraneous distractions, the learning points as very distinc-tive, the positive and negative versions as clearly distinguishable, and the models as appropriately reinforced for their correct (or incorrect) behavior.

In addition, pilot testing demonstrated that the subject pool had low baseline skills in the specific assertive skills to be trained. That is, given the learning points but without any training, subjects were poor at trying to effectively role play an assertive situation. These findings are consistent with previous research (e.g., Decker, 1980; Smith, 1975), which found that a low baseline rate does exist for the type of assertive communica-tion skills taught in this program.

Measures

Consistent with conventional criteria prescribed for training evalu-ation (cf. Kirkpatrick, 1967) and specifically with those criteria used previously to evaluate modeling programs (Decker & Nathan, 1985), five measures were obtained. A description of those measures and their timing is provided in the following paragraphs.

Reaction. The reaction measure was a 10-item, 5-point Likert scale assessing trainees' perceptions of the value of their training module, the predicted use of the skills taught, and the effectiveness and contribution of the trainer, method, and videos. The reaction measure was collected immediately after the training session. The alpha coefficient for this measure was .92.

Learning. The learning measure was also administered immediately after the conclusion of the training session; it asked each trainee to define 12 items derived directly from the six learning points of the program. The 12 items consisted of 2 items associated with each of the six learning points. Scoring was done on a 4-point scale (0 = *no understanding* to 3 = *mastery*) by two graduate students blind to the training conditions. The interrater agreement on this measure was .89.

Retention. The learning retention measure was the same 12-item paper-and-pencil learning measure given immediately after the program, but was administered 4 weeks after training. The retention measure was scored on the same 4-point scale as the initial learning measure. The interrater agreement on this measure was .88.

Behavioral reproduction. This measure assessed the extent to which trainees could demonstrate assertiveness skills in a situation closely related to the training environment. To simulate the assertiveness scenario, each trainee was asked to participate in a role play wherein a confederate acted out the same situation (using the same words and responses as the video models) that all trainees had viewed in their program. The role play was held on the same day of the training, and participants were randomly scheduled for a role-play time slot. Each role play was videotaped for later scoring. A 12-item scoring scale, corresponding to the 12 possible assertive responses, was constructed, and the taped scenarios were rated by two trained graduate students blind to condition. The average interrater agreement for this measure was .94.

Behavioral generalization. As discussed earlier, most reservations about behavior modeling training center around trainees' ability to generalize learning to contexts outside of training. Generalization has been defined as a necessary, though not sufficient, condition of transfer of training, which is of paramount concern in industrial contexts (Baldwin & Ford, 1988). That is, transfer is also dependent on motivation and opportunity to use the skills learned. However, the ability to generalize learning must be present to create the conditions for transfer. Therefore, it was critical to obtain some evidence of trainees' assertive behavior outside of simulated study conditions. With this in mind, an unobtrusive measure of generalization was created; the procedure used to obtain that measure is described in the following paragraph.

After completing a poststudy questionnaire, which included the retention measure (one month after the training), each trainee was thanked and permitted to leave. However, on the way out of the building, each trainee walked by a graduate student (actually playing the role of a confederate), who asked for a few minutes with each of them. The confederate explained that he was trying to raise money for his master's thesis by promoting the sale of business publications (pilot testing revealed that the price was prohibitively high for students). Recognizing that all subjects would respond, but in different ways, the confederate was provided with a set script that directed him to use the same manipulative pleas regardless of the nature of subject response. The debates were audiotaped and subsequently rated by two trained graduate students blind to condition. The scoring scale was a five-item rating scale corresponding to the five possible learning points deemed potentially appropriate for trainee use in this situation. The average interrater agreement on this scale was .92.

Results

The intercorrelation matrix of all variables is presented in Table 1.1. As the table indicates, significant intercorrelations were observed between trainee reaction and learning and between learning and retention. In addition, a significant negative relationship ($r = -.22$) was found between trainee reproduction and generalization. This suggests that trainees' ability to reproduce modeled skills was inversely related to their ability to transfer skills to a novel context.

The means and standard deviations, broken down by training condition, are shown in Table 1.2. Consistent with previous evaluation research on modeling programs, means for the reaction and paper-and-pencil learning measures were generally high. This suggests that the trainees were generally satisfied with their experience and that the training was quite successful in teaching the major learning points.

To test for the effects of modeling strategy on training outcomes, multivariate analysis of variance (MANOVA) was conducted; the overall test was significant, Wilks's lambda $F(2, 70) = 4.63$, $p < .001$. This was followed by separate univariate analyses of variance (ANOVAs) to test for differences across condition on the multiple dependent variables.

Results of ANOVA on trainee reaction, learning, and retention indicated that type of model strategy did not have a significant effect on any of those three variables. That is, although the positive and negative manipulation (Conditions 3 and 4) did yield higher average learning and retention scores, neither manipulation reached a conventional level of significance in its effect on trainee reaction, learning, or retention. There were also no significant interactions.

Results of ANOVA on trainee reproduction and generalization were significant, and results of those analyses are presented in Table 1.3. ANOVA using reproduction score as the dependent variable indicated joint main effects for positive and negative displays, $F(1, 68) = 24.86$, $p < .01$, and two scenarios, $F(1, 68) = 3.76$, $p < .05$, but no significant interaction. Subsequent mean comparisons revealed that reproduction proficiency was significantly higher for trainees in Condition 1, exposed to a minimum amount of variability, than for those in either Condition 3, $t(68) = 3.79$, $p < .01$, or Condition 4, $t(68) = 4.77$, $p < .01$, both of which included trainees exposed to a negative and positive combination. Reproduction proficiency was also significantly greater for trainees in Condition 2 than for trainees in Condition 3, $t(68) = 2.07$, $p < .05$, or

TABLE 1.1 Intercorrelations for All Variables

Variable	1	2	3	4	5
1. Reaction	.80				
2. Learning	.29*	.86			
3. Retention	−.13	.30*	.86		
4. Reproduction	−.04	.10	−.02	.94	
5. Generalization	.03	.06	.00	−.22*	.90

NOTE: $N = 72$. Reliability coefficients are on the diagonal.
*$p < .01$.

TABLE 1.2 Means and Standard Deviations for All Variables

	Overall		Condition 1		Condition 2		Condition 3		Condition 4	
Variable	M	SD	M	SD	M	SD	M	SD	M	SD
Reaction	4.06	0.38	3.93	0.38	4.09	0.47	4.16	0.31	4.07	0.33
Learning	25.82	5.01	25.50	3.94	24.06	5.99	26.28	5.14	27.44	4.51
Retention	17.22	4.70	15.94	4.85	16.33	4.83	18.67	3.24	17.94	5.45
Reproduction	2.90	0.53	3.27	0.58	3.02	0.46	2.72	0.29	2.58	0.36
Generalization	2.85	0.63	2.58	0.65	2.53	0.53	3.06	0.47	3.22	0.57

NOTE: $N = 72$ (18 per condition). Condition 1 = one scenario demonstrated with a purely positive model; Condition 2 = two scenarios demonstrated with purely positive models; Condition 3 = one scenario demonstrated with a positive and a negative display; and Condition 4 = two scenarios, each demonstrated with a positive and a negative display.

TABLE 1.3 Results of Analysis of Variance on Trainee Reproduction and Trainee Generalization

Source of variation	df	MS	F	p	ω^2
	Trainee reproduction				
Positive and negative models	1	4.772	24.862	.01	.25
No. of scenarios	1	0.617	3.664	.05	.05
Interaction	1	0.051	0.265	ns	
	Trainee generalization				
Positive and negative models	1	5.497	17.364	.01	.23
No. of scenarios	1	0.021	0.067	ns	
Interaction	1	0.122	0.387	ns	

Condition 4, $t(68)$ = 3.05, $p < .01$. There was also a difference in the reproduction scores for trainees who viewed only a single scenario (Condition 1) and those who saw two scenarios (Condition 2), though this difference did not reach a conventional level of significance. In summary, reproduction was inversely related to the amount of variability in the modeled stimuli, and, in particular, subjects exposed to a combination of positive and negative models achieved significantly lower mean scores on the reproduction measure.

ANOVA using the generalization role play as a dependent measure revealed a highly significant main effect for model competence, $F(1, 68)$ = 17.36, $p = .01$, explaining 23% of the variance. No main effect for multiple scenarios was found, nor was there an interaction. Subsequent mean comparisons supported the principal hypothesis of the study, revealing a significant generalization score difference in favor of trainees who viewed two scenarios and the negative and positive displays (Condition 4), compared with trainees in Condition 1, $t(68)$ = 3.43, $p < .01$, and Condition 2, $t(68)$ = 3.72, $p < .01$. Greater proficiency in generalization was also observed for trainees in Condition 3 than for trainees in Condition 1, $t(68)$ = 2.53, $p < .01$, and Condition 2, $t(68)$ = 2.83, $p < .01$. In summary, trainees exposed to both positive and negative model displays, either with or without multiple scenarios, achieved the highest average score on the generalization measure.

Discussion

What stands out most from the results of this study are the significant effects of the positive and negative modeling strategy on trainee reproduction and generalization. More specifically, trainees exposed to a combination of both positive and negative model displays scored significantly higher on a behavior generalization measure, taken 4 weeks after training, than did trainees who viewed only positive models. On the other hand, trainees exposed to only positive models scored significantly higher on the measure of behavioral reproduction than did trainees who viewed a combination of models. These results have several important implications for research and practice in behavior modeling training.

First, the finding that trainee generalization was enhanced by the use of a positive and negative model combination supports conceptual work, which suggests that such a learning stimulus may enhance understanding of concepts and foster a higher degree of mastery. In part, the value of the positive and negative strategy may stem from the fact that trainees are presented with a broader range of cues in the learning environment. However, if it were simply stimulus variability that made the difference, then the multiple scenario conditions would have been equally effective.

The results indicate that, in this case, it was not simply the variability per se that was of primary importance. Rather, it was the synthesis of exemplary and non-exemplary information that apparently facilitated generalization.

Perhaps part of the explanation for the superior generalization observed in the positive and negative conditions concerns the distinctiveness of the stimuli. Bandura (1977) noted that the distinctiveness of the stimuli is a key factor in social learning such that, if the stimuli presented induce the observer to form a distinctive mental script, then he or she will subsequently be better able to identify and remember desired learning. Similarly, Battig (1972) proposed that inclusion of task-related interference (e.g., a negative model) in a learning context forces the learner to actively concentrate and refine information to comprehend the underlying principles.

Consistent with such propositions, Mann and Decker (1984) found that including learning points on the video display itself increased the distinctiveness of those learning points and consequently enhanced trainee outcomes. It seems quite plausible that the contrast evoked by the positive and negative combination in the present study may have served to increase the distinctiveness of the stimuli and thus contributed to the positive effects on generalization.

Although the findings regarding trainee generalization are interesting, it is worth restating the point that generalization is not always (and should not always be) the primary objective of modeling programs. In contrast, when reproduction of skills is the paramount concern, then these results suggest that a minimum amount of variability and avoidance of negative examples would be appropriate. This finding is consistent with a substantial body of basic learning research, which has documented that stimulus similarity and repetition foster reproduction (Adams, 1987; Bandura, 1977; Hagman & Rose, 1983; Kazdin, 1975).

The different trainee outcomes attributable to alternative model display strategies is parallel to Decker's (1980, 1982) work on the effects of alternative learning point strategies. More specifically, Decker demonstrated that different types of learning points (e.g., behavioral, rule oriented) have different effects on reproduction and generalization. In particular, he found that some types of learning points enhance generalization but do not foster reproduction and vice versa.

The clear implication from both Decker's (1980, 1982) research and the present study is that there may well be an inverse relationship in modeling such that generalization is achieved at the expense of reproduction and vice versa. That is, although the evidence does not suggest that reproduction and generalization are mutually exclusive (i.e., both strategies result in some of each outcome), there is support for the notion that they may be somewhat antagonistic ends of a continuum and cannot be expected to build on one another (Clark & Voogel, 1985). Furthermore, we are now beginning to understand the nature of modeling configurations that will promote each outcome.

From a practical viewpoint, the superior generalization performance of trainees exposed to both positive and negative models suggests that the inclusion of negative models in the behavior modeling process may often be well directed. Filming negative versions of scenarios is already being done by some progressive training providers and should not add prohibitively to the development of training materials. Because the superior performance on the generalization measure was achieved without any significant detrimental effect on trainee learning, reaction, or retention, it is argued here that the traditional bias against nonexemplary information in training contexts should be reconsidered.

Clearly, the idea of mixing positive and negative examples in a learning context is not new. The informal inclusion of instructional examples of how not to do something (e.g., swing a golf club, conduct an employment interview) is commonplace. Nonetheless, one of the persistent criticisms of training and development design and practice is that it is too often based on trainer intuition and too infrequently supported by empirical evidence (Campbell, 1971).

The results of the present study also clearly document the critical need to obtain measurement of different types of training criteria and to understand the relationship between those criteria. Training researchers have perennially argued that reaction and learning criteria are, by themselves, inadequate criteria to assess training outcomes (Campbell, 1971; I. L. Goldstein, 1980; Kirkpatrick, 1967; Wexley, 1984). In this case, an evaluation relying solely on the criteria of reaction and learning would have failed to uncover important information. Even using the measurement of behavioral reproduction as the highest criterion, as is often done in the evaluation of modeling training, could have prompted inappropriate prescriptions for training design.

These results await replication in other settings and, as with any controlled experiment, some caution is warranted in generalizing to other training contexts. First, significant costs involved in filming, taping, and training time and resources restricted the feasible size of the sample. Therefore, although 72 trainees is well above average for training studies, it is still a small enough sample to warrant some caution concerning statistical power (Arvey, Cole, Hazucha, & Hartanto, 1985). Of course, the finding of several significant effects reduces this concern. Nonetheless, the presence of some nearly significant findings, such as those for trainee retention, suggests that even more significant effects might have been observed with a larger sample.

Second, the effects of differences between students and employed individuals is an unresolved issue. Of particular concern in training investigations are potential differences in ability and motivation to learn. It might be argued, for example, that college admission requirements generally ensure that students will be above average in cognitive ability and thus better suited to handling the complexity of alternative modeling strategies.

In this vein, Hovland (1953) found that the effectiveness of persuasive arguments was moderated by the intelligence of the listeners. One-sided arguments were found to be most persuasive for low-intelligence listeners, whereas more complex two-sided arguments were found most persuasive for those high in intelligence. Therefore, it is conceivable that intelligence level may be a boundary condition of these findings though, to the extent that industrial trainees are college trained, this should not be an issue.

In addition, Decker (1980, 1982) provided some limited evidence that suggests that the use of students may not lower the external validity of behavior modeling research. Provided the modeling stimulus is of general interest to the subject population, includes all of the attentional processes outlined by Bandura (1977), and has a low baseline rate of occurrence, it appears that procedural results can be generalized from students to industrial trainees (Decker, 1982). In the present study, each of those conditions was specifically addressed in a pilot study prior to the development of the actual training program used.

Given the popularity of the behavior modeling technique and the potential impact on the training community, future research should continue to explore improvements and refinements to the process. Related to the present findings, there are a number of unresolved questions about the design and presentation of model displays. For example, one interesting question involves the utility of having a model initially show uncertainty and apprehensiveness about applying the skill (to be more like the trainees) but then demonstrating confidence and competence with it. A related question concerns the utility of having a model receive clear outcomes from applying the behavior (e.g., for a positive model a problem is resolved, for a negative model the problem escalates).

The utility of different modeling strategies may be partially contingent on observer characteristics. As Campbell (1989) noted, it is unrealistic to assume that all trainees "just fall out of some great trainee bin in the sky," (p. 479). Rather, trainees bring long and varied histories, which have created certain attitudes, values, and behaviors relative to specific training experiences. For example, even in view of the present findings, there may be certain conditions under which one would want to exclusively use positive models, perhaps to avert the surfacing of past conflict or to avoid embarrassing a novice group.

Finally, the cognitive processes that occur under different modeling conditions, both intended and unintended (Manz & Sims, 1986), need to be better understood. Although these and other findings clearly establish that variants in modeled stimuli can affect trainee outcomes, future research directed at understanding the underlying cognitive explanations for such effects would be well directed.

References

Adams, J. A. (1987). Historical review and appraisal of research on the learning, retention, and transfer of human motor skills. *Psychological Bulletin, 101,* 41-74.

Alssid, L. L., & Hutchison, W. R. (1977). Comparison of modeling techniques in counselor training. *Counselor Education and Supervision, 17,* 36-41.

Arvey, R. D., Cole, D. A., Hazucha, J. F., & Hartanto, F. M. (1985). Statistical power of training evaluation designs. *Personnel Psychology, 38,* 493-507.

Baldwin, T. T., & Ford, J. K. (1988). Transfer of training: A review and directions for future research. *Personnel Psychology, 41,* 63-105.

Bandura, A. (1977). *Social learning theory.* Englewood Cliffs, NJ: Prentice Hall.

Bandura, A., & Menlove, F. L. (1968). Factors determining vicarious extinction of avoidance behavior through symbolic modeling. *Journal of Personality and Social Psychology, 8,* 99-108.

Battig, W. F. (1972). Intratask interference as a source of facilitation in transfer and retention. In R. F. Thompson & J. F. Voss (Eds.), *Topics in learning and performance* (pp. 131-159). San Diego, CA: Academic Press.

Becker, W. C., & Engelmann, S. (1977). *Systems for basic instruction: Theory and applications.* Palo Alto, CA: SRA Publishers.

Berliner, D. (1969). *Microteaching and the technical skills approach to teacher training.* Stanford, CA: Stanford Center for Research and Development in Teaching. (ERIC Document Reproduction Service No. ED 034 707)

Bourne, L. E., & Guy, D. E. (1968). Learning conceptual rules: The role of positive and negative instances. *Journal of Experimental Psychology, 77,* 488-494.

Bruner, J. S., Goodnow, J. J., & Austin, G. A. (1956). *A study of thinking.* New York: Wiley.

Burke, M. J., & Day, R. R. (1986). A cumulative study of the effectiveness of managerial training. *Journal of Applied Psychology, 71,* 232-246.

Calkin, A. B. (1979). *Measuring and comparing perceived facts, fun and freedom.* Unpublished doctoral dissertation, University of Kansas.

Campbell, J. P. (1971). Personnel training and development. *Annual Review of Psychology, 22,* 565-602.

Campbell, J. P. (1989). The agenda for theory and research. In I. Goldstein (Ed.), *Training and development in organizations* (pp. 469-486). San Francisco: Jossey-Bass.

Clark, R. E., & Voogel, A. (1985). Transfer of training principles for instructional design. *Educational Communication & Technology Journal, 33*(2), 113-123.

Cominsky, I. J. (1982). Transfer of training in counselor education programs: A study of the use of stimulus variability and the provision of general principles to enhance the transfer of the skill reflection of feeling. *Dissertation Abstracts International, 43,* 76A.

Decker, P. J. (1980). Effects of symbolic coding and rehearsal in behavior modeling training. *Journal of Applied Psychology, 65,* 627-634.

Decker, P. J. (1982). The enhancement of behavior modeling training of supervisory skills by the inclusion of retention processes. *Personnel Psychology, 32,* 323-332.

Decker, P. J., & Nathan, B. R. (1985). *Behavior modeling training.* New York: Praeger Publishers.

Duncan, C. P. (1958). Transfer after training with single versus multiple tasks. *Journal of Experimental Psychology, 55,* 63-72.

Ellis, H. C. (1965). *The transfer of learning.* New York: Macmillan.

Goldstein, A. P., & Sorcher, M. (1974). *Changing supervisory behavior.* New York: Pergamon Press.

Goldstein, I. L. (1980). Training in work organizations. *Annual Review of Psychology, 21,* 229-273.

Hagman, J. D., & Rose, A. M. (1983). Retention of military tasks: A review. *Human Factors, 25*(2), 199-213.

Hogan, P. M., Hakel, M. D., & Decker, P. J. (1986). Effects of trainee-generated versus trainer-provided rule codes on generalization in behavior-modeling training. *Journal of Applied Psychology, 71,* 469-473.

Hovland, C. I. (1953). *Communication and persuasion: Psychological studies of opinion change.* New Haven, CT: Yale University Press.

Kazdin, A. E. (1975). *Behavior modification in applied settings.* Homewood, IL: Dorsey Press.

Kirkpatrick, D. L. (1967). Evaluation of training. In R. L. Craig (Ed.), *Training and development handbook* (pp. 18-1—18-27). New York: McGraw-Hill.

Kraut, A. J. (1976). Developing managerial skills via modeling techniques: Some positive research findings. *Personnel Psychology, 29,* 325-328.

Latham, G. P., & Saari, L. M. (1979). Application of social-learning theory to training supervisors through behavior modeling. *Journal of Applied Psychology, 64,* 239-246.

Lewin, K. (1951). *Field theory in social science.* New York: Harper-Row.

Lumsdaine, A. A., Sulzer, R., & Kopstein, F. (1961). The effect of animation cues and repetition of examples on learning from an instructional film. In A. A. Lumsdaine (Ed.), *Student response in programmed instruction* (pp. 241-269). Washington, DC: National Academy of Sciences.

Mann, B., & Decker, P.J. (1984). The effect of key behavior distinctiveness on generalization and recall in behavior modeling training. *Academy of Management Journal, 27,* 900-910.

Manz, C. C., & Sims, H. P. (1986). Beyond imitation: Complex behavioral and effective linkages resulting from exposure to leadership training models. *Journal of Applied Psychology, 71,* 571-578.

McFall, R. M., & Twentyman, C. T. (1973). Four experiments on the relative contribution of rehearsal, modeling, and coaching to assertion training. *Journal of Abnormal Psychology, 81,* 199-218.

McGehee, W., & Tullar, W. L. (1978). A note on evaluating behavior modification and behavior modeling as industrial training techniques. *Personnel Psychology, 31,* 477-484.

McGuire, W. J. (1964). Inducing resistance to persuasion: Some contemporary approaches. In L. Berkowitz (Ed.), *Advances in experimental social psychology* (Vol. 1, pp. 191-229). New York: Academic Press.

Meyer, H. H., & Raich, M. S. (1983). An objective evaluation of a behavior modeling program. *Personnel Psychology, 36,* 755-762.

Newman, J. L., & Fuqua, D. R. (1988). A comparative study of positive and negative modeling in counselor training. *Counselor Education and Supervision, 28,* 121-129.

Parry, S. B., & Reich, L. R. (1984). An uneasy look at behavior modeling. *Training and Development Journal, 30*(3), 57-62.

Robinson, J. (1980). Will behavior modeling survive the 80's? *Training and Development Journal, 26*(1), 22-28.

Russell, J. S., & Mayer, S. (1985). *Behavior modeling: A review and future directions.* Unpublished manuscript, University of Oregon.

Russell, J. S., Wexley, K. N., & Hunter, J. E. (1984). Questioning the effectiveness of behavior modeling training in an industrial setting. *Personnel Psychology, 37,* 465-481.

Skinner, B. F. (1938). *The behavior of organisms.* New York: Appleton.

Smith, M. J. (1975). *When I say no, I feel guilty.* New York: Bantam.

Stokes, T.F., & Baer, D. M. (1977). An implicit technology of generalization. *Journal of Applied Behavioral Analysis, 10,* 349-367.

Stone, G. L., & Vance, A. (1976). Instructions, modeling, and rehearsal—Implications for training. *Journal of Counseling Psychology, 23,* 272-279.

Trimble, S. K., Nathan, B. R., & Decker, P. J. (1991). The effect of positive and negative models on learning in behavior modeling training: Testing for proactive and retroactive interference. *Journal of Human Behavior and Learning, 7*(2), 1-12.

Wexley, K. N. (1984). Personnel training. *Annual Review of Psychology, 35,* 519-551.

Whetten, D. A., & Cameron, K. S. (1984). *Developing management skills.* Glenview, IL: Scott, Foresman.

IMPLICATIONS FOR HUMAN RESOURCE DEVELOPMENT PROFESSIONALS

The Baldwin article focuses on a popular training method, that of behavior modeling. For HRD, this article helps to confirm that this long-standing method still shows promising results in terms of learning, retention, reproduction, and generalization. Such evidence is important to have available when others in the organization begin to criticize the "fad of the month."

In addition, the findings add to the body of knowledge about the behavior modeling method. In this case, we learn that the presentation of a positive model only leads to higher levels of behavioral reproduction. The use of both a positive and a negative model leads to enhanced generalization, or application, of the skill but does not have similar effects on behavioral reproduction. The HRD professional should determine the outcomes needed from the training. If behavioral reproduction is the desired outcome (assuming only minimal differences between the training setting and the job setting), then the use of behavioral models should be limited to positive models only. If, on the other hand, generalization is desired, then the behavioral models should include both positive and negative models. Indeed, the variability of the models will enhance the trainee's ability to transfer and generalize the behaviors to other situations.

Another critical implication for HRD professionals is the finding that no differences in trainee reaction, learning, or retention appeared based on model strategy but did emerge based on reproduction and generalization. Such findings again raise questions about the extensive use of trainee reaction forms as the only means of evaluating training. Trainees' reactions to the training yield no information as to how much has been learned or how much will be applied on the job. The use of trainee reaction forms as the primary means of evaluating training simply provides the message that the only expected outcome of training is a happy trainee.

IMPLICATIONS FOR RESEARCH DESIGN AND METHODOLOGY

Baldwin's research demonstrates how one research design can yield answers to several different questions. The design provided information on the effects of using one versus two scenarios and of using only positive behavioral models versus using positive and negative models. Furthermore, the researcher controlled for time exposure by ensuring that trainees in each of the four conditions saw a total of four video showings. For example, in one condition, subjects saw one positive scenario four times, whereas subjects in another condition saw a positive and a negative model of two different scenarios.

Baldwin's research provides an excellent model for measuring multiple outcomes of training. Not only did the researcher measure trainee reactions and learning but the study included measures of retention after four weeks of training, of behavioral reproduction, and of generalization. Use of such multiple measures is of particular importance in determining specific outcomes. As the Baldwin article shows, a method that affects behavioral reproduction may not affect generalization, whereas a method that affects generalization may not affect behavioral reproduction. As HRD researchers, we should test the various types of outcomes because this will add to our theoretical knowledge. In addition, practitioners will be interested in the different types of outcomes.

IMPLICATIONS FOR FUTURE INQUIRY

Given the extensive use of behavior modeling in organizational training, empirical research on the technique continues to be needed to yield the most effective results. The end of the Baldwin article suggests some continuing questions regarding behavior modeling. These include questions concerning the uncertainty and apprehension displayed by the model and the usefulness of models that receive clear positive or negative outcomes versus those that receive ambiguous outcomes.

Another issue of concern to HRD practitioners involves the degree of similarity between the model and the trainee in terms of both physical characteristics and setting. Another issue raised by recent research on distributed practice (Bahrick, Bahrick, Bahrick, & Bahrick, 1993; Dempster, 1988) suggests the importance of distributed practice for long-term retention. Within the context of behavior modeling training, issues arise concerning the length of retention. Perhaps some combination of model variability and distributed practice would yield superior retention, reproduction, and generalization. Unfortunately, little current research examines the various facets of this type of training.

One suggestion for improvement to this research involves the use of pretesting and an examination of pretest and posttest gains (perhaps using a research design as done in Bretz & Thompsett, Chapter 3). In this article, Baldwin assumed that all groups started at the same level of skill, which may or may not be accurate. A second suggestion involves the use of actual trainees in an organizational setting rather than students at a university. (Note that the author does address this issue in the discussion of the research findings.) Finally, inclusion of some demographic variables (such as education, intelligence, on-the-job experience, and supervisory support) may show differential effects on reproduction and generalization.

OTHER RESOURCES

Bahrick, H. P., Bahrick, L. E., Bahrick, A. S., & Bahrick, P. E. (1993). Maintenance of foreign language vocabulary and the spacing effect. *Psychological Science, 4,* 316-321.

Baldwin, T. T., & Ford, J. K. (1988). Transfer of training: A review of directions for future research. *Personnel Psychology, 41,* 63-105.

Dempster, F. N. (1988). The spacing effect: A case study in the failure to apply the results of psychological research. *American Psychologist, 43,* 627-634.

Mills, G. (1985). *The effects of positive and negative models in learning and displaying basic communication skills.* Provo, UT: Brigham Young University, Department of Communications.

Russ-Eft, D. F., & Zenger, J. H. (1995). Behavior modeling training in North America. In Nijhof, W., Mulder, M., & Brinkerhoff, R. (Eds.), *Corporate training for effective performance* (pp. 89-109; Appendix). Dordrecht, The Netherlands: Kluwer Academic.

Werner, J. M., O'Leary-Kelly, A. M., Baldwin, T. T., & Wexley, K. N. (1994). Augmenting behavior-modeling training testing the effects of pre- and post-training interventions. *Human Resource Development Quarterly, 5,* 169-183.

Enhancing Human Performance

An Evaluation of "New Age" Techniques Considered by the U.S. Army

John A. Swets
Bolt Beranek and Newman, Inc.

Robert A. Bjork
University of California, Los Angeles

UNCONVENTIONAL TECHNIQUES CONSIDERED BY THE UNITED STATES ARMY for enhancing human performance were reviewed during a two-year study by a committee of the National Research Council. Little or no scientific evidence was found to support the effectiveness of several, including neurolinguistic programming in interpersonal influence and such paranormal techniques as remote viewing and psychokinesis. Mixed results were seen to characterize other techniques, for example, group-cohesion procedures. Further study was suggested for a few, including mental practice of motor skills. Guidelines requested of the committee for future army evaluation of enhancement techniques stressed the need for, and the conduct of, both laboratory and field research. The committee recommended further consideration of main-

Source: Swets, J. A., & Bjork, R. A. (1990). Enhancing human performance: An evaluation of "New Age" techniques considered by the U.S. Army. *Psychological Science, 1*, 2, 85-96. Used by permission.

Authors' Note: This chapter is based on a study conducted by the National Research Council for the Army Research Institute and reported in Druckman and Swets (1988). The authors thank Daniel Druckman, Edgar M. Johnson, Alvin M. Liberman, Raymond S. Nickerson, and Jerome E. Singer for comments on a draft of the article.

stream research in the behavioral sciences as a basis for effective
performance enhancements.

Five years ago the Army Research Institute (ARI) asked the National
Research Council to assess a field of techniques designed to enhance
human performance. As a class, these techniques are extraordinary in
that they were developed outside of mainstream research in the behavioral sciences and are accompanied by strong claims for high effectiveness. The ARI wanted a committee to examine the potential of certain
specified techniques, to recommend appropriate criteria for evaluating
such techniques, and, where possible, to specify the research necessary
to advance understanding of performance enhancements in areas of
behavior related to the proposed techniques. In pursuing this line of
investigation, the ARI was reacting to broad and substantial advocacy in
the army of trying to gain large enhancements of human performance
by any conceivable means.

The army's interests, as summarized by ARI, included more efficient
learning, improved motor skills, altered mental states, stress reduction,
interpersonal influence, group cohesion, and certain parapsychological
processes. More specifically, the army was considering the possibilities
that learning could take place during sleep, that learning might be
accelerated via packaged programs designed for that purpose, and that
motor skills might be enhanced by guided imagery, mental practice,
visual concentration, and biofeedback. Further, it wished to pursue the
possibility that mental states could be altered by self-induced hypnotism,
meditation, focused concentration, or the integration of activity in the
brain's hemispheres, in order to promote periods of peak performance.
The army was also interested in whether biofeedback and methods that
purport to alter mental states might be useful in managing stress. Certain
aspects of interpersonal and group processes were under examination
as well, including whether group cohesion, which might be fostered by
keeping army units intact, enhances group and individual performance.
Finally, the army had an interest in such parapsychological processes as
remote viewing and psychokinesis, or mind over matter, especially
mental influence on the functioning of remote machines.

It may at first seem strange that anyone in the army was interested
in the panoply of behavioral processes and techniques that characterized
the countercultural human-potential movement of the 1960s. However,
in the 1980s advocates of such techniques have had success with an
approach that is more entrepreneurial than ideological. Moreover, the
techniques are presented less as related to general well-being and more
as related to specific tasks, such as marksmanship, second-language

learning, and sleep inducement. The army is not alone in this interest: Private industry and the general public have also given much attention to these New Age techniques in commercially available programs of general training and self-help. The army's interest in extending human abilities through parapsychological processes originated primarily in intelligence circles rather than in training circles, but psychology soon became a bedfellow of the unconventional training techniques in the army.

Formation of the NRC Committee

In conversations between Edgar M. Johnson, technical director of ARI, and David A. Goslin, then executive director of the Commission on Behavioral and Social Sciences and Education (CBASSE) of the NRC, and in a formal letter request, it was indicated that the ARI leadership wanted help, not only to reduce broad pressures on it that had recently intensified, but also with an important national problem of interest to private industry and the public as well as the military. CBASSE members who evaluated this request included psychologists William K. Estes, Ira J. Hirsh, Lauren Resnick, and Stanley Schachter. In response to the request, CBASSE moved to set up a committee especially for the purpose, with suggestions for particular kinds of expertise also from other advisers including psychologists Robert Boruch, Wendell R. Garner, Bert F. Green, and Gardner Lindzey. The first author of this article was enlisted as committee chair and, together with Goslin, he developed the final recommendations for membership that were endorsed by the commission.[1] Daniel Druckman was appointed as the committee's study director.

The Committee on Techniques for the Enhancement of Human Performance (henceforth, the committee) met first in late July 1985. ARI's Johnson along with George Lawrence, its liaison to the committee, arranged for several speakers at the first meeting, who informed and sometimes perplexed the members. A few speakers described single techniques, others waxed enthusiastic about the full range of them, and one, a retired general, spoke eloquently of his own extensive psychokinetic powers.

General Maxwell R. Thurman was the motivational speaker at dinner the first evening. His graphs demonstrated that in terms of recruits' test scores, the army was doing increasingly better, and also better compared to the other services. His review of the traditional and growing demands placed on soldiers, however, made clear that these demands continued to outstrip abilities by a large margin.

The Committee's Approach

The committee could easily imagine the great difficulties faced in converting recruits, most of them with minimal education as well as short terms of duty, into soldiers who possess the personal and social skills needed in battle as well as the technical skills needed to operate and maintain complex equipment. It could understand urges to look beyond slow, narrow, and insufficiently targeted mainstream research on human performance to enhancements that could come from elsewhere. And it was aware that those in the army responsible for training and technique evaluation would face difficulties in responding to strong enhancement claims (both by army officers and outside vendors) for diverse and far-ranging techniques. The committee agreed that the general problem deserved objective and thorough examination and was willing to initiate such a study.

Subcommittees were formed on various facets of the problem, including evaluation issues, sleep learning, accelerated learning, guided imagery, biofeedback, split-brain effects, stress management, cohesion, influence, and parapsychology. The committee met as a whole six times in 2 years, in whole or part made ten site visits, invited twenty or so briefings, and commissioned ten background review papers.[2] It met twice with a Resource Advisory Group of army officers formed for the purpose.[3]

Army Background

The army's interest in parapsychology is reported to be longstanding, including, for example, sponsorship of ESP research by J. B. Rhine in the early 1950s. Remote-viewing experiments were conducted for the army by the Stanford Research Institute in the 1970s. A military concern has been that the Soviets have been active in the development of psychic abilities, including the ability to affect the behavior of others through mental telepathy. A proposal developed in the army for the First Earth Battalion envisioned warrior monks with a range of parapsychological abilities allowing them, for example, to leave their bodies and to walk through walls. (See, e.g., Squires, 1988.) These ideas and enhancement techniques of the sort mentioned above were advanced by an informal group of some 300 army officers known as the Delta Force (not to be confused with the antiterrorist unit having the same name). Several other task forces in the army were organized in the 1970s to examine and promote the techniques.

An influential memo pulling much of this together for the army was written in 1982 by General Thurman, then a lieutenant general and deputy chief of staff for personnel. (Thurman went on to become a four-star general and vice chief of staff, and was an architect of the army's very successful recruiting campaign with the slogan of "Be all that you can be.") He subsequently led the army's training effort as commander of the Training and Doctrine Command. His memo identified "accelerated learning, inferential focus, previsualization, psychokinetics and biokinetics, remote viewing, biophysical stress prevention, etc." as techniques that should be considered. It was based in part on a half-dozen commercially available techniques that may be characterized as follows.

Suggestive accelerative learning and teaching techniques (SALTT) combine physical relaxation, mental concentration, guided imagery, suggestion, and baroque music to improve classroom performance. The *Journal of the Society for Accelerative Learning and Teaching* publishes evaluations of applications of SALTT to language training, typing instruction, high-school science courses, and so forth.

Concentrix designates a specific procedure for training visual concentration on a target, broadly defined, and maximizing hand-eye coordination, balance, body control, and sensory and visualization skills. It is intended for application not only to marksmanship but to the operation of complex equipment, movement over long distances with the objectives of reducing fatigue, and intelligence gathering.

Hemi-Sync,™ short for hemispheric synchronization, consists of presenting tones of slightly different frequency to each ear to produce a beating sound. An EEG-measured brain response follows changes in the beat frequency and changing sound patterns are thought to change states of awareness. Recommended applications are for language learning, stress reduction, reading skills, problem solving, creativity, and sleep control.

Stress-management techniques are designed to alleviate anxiety and tension and are implemented by self-help books and groups and by clinics. They often emphasize fitness, nutrition, and lifestyles, as well as strategies such as progressive relaxation and image rehearsal. Promoters claim an interactive effect and put forth a particular package of techniques.

Neurolinguistic programming (NLP) is intended primarily to be a means of exerting influence over others. The skilled practitioner is supposed to be able to determine what representational system (e.g., visual, auditory, or kinesthetic) another person is using at the moment—by observing his or her speech, eye movements, and posture—and then to frame communications to that person in terms of the particular representational system in use. A national association is reported to have a membership of about 500 persons.

In 1983, an *ad hoc* subgroup of the Army Science Board, formed in response to General Thurman's memo, issued a report supportive of further consideration of these techniques. The group had been exposed to them in an "experiential workshop format" during a four-day meeting at the Monroe Institute of Applied Sciences, developer of Hemi-Sync. It recommended that formal mechanisms be established to undertake a major effort on "human technologies," that "technologies should be sorted into those which require a scientific base and need verifiable, repeatable data for evaluation versus those which are more analytic representing principles of good practice and are evaluated by consensus, acceptance and overall effectiveness," and, further, that research efforts be managed jointly by the Army Research Institute and the Medical R&D Command.

In 1984, ARI, which reported then to General Thurman, hired a program manager, commissioned review papers on five techniques, and requested of the National Research Council that a committee examine the area. In 1985, ARI initiated research on several of the techniques and reviewed army research in progress elsewhere.

The Committee's Specific Findings

Learning During Sleep

The committee recommended that the army give sleep learning a "second look." Considering only the sleep-learning literature, there seemed little basis for any kind of positive recommendation. This conclusion was reinforced in a detailed briefing by La Verne Johnson of the Naval Health Research Center. When all possible criteria are applied to verify that the learner is truly asleep, there appears to be no evidence of conscious recognition or recall of materials presented during sleep (for a thorough review, see Aarons, 1976). In fact, since the mid-1970s research activity on sleep learning has nearly stopped, at least in this country.

The committee, however, was influenced by recent developments in basic research on "implicit memory," "stimulus-driven processing," "learning without awareness," and related topics (for reviews, see Richardson-Klavehn & Bjork, 1988; Schacter, 1987; Shimamura, 1986; and the commissioned paper by Eich, see Note 2). That research, employing amnesic as well as normal subjects, has illustrated that certain indirect measures of memory (for example, perceptual identification, word-fragment completion, procedural skills) can show large effects of prior episodes when conventional recall and recognition measures fail to show any such effects. Viewed in that context, only certain types of learning should take place during true EEG-verified sleep, and learning should show up on only certain types of memory tests. In general, the past negative results were obtained with inappropriate presentation procedures and with testing procedures that were insensitive to any learning that might take place.

The committee's primary recommendation was that the degree of learning of materials presented during sleep be examined again as a basic research problem. Rather than looking at intentional recall or recognition of material presented during true sleep, the committee urged the army to look for effects such as lowering of perceptual thresholds for items presented during sleep, semantic or affective biasing in the postsleep interpretation of verbal items as a consequence of their being presented in biased contexts during sleep, repetition effects (enhancing postsleep performance on material studied before the sleep period by repeating the material during the sleep period), and priming effects (facilitating postsleep acquisition of material by presenting that material during the preceding sleep period).

Recent research on state dependencies in human learning (Eich, 1989) also influenced the committee. If learning during sleep is to some extent state-specific, then it might transfer more effectively to the states of drowsiness and semisleep that accompany exhaustion and sleep deprivation than it does to the normal waking state. Since cognitive performance deteriorates under sleep deprivation, such potential transfer of sleep-training might help the subject when he or she needs it most. Finally, the committee thought that learning that depends on sleep disruption might be examined from a cost-benefit standpoint; procedures that disrupt the quantity or quality of sleep might shorten training or have other benefits that could outweigh their costs.

Accelerated Learning

The committee focused primarily on one particular learning package, SALTT (Suggestive Accelerative Learning and Teaching Techniques). Literature in the *Journal of the Society of Accelerative Learning* was reviewed and committee member Schneider attended the society's national meeting in 1986. The commissioned paper by Slavin provided background information on the teacher's contributions to effective instruction and the paper by Harris and Rosenthal considered the potential contribution of the learner's expectations in the SALTT environment (see Note 2).

The committee concluded that the extravagant claims for accelerated learning programs are unjustified. The effectiveness of such programs did not exceed what might be expected on the basis of the mainstream instructional elements (for example, imagery, cooperative learning, tests as motivational devices and learning events) that are embedded in a non-traditional framework including relaxation exercises and special music. The committee did feel, however, that there was value in the kind of holistic approach to instruction exemplified by such programs. The army was encouraged to use its resources to evaluate competing training procedures in order to isolate the components of instruction that are effective in army settings.

Improving Motor Skills

The committee focused on three strategies to enhance motor skills: mental practice, visual concentration, and biofeedback. A background paper by Feltz, Landers, and Becker on the mental-practice literature was solicited by the committee (see Note 2), and there were four briefings: one on peak performance issues, and three by experts on or promoters of visual-training techniques. In addition, Landers and Bjork made site visits to the headquarters of SyberVision® and to the Vic Braden Tennis Academy. SyberVision is a highly successful marketer of audio and visual tapes designed to enhance skills such as golf, tennis, skiing, bowling, racquetball, and others. Tapes such as "The Neuropsychology of Achievement" address more global skills. What is shown on the tapes and the instructions to the learner are supposedly guided by a principle of "neuromuscular programming," which is in turn derived from Karl Pribram's holographic theory of brain function. The subcommittee interviewed Pribram, director of research for SyberVision, and Stephen DeVore, founder and president.

With respect to mental practice, defined as "the symbolic rehearsal of a physical activity in the absence of any gross muscular movements" (Richardson, 1967, p. 95), the committee's recommendations were quite positive. A meta-analysis of the relevant research literature revealed that mental practice yields a gain in performance on the order of half a standard deviation when compared to appropriate controls. The gain is somewhat greater for motor tasks that incorporate a substantial cognitive component, and the advantages of mental practice can be enhanced if physical practice and mental practice are interspersed. The committee recommended that the army evaluate mental practice as a training component in operational military tasks, and that the army pursue basic research to determine what mixture of mental and physical practice might be optimal (given considerations of expense, equipment availability, and so forth).[4]

Concerning visual-training programs, the committee concluded that there was no research base to suggest that such training leads to improved performance. There is evidence that certain visual abilities can be improved by training the eye muscles, but evidence that attentional skills can be enhanced by visual training is lacking.

The committee concluded that there remain too many loose ends for the relationship between biofeedback and skilled performance to be determined. Part of the problem is that biofeedback is often used as part of broader therapeutic programs that incorporate other, possibly effective, techniques. Another problem is that biofeedback is used to train physiological parameters (heart rate, for example) although clear knowledge of the most desirable levels of these parameters with respect to a given skill typically does not exist. In cases where that relationship is known (e.g., hand warmth and finger dexterity), there is evidence of performance benefit.

Altering Mental States

The idea that people can achieve an internal state that will be optimal for a broad range of performance has been appealing. Some level of arousal is optimal for performance of a given complexity (Duffy, 1962; Yerkers & Dodson, 1908) and, specifically, the optimal level decreases as task complexity increases (Easterbrook, 1959). This concept fits the behavior theories of the 1950s, which specified that a source of energy or drive is required to keep the organism active and was reinforced by the physiological discovery of a diffuse activating system in the brain (Moruzzi & Magoun, 1949). However, with new knowledge of the variety and specificity of neurotransmitter systems (Robbins & Everitt, 1982) and with psychological theory focused on cognition, we have begun to think of a large number of cortical computations in widely distributed neural systems (Rumelhart & McClelland, 1986). The view that cortical computations are modulated by different transmitter systems in varying ways makes it more difficult to suppose that any training technique will provide optimal states for all forms of physical and mental activity. An example comes from the finding that the optimal conditions of alertness for rapid responding differ from those for the best memory performance (Posner, 1975).

Unfortunately, the committee did not find time to explore the evidence for the wide variety of specific training or induction methods that might provide a basis for techniques for manipulating internal states. It recommended a literature review of links between such techniques and changes in performance and, in its next phase, will examine further the techniques of intensive meditation and self-hypnosis.

The committee considered issues of brain asymmetry in detail. It reviewed Hemi-Sync, in part through a visit by Springer, Thompson, Druckman, and Lawrence to the Monroe Institute in Virginia where it was developed. Although this technique is said to be valuable in therapeutic settings (pain control in cancer patients, alcohol abuse, retardation, autism, and seizure disorders) and though formal research designs have been approximated for its application in a few educational settings (courses in basic broadcasting, ear training, and introductory psychology), the committee concluded that current attempts to alter performance through coordinating the two hemispheres by an external or instructional device do not appear to be effective. It observed, more generally, that the scientific evaluation of claims for enhancing performance by involving the hemispheres differentially awaits the development of reliable measures of hemispheric activity in individuals.

Stress Management

The clear thrust of the evidence from various types of research on stress, from animal studies as well as human studies, is that an individual's uncertainty about impending events and sense of control over them are the main factors in perceived stress. This conclusion is supported by the extensive review paper on stress and performance prepared for the committee by Seymour Levine (see Note 2). A case in point is the study of hormonal and behavioral responses of Norwegian paratroop trainees as they made repeated jumps from a tower on a guide wire (Ursin, Baade, & Levine, 1978). Initially high elevations of cortisone in the blood were reduced to basal levels after the second jump and fear ratings changed similarly.

The implications of this research evidence for the army are complex. There surely are practical limitations on how much knowledge and understanding of the future can be disseminated during combat and on how much individual or group control can be permitted or demonstrated. Moreover, though the committee focused primarily on stress reduction, the army must also induce stress during training to prepare soldiers for real combat. A study by Novaco, Cook, and Sarason (1983) showed that providing marine recruits with more realistic information about what lies in store for them, and about the skills necessary for coping with the rigors of boot camp, led them to exhibit higher expectations of personal control and efficacy.

The committee reviewed individual and intrapsychic approaches to stress reduction, including arousal reduction (relaxation training and biofeedback), cognitive restructuring and problem solving, and behavioral skills training. Regarding biofeedback, on which a conclusion was specifically requested of the committee, it was found that although biofeedback can achieve a reduction of muscle tension, it does not reduce stress effectively.

Committee members' appreciation of military stress was enhanced by a visit to Fort Benning, Georgia, where they viewed paratroop training (and arranged, and then mercifully aborted, an opportunity for David Goslin to make a jump). They saw Bradley vehicles maneuvering under fire and then rode in one. They also heard a presentation and viewed a videotape on the extraordinarily demanding and stressful procedures of Ranger training, which centers on several weeks of long daily marches over difficult and hazardous terrains under severe environmental conditions.

Influence Strategies

The committee's treatment of strategies of social influence centered on neurolinguistic programming (NLP). NLP's wide use in the army was described by army representative Robert Klaus in two briefings; a background paper by Pruitt, Crocker, and Hanes was recruited by the committee (Note 2); and Singer, Davison, Mobley, and Druckmann attended a workshop on NLP techniques and interviewed Richard Bandler, one of the developers of NLP. The conclusion was that little if any evidence exists either to support NLP's assumptions or to indicate that it is effective as a strategy for social influence.

NLP has also been used as a means to model expert performance and the committee's visit to Fort Benning included a review of a test of this aspect of NLP as applied to marksmanship. Though the committee could find only one evaluation of NLP as a model of expert performance, and found that one wanting, it did conclude that the investigation of expert models constitutes a worthwhile activity for the army, and the continuing committee plans to pursue that topic.

Group Cohesion

The army is quite committed to developing group cohesion. Its current COHORT system of keeping units intact is motivated by the desire to enhance group performance by increasing group cohesion. The chair of the committee's resource advisory group, Lieutenant General Robert M. Elton, and the commander of the Army Research Institute, Colonel William Darryl Henderson, have written in support of it (Elton, 1984; Henderson, 1985). A technical report from the Walter Reed Army Institute for Research points out that civilian scholars as well as senior military officers accept that cohesion inhibits breakdown, without regard to the research community's ability to demonstrate relationships ("The New Manning System Field Evaluation," 1986, No. 3, p. 9). Peters and Waterman's *In Search of Excellence* (1982) may represent civilian scholars in this regard, and indeed, the research community has been supportive to a degree (e.g., Campbell, 1975; Katz & Kahn, 1966).

The committee, however, believed that the arguments in favor ought to be treated as hypotheses rather than conclusions, citing difficulties in separating consequences and indicators of cohesion, the gap between improved cohesion and better unit performance, the tendency to rely on single-factor explanations of group performance, and the possibility of reciprocal effects between cohesion and performance. The current evidence makes it necessary for organizations seeking to benefit from cohesion to proceed largely on faith; the committee referred to some possible negative consequences of cohesion as reviewed by Porter, Lawler, and Hackman (1975): ineffective handling of deviance, "group think," increased impact of any existing negative norms, and increased intergroup conflict. The committee also discussed issues of implementation that it saw as having received little attention. A background paper by Tamir and Kunda (Note 2) developed implications from the cultural perspective advanced by Schein (1985).

Parapsychology

The subcommittee on parapsychology made its principal site visits to the laboratories of Robert Jahn at Princeton University and Helmut Schmidt in San Antonio to discuss experiments on the psychokinetic control of random event generators. Experiments on remote viewing were also discussed at Princeton. Hyman and Humphreys were joined on both visits by Dr. Paul Horwitz, a consultant to the committee and a physicist at Bolt Beranek and Newman Inc., who had organized a 1979 symposium on "Physics and Parapsychology" for the American Physical Society that included as speakers Helmut Schmidt and Ray Hyman. Also visiting Professor Jahn were Druckman, Lawrence, and Paul Holland, then a member of the committee. Hyman visited Edward May at the Stanford Research Institute to discuss experiments on random event generators and remote viewing. Hyman and Horwitz were briefed by representatives of the U.S. Army Laboratory Command on parapsychology and military intelligence; Druckman and Swets were briefed on Soviet parapsychology by representatives of the Army Foreign Science and Technology Center and the Defense Intelligence Agency. In connection with a meeting held in San Diego, the entire committee, kindly accompanied by local psychology professors George Mandler and William McGill, visited the laboratory of Cleve Backster who suggests that the electrical activity of a preparation of leukocytes taken from the mouth of a human subject responds to the emotional states of the subject, at a later time and in a different place. For this visit, the promise to the committee, not fulfilled, was an observable demonstration of anomalous events.

Visitors to Professor Jahn's laboratory were shown how subjects sit in front of one of three kinds of random event generators and attempt to affect the behavior of the device in one of three ways: In the PK + mode, the subject tries to get a higher than chance level of hits; in PK − mode, a lower than chance level; and in baseline mode, a number of hits equal to the chance level. Under volitional conditions, the subject is free to select among the three modes; under instructed conditions, he or she is not. Horwitz observed that the investigators reported no differences in results occasioned by a transition from a true random event generator (an analogue electronic device or a mechanical device) to a pseudorandom event generator (a digital, programmed device) that is actually deterministic and nonrandom. They believed that their subjects could will changes in a voltage or voltage threshold of a noise source or changes in the trajectories of small balls falling down a chute with multiple obstacles and, equally well, changes in certain bits (from zeros to ones or vice versa) of predetermined and otherwise completely reproducible sequences as generated by an array of shift registers.

At his Mind Science Foundation in San Antonio, Dr. Schmidt described an experiment designed to permit a skeptical group of scientists to apply adequate controls to a psychokinesis experiment without destroying the psychological environment for a subject that is said by psi researchers to be critical for obtaining positive results. Both groups use a piece of data not yet available (e.g., specified weather data from the *New York Times* at some agreed-upon future date) as a pointer into a given table of random numbers, which will generate "seed numbers" to a pseudorandom number generator and hence produce a predetermined sequence of ones and zeros. Both groups follow a set procedure to assign PK + and PK − modes to the seed numbers and thereby instructions for the subject. An agreement made during the site visit to conduct a joint experiment with Dr. Horwitz as participant, which would be monitored by the committee, was not followed up by Dr. Schmidt.

The committee benefited from a review of the literature on remote viewing and random event generators prepared for the Army Research Institute by John Palmer and from a review of the same studies that it commissioned Alcock to make. The committee also reviewed the other main body of experimental research, namely, on Ganzfeld experiments, in which a homogeneous visual field is used to alter states of mind in the interest of receiving psi signals. A paper on intuitive judgment and the evaluation of evidence was prepared for the committee by Griffin (see Note 2).

With particular attention to the three sets of experimental studies, but including its other reviews and experiences, the committee found no scientific warrant for the existence of parapsychological phenomena. ("No scientific justification" was the phrase agreed on with NRC editors for the committee's report, but "warrant" captures better the intended sense.) Though the committee therefore saw no reason for direct army involvement, it felt that monitoring by the army of the main, current, experimental work would be prudent and suitable. If that monitoring led to the proposal of specific studies, the recommendations were that army and outside scientists arrive at an agreed-upon research protocol, that the research be conducted by proponents and skeptics, and that attention be given to the manipulability and practical application of any effects found to exist.

General Conclusions and Recommendations

Just like business

The committee observed a pervasive army tendency to accept and implement enhancement techniques on the basis of personal or clinical experience and marketplace popularity instead of on the basis of research evidence that could establish the existence and usefulness of an enhancement effect. In expressing its concern about this practice, the committee issued a list of questions about presumed enhancement techniques that had been prepared by scientists at the Walter Reed Army Institute for Research: What changes will the technique produce? What evidence supports the claims for the technique? What theories stand behind it? Who will be able to use it? What are its implications for army operations? How does it fit with army philosophy? What are the cost-benefit factors? (Hegge, Tyner, & Genser, 1983).

Because strong claims of support from basic research have been made for some of the techniques the committee examined, the committee reviewed in its report what it takes to justify a scientific claim. Specifically, it highlighted the need to conduct basic research so that inferences could be drawn in accordance with scientific standards—inferences about novel concepts, causation, alternative explanations of causal relations, and the generalizability of causal relations. Standards for evaluating field tests of enhancement programs were also reviewed, including such factors as immediate effects, side effects, assigning merit and meeting needs, likelihood of transfer, and contrast with alternatives.

The committee acknowledged the differences between rational decision making in science and in practical contexts, for example, differences in the benefits of correct decisions and the costs of incorrect decisions and in what is viewed as a timely decision. It recommended that the army acknowledge such differences explicitly in connection with decisions about particular techniques. It set forth an analysis of the unreliability of testimonies as evidence for enhancement effects. And it stipulated what it thought would be useful mechanisms for advice to different parts of the army as well as bidding procedures it felt would facilitate informed choices of programs and vendors.

The committee recommended that the army continue to examine vigorously enhancement techniques that appear promising. It added the advice that the examination should be systematic and should include techniques drawn from mainstream research as well as packages promoted by vendors. A main concern of the committee was to link more closely the army's great interest in enhancing human performance and its substantial resources for conducting tests to evaluate techniques. The committee remarked on the potential for transfer to the civilian sector.

Committee Publications

The committee's final report was published as a book by the National Academy Press in early 1988, entitled *Enhancing Human Performance: Issues, Theories, and Techniques,* edited by Druckman and Swets. (A second printing was made a year later.) With preliminary copies available, a briefing was given army officials and a press conference was held in December 1987, with Swets, Bjork, Hyman, Singer, and Druckman representing the committee. The press conference was attended by some fifty reporters who heard a 15-minute prepared statement and then raised questions for an hour or so. Primary articles appeared in the *New York Times* (Leary, 1987), *Washington Post* (Squires, 1987a, 1987b), *Washington Times* (Price, 1987), and *Los Angeles Times* (Gillette, 1987), and articles based on them appeared in many other local and regional newspapers. Other news articles were published in *Science* (Holden, 1987), *Science News* (Greenberg, 1988), *Science and Government Report* (Greenberg, 1987), *APA Monitor* (Hostetler, 1988), *Psychology Today* (Roberts, 1988), *The Chronicle of Higher Education* (Wheeler, 1987), Beijing's *Science and Technology Daily* for June 29, 1988, and the NRC's *News Report* (Jarmal, 1988). Swets and Druckman co-authored an op-ed article that was printed in 25 daily newspapers.

The press conference was videotaped by NBC, CNN, and the United States Information Agency. CNN replayed small segments for a few days. NBC's camera did not operate properly, so Tom Brokaw's evening news used file footage representing some of the army's more lurid past interests, for example, in walking through walls, and he commented in kind. National Public Radio presented for a few days an interview with Robert Bjork on learning techniques.

Public Reaction

The committee's book was reviewed descriptively under the heading "Briefly Noted" by Sheldon Zedeck (1988) in *Contemporary Psychology.* It was reviewed extensively by Philip Morrison (1988) in *Scientific American.* We appreciated his summary: "Among the most difficult lessons in science is how not to deceive yourself. This patient and judicious overview offers genuine help" (p. 109). Irwin Child (1988), in a review for *Choice,* complimented the exposition of general principles of evaluation but noted what he called the report's "bias against exploration of apparent anomalies not yet well attested" (p. 536). Kendrick Frazier (1988) reviewed the book extensively for the *Skeptical Inquirer,* with emphasis on paranormal phenomena.

Druckman and Swets received several phone calls and letters, many of them complimentary (wanting more information and making suggestions), for example, from the Los Angeles Police Department, and many of them expressing concern over negative treatment of particular techniques. In an interchange of several letters, Wilse Webb argued that we had been too generous to one technique, that sleep learning was not worth a "second look."

The strongest reactions came as expected from proponents of the paranormal and these tended to be in letters addressed to Frank Press, Chairman of the National Research Council. Robert Jahn, former Dean of Princeton's School of Engineering and Applied Science, wrote that a biased committee made factual errors in reviewing his experiments on mental biasing of random number generators. A copy from Jahn to Senator Claiborne Pell was followed by a letter from Pell to Press. The senator was concerned, among other things, about the possible impact of the committee's report on the National Science Foundation, which was said to be reconsidering support of parapsychological research, and he no doubt had in mind his plans to sponsor a bill to create a commission to study parapsychology and other performance-enhancement techniques, a bill co-sponsored by Senators Gore and Kassebaum and now in committee (e.g., *Newsweek,* June 26, 1989, p. 8). Not satisfied by the committee's detailed replies to Jahn's letters, Jahn and Pell carried their case to the undersecretary of the army, who responded that it would be improper for the army to insert itself in this argument and that failing direct resolution with the NRC, resolution could be pursued through scientific forums and journals.

The President of the Parapsychological Association, Inc., Richard S. Broughton, also wrote to Chairman Press, emphasizing what he and his associates saw as bias in the selection of the committee and an attempt by the committee's chair to suppress a positive evaluation of a set of parapsychology studies. Upon what it considered an inadequate response from the NRC, the association published a lengthy report as a "Reply to the National Research Council Study on Parapsychology." That reply was reviewed in *The Chronicle of Higher Education* (Wheeler, 1988) and in *Omni* magazine (Huyghe, 1989). Similarly, R.A. McConnell of the University of Pittsburgh wrote Druckman and Swets and then mailed an extensive set of his materials, including his correspondence with the NRC and an earlier article by him. Colonel John Alexander (Ret.), one of the briefers at the committee's first meeting, challenged the validity of its report in the periodical *New Realities* (Alexander, 1989). We should add that the NRC's executive office consistently supported the committee's conclusions (and, we understand, put off a potential donor as a result).[5]

The Army's Reaction

Army leadership was initially concerned about the early publicity, primarily the negative treatment by NBC News. Concern was expressed to and within the army by advocates of specific techniques that had received negative evaluations. Field leaders at first showed limited interest, largely through calls by users or opponents of specific techniques. As time went on, the army received favorable comments from several sources about the committee's report and the interest of field leaders increased. One apparently influential event was Druckman's briefing of the army's Human Factors Technical Group in May 1988; another was the favorable mention of the report in the chief of staff's monthly newsletter.

In September 1988, Bjork, Druckman, Johnson, and Swets went to General Thurman's headquarters at Fort Monroe, Virginia, to brief him on the study and to propose directions for further study. That meeting, scheduled for 45 minutes but lasting 3 hours and 45 minutes, was an exceptionally successful event. Thurman's ideas about follow-on ARI research projects were many and in knowledgeable and authoritative detail. He wanted the committee to continue and gave it a new charter: Rather than evaluating others' solutions to soldier-performance problems, it could choose from a list of general problems that the army would generate and develop its own proposed approaches. He was impressed, for example, that academic psychology had insights into training for skill retention instead of merely for rapid acquisition. And he offered to arrange the classroom and field resources required for tests of concepts and evaluation of larger-scale applications. General Thurman's comment about the generally skeptical or negative evaluation by the committee of several enhancement techniques, some of which he had personally considered seriously, was "I was listening to my gurus of the time and I was wrong."

Continuing Committee Activities

The second major phase of the committee's activities is now under way. A newly constituted committee met in July 1989 to put the final touches on an agenda that took shape over the 19 months that followed the release of *Enhancing Human Performance.*[6] A second meeting at General Thurman's headquarters in April 1989 was especially important in defining the committee's new tasks. The meeting was hosted by

Lieutenant General John Crosby, who has assisted General Thurman and the committee throughout its existence; the presentations focused on current uses of self-assessment and other approaches to individual development in the army, on the problems in maintaining high performance in situations of high stress and high risk, and on the problem of detecting deception. Subcommittees were appointed to consider the following problem areas.

Long-term retention of skills and knowledge

Skills and knowledge gained in army instructional programs are exercised often a year later. Therefore, the committee will examine procedures that appear to slow the acquisition rate initially but may be optimal for long-term, post-training effectiveness. Included, for example, are spacing of repetitions during practice, restricted feedback on the execution of motor skills (Schmidt, Young, Swinnen, & Shapiro, 1989), and requiring the learner to perform under conditions of restricted sensory input.

Training to optimize performance in special emotional, physical, and environmental states

Procedures that optimize the initial rate of acquisition are unlikely to be optimal in terms of improving later performance under conditions of stress and/or restricted information. Recent research on state dependencies in memory (body states, mood states, and environmental contexts) may have implications for training (Bjork & Richardson-Klavehn, 1989; Eich, 1989; Smith, 1988). Training techniques designed in sports psychology to enhance performance under pressure may have implications for army training programs.

Cognitive-motor preparation to perform under pressure

Beyond such training issues having to do with the acquisition of a skill, there are issues related to performing at the level one is capable of when it matters. There are indications that certain preparation strategies (such as mental rehearsal, or automating pre-performance motor routines) may prime or stabilize the cognitive motor programs that underlie skilled performance. Such strategies may help to induce or maintain bodily states that are correlated with high performance; recent psychophysiological studies suggest that certain patterns of heart-rate and EEG changes in the few seconds prior to the execution of a critical shot or stroke (in golf or archery) are correlated with better performance (Landers, personal communication).

Models of expert performance

The potential of modeling experts was suggested by the committee's prior review of neurolinguistic programming (NLP), by research developments, and by developments in sports training. In its otherwise fairly negative evaluation of NLP, the committee found promise in the importance NLP attributes to decoding an expert's behavior as a guide to training the beginner. Research on the nature of expertise has flourished in recent years (Chi, Glaser, & Farr, 1988) and may provide a foundation for training/performance programs. In addition, computer-aided representations of skilled performance have apparently been used with some success in sports psychology.

"Subliminal" methods to enhance mental states

As part of recent research activity employing a variety of nontraditional measures of memory (see the earlier discussion of learning during sleep) that seem sensitive to types of learning without awareness ("data-driven processing"), there is renewed interest in subliminal learning (e.g., Jacoby & Whitehouse,1989; Marcel, 1983). While such results suggest a new look at the subliminal-learning issue, a large variety of subliminal tapes designed to alter attitudes, enhance confidence, reduce anxieties, and so forth, have had striking success in the marketplace.

Manipulating mental, emotional, and arousal states

A draft review of the literature on techniques to change mental states, commissioned by ARI and prepared by J. Brener and S. R. Connally, was reviewed by Druckman and Posner for implications for task performance. Research developments in various fields, including health psychology, suggest that altered states of consciousness may affect a variety of physiological processes. The converse may be true as well; recent work suggests that mood states may be altered by influences on bloodflow that are a consequence of the differing facial muscular patterns corresponding to various emotional expressions (Zajonc, Murphy, & Inglehart, 1989). ARI, motivated by the problem of detecting deception (Hyman, 1989), has urged the committee to consider also the physical manifestations of mental and emotional states.

Career development

A class of techniques designed to improve performance through increased self-insight is widely used in public and private organizations; included are assessment batteries designed to facilitate leadership, interpersonal influence skills, team building, and decision making. Specific examples are the Myers-Briggs Type Indicator (Myers & McCaulley, 1985), the Managerial Grid (Blake & Mouton, 1964), and the Social Styles Profile (Merrill & Reid, 1981). These techniques have considerable appeal to trainers as well as to the trainees because of high "face validity," but they have been subject to little rigorous research. To help define the questions, the committee commissioned Paul Thayer to write a critical review of the relevant literature.

Part-whole methods to enhance group processes

At its first meeting the continuing committee became convinced that certain issues of group performance deserved study. Should the members of a working group be trained as a team or individually? If team training facilitates initial performance, is that advantage offset by greater disruption when original members of the team need to be replaced by new members? Should the individuals in a group be trained in only their task, or should there be backup training to increase the flexibility of the group? Current research may not supply definitive answers to these and a number of related questions, but the issues are important enough to army functioning to be addressed, if only to clarify the questions and to outline needed research.

Conclusion

Although other arrangements might be workable, we found that the National Research Council provides an ideal setting for a study of this sort. The Council was designed expressly for the purpose, first under the sponsorship of the National Academy of Science and now administered as well by the National Academy of Engineering and the Institute of Medicine. The NAS was chartered by Congress in 1863; the NRC was established in 1916. Among the NRC's strengths are that it spans the scientific and professional disciplines; it benefits from the prestige of its governing academies; it provides in competent fashion the services required by committee function; and it follows guidelines to promote thorough and objective reports, including procedures for proposal and report review. Committee members are suggested by broadly based advisers, proposed by a commission's staff and executive director working with the committee's chairperson, nominated by the commission, and appointed by the NRC's chairperson in the interests of competence, relevance, and diversity of viewpoints. They are asked to verify that they have no conflict of interest and they serve without financial compensation.

Members of the committee generally regarded their task as challenging and they demonstrated consistently that it was engaging. They came to the meetings almost without exception, made site visits willingly, submitted draft sections of the report nearly on time, and achieved consensus in an advised, efficient, and congenial way. They feel that their training and experience were adequate to the task and they are pleased to recommend the process to psychologists and scientists in related fields. The continuing committee can reasonably anticipate that it will contribute more by steering the army toward promising new ways to enhance training and performance and less by saving the army from investing in ineffective techniques. It will likely also serve an advisory role for some specific enhancement projects undertaken in the army.

A long-term, successful impact of the committee's work, in both of its phases, is hardly assured. The power of the human-potential movement in the minds of the citizenry, as evidenced by its marketplace popularity, dwarfs the force of mainstream psychology. New Age techniques are also apparently making substantial inroads on the more than $30 billion a year that the American Society for Training and Development estimates to be spent on formal courses in industry (*Wall Street Journal*, August 5, 1986). The army, of course, will continue to have serious needs for performance enhancement and will continue to be bombarded by strong, new claims for existing and new techniques. The lack of theoretical and empirical support for many such techniques does not stifle their ability to capture the imagination of consumers.

Still, the Condon Report of 1968 on unidentified flying objects was cited recently (Alexander, 1989) as continuing to depress the government's interest in that subject, and we note that the Condon Committee had nothing positive to substitute. The continuing challenge to mainstream psychology will be to translate its findings and concepts into practical enhancement techniques and to package those techniques so it can "give psychology away"—or sell it, for that matter. The committee's efforts, we submit, should be only an installment.

Notes

1. The committee consisted of John A. Swets, chair, Robert A. Bjork, Thomas D. Cook, Gerald C. Davison, Lloyd G. Humphreys, Ray Hyman, Daniel M. Landers, Sandra

A. Mobley, Lyman W. Porter, Michael I. Posner, Walter Schneider, Jerome E. Singer, Sally P. Springer, and Richard F. Thompson.

2. Ten commissioned papers, available from the National Academy Press, are these: Eric Eich, Learning during sleep; Robert E. Slavin, Principles of effective instruction; Deborah L. Feltz, Daniel M. Landers, and Betsy J. Becker, A revised meta-analysis of the mental practice literature on motor skill learning; Seymour Levine, Stress and performance; Raymond W. Novaco, Stress reduction and the military; Dean G. Pruitt, Jennifer Crocker, and Deborah Hanes, Matching and other influence strategies; Boaz Tamir and Gideon Kunda, Culture and military performance; James E. Alcock, A comprehensive review of major empirical studies in parapsychology involving random event generators and remote viewing; Monica J. Harris and Robert Rosenthal, Interpersonal expectancy effects and human performance research; Dale Griffin, Intuitive judgment and the evaluation of evidence.

3. The Resource Advisory Group consisted of general officers who held the positions of Deputy Chief of Staff for Personnel, Deputy Chief of Staff for Intelligence, Director of Army Research and Technology, Commander of the Soldier Support Center, and Commander, Medical Research and Development Command and as well the Assistant Secretary of the Army for Manpower and Reserve Affairs.

4. Following on that recommendation, an experiment is underway at the Redstone Arsenal in Alabama to evaluate mental practice as a component in the training of complex soldering of electronic circuits. Landers guided the design of conditions that will permit a comparison of mental-practice, placebo, and standard training groups.

5. Colonel Alexander, who co-hosted the committee at Cleve Backster's laboratory test of the emotional response of Posner's leukocytes, wrote that the committee denigrated such scientific research by mentioning also the scientifically unsupported ideas of psychic warfare and psychotronic weapons. Meanwhile, R.A. McConnell wrote that the committee's mention of Backster's research was an attempt to taint legitimate research on parapsychology. We noticed that the Parapsychological Association, Inc., did not collaborate with McConnell in its complaint about the committee's report and that Robert Jahn chose to keep his adverse reaction separate from that of the Parapsychological Association, Inc.

6. Five new members were added to the committee to bolster its expertise in the new problem areas on its agenda. Michelene Chi, Robert Christina, James Davis, Eric Eich, and Francis Pirozzolo joined seven members of the original committee (Bjork, Davison, Hyman, Landers, Porter, Singer, and Thompson), whose expertise remains appropriate to the committee's new tasks and who were willing to continue on the committee through the next phase. Bjork replaced Swets as committee chair, Druckman remains as study director, and Judith Orasanu is now the committee's liaison with ARI.

References

Aarons, L. (1976). Sleep-assisted instruction. *Psychological Bulletin, 83,* 1-40.

Alexander, J. (1989, March/April). Enhancing human performance: A challenge to the report. *New Realities,* pp. 10-15, 52-53.

Blake, R. R., & Mouton, J. S. (1964). *The managerial grid.* Houston, TX: Gulf.

Bjork, R. A., & Richardson-Klavehn, A. (1989). On the puzzling relationship between environmental context and human memory. In C. Izawa (Ed.), *Current issues in cognitive processes: The Tulane Floweree symposium on cognition* (pp. 313-344). Hillsdale, NJ: Lawrence Erlbaum.

Campbell, D. T. (1975). On the conflicts between biological and social evolution and between psychology and moral tradition. *American Psychologist, 30,* 1103-1126.

Chi, M. T. H., Glaser, R., & Farr, M. (Eds.). (1988). *The nature of expertise.* Hillsdale, NJ: Lawrence Erlbaum.

Child, I. (1988, May). Review of *Enhancing human performance. Choice,* p. 536.

Druckman, D., & Swets, J. A. (Eds.). (1988). *Enhancing human performance: Issues, theories, and techniques.* Washington, DC: National Academy Press.

Duffy, E. (1962). *Activation and behavior.* New York: Wiley.

Eich, E. (1989). Theoretical issues in state-dependent memory. In H. L. Roediger & F. I. M. Craik (Eds.), *Varieties of memory and consciousness: Essays in honour of Endel Tulving* (pp. 331-354). Hillsdale, NJ: Lawrence Erlbaum.

Easterbrook, J. A. (1959). The effect of emotion on cue utilization and the organization of behavior. *Psychological Review, 66,* 183-201.

Elton, R. M. (1984, October). Cohesion and unit pride aims of the new manning system. *Army Magazine,* pp. 218-228.

Frazier, K. (1988, Fall). Improving human performance: What about parapsychology? *Skeptical Inquirer,* pp. 13, 34-45.

Gillette, R. (1987, December 4). Exotic ways to learn doubted by U.S. Study. *Los Angeles Times,* pp. 1, 32.

Greenberg, D. (Ed.). (1987, December 15). Science panel chilly on paranormal weapons for army. *Science and Government Report,* p. 7.

Greenberg, J. (Ed.) (1988, January 2). Offbeat learning methods off target. *Science News,* p. 9.

Hegge, F. W., Tyner, C. F., & Genser, S. (1983). Evaluating human technologies: What questions should we ask? Memorandum, Walter Reed Army Institute for Research, Washington, DC.

Henderson, W. D. (1985). *Cohesion: The human element in combat.* Washington, DC: National Defense University Press.

Holden, C. (1987). Academy helps army be all that it can be. *Science, 238,* 1501-1502.

Hostetler, A. J. (1988, January). Army eyes novel learning methods. *A.P.A. Monitor,* p. 7.

Huyghe, P. (1989, April). Parapsychology vs. the NRC. *Omni,* pp. 90-91.

Hyman, R. (1989). The psychology of deception. *Annual Review of Psychology, 40,* 133-154.

Jacoby, L. L., & Whitehouse, K. (1989). An illusion of memory: False recognition influenced by unconscious perception. *Journal of Experimental Psychology: General, 118,* 126-135.

Jarmal, D. (December 1987/January 1988). There are no easy ways to make better soldiers. National Research Council *News Report,* pp. 2-6.

Katz, D., & Kahn, R. L. (1966). *The social psychology of organizations.* New York: Wiley.

Leary, W. E. (1987, December 4). Army's learning panel urges offbeat studies. *New York Times,* p. B5.

Marcel, A. J. (1983). Conscious and unconscious perception: An approach to the relations between phenomenal experience and perceptual processes. *Cognitive Psychology, 15,* 238-300.

Merrill, D. W., & Reid, R. H. (1981). *Personal styles and effective performance.* Radnor, PA: Chilton.

Morrison, P. (1988, August). Review of *Enhancing human performance. Scientific American,* pp. 108-109.

Moruzzi, G., & Magoun, H. W. (1949). Brainstem reticular formation and activation of the EEG. *EEG and Clinical Neurophysiology, 1,* 455-473.

Myers, I. B., & McCaulley, M. A. (1985). *A guide to the development and use of the Myers-Briggs Type Indicator.* Palo Alto, CA: Consulting Psychologist Press.

Novaco, R. W., Cook, T. M., & Sarason, I. G. (1983). Military recruit training: An arena for stress-coping skills. In D. Meichenbaum & M. E. Jaremko (Eds.) *Stress reduction and prevention.* New York: Plenum.

Peters, T. J., & Waterman, R. H. (1982). *In search of excellence.* New York: Harper & Row.

Price, J. (1987, December 4). Panel rejects mental telepathy, ESP for practical military use. *Washington Times,* p. A6.

Porter, L. W., Lawler, E. E., & Hackman, J. R. (1975). *Behavior in organizations.* New York: McGraw-Hill.

Posner, M. I. (1975). Psychobiology of attention. In M. S. Gazzaniga & C. Blakemore (Eds.), *Handbook of psychobiology.* New York: Academic Press.

Richardson, A. (1967). Mental practice: A review and discussion. *Research Quarterly, 38,* 95-107, 263-273.

Richardson-Klavehn, A., & Bjork, R.A. (1988). Measures of memory. *Annual Review of Psychology, 39,* 475-543.

Robbins, T. W., & Everitt, B. J. (1982). Functional studies of the central catecholamines. *International Review of Neurobiology, 23,* 303-365.

Roberts, M. (1988, March). Be all that you can be. *Psychology Today,* pp. 22, 28-29.

Rumelhart, D. E., & McClelland, J. L. (1986). *Parallel distributed processing.* Cambridge, MA: Bradford Brooks, MIT Press.

Schacter, D. L. (1987). Implicit memory: History and current status. *Journal of Experimental Psychology: Learning, Memory, and Cognition, 13,* 501-518.

Schein, E. H. (1985). *Organizational culture and leadership.* San Francisco: Jossey-Bass.

Schmidt, R. A., Young, D. E., Swinnen, S., & Shapiro, D. C. (1989). Summary knowledge of results for skill acquisition: Support for the guidance hypothesis. *Journal of Experimental Psychology: Learning, Memory, and Cognition, 15,* 352-359.

Shimamura, A. P. (1986). Priming effects in amnesia: Evidence for a dissociable memory function. *Quarterly Journal of Experimental Psychology, 38A,* 619-644.

Smith, S. M. (1988). Environmental context-dependent memory. In D. M. Thompson & G. M. Davies (Eds.), *Memory in context: Context in memory* (pp. 13-34). New York: Wiley.

Squires, S. (1987a, December 4). Army research finds possible military use for sleep learning: Parapsychology's validity doubted. *Washington Post,* p. A23.

Squires, S. (1987b, December 8). Biofeedback: Even the army is interested, but . . . *Washington Post,* p. Z11.

Squires, S. (1988, April 17). The pentagon's twilight zone. *Washington Post,* p. C3.

Ursin, H., Baade, E., & Levine, S. (Eds.). (1978). *Psychobiology of stress: A study of coping men.* New York: Academic Press.

Wheeler, D. L. (1987, December 9). New study for National Academy of Sciences debunks many methods for enhancing human performance. *Chronicle of Higher Education,* p. A4.

Wheeler, D. L. (1988, September 14). Parapsychologists fire back at National Academy report that called field unscientific and experiments flawed. *Chronicle of Higher Education,* pp. A5, A10.

Yerkers, R. M., & Dodson, J. P. (1908). The relationship of strength of stimulus to rapidity of habit formation. *Journal of Comparative Neurological Psychology, 18,* 458-482.

Zajonc, R. B., Murphy, S. T., & Inglehart, M. (1989). Feeling and facial efference: Implications of the vascular theory of emotion. *Psychological Review, 96,* 395-416.

Zedeck, S. (1988). Review of *Enhancing human performance. Contemporary Psychology, 33,* 727.

IMPLICATIONS FOR HUMAN RESOURCE DEVELOPMENT PROFESSIONALS

The major message from the Swets and Bjork work is that HRD practitioners should not adopt methods simply because developers of these methods say that they work. The authors showed the importance of undertaking a thorough review of previous research and examining rigorous scientific studies in addition to personal experience and marketplace popularity.

The National Research Council committee provided a series of questions that HRD practitioners should use to make decisions regarding proposed training and development methods:

- ♦ What changes (in learning, retention, reproduction, and generalization) will the method produce?
- ♦ What evidence exists to support claims for the method?
- ♦ What theories support the method or components of the method?
- ♦ Who will be able to use it?
- ♦ What are its implications for the organization's operations?
- ♦ How does the method fit with the organization's philosophy?
- ♦ What are the costs and benefits?

By answering these questions, the HRD professional can make an informed decision for the organization regarding training approaches that will yield what the organization needs in terms of learning and performance outcomes.

IMPLICATIONS FOR RESEARCH DESIGN AND METHODOLOGY

For researchers, this work provides an important model. These authors did not immediately begin primary studies to answer important questions. Instead, they undertook a thorough review of previous research, focusing primarily on what they called "rigorous scientific studies."

Their review was not, however, limited to scientific studies. They also examined evidence gathered from personal experience and marketplace popularity. HRD researchers may want to consider similar reviews or meta-analyses of the literature on specific popular training and development approaches. Written material on a particular method may contain extensive reports of personal experience and popularity yet lack experimental testing. In such cases, HRD researchers can make important contributions to the field by designing and conducting experiments evaluating the method and using appropriate controls.

IMPLICATIONS FOR FUTURE INQUIRY

Swets and Bjork have suggested that some of the methods need further experimental tests (as in Baldwin's article, Chapter 1) or field tests (as in the Bretz and Thompsett article, Chapter 3). HRD researchers may want to examine some of the most promising methods to determine their effect within organizational settings. Sleep learning methods, for example, may be useful in situations where training must be completed in a short period of time and where trainees may need to function in sleep-deprived states. Some examples outside the military include the learning of new techniques needed by emergency room staff or those engaged in shift work.

In addition to the "New Age" methods discussed in the article, researchers should examine the alternative technologies being touted for their efficacy and cost-effectiveness. Such technologies as CD-ROM, the Internet, and distance learning may prove useful, but only for certain people and certain situations.

OTHER RESOURCES

Bjork, R. A., & Swets, J. A. (Eds.). (1992). *In the mind's eye.* Washington, DC: National Academy Press.

Druckman, D., & Swets, J. A. (Eds.). (1988). *Enhancing human performance: Issues, theories, and techniques.* Washington, DC: National Academy Press.

Comparing Traditional and Integrative Learning Methods in Organizational Training Programs

Robert D. Bretz, Jr.
Cornell University

Robert E. Thompsett
Eastman Kodak Company

PREVIOUS RESEARCH AND ANECDOTAL REPORTS HAVE SUGGESTED THAT WHEN certain teaching approaches are used, students not only learn more but also experience greater satisfaction with the training process. This study examined the effects of integrative-learning-based (IL) training in relation to lecture-based training. Employees enrolled in a three-day manu-

Source: Bretz, R. D., & Thompsett, R. E. (1992). Comparing traditional and integrative learning methods in organizational training programs. *Journal of Applied Psychology,* 77(6), 941-951. Used by permission.

Authors' Note: Funding for this research was provided by the Center for Advanced Human Resource Studies, School of Industrial and Labor Relations, Cornell University, Ithaca, New York, and by Eastman Kodak Company. The views, opinions, and findings contained in this article are ours and do not reflect official Eastman Kodak Company policy or opinion.

We thank Dennis Lyons, Robert Keller, Robert Cournoyer, and Sharon Weins of Eastman Kodak Company for their administrative and logistical support. We also thank Frank Voullo, Laurence Martel, Laurence VanEtten, and Peter Kline of the National Academy of Integrative Learning for their insights and cooperation. We are especially grateful to Albert Brault, Executive Director of the Center for Advanced Human Resource Studies, for his assistance and support throughout this project. Dann Hayes and Collete Mike deserve special thanks for their assistance in data collection and processing. Finally, we thank John Bishop, John Boudreau, Leo Flanagan, Barry Gerhart, and two anonymous reviewers for their helpful comments on earlier drafts of this article.

facturing resource planning training course were randomly assigned to either IL or traditional training. Subjects reacted more favorably to IL-based training. Trained subjects performed significantly better than those in a no-treatment control group, but no differences were noted between training interventions.

By all accounts, training in U.S. organizations is big business. More than 90% of all private organizations have some type of systematic training program (Goldstein, 1986), and virtually all organizations with more than 1,000 employees systematically train managerial personnel (Saari, Johnson, McLaughlin, & Zimmerle, 1988). It is estimated that more than $44 billion per year are spent on training initiatives (Carnevale & Gainer, 1989). Moreover, employee training and development is often identified as the most critical priority organizations will need to address in the coming decade (e.g., Goldstein, 1991; Milkovich & Boudreau, 1991). In spite of this perceived importance, however, training methods are often seen as fads, training program evaluation is rare, and rigorous evaluation is virtually nonexistent (Goldstein, 1986, 1991).

A training approach referred to as *integrative learning* (IL, also referred to as *accelerated learning* or *super learning*) has been used for many years in educational settings. For example, the United Nations Education and Scientific Cultural Organization (UNESCO) has reported dramatic results with IL in foreign language courses (Rose, 1985). In addition, public school systems in Finland, Chicago, Detroit, Boston, and Jacksonville, and in Brooklyn, Oswego, Syracuse, Rochester, and Utica, New York, have implemented IL-based curriculums (Martel, 1989). Moreover, IL is increasingly being used in U.S. industry. Many organizations (both public and private) believe that training programs that are based on the IL approach may offer substantially better learning and retention rates than those achieved by traditional training methods. There are IL-based training initiatives in place in dozens of U.S. government agencies and embassies and in several large organizations, including Alcan, Apple, AT&T, Bell Atlantic, Eastman Kodak, General Motors, Hilton Hotels, Johnson Controls, Sandia Laboratories, Shell Oil, and US West, among others (The Center for Accelerated Learning, 1989; Martel, 1989; Rose, 1985).

The IL approach is firmly rooted in Lewin's (1951) equation $B = f(P, E)$—behavior is a function of the person and the environment. In fact, because the learning environment is viewed as so important, IL places extreme emphasis on creating environmental conditions believed to maximize learning potential. Integrative learning is based on a belief that environments that minimize or eliminate traditional barriers to learning allow students to use more of their cognitive potential and cause greater learning and retention to occur. Learning barriers include negative reinforcement, fear of failure, boredom, and anxiety. Proponents of IL argue that most educational institutions and corporate training programs are characterized by environments that impose rather than eliminate these barriers.

The IL approach relies on the "combination of physical relaxation, mental concentration, guided imagery, suggestive principles, and baroque music" (Druckman & Swets, 1988, p. 6) to replicate the environments in which children learn basic life skills. A wide variety of instructional components are used to make the learning environment more relaxing and enjoyable. These components include supportive comfortable surroundings, music, rhythmic mnemonics, games, stories, poetry, background posters and peripherals, and group interactions. Performance is enhanced through self-monitoring, data feedback, and positive reinforcement. Advanced organizers, student participation, and timing of instructional elements provide a structure that prepares the students to learn, gets them involved in the learning, and allows for both mental and physical "practice." Enjoyable and positive learning experiences are then supposed to lead to further learning.

[handwritten margin note: definition of Integrative Learning]

Many of these IL instructional components have been shown to increase learning effectively. For example, the ability to remember information about objects can be improved through guided imagery and also appears to be enhanced by songs and rhythm (Paivio, 1971; Paivio & Desrochers, 1979). Cooperative learning exercises, in which students work together to learn and then present the material (Slavin, 1983), and the use of advanced organizers (an overview of which is to come; Mayer, 1979) also appear to enhance learning. A critical component of IL-based training, the repetition of material through diverse media, is based on research showing that long-term memory is enhanced when material is repeated at optimal intervals rather than under massed practice conditions (Crowder, 1976; Goldstein, 1986). In addition, heavy reliance on student-generated elaboration of the material rather than trainer-generated explanations facilitates learning (Reder, Charney, & Morgan, 1986), as would be expected under conditions that allow additional practice (e.g., Digman, 1959).

The IL instructional components appear to work through their impact on affectivity. The IL classroom atmosphere and the mix of instructional components are designed to minimize learning barriers (negative reinforcement, fear of failure, boredom, anxiety) and to create positive affect among participants. Although intense emotional states tend to interrupt normal processing of information (e.g., Simon, 1967), mild positive affective states have been shown to change not only the content of thoughts but also the nature of the cognitive process itself. Recent research indicates that positive affect influences the manner in which information is organized and improves the ability to integrate divergent information (Isen & Daubman, 1984; Isen, Johnson, Mertz, & Robinson, 1985).

Recently, Ree and Earles (1991) reported that general cognitive ability was the best predictor of training success. The philosophy underlying IL, however, rejects the commonly held understanding of intelligence. In the IL framework, general cognitive ability, or psychometric g (Jensen, 1986), is seen as only one of many faculties that meet the criteria for intelligence (Martel, 1989). Proponents of IL accept the premise that seven separate and distinct intelligences exist and that people can learn and express their knowledge in linguistic, logical-mathematical, musical, spatial, bodily-kinesthetic, interpersonal, or intrapersonal ways (Gardner, 1983). They argue that traditional instructional techniques that focus on linguistic, mathematical, and logical abilities, to the exclusion of the others, limit the learning that occurs by neglecting the other intelligences. Moreover, students are purported to be differentially affected depending on their dominant learning style. That is, students with primarily visual-auditory learning styles may be less affected by this neglect than students with primarily kinesthetic learning styles. IL instructional methods purport to integrate the power of multiple intelligences, thereby allowing exponential increases in learning and retention.

The popular press has reported remarkable success with IL-based instruction. For example, UNESCO claimed that this approach allowed students to "absorb and retain a two year language course in as few as 20 days" (Rose, 1985, p. 3), and Ostrander and Schroeder (1975) reported that just the suggestive principles used in IL increase learning "from five to fifty times, increase retention, [and] require virtually no effort on the part of students" (p. 15). Several research studies have attempted to document reports such as these; however, though the principles are appealing and the claims ambitious, the empirical support has been less than convincing. Kirkpatrick (1959) suggested that evaluation procedures could consider four levels of criteria: reaction, learning, behavior, and results. Most of the support for the IL approach is based on reaction measures. Testimonials abound, and examinations of learning criteria have typically used experimental designs that lack the control necessary to eliminate alternative explanations.

Perhaps the most frequently cited testimonial regards the rejuvenation of Chicago's Guggenheim School, an inner-city school (Grades kindergarten–8). Prior to 1985, the school was plagued by poor student performance. The entire teaching staff was trained in IL methods and began applying IL techniques in 1986. Reports indicated that average reading performance doubled, mathematic performance increased by approximately 50%, and the school's ranking within its district, based on student performance, increased dramatically (Martel, 1989). However, though it is possible that the introduction of the IL techniques caused the increase, it is also possible that the results were due to administrative changes that accompanied the transition, teacher enthusiasm, or Hawthorne effects.

The research that has addressed IL has been criticized for several reasons. First, almost all of the experimental studies that exist failed to control for instructor (e.g., Gasser-Roberts, 1985; Schuster & Prichard, 1978) or Hawthorne (e.g., Knibbeler, 1982) effects that may have confounded the instructional effects. Second, weak experimental designs (e.g., posttest only or one-group designs) have led to uninterpretable and unsupportable conclusions (Cook & Campbell, 1979). Finally, small sample sizes typically have not provided the statistical power to detect significant differences that might have actually existed.

Limited evidence exists with regard to the application of IL techniques in corporate training programs. For example, Bell Atlantic recently converted two customer-service training courses from traditional teaching methods to an IL-based format. Gill and Meier (1989) reported that "the satisfaction of students and trainers greatly improved, as did their job performance" (p. 63). The results are difficult to interpret, however, because the performance increases were inferred from posttest-only supervisory responses to the question "do your newly-trained employees perform better, the same, or worse than those previously trained?" The absence of pretests and control groups, combined with the informational campaign that accompanied the new training intervention, makes it impossible to determine if the use of IL caused increased performance. What is clear, and consistent with other studies, is that reaction measures indicated that students like this type of training. It is not clear whether participant reactions lead to any tangible differences in learning, retention, behavior, or impact.

In 1984, the National Academy of Sciences (NAS) began to examine the potential of several approaches, including IL-based techniques, that were purported to enhance human performance (Druckman & Swets, 1988). The NAS committee concluded that although the approach was based on sound instructional components that should improve learning (e.g., imagery, cooperation, repetition), the research to date was sufficiently flawed to prevent sound conclusions from being drawn regarding the effectiveness and the utility of IL-based training programs. The committee called for scientifically controlled studies in applied settings. In the current study, we respond to that call by directly comparing IL-based and traditional training methods through an experimental design in an organizational setting.

Hypotheses

Direct comparison of training interventions yields many testable hypotheses. We focus on the issues that have received the most attention and appear to be most central to the IL approach: student reaction and student learning. Research, though inconclusive, and the plethora of testimonials indicate that IL-based training will lead to greater comprehension. These sources also strongly suggest that participants react very favorably to IL-based training. Therefore, we present the following hypotheses.

Hypothesis 1

Students trained using IL methods will learn more than students trained with traditional methods.

Hypothesis 2

Students in IL-based training will have more positive reactions to the training than will students trained with traditional methods.

Method

Setting

Technical Educational Resources (TER) at Kodak is responsible for supplying training to Kodak divisions in a timely, competitive fashion. One of the major ongoing training initiatives at Kodak during the late 1980s and early 1990s has been manufacturing resource planning (MRP-II). This is a method for effectively planning, coordinating, and integrating the use of all resources of a manufacturing company (Wallace, 1985).

As is true of most subject matter, MRP-II training can be delivered at introductory, intermediate, or advanced levels, depending on the individual's needs and the organization's goals. Successful full-scale implementation of MRP-II depends on each employee understanding and following procedural guidelines. The 3-day training program assessed in this study had been designed to provide employees with an introduction to MRP-II and to transmit the fundamental knowledge necessary to contribute to implementing the system. This training is particularly important to Kodak because the organization views successful full-scale implementation as necessary to maintaining its competitive advantage in the coming decade.

At the time planning for this study began (mid-1989), the three-day MRP-II training program was being offered in both traditional and IL-based formats, and TER officials estimated that approximately 10,000 Kodak employees would receive MRP-II training over the next two years. Kodak contemplated converting all MRP-II training from a traditional to an IL-based format. Because of the scope of the training, the perceived importance of MRP-II in Kodak's business plan, and the potential benefits

IL purported to offer in terms of greater learning and attitudinal improvements, Kodak officials were interested in rigorous documentation of the effects of IL in relation to the traditional manner (lecture) in which MRP-II training was delivered. To achieve this objective, the principal investigator served as an impartial mediator in a series of meetings during which the hypotheses to be tested, the research design, the measures, and the procedure were agreed to by the proponents of both traditional and IL-based training. This method, in which the concerned parties jointly design the study, has been shown to be effective for resolving scientific disputes (Latham, Erez, & Locke, 1988).

The traditional method of teaching was a lecture-based delivery of the primary elements of MRP-II. It incorporated many examples and allowed participants to ask questions as they arose. The content of the IL-based approach was derived from the traditional approach and covered exactly the same material. Even though the content of the courses was similar, however, the delivery of the material was radically different.

Each IL-based training session began with a series of activities intended to create a relaxed, positive environment for learning. Before the students arrived, the facilitators (trainers) removed the desks and tables from the room, put up several posters containing important MRP-II elements and concepts, and set the chairs in a circle. The intent was not only to improve communication between students but also to suggest that the facilitator was only one of many potential sources from which to learn. When they arrived, subjects first engaged in a relaxation exercise that involved tossing a ball around the room. The person catching the ball introduced himself or herself and told the group something "good or new" that had happened in the past couple of days. Then, students were asked what MRP-II meant to them, and attempts were made to reaffirm their beliefs (show them that their preconceptions were "correct") and unite the group around a common understanding of MRP-II. Finally, the facilitators provided a global overview of MRP-II. This overview was intended as a framework on which the students could organize the material that would follow.

The major portion of the IL-based course focused on the primary elements of MRP-II. Each element was presented in a module (lasting from 20 minutes to 1.5 hours) that included facilitator explanation of the concepts followed by an activity intended to reinforce the concepts in a fun or relaxing way. The activities included group discussions, games (e.g., Win-Lose-or-Draw and Charades), stories and poetry, and an elaborate business game that involved producing and distributing a product. The nature and complexity of each activity was matched to the nature and complexity of the MRP-II element that it reinforced.

Another primary segment of the IL-based training involved student presentation of the material. From 1 to 2 hours on the afternoon of the second day and again on the morning of the final day were set aside for groups of students to prepare skits or games depicting "life at the shop" both before and after implementation of MRP-II. A significant portion of the final day was set aside for group presentations.

Each day of training ended with a concert session in which the facilitator, to the accompaniment of background baroque music, read a story that incorporated the important elements discussed that day. The tempo and intonation of the story were matched to that of the music. The final day of training concluded with a session in which each student was required to set goals regarding specific MRP-II activities and outcomes they planned to accomplish over the next six months. Finally, facilitators reviewed MRP-II, discussed the audit process for certification, and ended with a concert.

Research Design

A Solomon four-group research design was used (Cook, Campbell, & Peracchio, 1990). This design controls for most threats to internal and external validity and represents a significant improvement over typical training evaluation designs (Goldstein, 1986, 1991). The groups consisted of (a) a group that received pretests, IL-based training, and posttests; (b) a group that received pretests, traditional training, and posttests; (c) a group that received IL-based training and posttests only; and (d) a group that received traditional training and posttests only. Because the hypotheses concerned the effects of IL in relation to traditional training methods, it was determined that the most appropriate control group was traditional training rather than no treatment. A no-treatment group was included, however, so that the absolute effects of the training might be ascertained. Membership in Groups 1–4 was determined by random assignment. The organization was unwilling to assign employees randomly to a no-treatment group. Therefore, the no-treatment group consisted of volunteers (all from TER) and was significantly smaller than the treatment groups.

Subjects

Group size was determined through power analysis. One hundred eighty employees were scheduled to be trained, and 172 actually completed the training. Twelve subjects in the no-treatment group brought the total sample size to 184. With this sample size, if the reports of extraordinary improvements over traditional methods were true, assuming Cohen's (1988) convention of a large effect size (one that explains 14% or more of total variation in the dependent variable), power to detect the effect at the .05 level of significance would be greater than .95. Assuming a moderate effect size, again relying on Cohen's convention (one that explains approximately 6% of the variance), at the .05 level of significance, power to detect the effect would be approximately .70-.80.

Subjects were a representative sample of the Kodak population that was expected to be trained in MRP-II. They were mostly male (73%), currently married (74%), and predominantly White (91%). Average age was 42 years and average tenure with Kodak was 18 years. All subjects were high school graduates, most (53%) had attended some college, and 26% were college graduates. Average educational attainment was 14.5 years. Job levels were distributed throughout the organizational hierarchy and salaries ranged from $16,500 to $98,000, with an average of $37,227.

Measures

To measure the amount of material learned, it was necessary to create a test that assessed the subset of MRP-II knowledge addressed in this particular training program. Standardized examinations currently existed for MRP-II certification purposes. Because this course covered only a portion of possible MRP-II subject matter, however, existing competency examinations contained extraneous information that this training program did not contain. Therefore, these examinations were not suitable for determining learning in this context.

To create an appropriate test, an MRP-II expert within Kodak who had had several years' experience in teaching MRP-II and designing, implementing, and evaluating MRP-II in Kodak facilities worldwide reviewed the course content and chose approximately 100 multiple-choice items from those on the certification examinations. These items were then reviewed with four other MRP-II experts who were familiar with the content of the three-day training program. Because testing was uncommon in this organization and because we were instructed to keep testing time to a minimum, it was determined that no more than 30 minutes could be dedicated to assessing learning. Therefore, with input from the other four experts, Kodak's primary MRP-II expert chose 40 items that best represented the content of the three-day training program.

This examination was pilot tested by administering it to 40 individuals who had been certified as MRP-II facilitators at some time in the past (subject-matter experts) and a random sample of 40 other Kodak employees who had had no formal MRP-II training. The experts averaged 81% correct (range, 24-37; SD = 3.38) compared with 50% correct (range, 8-29; SD = 5.18) for the untrained sample, $t(78)$ = 11.63, p < .01. No member of the novice group scored above the expert group mean, and no member of the expert group scored below the novice group mean. Because the untrained group did significantly better than chance, it appeared that the test may have been somewhat lenient. Because MRP-II training is an ongoing initiative, however, and because MRP-II knowledge is considered valuable within Kodak, it is believed that employees acquire some MRP-II knowledge on their own. Because the experts averaged only 81% correct, it appeared that the exam items might have been measuring something other than MRP-II knowledge; however, this was determined to be unlikely for three reasons. First, the items were selected on the basis of content validity, as suggested by Nunnally (1978). Second, when the expert sample was constrained to include only those who used MRP-II regularly as a part of their current job, the average score rose to 87.5% ($SD = 1.41$, $n = 20$). Third, item analysis indicated that the discrimination coefficients on all items were positive, as were the item-total correlations generated by the reliability analysis ($\alpha = .75$). Therefore, on these bases it was determined that the examination demonstrated sufficient content validity and reliability to warrant its use (Ackerman & Humphreys, 1990; Kerlinger, 1986; Nunnally, 1978).

The G.M. Faces scale (Kunin, 1955) was modified to elicit reaction to the training intervention. Specifically, it asked "Which face comes closest to expressing how you feel about the training program you are currently attending?" The scale was anchored by six faces, arranged from sad to happy, and the subject was instructed to check the face that best portrays how he or she felt about the training. To control for the possibility that attitudes about training in general might confound responses to this question, another item, also based on the G.M. Faces scale format, asked "Which face comes closest to expressing how you feel about your training opportunities at Kodak?"

The reliability of single-item measures is often questioned. Single-item responses, however, are most appropriate when the use of faceted measures might reasonably omit some aspect of the phenomenon (e.g., when the dimensionality of a construct is unknown or not clear) or when individuals are asked to make summary judgments about their own level of satisfaction or affect (Scarpello & Campbell, 1983). Scarpello and Campbell (1983) concluded that the G.M. Faces scale was not unreliable as a single-item measure of job satisfaction. Moreover, a modification of the G.M. Faces scale has also been shown to be a reliable and valid measure of life satisfaction (Andrews & Withey, 1976; Judge & Hulin, 1993). Because training reaction requires a summary judgment about how well the subject liked the training, single-item measures are not inappropriate (Alliger & Janak, 1989). Because the G.M. Faces scale has been shown to be reliable in other contexts requiring affect-based summary judgments, it seemed an appropriate measure of training reaction, particularly given the organization's desire to keep testing time to a minimum.

Several control measures were taken. The Wonderlic Personnel Test (Wonderlic, 1983) was administered to control for general cognitive ability. As a measure of cognitive ability, the Wonderlic test fares well and has been shown to correlate between .56 and .80 with Aptitude G of the General Aptitude Test Battery (U.S. Department of Labor, 1967) and between .91 and .93 with the Wechsler Adult Intelligence Scale (Dodrill, 1983). One advantage the Wonderlic test has over other cognitive ability measures is that it takes only 12 minutes to administer.

Because the IL approach accepts the premise that learning styles affect the degree to which material presented through particular media will be assimilated, the Productivity Environmental Preference Survey (PEPS) was used to identify the conditions under which individuals are most likely to achieve or learn (Price, Dunn, & Dunn, 1991). Freedman and Stumpf (1980) suggested that the use of learning style measures should be suspended because of unreliable instrument design. However, because newly developed instruments such as the PEPS report acceptable internal consistency coefficients and are fundamental to the training approach being studied, it seemed appropriate to include this control. The PEPS contains scales that, among other things, assess preference for different environmental conditions such as light ($\alpha = .84$), noise level ($\alpha = .83$), time of day ($\alpha = .84$), and temperature ($\alpha = .85$). Other scales assess preference for cooperative learning ($\alpha = .84$), auditory stimuli ($\alpha = .78$), visual stimuli ($\alpha = .67$), tactile involvement ($\alpha = .78$), and kinesthetic activity ($\alpha = .58$). Although many of the variables were held constant by fixing the time and place of the training, others such as preference for cooperative learning and type of stimuli varied considerably by treatment. Therefore, it was deemed appropriate to control for individual preferences for these conditions.

Affective disposition is the "tendency to respond to classes of environmental stimuli in a predetermined, affect-based manner" (Judge & Hulin, in press). Positive affect is a state of high energy, full concentration, and pleasurable engagement, whereas negative affectivity is characterized by distress, unpleasurable engagement, and nervousness (Watson, Clark, & Tellegen, 1988). Affectivity has been shown to affect learning through its influence on how information is coded and recalled (Isen & Daubman, 1984). Affectivity may also affect attitudes toward training. Therefore, we assessed the subject's affective state during training by using the Watson et al. (1988) Positive and Negative Affectivity Scale (PANAS).

In addition, subjective well-being, the ongoing state of psychological wellness (Diener, 1984), might affect both reaction and learning. Therefore, the aforementioned G.M. Faces scale was used to assess subjective well-being. Again, this item has been shown to be a valid and reliable measure of life satisfaction that compares favorably with several faceted measurements of this construct (Andrews & Withey, 1976; Diener, 1984; Judge & Hulin, in press).

Procedure

Employees (n = 180) were randomly assigned to receive either IL-based or traditional training, but they were not informed of the type of training they would receive until the day training began. Because it was not customary at Kodak to evaluate student performance in training programs (i.e., to administer tests), at the time of enrollment all potential students were informed that the MRP-II course they would be attending was part of a large-scale study on the effectiveness of Kodak training programs. They were also informed that the study would include assessments about how they felt about the course and how much they learned. All students were given the opportunity to withdraw at any time without penalty and receive the training at a later date. Although no participants announced their intention to withdraw, eight employees did not report for their scheduled training session.

Employees were notified by electronic mail of the time and place to report for the three-day training session. To accommodate the number of students, six classes were needed. Traditionally, MRP-II training was conducted with a lecture format. The number of students per class was therefore constrained only by classroom size. Because this type of training had typically been offered to groups of 40–50, we maintained that convention. Actual class sizes for the two traditional training groups were 40 (Class 1) and 44 (Class 2). Classes that are IL-based require significant student interaction and kinesthetic activity. For this reason, proponents recommend that class sizes be kept in the range of 15–30 students. Differences in the physical sizes of the classrooms and accommodating a few schedule changes resulted in actual IL class sizes of 29 (Class 3), 22 (Class 4), 22 (Class 5), and 15 (Class 6).

Five subjects came to the wrong session. Rather than losing subjects (because they arrived for a later session) or asking them to return 1–3 hours later (because they arrived for an earlier session), we accommodated them as best we could. All five of the subjects who reported at the wrong time were placed into a class that was receiving the type of treatment to which they had originally been assigned. Therefore, accommodating them changed our anticipated class sizes but did not distort the random assignment.

Two methods were used to determine which subjects would be pretested. For the two larger, traditional training classes, the students were split into two groups through a process of counting off (1-2-1-2-1-2 . . .). One-half left the room and engaged in an unrelated exercise, and the other half was pretested. Those who were pretested were asked not to discuss any part of the pretest with the other students. For the smaller, IL-based classes, a coin flip determined which two of the four classes would receive the pretest–posttest condition and which two would receive the posttest-only condition. Because of the high level of interaction among students in the IL treatment, it was believed that this process would reduce the likelihood of pretest recipients discussing the pretest content with those who were not pretested.

These procedures resulted in somewhat unequal group sizes. The 51 subjects in Group 1 (pretest–IL training-posttest) consisted of all subjects in Classes 3 and 5. The 42 subjects in Group 2 (pretest–traditional training–posttest) consisted of half of the students from Classes 1 and 2. The 37 subjects in Group 3 (IL training–posttest only) consisted of all subjects in Classes 4 and 6. Finally, the 42 subjects in Group 4 (traditional training–posttest only) consisted of half of the students in Classes 1 and 2.

To minimize instructor effects, different instructors taught each of the six classes. All instructors had had previous experience teaching MRP-II, had experience with either traditional or IL-based instruction (although the traditional instructors had significantly more experience), and were randomly chosen from two pools (one for each of the training methods). Because the IL-based training was designed to be presented by teams of two instructors per class, we maintained that convention. The traditional classes were taught by a single instructor. Because this was the method by which future IL training would be offered, maintaining this convention added to the generalizability of the results. The classes were scheduled so that both types of training were offered concurrently.

On the day the training began, the start times were staggered so that the principal investigator could personally meet each class (and the no-treatment group) and administer the measures. Absolute confidentiality of individual responses was assured, and subjects were told that nobody at Kodak would ever see their individual information. Subjects were informed that upon completion of the study, their personal information would be returned to them along with a summary of the results. Time was then provided for questions and comments. Most questions involved how the material would be returned so that confidentiality would be maintained. In response, subjects were ensured that the principal investigator would maintain possession of all test materials and would be available upon completion of the study to personally return the materials and discuss them.

The pretest consisted of the MRP-II comprehension exam, the PANAS, and the reaction measures. One hour was set aside for the pretest. Most subjects finished in 30–40 minutes.

At the end of the three-day training session, all subjects received posttests. Coinciding with the staggered starting times, the classes ended at different times so that the principal investigator could administer the posttests. There were 1.5 hours allowed for the posttest, and most subjects used the entire time period. Posttest measures included all of the pretest measures plus the Wonderlic, the PEPS, and demographic information.

Analyses

Ordinary least squares regression analysis was used to examine the relative effects of the training interventions. Two dummy variables were created: IL training was set equal to 1 if the subject received IL-based training and set equal to 0 otherwise; TR training was set equal to 1 if the subject received traditional training and set equal to 0 otherwise. These two dummy variables allowed the independent effects of each type of training to be ascertained. The no-treatment condition served as the excluded group. In addition, to assess whether the pretest had any effect on learning or reaction, a dummy variable (pretest) was created and set equal to 1 if the subject was pretested and set equal to 0 otherwise.

A learning style index that included preference for learning with peers, preference for several types of stimuli, preference for mobility, preference for tactile manipulation while learning, and preference for kinesthetic activity was created by combining subjects' scores on the PEPS scales that assessed these preferences. On the basis of the content of the two training treatments, this combination emphasized the differences between the IL and the traditional training environments. Specifically, the IL instructional environment included all of these components, whereas the traditional environment contained virtually none of them.

When MRP-II comprehension was specified as the dependent variable, the other control variables included cognitive ability, affectivity, subjective well-being, preference for particular learning environments, attitudes toward the training and toward general training opportunities, and individual demographic variables such as sex, race, age, organizational tenure, marital status, education, and income.

When reaction to the training was specified as the dependent variable, the other control variables included amount of material learned, cognitive ability, affectivity, subjective well-being, preference for particular learning environments, attitudes toward general training opportunities, and the individual demographic variables.

Results

A one-way analysis of variance indicated that the three groups (IL trained, traditionally trained, and no treatment) were similar in most regards at the pretest. No differences were noted on MRP-II pretest scores, attitudes about training opportunities, expectations about the forthcoming training session, subjective well-being, learning style, or positive affectivity. The only difference that was found concerned negative affectivity. Specifically, the no-treatment group exhibited a higher level of negative affectivity than did the IL and traditional-training groups, $F(2, 104) = 3.85$, $p < .05$. There was no difference between the IL and the traditional treatment groups on pretest negative affectivity.

In addition, although the IL and traditional training groups were virtually identical on the demographic variables, the no-treatment group differed in some meaningful ways. Specifically, the training groups were predominately male (IL = 74%; traditional = 79%), but the no-treatment group was 77% female, $F(2, 104) = 6.1$, $p < .01$. The training groups had significantly more organizational tenure (IL = 18 years; traditional = 16.5 years) than the no-treatment group (12.6 years), $F(2, 104) = 3.4$, $p < .05$. Greater percentages of the training groups were married (IL = 80%; traditional = 75%) compared with 42% of the no-treatment group, $F(2, 104) = 4.2$, $p < .05$. Finally, the subjects in the training groups tended to earn more (IL = \$39,489; traditional = \$42,631) than those in the no-treatment group (\$33,449 average), $F(2, 104) = 3.5$, $p < .05$. These differences reflect the random assignment to training versus the voluntary makeup of the no-treatment group. Because of the nonrepresentative nature of the no-treatment group, we recommend cautious interpretation of no-treatment group outcomes.

Because some differences between the no-treatment group and the training groups did exist, these variables were included as controls in the analyses. No differences between treatments were noted on the variables that were thought most likely to influence learning, such as cognitive ability scores (IL = 21.2; traditional = 21.8; no treatment = 24), years of education (IL = 13.3; traditional = 13.8; no treatment = 14), age (IL = 41.9; traditional = 40.5; no treatment = 40.3), or any of the other variables.

Correlational analyses indicated that cognitive ability, amount of material learned, and years of formal education were all significantly positively related. Reaction to the training was significantly positively related to positive affectivity, subjective well-being, and perceived training opportunities but was unrelated to learning ($r = .02$). The very small, nonsignificant correlation between reaction and learning apparently contradicts the assumption of successive causality in Kirkpatrick's (1959) hierarchical model of training criteria but is consistent with Alliger and Janak's (1989) assertion that reactions need not be related to learning. The correlations between variables in the analyses are presented in Table 3.1.

For the subjects who received both pre- and posttests ($N = 107$), Table 3.2 shows average scores on the dependent measures. On the

TABLE 3.1 Correlation Matrix

Variable	1	2	3	4	5	6	7	8	9	10	11	12	13	14	15	16
1. IL training	—	-.88**	-.07	-.08	.42**	.03	.01	.14	.05	-.00	.01	.10	.15	.10	-.08	.15*
2. Traditional training		—	.02	.19**	-.28**	-.02	-.07	-.12	-.06	.12	-.06	-.08	-.07	.00	.15*	.12
3. Cognitive ability			—	.57**	-.08	.03	.01	.01	.00	.09	-.20**	-.11	-.12	-.05	.28**	.60**
4. MRP-II learning[a]				—	.02	.00	.00	.11	-.05	.01	-.22**	-.19**	-.04	.06	.24**	.51**
5. Reaction					—	.24**	-.08	.44**	.29**	-.12	-.01	-.01	.01	-.04	-.02	-.07
6. Positive affectivity[b]						—	-.13	.31**	.39**	-.01	.06	.05	-.01	-.00	.02	.08
7. Negative affectivity[b]							—	-.17*	-.41**	-.09	-.06	-.14	-.09	-.00	-.05	.08
8. Perceived training opportunity								—	.33**	-.03	.05	.01	-.01	.01	-.01	.11
9. Subjective well-being									—	.06	.00	.06	.02	-.06	.02	.06
10. Sex										—	-.20**	.14	.25**	.34**	.35**	.00
11. Race											—	-.14	-.18*	-.12	-.07	.01
12. Age												—	.72**	.21**	.28**	-.12
13. Tenure													—	.17*	.36**	-.21**
14. Marital Status														—	.18*	.03
15. Income															—	.38**
16. Education																—
M	0.48	0.46	21.7	28.9	2.3	34.6	17.3	2.3	2.4	0.74	0.08	41.0	17.0	0.75	40,530	13.6
SD	0.50	0.50	6.6	5.0	1.0	7.2	6.6	1.0	0.9	0.44	0.27	7.5	7.4	0.43	12,582	2.0

NOTE: $N = 184$. Sex coded 0 = female, 1 = male. Race coded 0 = White, 1 = non-White. IL = integrative learning; MRP-II = manufacturing resource planning.
a. $\alpha = .75$.
b. $\alpha = .89$.
*$p < .05$; **$p < .01$.

72

TABLE 3.2 Dependent Variable Scores and Standardized Effects

Variable	IL Based (N = 51)	Traditional (N = 44)	No Treatment (N = 12)
Prelearning			
M	23.88	24.75	25.65
SD	5.34	5.55	2.46
Postlearning			
M	28.16	30.23	24.58
SD	5.19	5.38	3.99
Effect	0.80	0.98	−0.43
Prereaction			
M	3.04	2.86	3.00
SD	0.92	0.88	1.10
Postreaction			
M	1.88	2.55	3.33
SD	0.95	0.76	1.07
Effect	1.26	0.35	−0.30

NOTE: Effect = (post − pre)/pre SD. For reaction, lower scores indicate more positive reaction. IL = integrative learning.

basis of these results, we calculated gain scores and expressed them in terms of standard deviation units. For example, the IL-trained group experienced a positive learning effect of 0.80 *SD* compared with a positive 0.98-*SD* effect on learning in the traditional training treatment and a 0.43-*SD* decrease for the no-treatment group. The difference in gains between the traditional and the IL groups was not significant, $t(92) = 1.74$, $p = .085$. Similarly, the effect of training on reaction was a 1.26-*SD* increase in the IL treatment compared with a 0.35-*SD* increase in the traditional training treatment and a 0.30-*SD* decrease in the no-treatment group. The difference in gains between the traditional and IL-based groups was significant, $t(93) = 3.96$, $p < .01$.

Learning

Regression results indicated that both types of training had significant, positive effects on learning (see Table 3.3). Training was the most powerful predictor of performance level on the MRP-II comprehension test. Tukey multiple comparison analyses ($\alpha = .05$) indicated that both training groups differed significantly from the no-treatment group, $F(2, 180) = 6.95$, $p < .01$, but were not significantly different from one another. Thus, Hypothesis 1 was not supported. The nonsignificant coefficients on the pretest dummy variable and on learning style indicated that neither the pretest nor preference for particular learning environments had an effect on the amount of material learned.

TABLE 3.3 Regression Results for Learning Measure

Variable	Full Sample (N = 173)		Pretest–Posttest Sample (N = 100)	
	β	t ratio	β	t ratio
Pretest dummy	-.009	-0.169	—	—
Pretest score	—	—	.536	7.134**
Traditional training	.557	4.511**	.370	3.313**
IL-based training	.466	3.621**	.252	2.024*
Cognitive ability	.445	6.253**	.195	2.497*
Years of education	.268	3.406**	.182	2.120*
Reaction to training	.009	0.121	.126	1.456
Positive affect	-.031	-0.524	-.059	-0.884
Negative affect	-.077	-1.288	-.085	-1.357
Subjective well-being	-.101	-1.543	-.134	-1.827
Perceived training opportunities	.132	2.053*	-.029	-0.379
Learning style	.055	0.927	.041	0.668
Age	-.291	-3.653**	-.310	-3.578**
Sex	-.173	-2.724**	.016	0.221
Race	-.141	-2.461*	-.104	-1.658
Tenure	.297	3.491**	.229	2.369*
Marital status	.071	1.201	.042	0.651
Income	-.036	-0.521	-.063	-0.749
R^2	.571		.756	
Adjusted R^2	.524		.706	

NOTE: t ratio = regression coefficient/standard error.
*$p < .05$; **$p < .01$.

The practical significance of the training intervention was that the no-treatment group averaged 61% correct on the post-test learning measure, whereas the IL group and the traditional training group averaged 71% and 75% correct, respectively. Although the difference between the no-treatment group and the trained groups was only 10%–14%, it represents performance at a level 1 *SD* better than the performance of the no-treatment group. In addition, recall that the no-treatment group consisted of volunteers from TER. Because MRP-II is such an important training initiative for TER, it is likely that in the course of their day-to-day work, the members of the no-treatment group were exposed to a significant amount of the course content. Therefore, the difference between the trained and untrained groups may be understated.

The variables that tend to be associated with learning were significant predictors of performance on the MRP-II exam. As expected (e.g., Ree & Earles, 1991), cognitive ability accounted for significant variation in performance. Next to content-specific training, general cognitive ability had the most significant effect. Years of formal education was also significant.

Subjects' perceptions of their general training opportunities had significant effects, but their feelings about the course they were attending did not. Finally, some demographic characteristics were significant. The coefficient on race (0 = White, 1 = non-White) indicated that Whites tended to score better than non-Whites. In addition, women tended to score higher than men (0 = female, 1 = male), and younger subjects scored better than older ones.

Reaction

As Table 3.4 indicates, IL-based training had an effect on participant reaction. The coefficients on both of the training intervention variables were positive and significant. Tukey's multiple comparison procedure (α = .05) indicated that all three groups differed significantly in their reactions to the training, $F(2,181) = 23.05$, $p < .01$. Thus, Hypothesis 2 was supported. Attitudes about general training opportunities and subjective well-being also influenced reaction to training.

Discussion

Predictions that the IL-trained subjects would learn significantly more than the traditionally trained subjects were not supported by this study. Subjects who were randomly assigned to the IL-based training learned slightly less than subjects who received traditional lecture-based training. Subjects in the IL-based training, however, had much more positive reactions to the intervention than did those in the traditional training.

The similar amount of material learned through IL and traditional interventions is inconsistent with previous claims and may have been observed in the current study for many reasons. One explanation may be that IL works better for particular types of subject matter than for others. Specifically, the MRP-II knowledge assessed in the current study was very cognitive, whereas some previous studies (e.g., Gill & Meier, 1989) assessed training that was more interpersonal or behavioral. Although current IL philosophy does not specify that the approach is superior for behaviorally based topics, the instructional components do appear to be better suited to behavioral or skill-based training.

Given the role of affect in IL-based training, the intervention may work better for topics that tend to cause apprehension or anxiety, or those topics that are generally disliked. For example, many people express dislike for certain subjects (e.g., foreign languages, mathematics) generally because they are perceived to be difficult. The IL focus on

TABLE 3.4 Regression Results for Reaction Measure

Variable	Full sample (N = 173) β	Full sample (N = 173) t ratio	Pretest–Posttest Sample (N = 100) β	Pretest–Posttest Sample (N = 100) t ratio
Pretest dummy	.021	0.341	—	—
Learning score	.011	0.121	-.100	-0.941
Pretest reaction	—	—	.144	1.763
Traditional training	.434	3.005**	.256	1.801
IL-based training	.736	5.277**	.634	4.474**
Cognitive ability	-.017	-0.194	-.111	-1.126
Years of education	-.124	-1.347	-.139	-1.285
Positive affect	.082	1.228	.020	0.243
Negative affect	.057	0.853	-.033	-0.421
Subjective well-being	.168	2.300*	.124	1.353
Perceived training opportunities	.348	5.112**	.452	5.529**
Learning style	.041	0.617	.159	2.111*
Age	-.018	-0.191	.000	0.000
Sex	-.182	-2.523*	.109	1.273
Race	-.057	-0.868	-.115	-1.470
Tenure	-.071	-0.715	.020	0.157
Marital status	-.049	-0.725	-.115	-1.450
Income	.140	1.769	.152	1.467
R^2	.451		.624	
Adjusted R^2	.391		.546	

NOTE: t ratio = regression coefficient/standard error. IL = integrative learning.
*$p < .05$; **$p < .01$.

making the learning experience fun and eliminating negative feedback suggests that these types of topics may be best suited to its application. Alternatively, a topic that everyone finds enjoyable and interesting to begin with probably presents fewer learning barriers to overcome and therefore may offer little opportunity for improved learning.

The current training topic may not have been particularly well suited to the IL intervention. In fact, this topic seems to represent the type of training that should prove most challenging for IL to achieve significantly better learning effects. It was cognitive and was designed to impart knowledge rather than change behavioral patterns or skills. In addition, because much of the MRP-II material presented in the current training can be defined as "organized common sense" (Wallace, 1985, p. 262), subjects may have had very little anxiety or apprehension about the topic. Moreover, because MRP-II outcomes are unit based, it is unlikely that any particular individual could be singled out as the reason for meeting (or not meeting) goals. Therefore, subjects may not have felt much pressure to learn the material. Given these conditions, the traditional learning barriers that IL purports to overcome may not have been much of a factor.

Another explanation for the similar results may be that the traditional lecture-based method incorporated some of the instructional components that IL relies on (e.g., advanced organizers, relaxation, affect, imagery, cooperation, participation, and practice). Examination of the traditional method found no evidence to support this suspicion. Although it was a thoughtful, interesting, organized presentation, it was nonetheless a lecture. It is possible, however, that the attitude of the instructors in the traditional intervention did have an effect. Specifically, both instructors tended to be very positive, tried to make the material interesting and enjoyable, and relied heavily on positive reinforcement. Therefore, the nature of the traditional instructors may have minimized the learning barriers that IL purports to overcome, and this may have had a suppressing effect on the power of the IL intervention.

did not control for instructors

Another possible explanation is that IL has not operationalized its component parts as effectively as possible. Previous research has shown (often in laboratory settings) that the instructional components on which IL relies facilitate learning. However, although it is true that IL uses these components, at least as applied to the MRP-II training assessed in this study, the approach does not appear to emphasize any of them. It is possible that the components work in a compensatory way or that the effects of some components either offset the effects of others or add little above the effects already achieved by others. This possibility deserves future research attention. For example, it is possible to assess the unique effect of each component by offering a set of IL-based training sessions in which one component at a time was systematically omitted. By measuring the learning that occurs in the absence of particular components, it is possible to ascertain the independent effects of each instructional component in the IL environment.

It is also possible that particular instructional components may be differentially effective, depending on the type of material being taught. For example, kinesthetic activity may be more effective for learning specific skills or behaviors than for learning the types of principles and procedures taught in the MRP-II course described in this study. Examining unique effects of each of the instructional components within the context of the others and further exploring the types of subject matter best suited to the specific components seems to offer the greatest potential for understanding which combination of learning components have the greatest impact for specific purposes.

Finally, claims made on the basis of results from previous research have typically far exceeded the legitimate conclusions that the research designs permitted. Past research is dominated by single-group and post-test-only research designs. Cook and Campbell (1979, p. 96) referred to these types of research designs as "generally uninterpretable." The highly controlled research design used in the current study eliminates most threats to internal and external validity and permits more rigorous documentation of training effects.

The significantly more positive reaction expressed by the IL-trained subjects is consistent with reactions reported in prior descriptions of IL interventions. Both students and teachers enjoyed the informal class-room atmosphere and the variety of activities. It is not surprising that games, music, imagery, physical activity, and substantial interaction elicited more positive reactions than did three days of listening to lectures. The favorable reactions (both measured reactions and those articulated by the participants) are consistent with the existing over-whelming testimonial support for this approach. In relation to the tradi-tionally trained subjects, participants in the IL-based approach not only liked the training better but also tended to believe they had learned more.

This study examined the relative effects of IL and traditional training methods on participant reaction and learning. Additional research is needed to examine possible differences on other criteria such as reten-tion of material, job-relevant behavior, and organizational impact. It is possible that even though no differences were observed on the amount of material learned, differences may emerge if one group retains more of the learned material than the other group. Because IL-based training uses components that have been shown to increase retention (e.g., spaced practice, advanced organizers), some bases exist for expecting IL-trained subjects to remember more than traditionally trained subjects. This possibility could be explored by subsequently assessing subjects' knowledge of the training content. To avoid instrumentation effects, the same instrument (or equivalent form) used to assess learning at the posttest stage should be used to assess retention. Retention could then be expressed as a percentage of learning.

This study would have been strengthened if the behavioral effects of training could have been assessed. Unfortunately, a major organizational restructuring prevented the collection of supervisory ratings of trainee performance on MRP-II-related activity. Future research, however, should attempt to assess both pre- and posttraining behaviors. The process of assessing training needs and enrolling an employee for training provides the opportunity to obtain pretraining assessments of behavior. At the time an employee is enrolled for training, the supervisor might be asked to provide a brief, though systematic, assessment of the employee's behavior on course-relevant dimensions. Posttraining behavior might be assessed by asking the supervisor to complete a similar questionnaire at a later date. Alternatively, it might be assessed as part of the formal per-formance appraisal process and then matched to pretraining assessments.

The MRP-II comprehension test was designed to measure how much of the training program content was assimilated by the subjects. Because trainees can transfer only what they have learned, the test score provided an indication of the maximum amount of training program content that the subject would be able to transfer to the job. Because many things restrict the transfer of training content, however, test scores probably over-estimate the transfer that would actually occur. Direct measurement of job behaviors would address this issue. For example, although no differences between groups were observed on test scores, perhaps through differences in attitudes or interpersonal relationships one group may be more or less able to effect greater changes in job behavior. It is also possible that the more favorable reaction to the IL-based training might make employees more motivated to undertake future training and might facilitate transfer. This seems particularly likely in organizational environments in which mandatory training is perceived as boring or as being a chore. If so, different conclusions about the effectiveness of the intervention would be warranted. Because IL-based training emphasizes interaction and interpersonal relationships to a much greater extent than does lecture-based training, it is possible that transfer to the job may be greater for IL-trained subjects.

Direct comparisons of different training programs also offer opportunities to study the impact of training interventions. Although a complete utility analysis is beyond the scope of this study, it appears that analyses of the relative costs and benefits of each approach might be the most effective way of determining the value of different training approaches in particular organizational settings. For example, in the current study the teacher:student ratio for the IL-based approach was approximately $\frac{1}{10}$, compared with $\frac{1}{44}$ for the traditional approach. Other costs included acquiring the IL technology. Therefore, the costs of each approach can be objectively determined. It seems possible to determine subjectively the value of material learned, behavioral changes, and participant attitudes. Once done, it would be possible to form a more holistic opinion of the contextual merits of alternative training interventions.

Future research might consider alternative methods for measuring what was learned. This study assessed MRP-II knowledge with a multiple-choice test that relied on linguistic and logical-mathematical abilities. It is possible that this type of examination did not allow all subjects to express their knowledge to its fullest extent. Even though all parties involved with the design of this study agreed to this method of testing, because the IL approach accepts the premise of multiple intelligences, future research should consider how to measure learning in a variety of ways.

In conclusion, when subjected to a very tightly controlled experimental design and a decidedly cognitive topic, claims of greater learning in IL-based training were not supported. For the reasons discussed previously, however, this study appears to have been a very challenging test for IL. Different results may be observed for more task-oriented or behavioral training interventions, or when greater learning barriers are present or perceived. It is possible that the assessment of different criteria (e.g., behaviors) might have yielded other conclusions, or that the unmeasured effects of enhanced participant reaction return significant benefits to the organization. Even so, IL yielded similar learning results with less experienced instructors and with significantly more positive reactions. Therefore, additional research with different samples in different types of training and in other settings is needed to substantiate or refute these findings.

References

Ackerman, P. L., & Humphreys, L. G. (1990). Individual differences theory in industrial and organizational psychology. In M. Dunnette & L. Hough (Eds.), *Handbook of industrial and organizational psychology* (Vol. 1, pp. 223-282). Palo Alto, CA: Consulting Psychologists Press.

Alliger, G. M., & Janak, E. A. (1989). Kirkpatrick's levels of training criteria: Thirty years later. *Personnel Psychology, 42,* 331-342.

Andrews, F. M., & Withey, S. B. (1976). *Social indicators of well-being: America's perception of life quality.* New York: Plenum Press.

Carnevale, A. P., & Gainer, L. J. (1989). *The learning enterprise.* Alexandria, VA: American Society for Training and Development.

The Center for Accelerated Learning. (1989, Winter). *A.L. Network News.* Lake Geneva, WI: Author.

Cohen, J. (1988). *Statistical power analysis for the behavioral sciences* (2nd ed.). Hillsdale, NJ: Lawrence Erlbaum.

Cook, T. D., & Campbell, D. T. (1979). *Quasi-experimentation.* Boston: Houghton Mifflin.

Cook, T. D., Campbell, D. T., & Peracchio, L. (1990). Quasi-experimentation. In M. Dunnette & L. Hough (Eds.), *Handbook of industrial and organizational psychology* (Vol. 1, pp. 491-576). Palo Alto, CA: Consulting Psychologists Press.

Crowder, R. G. (1976). *Principles of learning and memory.* Hillsdale, NJ: Lawrence Erlbaum.

Diener, E. (1984). Subjective well-being. *Psychological Bulletin, 95,* 542-575.

Digman, J. M. (1959). Growth of a motor skill as a function of distribution of practice. *Journal of Experimental Psychology, 57,* 310-316.

Dodrill, C. B. (1983). Long-term reliability of the Wonderlic Personnel Test. *Journal of Consulting and Clinical Psychology, 51,* 316-317.

Druckman, D., & Swets, J. A. (1988). *Enhancing human performance.* Washington, DC: National Academy Press.

Freedman, R. D., & Stumpf, S. A. (1980). Learning style theory: Less than meets the eye. *Academy of Management Review, 5,* 445-447.

Gardner, H. (1983). *Frames of mind: The theory of multiple intelligences.* New York: Basic Books.

Gasser-Roberts, S. (1985). SALT, suggestopedia and other accelerative learning methods in Japan and Europe. *Journal of the Society for Accelerative Learning and Teaching, 10,* 131-146.

Gill, M. J., & Meier, D. (1989). Accelerated learning takes off. *Training & Development Journal, 43*(1), 63-65.

Goldstein, I. L. (1986). *Training in organizations* (2nd ed.). Pacific Grove, CA: Brooks/Cole.

Goldstein, I. L. (1991). Training in work organizations. In M. D. Dunnette & L. M. Hough (Eds.), *Handbook of industrial and organizational psychology* (Vol. 2, pp. 507-620). Palo Alto, CA: Consulting Psychologists Press.

Isen, A. M., & Daubman, K. A. (1984). The influence of affect on categorization. *Journal of Personality and Social Psychology, 47,* 1206-1217.

Isen, A. M., Johnson, M. M. S., Mertz, E., & Robinson, G. F. (1985). The influence of positive affect on the unusualness of word associations. *Journal of Personality and Social Psychology, 48,* 1413-1426.

Jensen, A. R. (1986). g: Artifact or reality? *Journal of Vocational Behavior, 29,* 301-331.

Judge, T. A., & Hulin, C. L. (1993). Job satisfaction as a reflection of disposition: A multiple source causal analysis. *Organizational Behavior and Human Decision Processes, 56*(3), 388-421.

Kerlinger, F. N. (1986). *Foundations of behavioral research.* Fort Worth, TX: Holt, Rinehart & Winston.

Kirkpatrick, D. L. (1959). Techniques for evaluating training programs. *Journal of the American Society of Training Directors, 13,* 3-26.

Knibbeler, W. (1982). Suggestopedia applied to an English-as-a-second-language setting. *Journal of the Society for Accelerative Learning and Teaching, 9,* 61-77.

Kunin, T. (1955). The construction of a new type of attitude measure. *Personnel Psychology, 8,* 65-78.

Latham, G. P., Erez, M., & Locke, E. A. (1988). Resolving scientific disputes by the joint design of crucial experiments by the antagonists: Application to the Erez-Latham dispute regarding participation in goalsetting [Monograph]. *Journal of Applied Psychology, 73,* 753-772.

Lewin, K. (1951). *Field theory in social science: Selected theoretical papers.* New York: Harper & Row.

Martel, L. D. (1989). *A working solution for the nation's schools.* Syracuse, NY: Syracuse University Center for the Study of Learning and Retention.

Mayer, R. E. (1979). Can advanced organizers influence meaningful learning? *Review of Educational Research, 49,* 371-383.

Milkovich, G. T., & Boudreau, J. W. (1991). *Human resource management.* Homewood, IL: Irwin.

Nunnally, J. C. (1978). *Psychometric theory.* New York: McGraw-Hill.

Ostrander, S., & Schroeder, L. (1975). *Superlearning.* New York: Dell.

Paivio, A. (1971). *Imagery and verbal processes.* New York: Holt, Rinehart & Winston.

Paivio, A., & Desrochers, A. (1979). Effects of an imagery mnemonic on second language recall and comprehension. *Canadian Journal of Psychology, 33,* 17-27.

Price, G. E., Dunn, R., & Dunn, K. (1991). *Productivity Environmental Preference Survey manual.* Lawrence, KS: Price Systems.

Reder, L. M., Charney, D., & Morgan, K. (1986). The role of elaboration in learning a skill from instructional text. *Memory & Cognition, 14,* 64-78.

Ree, M. J., & Earles, J. A. (1991). Predicting training success: Not much more than g. *Personnel Psychology, 44,* 321-332.

Rose, C. (1985). *Accelerated learning.* New York: Dell.

Saari, L. M., Johnson, T. R., McLaughlin, S. D., & Zimmerle, D. M. (1988). A survey of management training and education practices in U.S. companies. *Personnel Psychology, 41,* 731-743.

Scarpello, V., & Campbell, J. P. (1983). Job satisfaction: Are all the parts there? *Personnel Psychology, 36,* 577-600.

Schuster, D. H., & Prichard, R. A. (1978). A two-year evaluation of the Suggestive Accelerative Learning and Teaching (SALT) method in a central Iowa public school. *Journal of the Society for Accelerative Learning and Teaching, 3,* 108-121.

Simon, H. A. (1967). Motivational and emotional controls of cognition. *Psychological Review, 74,* 29-39.

Slavin, R. E. (1983). When does cooperative learning increase student achievement? *Psychological Bulletin, 94,* 429-445.

U.S. Department of Labor. (1967). *Manual for the General Aptitude Test Battery Section III: Development.* Washington, DC: U.S. Government Printing Office.

Wallace, T. F. (1985). *MRP II: Making it happen.* Essex Junction, VT: Oliver Wright.

Watson, D., Clark, L. A., & Tellegen, A. (1988). Development and validation of brief measures of positive and negative affect: The PANAS scales. *Journal of Personality and Social Psychology, 54,* 1063-1070.

Wonderlic, E. F. (1983). *Wonderlic Personnel Test manual.* Northfield, IL: E. F. Wonderlic & Associates.

IMPLICATIONS FOR HUMAN RESOURCE DEVELOPMENT PROFESSIONALS

The Bretz and Thompsett article, as the Swets and Bjork article (Chapter 2), emphasized the importance of taking a closer look at the claims made for each training method. Evidence provided by the developer or supplier may or may not yield a complete picture of the effect. In some cases, testimonials focus on reactions. As seen in the Baldwin article (Chapter 1) and in Bretz and Thompsett, results from trainee reactions were not predictive of or correlated with learning, behavior reproduction, or generalization. This research suggests that the HRD practitioner should view evidence regarding trainee reaction as tangential in decision making, particularly if the primary outcome being demanded is learning and performance.

In addition, HRD practitioners should demand solid evidence from developers and suppliers. In many instances, developers and suppliers tend to rely on the single group, post-test-only design. With this approach, a group or even an individual receives training using that method, reports favorable reactions, and testifies to improved learning and performance. As shown by Bretz and Thompsett, however, such reports can prove false or, at the very least, misleading. Though the group receiving the integrative learning method believed that they had learned more than did the group receiving the lecture method, their learning was at a lower level and showed less gain than did that of the group receiving the lecture method (though not at a statistically significant level).

This research could have simply used one group, that receiving the integrative learning method. The results would have supported the use of the integrative method because gains were achieved. What was critical was the use of the group using the lecture and the no-treatment control. The results were able to show no differences between the two training methods in terms of learning outcomes and to demonstrate that the integrative method actually cost more to implement.

IMPLICATIONS FOR RESEARCH DESIGN AND METHODOLOGY

One of the major implications for the HRD researcher is similar to that mentioned for the practitioner. Rather than simply comparing a new method or treatment group to a control group, HRD researchers should include some baseline method or treatment (in this case, the use of the lecture method). Rather than concluding that some training is better than duh! no training, researchers can advance the practice by identifying the most promising of a variety of methods.

This research makes an important contribution to the field by demonstrating that it is possible to conduct rigorous empirical research within an organizational context. Bretz and Thompsett randomly assigned trainees to conditions, gathered extensive background information, and collected measures before and after training. At the same time, they pointed out some problems that emerged from field research. In some cases, trainees came to the wrong session. In another example, the researchers recognized the importance of measuring behavior changes resulting from training. "Unfortunately, a major organizational restructuring prevented the collection of supervisory ratings of trainee performance on MR P-II-related activity" (p. 78). HRD researchers must be bold in their attempts to conduct rigorous empirical research, but at the same time they must be realistic about the barriers that confront them in such a pursuit.

The Bretz and Thompsett article provides a good model for the use of control variables. Rather than simply testing the different treatment methods, the researchers gathered background information on the trainees, such as cognitive ability, years of education, learning style, and tenure. HRD researchers should include such demographic and background variables in their data collection efforts. Thus, if some differences do emerge in these variables, appropriate statistical controls can be used to obtain meaningful results.

IMPLICATIONS FOR FUTURE INQUIRY

Bretz and Thompsett were unable to examine behavioral reproduction or generalization, as had Baldwin (Chapter 1). Because the Baldwin article showed reproduction and generalization results but not learning results, a similar finding might emerge from the study on integrative learning. Perhaps the integrative method would yield superior results in both reproduction and generalization or perhaps the lecture method would prove superior in reproduction and the integrative method superior in generalization. On the other hand, such a study might find no differences between the integrative and lecture approaches in either reproduction or generalization.

Future research on the integrative learning method may reveal that such an intervention works best in certain situations. The researchers suggested that, because the method makes learning fun, it may be most effective for topics that are disliked or that cause some anxiety. Such research would show what topics and what circumstances, if any, lead to improved learning and performance for the integrative method.

This article, along with the article by Swets and Bjork (Chapter 2), reveals a desperate need for researchers to test the exaggerated claims made by some training developers and some training methods. Unless researchers undertake the necessary testing, ineffective methods will continue to be promulgated.

OTHER RESOURCES

Burke, M. J., & Day, R. R. (1986). A cumulative study of the effectiveness of managerial training. *Journal of Applied Psychology, 71*, 232-245.

Measuring Mental Models

Choosing the Right Tools for the Job

Anna L. Rowe
Brooks Air Force Base, Texas

Nancy J. Cooke
New Mexico State University, Las Cruces

WITH THE EVOLVING NATURE OF HIGH-TECHNOLOGY WORKPLACES, PERSONNEL are continually confronted with new, complex systems. Possession of accurate mental representations or "mental models" of these systems should enhance workers' understanding and use of the equipment. Incorporating mental model assessment, diagnosis, and instruction into training requires the selection of an appropriate measure of mental model knowledge. Because there is no agreed-upon measure of this knowledge, selection can be difficult. This study evaluated four mental model measures, with performance as the criterion. Three of the evaluated techniques were predictive of performance; two of these were independently predictive. Determining the relationship between

Source: Rowe, A. L., & Cooke, N. J. (1995). Measuring mental models: Choosing the right tools for the job. *Human Resource Development Quarterly, 6*(3), 243-255. Used by permission.

Authors' Note: Dr. Rowe's doctoral dissertation, on which this article is based, received the 1994 Donald Bullock Award from the American Society for Training and Development for the outstanding dissertation in HRD completed in 1994. The study was sponsored by the Air Force Office of Scientific Research, Bolling AFB (Contract No. F49620-90-C-09076), and the Air Force Armstrong Laboratory, Human Resources Directorate.

Thanks are due to Ellen Hall, Bob Pokorny, Emily Dibble, reviewers from the Donald Bullock Award Committee, and the HRDQ editors for their valuable comments on this work.

a knowledge representation and performance can offer valuable infor-
mation for designing and evaluating a training intervention.

With the evolving nature of high-technology workplaces, personnel must readily adapt to changing technologies. The impact of technology has been dramatic in a variety of workplaces, ranging from office settings to hospitals, manufacturing plants (Schendel, 1994), and urban mass transit (Clark, 1982). For example, workers in manufacturing plants are no longer required to lift heavy loads. Instead, they must understand and operate equipment that lifts the load for them.

When incorporating high-technology equipment into a particular work setting, the goal is to increase productivity. Although the equipment is designed to enhance workers' capabilities, it typically introduces complexity into the workplace. Workers must often acquire new skills and knowledge to effectively use the equipment. As the workplace becomes more cognitively complex and demands more specialized skill, training issues are increasingly critical.

How can training programs prepare workers to effectively interact with these complex systems? Recent research in psychology may guide these training efforts. This research indicates that understanding a complex system and successfully interacting with it requires several different types of knowledge, including knowledge of the basic system components, the possible states of those components, and how the components are interrelated (Hegarty, 1991). Such knowledge forms an internal mental representation, or "mental model," of the system (Gentner & Stevens, 1983; Staggers & Norcio, 1993). Mental models are acquired through interactions with the system, and possession of a mental model provides the system user with predictive and explanatory power (Norman, 1983). A worker operating complex equipment uses a mental model to understand the equipment and any feedback that it provides (Rasmussen & Jensen, 1974). Although a mental model is not always necessary for effective interactions with complex equipment, mental models are assumed to play an important role in facilitating most human-equipment interactions, particularly when the equipment does not behave in an expected manner. In essence, a worker uses a mental model of a system to anticipate what needs to be done with the system before actually physically interacting with it.

For example, office workers routinely use, and sometimes have difficulties with, their computer printer. When the printer behaves in an unexpected manner, the office worker may turn to a mental model of the printer in an attempt to understand the printer's "misbehavior." The worker may mentally visualize the printer's internal workings and, based on this mental representation, choose some corrective action. The worker who is unfamiliar with the printer's internal workings may only be capable of visualizing the printer as a "black box." Using such a coarse mental model, the worker's attempts to solve the problem may not extend beyond determining if the printer has been turned on. Conversely, the worker who is very familiar with the printer may mentally visualize the printer's function at a deeper level, that is, as signals passing from the computer to the printer that affect paper moving through the printer. Here, attempts to solve the problem would likely expand to include looking for jammed paper, determining if the printer is "on-line," or checking cable connections between the computer and the printer. Thus, the worker's mental model guides corrective actions when the system behaves in an unexpected manner.

Incorporating mental model assessment, diagnosis, and instruction into training programs should enhance workers' understanding and subsequent use of complex systems. In fact, use of the mental model construct for pragmatic purposes such as improvement of system design and instruction has been promoted (Rouse & Morris, 1986). Researchers have examined the effect of mental model instruction in a variety of domains, including calculator use (Bayman & Mayer, 1984; Halasz & Moran, 1983), electronic circuitry (Gentner & Gentner, 1983), a control panel device (Kieras & Bovair, 1984), an electronic mail filing system (Sein & Bostrom, 1989), and a word processing system (Frese et al., 1988). In general, the results of these studies indicate that mental model instruction enhances interactions with the complex systems: trainees receiving mental model instruction tend to exhibit more sophisticated performance, they learn and execute procedures faster, and they exhibit improved performance for novel problems. Thus, mental model instruction can provide an effective and robust basis for operating complex equipment.

To effectively incorporate the mental model construct into a training program, measures of mental model knowledge appropriate to the domain must be identified. These measures can be used to inform the training development process and to determine training effectiveness. Assessing trainees' mental models before and after training would offer insight for the development of training materials and for evaluating the effectiveness of the training materials. Important questions include: Are there aspects of the system that trainees simply do not understand before training? Does the instruction change this? Do trainees hold misconceptions about the system before training? Are these misconceptions corrected following training? Gathering these pieces of information before and after training will ensure successful training development and implementation.

Measurement is an important component of an effective training program. But herein lies the problem. The mental model construct is associated with varied and often vague definitions (Rouse & Morris, 1986; Wilson & Rutherford, 1989). Furthermore, mental models are not directly observable—they must be inferred from performance on some measure. There is, however, no single agreed-upon measure of mental model knowledge. Some researchers use think-aloud protocols or interviews, whereas others use multivariate statistical techniques to "capture" mental models (Rowe, 1994). The human resource professional attempting to identify the most appropriate mental model measure for a given situation faces a difficult task, and empirical studies are not available to offer direction in such decision making. This study was undertaken in response to that need.

The study evaluated several common measures of mental model knowledge in the domain of electronics troubleshooting. Technicians in the U.S. Air Force must troubleshoot complex electronic equipment, and research has shown that mental model knowledge is a vital component in this kind of problem solving (Hall, Gott, & Pokorny, 1995; Rasmussen & Jensen, 1974). Incorporating mental model assessment, diagnosis, and instruction into their training program should enhance technicians' troubleshooting performance. However, before this can be done, a comparison of mental model measures must be undertaken.

Mental model measures can be compared across a number of criteria, including ease of use, intuitive appeal, and ability to discriminate between individuals or predict performance (Cooke, 1994). As in most human resource problems, the ultimate goal in this situation is performance improvement. A "good" mental model measure should provide output that predicts performance differences. Thus, a comparison of mental model measures was undertaken in which the measures were evaluated on the basis of their ability to predict troubleshooting performance. Subjects' mental models of a complex electronics system were measured. In addition, each subject worked to troubleshoot a problem that occurred in the electronics system. If mental model knowledge underlies successful troubleshooting, then relating the results of each of the mental model measures to troubleshooting performance should offer insight into the strengths and weaknesses of each of the measures for accessing mental model knowledge pertinent for skillful troubleshooting.

Method

Participants

Nineteen technicians in the airborne electronic troubleshooting career field of the Air Force voluntarily participated in this study. All of the technicians had been through a technical training school designed to prepare them for their specialty and had received subsequent on-the-job training. These technicians are responsible for the identification, isolation, and repair of airborne electronic equipment systems. Technicians were selected to achieve a range of troubleshooting proficiency; some had been on the job for as little as two months, whereas others had more than ten years of job experience. All participating technicians but one were male.

Troubleshooting Problem. All experimental materials were developed in the context of a single troubleshooting problem, selected based on an extensive PARI (Precursor, Action, Result, Interpretation) cognitive task analysis of the flightline electronics troubleshooting job (Hall, Pokorny, & Kane, 1994). Developed by Hall, Gott, and Pokorny (1995), the PARI methodology is used by the Air Force as an integrated skill analysis and instructional development tool. PARI involves the development of problem-solving scenarios and the collection of problem-solving interview data from experts and novices. In these semistructured problem-solving interviews, technicians describe each troubleshooting action they would take and their associated rationale. They then receive feedback on the "result" of each action, which they must explain before moving on to the next action.

PARI data collected from flightline technicians (Hall, Pokorny, & Kane, 1994) were used to select a moderately difficult troubleshooting problem. Presumably, technicians who successfully troubleshoot a moderately difficult problem must use their mental model knowledge while troubleshooting. Furthermore, such a problem should distinguish expert from novice technicians. The selected problem occurred in the Radar Warning Receiver (RWR) system, part of a larger system on the F-15 aircraft. The RWR system shows the pilot whether the aircraft has been detected by enemy radar. The fault to be isolated in the troubleshooting problem involved a short-circuited video cable between two components of the system.

Procedure

Laddering Interview. Upon arriving at the testing session, the technician completed a four-step laddering interview. The technician was given a troubleshooting problem statement: "In debrief the pilot reports that the RWR is inoperative, the BIT light is on, and the TEWS display is blank." The technician was asked (1) to identify the major system important in troubleshooting this problem, (2) to name the major components of the identified system in the context of the troubleshooting problem, and (3) to list all the major components of the identified system, regardless of the problem's context. Finally, the technician named the major systems with which the identified system interfaced.

Relatedness Ratings. Following the laddering interview, the technician completed a component-relatedness ratings task. Here, the technician used a six-point scale to rate the functional relatedness of all pairs of the eleven RWR system components. Pairs were presented randomly, and technicians were told to rate them in terms of their first impression of functional relatedness, within the context of the troubleshooting problem.

Diagramming. Next, the technician completed a diagramming task, using the component set just rated. The technician arranged and connected index cards, with a component name printed on each, in a manner representing the way in which the RWR system functions, in general. Connections and their directionality were represented with a set of directional and bidirectional arrows. The technician was then asked to create a second diagram designating the components and/or connections that were most important in troubleshooting the problem.

Think-Aloud and Verbal Troubleshooting. Finally, the technician proceeded to the think-aloud and verbal troubleshooting tasks. The troubleshooting problem statement was presented to the technician, who was instructed to isolate the fault and repair the equipment. The technician stated the troubleshooting actions he or she would take, and a subject matter expert stated the results of those actions. This constitutes the verbal troubleshooting task. The technician was also instructed to verbally express all thoughts, or think aloud, while working to solve the problem. This is the think-aloud measure. The technician worked until the problem was solved, he or she gave up, or the forty-five-minute time limit had expired.

Results

Overview of Analyses

Comparing the results obtained from the mental model measures with the results from the troubleshooting task provides a pragmatic means of assessing the mental model measurement techniques. This approach assumes that a high-quality mental model is associated with high-quality troubleshooting performance. It requires two assessments: an evaluation of troubleshooting performance and an assessment of the technicians' mental model knowledge.

Troubleshooting Performance

To obtain a troubleshooting performance measure, two subject matter experts independently scored the technicians' troubleshooting action protocols, using a modified Q sort. These protocols contained the actions verbalized by individual technicians, along with the corresponding results of those actions. The experts read each of the protocols and rank-ordered them according to the troubleshooting proficiency displayed. They then reread the protocols and assigned a score to each one, using a 100-point scale, where 100 indicated correct and efficient fault isolation. The scores awarded by the two experts were significantly correlated, with r (17) = .883, p < .0001, as were their rank-orderings, with Spearman's r (17) = .847, p < .0005. (All correlations reported in this article are Pearson product moment correlations unless otherwise specified. In addition, because correlations between performance and knowledge were expected in particular directions, they were tested for significance using one-tailed probabilities.)

A single performance score was created for each technician by averaging the troubleshooting scores given by the two experts. This score was then used as the performance score in all subsequent analyses. Four high performers emerged from this analysis who had performance scores one standard deviation greater than the mean (all scores were 95 or above).

Mental Model Knowledge

Because the knowledge measures only offer information regarding the content of the technicians' knowledge, a quantitative assessment of their knowledge is also necessary. Such an assessment requires an ideal or standard mental model. A standard was created for each mental model measure by combining the data from the four technicians who scored the highest on the performance measure, the verbal troubleshooting task. (Extracting the data from the four highest performers restricted the range of data on which the correlations were based. Thus, the correlations reported in this study may be underestimated.) In cases in which there was little agreement across high performers, several standards were constructed, each based on a group of technicians whose results were similar. The quality of each technician's mental model knowledge was then assessed in terms of the overlap between this standard and the technician's response to the measure. This procedure was completed for each measure. The resulting knowledge assessment scores were then correlated with the performance score. This comparison, repeated for each measurement technique, provides a means of quantitatively assessing the mental model measures.

Predictiveness of the Mental Model Measures

Laddering Interview. To determine the level of agreement between the four high performers, the proportion of shared items across lists for each pair of high performers was calculated for each interview step. The resulting proportions indicated that the high performers agreed on the important components or systems for each step. Thus, a composite list of components found in the lists of the four high performers was created for use as the standard. The quality of a technician's mental model was then assessed in terms of the overlap between this standard list and the technician's list.

The overlap between a technician's list of components and the standard list was significantly correlated with verbal troubleshooting performance for step 2 of the laddering interview with r (13) = .542, p < .025. This positive relationship indicates that good troubleshooters agreed with the high performers on the components important for troubleshooting the problem, whereas poor troubleshooters did not. The data resulting from the remaining steps were not predictive of troubleshooting performance.

Relatedness Ratings. In order to generate a graphic summary of the ratings, the ratings data were submitted to the Pathfinder network scaling procedure, a descriptive multivariate statistical technique that represents pairwise proximities in a network form (Schvaneveldt, 1990). In the networks, concepts (or components, in this case) are represented as nodes, and relations (functional relations, in this case) are represented as links between nodes. These network representations not only summarize the data but have been shown to convey information about conceptual relatedness that is not seen in the ratings themselves (Cooke, 1992; Cooke, Durso, & Schvaneveldt, 1986).

The C statistic (Goldsmith & Davenport, 1990), a measure of shared links for matching nodes across two different networks, was calculated between each of the four high performers. This measure ranges from 0 (low similarity) to 1 (high similarity) and can be viewed as a measure of association between two networks. The resulting C values indicated that technician 8 shared fewer links with the other three high performers than the other three shared with each other (technician 8 had a mean C value of .415 compared to .838 for other pairs of high performers). Therefore, the standard network was created in several ways: (1) from the averaged ratings of all four high performers, (2) using ratings of technician 8 only, and (3) from the averaged ratings of all high performers, excluding technician 8. The quality of a technician's mental model was then assessed in terms of the C value between these standard networks and the technician's network.

Correlations between these *C* values and verbal troubleshooting performance indicated that pairwise relatedness ratings are predictive of troubleshooting performance: the similarity between technicians' individual networks and the network of technician 8 (standard network 2) was significantly correlated with troubleshooting performance, with $r(13) = .527$, $p < .05$. This positive relationship indicates that good troubleshooters made ratings like those given by technician 8, whereas poor troubleshooters did not. Interestingly, when standard networks 1 or 3 were used to assess mental model quality, ratings were not predictive of troubleshooting performance.

Diagramming Task. The following analyses are based on the general (problem-independent) diagrams of the RWR system. The diagrams that were specific to the troubleshooting problem did not distinguish between the technicians because there was little variance between the technicians' responses, and the majority of the technicians deemed that only three to five system components were relevant to this problem. Each of the 19 technicians' general system diagrams was converted to an 11-by-11 asymmetric matrix, with ones representing the presence of a connection between components and zeros indicating no connection.

To determine the level of similarity between the diagrams of the four high performers, the proportion of shared connections was computed for each pair of diagrams. In general, pairs of high performers shared about half of the links present in the two diagrams. However, technician 8's diagram shared the fewest connections with those of the other high performers (technician 8 had a mean proportion of .42 compared to .68 for other pairs of high performers). For this reason, three standard diagrams were created parallel to the three standards for the relatedness ratings: (1) a diagram based on all four high performers, (2) technician 8's diagram, and (3) a diagram based on all high performers, excluding technician 8. The matrix representing the group diagrams (that is, standards 1 and 3) consisted of ones, indicating that the connection existed in at least one diagram, and zeros otherwise. Again, these matrices were asymmetric. The quality of a technician's mental model was then assessed in terms of the overlap between these standard diagrams and the technician's diagram. Specifically, the number of different connections across diagrams was counted.

Correlations between these difference scores and verbal troubleshooting performance indicated that the diagramming task was predictive of performance, with $r(13) = -.464$, $p < .05$, for standard 1 and $r(13) = -.440$, $p = .05$, for standard 2. In the diagramming task, a negative correlation is anticipated because a large number of differences between the standard diagram and a technician's diagram should be associated with a low performance score. The low correlation between standard 3 and performance (r = .089), as well as a nonsignificant correlation of r = -.181 when technician 8's diagram is partialed out of standard 1, suggests that the predictability of the high performers in this technique can be attributed to technician 8. In fact, when the contribution of the three other high performers is removed from the correlation between technician 8 and performance, the resulting correlation is high and significant, with r (12) = -.538, p = .02. Thus, as with relatedness ratings, technician 8 is more predictive of technician performance than the other three high performers.

Think-Aloud Task. In order to assess the quality of the mental model measured by the think-aloud technique, the verbal protocols that were generated were subjected to a content analysis (see Rowe, 1994, for details). The coded protocols were then analyzed in terms of transition probabilities for pairs of utterances. In general, this analysis focuses on recurring sequential patterns of utterances (verbalized thoughts and specified actions) in the coded protocols.

The Pathfinder network scaling algorithm was again used to summarize the transition probabilities. Although the Pathfinder procedure has typically been used to represent knowledge in the form of conceptual or declarative relationships (Schvaneveldt and others, 1985), it has also been used to represent sequences (McDonald & Schvaneveldt, 1988; Cooke, Neville, & Rowe, in press). C values among pairs of networks for high performers indicated that the high performers conveyed very different sequences of thoughts in their verbalization, with mean inter-high-performer C = .06. Because no high performer seemed different from the rest, however, the transition frequencies of all four high performers were combined, and a standard network was created from these data.

The quality of a technician's mental model as measured by the think-aloud task was then assessed by calculating a C value between the standard network and each technician's network. A correlation between these C values and verbal troubleshooting performance indicated that the think-aloud task was not predictive of performance, with r (13) = .026. Furthermore, using a standard based on any one of the high performers' think-aloud protocols did not enhance predictability. This result may seem puzzling: Why did the transition analysis of utterances prove unrelated to performance when the performance measure is based on a portion of those utterances (that is, the specified actions)?

This result can be explained in several ways. First, the performance measure was based on expert judgments, and experts base their judgments on more than the sequences in which actions were taken. In addition, the technicians had difficulty thinking aloud. They tended to speak very little beyond specifying actions, and when they did speak, they usually chose to read aloud technical documents that were available for their use. Furthermore, the think-aloud procedure used in this study did not attempt to structure technicians' verbalizations in any way; this lack of structure may have contributed to the lack of predictiveness associated with this measure. Structuring technicians' verbalizations may enhance the predictiveness of this technique (for example, prompting them with questions such as "What will this action tell you?" or "How would you interpret that result?").

Finally, this result is a good example of the kinds of dissociations researchers have noted between task performance and verbalizable knowledge about that task (Broadbent, FitzGerald, & Broadbent, 1986; Reber, 1989). Technicians may be unaware of much of the knowledge that underlies their troubleshooting performance and, when they are asked to think aloud, they verbalize thoughts that are independent of task performance. Thus, an unstructured think-aloud task like the one used here does not appear to assess mental model knowledge that is critical for troubleshooting performance in this domain.

Comparing the Techniques

Of the four techniques tested, all but the think-aloud technique were predictive of this task and criterion. Partial correlations, however, indicate that only the relatedness ratings and laddering tasks are independently predictive of troubleshooting performance. Specifically, the relatedness ratings are predictive of performance either with the contribution of the laddering task partialed out, r (12) = .461, p = .042, or with the diagramming task partialed out, r (12) = .471, p = .039. Similarly, laddering is independently predictive of performance with the contribution of the rating task partialed out, r (12) = .480, p = .035, or with the diagramming task partialed out, r (12) = .421, p = .057, although the significance of this second correlation is marginal. On the other hand, the diagramming task is not independently predictive of performance once the contributions of the laddering or rating task are removed. Thus, the laddering and rating tasks each assessed mental model information that is independently predictive of performance, whereas the diagramming technique did not. These two measures appear to capture different aspects of a mental model, each of which is important to the troubleshooting task.

Discussion and Implications

Identifying Mental Model Knowledge

The purpose of this study was to evaluate several mental model measures, with performance as the criterion. Of the four techniques assessed, all but the think-aloud technique were predictive of troubleshooting performance. Although the think-aloud verbal reports yielded mental models, these models were not predictive of performance. This finding points to the limitations of purely unstructured interviews. Structuring the think-aloud interview might have resulted in data more closely related to performance. This finding also emphasizes the importance of verifying that your mental model measure is related to the criterion of interest. Suppose that only the think-aloud measure had been used here and that this measure had been evaluated in reference to a nonperformance criterion such as ease of implementation. Conclusions about technicians' mental models based only on this information would have had little or no relation to their ultimate troubleshooting performance.

On the other hand, the laddering (step 2), relatedness ratings, and diagramming techniques were all predictive of troubleshooting performance. Furthermore, the laddering and ratings techniques were independently predictive of performance, suggesting that these two measures capture different aspects of a mental model, each of which is important to the troubleshooting task. The laddering task appears to tap into knowledge about existing components, whereas the ratings task accesses knowledge about the interfaces or connections between components. Both of these measures appear to be good choices for identifying mental model knowledge when the goal is to affect troubleshooting performance.

The procedural features of these two techniques may also be used to inform decisions about which measure to use. Specifically, the laddering technique should be used in cases in which both ratings and laddering cannot be used. Relatedness ratings can become unwieldy: presenting all pairs of a concept set quickly leads to an unmanageable number of pairs as the number of concepts increases, making this technique nearly impossible to use with large sets of concepts. Even with a smaller number of concepts (around twenty), the pairwise ratings task may seem quite long and tedious to subjects. On the other hand, the laddering technique is easier to implement. It requires less background knowledge on the part of the researcher, especially when ratings are followed by Pathfinder analysis. There is a tradeoff to be considered, however. Whereas the ratings technique is more difficult than the laddering technique in terms of the effort required from subjects and the data analysis, it provides a graphic representation of knowledge that is much richer than the list produced using the laddering technique.

Research Issues

Several other interesting issues were revealed in this study. In particular, it was interesting that the mental model of one high performer, technician 8, offered optimal predictability for two of the measures.

Although technician 8 and the other three high performers all did well on the troubleshooting problem, their performance on the knowledge measures was different. It turns out that technician 8 was, in fact, less experienced than the other three high performers. Thus, he appears to be a very good "intermediate"-level technician rather than an "expert"-level technician. The fact that an intermediate model would be a better predictor of novice performance than an expert model has a number of implications regarding the development of expertise. One possibility is that the mental models of the expert technicians are too far removed from those of novices. Perhaps they even differ qualitatively, whereas intermediate and novice models differ only by degree, a perspective espoused by phase theorists (Karmiloff-Smith, 1986; Shuell, 1990). This and other possibilities remain for further investigation.

Implications for Human Resources

Although incorporating complex equipment into the workplace generally increases productivity, it also tends to increase the cognitive difficulty of the job, and workers must be trained to use the new equipment. Targeting workers' mental models of the equipment in this training should enhance their understanding and subsequent use of the equipment. Successfully incorporating the mental model construct into training, however, requires an appropriate measure of mental model knowledge. Because the goal is typically performance improvement in human resource problems, selection of a mental model measure or measures should be made with this goal in mind.

This study offers a good example of assessing knowledge measures by using performance as the criterion. It may be tempting to evaluate knowledge measures by determining how well a given measure discriminates between two or more groups with respect to an easily measured variable such as experience or type of training. However, experience and type of training are not necessarily correlated with performance. Furthermore, the knowledge that differentiates groups may not be causally related to performance. Simply having the ability to categorize people may not offer information directly relevant to training interventions. For example, the results from the think-aloud technique distinguished novices from experts in that novices read available technical materials aloud and experts did not. This difference, however, would not aid in the development of instructional materials.

In contrast, using performance as the final criterion can provide valuable information in designing a training intervention. If a particular type of knowledge is associated with successful performance, then training incorporating this knowledge should result in performance improvements. In this study, three of the evaluated measures were predictive of performance. Being able to list the RWR system components was predictive of troubleshooting performance, indicating that learning to identify pertinent components is a good first step in developing a good mental model. Diagram quality was related to troubleshooting performance; therefore, training technicians in diagramming to increase their awareness of the relationships between RWR components may be a valuable instructional intervention. Additionally, studying expert networks resulting from the ratings task could assist technicians in improving their own mental models. Understanding the relationship between a knowledge representation and performance can offer valuable information for both designing and evaluating training interventions to improve job performance.

References

Bayman, P., & Mayer, R. E. (1984). Instructional manipulation of users' mental models for electronic calculators. *International Journal of Man-Machine Studies, 20,* 189-199.

Broadbent, D. E., FitzGerald, P., & Broadbent, M. H. P. (1986). Implicit and explicit knowledge in the control of complex systems. *British Journal of Psychology, 77,* 33-50.

Clark, F. (1982). Improving technical skills in an urban transit environment. *Training and Development Journal, 36* (9), 58-63.

Cooke, N. J. (1992). Predicting judgment time from measures of psychological proximity. *Journal of Experimental Psychology: Learning, Memory, and Cognition, 18,* 640-653.

Cooke, N. J. (1994). Varieties of knowledge elicitation techniques. *International Journal of Human Computer Studies, 41,* 801-849.

Cooke, N. J., Neville, K. J., & Rowe, A. L. (in press). Procedural network representations of sequential data. *Human-Computer Interaction.*

Cooke, N. M., Durso, F. T., & Schvaneveldt, R. W. (1986). Recall and measures of memory organization. *Journal of Experimental Psychology: Learning, Memory and Cognition, 12,* 538-549.

Frese, M., Albrecht, K., Altmann, A., Lang, J., Papstein, P. V., Peyerl, R., Prumper, J., Schulte-Gocking, H., Wankmuller, I., & Wendel, R. (1988). The effects of an active development of the mental model in the training process: Experimental results in a word processing system. *Behaviour and Information Technology, 7,* 295-304.

Gentner, D., & Gentner, D. R. (1983). Flowing waters or teeming crowds: Mental models of electricity. In D. Gentner & A. L. Stevens (Eds.), *Mental models* (pp. 99-129). Hillsdale, NJ: Lawrence Erlbaum.

Gentner, D., & Stevens, A. L. (Eds.). (1983). *Mental models.* Hillsdale, NJ: Lawrence Erlbaum.

Goldsmith, T. E., & Davenport, D. M. (1990). Assessing structural similarity of graphs. In R. Schvaneveldt (Ed.), *Pathfinder associative networks: Studies in knowledge organization* (pp. 75-87). Norwood, NJ: Ablex.

Halasz, F. G., & Moran, T. P. (1983). Mental models and problem solving in using a calculator. In A. Janda (Ed.), *Human factors in computing systems: Proceedings of CHI 1983 conference* (pp. 212-216). New York: Association for Computing Machinery.

Hall, E. M., Gott, S. P., & Pokorny, R. A. (1995, October). *A procedural guide to cognitive task analysis: The PARI methodology.* (Air Force Technical Report No. AL/HR-TR-1995-0108; National Technical Report No. AD-A303654). Brooks Air Force Base,

TX: Air Force Armstrong Laboratory, Human Resources Directorate, Manpower and Personnel Division.

Hall, E. M., Pokorny, R. A., & Kane, R. (1994). [Identification of instructional goals: A qualitative and quantitative analysis of problem-solving problems]. Unpublished raw data.

Hegarty, M. (1991). Knowledge and processes in mechanical problem solving. In R. J. Sternberg & P. A. Frensch (Eds.), *Complex problem solving: Principles and mechanisms* (pp. 253-285). Hillsdale, NJ: Lawrence Erlbaum.

Karmiloff-Smith, A. (1986). Stage/structure versus phase/process in modelling linguistic and cognitive development. In I. Levin (Ed.), *Stage and structure* (pp. 164-190). Norwood, NJ: Ablex.

Kieras, D. E., & Bovair, S. (1984). The role of a mental model in learning to operate a device. *Cognitive Science, 8,* 255-273.

McDonald, J. E., & Schvaneveldt, R. W. (1988). The application of user knowledge to interface design. In R. Guindon (Ed.), *Cognitive science and its applications for human-computer interaction* (pp. 289-338). Hillsdale, NJ: Lawrence Erlbaum.

Norman, D. A. (1983). Some observations on mental models. In D. Gentner & A. L. Stevens (Eds.), *Mental models* (pp. 7-14). Hillsdale, NJ: Lawrence Erlbaum.

Rasmussen, J., & Jensen, A. (1974). Mental procedures in real-life tasks: A case study of electronic troubleshooting. *Ergonomics, 17,* 293-307.

Reber, A. S. (1989). Implicit learning and tacit knowledge. *Journal of Experimental Psychology: General, 118,* 219-235.

Rouse, W. B., & Morris, N. M. (1986). On looking into the black box: Prospects and limits in the search for mental models. *Psychological Bulletin, 100,* 349-363.

Rowe, A. L. (1994). *Mental models of physical systems: Examining the relationship between knowing and doing.* Unpublished doctoral dissertation, Rice University, Houston, TX.

Schendel, J. D. (1994). Training for troubleshooting. *Training and Development, 48* (5), 89-95.

Schvaneveldt, R. (Ed.). (1990). *Pathfinder associative networks: Studies in knowledge organization.* Norwood, NJ: Ablex.

Schvaneveldt, R. W., Durso, F. T., Goldsmith, T. E., Breen, T. J., Cooke, N. J., Tucker, R. G., & DeMaio, J. C. (1985). Measuring the structure of expertise. *International Journal of Man-Machine Studies, 23,* 699-728.

Sein, M. K., & Bostrom, R. P. (1989). Individual differences and conceptual models in training novice users. *Human-Computer Interaction, 4,* 197-229.

Shuell, T. J. (1990). Phases of meaningful learning. *Review of Educational Research, 60,* 531-547.

Staggers, N., & Norcio, A. F. (1993). Mental models: Concepts for human-computer interaction research. *International Journal of Man-Machine Studies, 38,* 587-605.

Wilson, J. R., & Rutherford, A. (1989). Mental models: Theory and application in human factors. *Human Factors, 31,* 617-634.

IMPLICATIONS FOR HUMAN RESOURCE DEVELOPMENT PROFESSIONALS

The Rowe and Cooke article provides evidence of the existence of mental models for troubleshooting performance. Other forms of mental models may also exist and be used by individuals in their jobs. HRD practitioners may want to consider the use of expert mental models in training and development efforts. Practitioners can thus use some of the methods described by Rowe and Cooke to describe the mental models of top performers in specific jobs. These mental models may help novices circumvent long hours of training or trial and error.

As shown by Rowe and Cooke, not all mental models are of equal value. Rowe and Cooke's results suggest that the mental model of someone of intermediate expertise may prove more useful to novices than the mental models of the high-performing expert. Similar to Rowe and Cooke, Hall, Rowe, Pokorny, and Boyer (1996) found that a tutoring system that focused on strategy led to performance that was superior to that achieved by a system that focused on tactical performance.

IMPLICATIONS FOR RESEARCH DESIGN AND METHODOLOGY

Rowe and Cooke identified mental models that were in use during troubleshooting tasks. Researchers should begin to identify further the variety of tasks in which workers use mental models. As with Rowe and Cooke, what is of interest are mental models that are related to some desired outcome in terms of learning or performance. Furthermore, this study suggests that researchers should use at least two separate measures of mental models to determine the reliability and validity of the measures.

Of interest to researchers is the use of both qualitative and quantitative methods to answer questions regarding mental models. Given the verbal protocols involved in determining the existing mental model, standard qualitative methods seem most appropriate. When examining the effect of those mental models on specific outcomes, quantitative methods may be more appropriate.

IMPLICATIONS FOR FUTURE INQUIRY

In addition to investigating the existence of mental models, researchers should determine what differences arise in mental models between expert performers, intermediate performers, and novices. Of interest is not only descriptive research concerning the models of different levels used by performers, but also theoretical work regarding how people develop mental models. Some questions that arise concern whether mental models proceed through certain phases and, if so, how such models move from one phase to the next.

Having defined different levels or phases of mental models and the mechanisms that shape their development, researchers could then examine the use of mental models in training and development efforts. Of particular interest in the research done by Rowe and Cooke was the finding that the mental model of an intermediate performer was more predictive of enhanced novice performance. This implies that the mental models of "true" experts may be too different from those of novices to be of use in training or developing these novices. Researchers should investigate the use of the mental models of both expert performers and intermediate performers in the training of novices.

OTHER RESOURCES

Ericsson, K. A., & Charness, N. (1994). Expert performance: Its structure and acquisition. *American Psychologist*, pp. 725-747.

Ericsson, K. A., & Lehmann, A. C. (1996) Expert and exceptional performance: Evidence of maximal adaptation to task constraints. *Annual Review of Psychology, 47*, 273-305.

de Groot, A. D. (1978). *Thought and choice and chess.* The Hague, Netherlands: Mouton. (Original work published 1946)

Gardner, H. (1991). *The unschooled mind: How children think and how schools should teach.* New York: Basic.

Gentner, D., & Stevens, A. L. (Eds.). (1983). *Mental models.* Hillsdale, NJ: Lawrence Erlbaum.

Glaser, R. (1990). The reemergence of learning theory within instructional research. *American Psychologist, 45*, 29-39.

Hall, E. P., Rowe, A. L., Pokorny, R. A., and Boyer, B. S. (1996, April). A field evaluation of two intelligent tutoring systems. In J. Ellis (Chair), *Instructional strategies, retraining, and training evaluation.* Symposium conducted at the annual meeting of the American Educational Research Association, New York.

Sein, M. K., & Bostrom, R. P. (1989). Individual differences and conceptual models in training novice users. *Human-Computer Interaction, 4*, 197-229.

Testing Common Sense

Robert J. Sternberg
Yale University

Richard K. Wagner
Florida State University

Wendy M. Williams
Yale University

Joseph A. Horvath
Yale University

PREDICTORS OF SUCCESS IN SCHOOL, SUCH AS CONVENTIONAL PSYCHOMETRIC intelligence (e.g., IQ) tests, are less predictive of success out of school. Even the most charitable estimates of the relation between intelligence test scores and real-world criteria such as job performance indicate that approximately three fourths of the variance in real-world performance is not accounted for by intelligence test performance. Researchers have begun to explore new constructs in search of measures to supplement existing cognitive ability tests as predictors of real-world performance. Among the most promising constructs is practical intelligence, or common sense. Performance on measures of practical intelligence predicts real-world criteria such as job performance but is relatively unrelated to performance on intelligence tests and other common selection measures. Consequently, its contribution to prediction is largely independent of the contributions of existing measures, including measures of cognitive ability.

Source: Sternberg, R. J., Wagner, R. K., Williams, W. M., & Horvath, J. A. (1995). Testing common sense. *American Psychologist, 50*(11), 912-927. Used by permission.

Each of us knows individuals who succeed in school but fail in their careers, or conversely, who fail in school but succeed in their careers. We have watched as graduate students, at the top of their class in the initial years of structured coursework, fall by the wayside when they must work independently on research and a dissertation. Most of us know of colleagues whose brilliance in their academic fields is matched only by their incompetence in social interactions. There are any number of reasons why someone might succeed in one environment but fail in another. A growing body of research, summarized in this article, suggests that differential success in academic and nonacademic environments reflects, in part, differences in the intellectual competencies required for success in these arenas.

Academic psychologists enjoy few perks, but one is the occasional opportunity to be thankful about their career choice. Consider the plight of the garbage collector, particularly in Tallahassee, Florida. If it is not enough that the summer heat makes any outdoor work unbearable, the city of Tallahassee adds insult to injury. Priding itself on the service it provides its citizens, Tallahassee requires physical labor far beyond the ordinary lifting and tossing of the standard-sized garbage cans placed carefully at curbside in other cities. In Tallahassee, each household fills a huge, city-issued trash container kept in its backyard. Trash collectors are required to locate and retrieve each full container from each backyard, heave them into the truck, and then drag back the empty containers to each yard.

Many of the garbage collectors are young high school dropouts who, because of their lack of education, might not be expected to do well on intelligence tests. And on the surface, the job appears to be physically but not intellectually challenging. Each stop simply requires two trips to the backyard, one to retrieve the full can, another to replace it when empty. Or so we thought.

After observing this collection routine one summer, we noticed that a new, older man joined the crew, and the routine changed. The change involved relaxing the constraint that each household retain the same garbage container. After all, the trash bins are identical, issued by the city rather than purchased with personal funds. The new routine consisted of wheeling the last house's empty can into the current house's backyard, leaving it to replace the full can that was in turn wheeled to the truck to be emptied. Once emptied, this can was now wheeled to the backyard of the next household to replace its full can, and so on. What had required two trips back and forth to each house now required only one. The new man's insight cut the work nearly in half.

What kind of intelligence enables a person to come up with this kind of strategy for reducing effort by half, a strategy that had eluded well-educated observers such as the present authors, other garbage collectors, and the managers who trained them? And how well is this kind of intelligence reflected in an IQ score? An anecdote by Seymour Sarason, a psychologist at Yale, provides little grounds for optimism. When he reported to his first job—administering intelligence tests at a school for the mentally retarded—he could not begin testing because the students had cleverly eluded elaborate security precautions and escaped. When the students were rounded up, Sarason proceeded to administer the Porteus Maze Test, a paper-and-pencil intelligence test that involves finding the way out of labyrinths. To his surprise, Sarason discovered that the very same students who had been able to outwit the staff and escape from the facility were unable to find their way out of the first maze on the test.

The degree to which intelligence tests predict out-of-school criteria, such as job performance, has been an area of longstanding controversy. Opinions range from the view that there is little or no justification for tests of cognitive ability for job selection (McClelland, 1973) to the view that cognitive ability tests are valid predictors of job performance in a wide variety of job settings (Barrett & Depinet, 1991) or even in all job settings (Schmidt & Hunter, 1981; see also Gottfredson, 1986; Hawk, 1986).

For the purpose of this article, one can sidestep the debate about the degree to which intelligence test scores predict real-world perfor-mance. Even the most charitable view of the relation between intelli-gence test scores and real-world performance leads to the conclusion that the majority of variance in real-world performance is not accounted for by intelligence test scores. The average validity coefficient between cognitive ability tests and measures of job performance is about .2 (Wigdor & Garner, 1982). At this level of validity, only 4% of the variance in job performance is accounted for by ability test scores. The average validity coefficient between cognitive ability tests and measures of performance in job training programs is about double (.4) that found for job performance itself, a fact that suggests the magnitude of prediction varies as a function of how comparable the criterion measure is to schooling. Hunter, Schmidt, and their colleagues have argued that better estimates of the true relation between cognitive ability test performance and job performance are obtained when the validity coefficients are corrected for (a) unreliability in test scores and criterion measures and (b) restriction of range caused by the fact that only high scorers are hired. Employing these corrections raises the average validity coefficient to the level of about .5 (Hunter & Hunter, 1984; Schmidt & Hunter, 1981). Of course, this validity coefficient represents a hypothetical level, not one that is routinely obtained in practice. But even if one adopts the more optimistic hypothetical figure of .5, intelligence test scores account for only 25% of the variance in job performance. Whether you view the glass as being one-quarter filled or three-quarters empty, room for improvement exists. Researchers have therefore begun to explore new constructs in search of measures to supplement existing cognitive ability tests. Among the most promising constructs is practical intelligence, or common sense.

Practical Intelligence

Neisser (1976) was one of the first psychologists to press the distinction between academic and practical intelligence. Neisser described academic intelligence tasks (common in the classroom and on intelligence tests) as (a) formulated by others, (b) often of little or no intrinsic interest, (c) having all needed information available from the beginning, and (d) disembedded from an individual's ordinary experience. In addition, one should consider that these tasks (e) usually are well defined, (f) have but one correct answer, and (g) often have just one method of obtaining the correct solution (Wagner & Sternberg, 1985).

Note that these characteristics do not apply as well to many of the problems people face in their daily lives, including many of the problems at work. In direct contrast, work problems often are (a) unformulated or in need of reformulation, (b) of personal interest, (c) lacking in information necessary for solution, (d) related to everyday experience, (e) poorly defined, (f) characterized by multiple "correct" solutions, each with liabilities as well as assets, and (g) characterized by multiple methods for picking a problem solution.

Laypersons have long recognized a distinction between academic intelligence (book smarts) and practical intelligence (street smarts). This distinction is represented in everyday parlance by expressions such as "learning the ropes" and "getting your feet wet." This distinction also figures prominently in the implicit theories of intelligence held by both laypeople and researchers. Sternberg, Conway, Ketron, and Bernstein (1981) asked samples of laypeople in a supermarket, a library, and a train station, as well as samples of academic researchers who study intelligence, to provide and rate the importance of characteristics of intelligent individuals. Factor analyses of the ratings supported a distinction between academic and practical aspects of intelligence for laypeople and experts alike.

Older adults commonly report growth in practical abilities over the years, even though their academic abilities decline. Williams, Denney, and Schadler (1983) interviewed men and women over the age of 65 about their perception of changes in their ability to think, reason, and solve problems as they aged. Although performance on traditional cognitive ability measures typically peaks at the end of formal schooling,

76% of the older adults in the Williams et al. (1983) study believed that their ability to think, reason, and solve problems had actually increased over the years, with 20% reporting no change and only 4% reporting that their abilities had declined with age. When confronted with the fact of decline in psychometric test performance upon completion of formal schooling, the older sample said that they were talking about solving different kinds of problems than those found on cognitive ability tests—problems they referred to as "everyday" and "financial" problems.

Horn and Cattell (1966), in their theory of fluid and crystallized intelligence, provided a theoretical language with which to describe age-related changes in intellectual ability. According to their theory, *fluid abilities* are required to deal with novelty in the immediate testing situation (e.g., induction of the next letter in a letter series problem). *Crystallized abilities* reflect acculturated knowledge (e.g., the meaning of a low-frequency vocabulary word). A number of studies have shown that fluid abilities are vulnerable to age-related decline but that crystallized abilities are maintained throughout adulthood (Dixon & Baltes, 1985; Horn, 1982; Labouvie-Vief, 1982; Schaie, 1977/1978).

Recall that practical problems are characterized by, among other things, an apparent absence of information necessary for a solution and for relevance to everyday experience. By contrast, academic problems are characterized by the presence, in the specification of a problem, of all the information necessary to solve the problem. Furthermore, academic problems are typically unrelated to an individual's ordinary experience. Thus, crystallized intelligence in the form of acculturated knowledge is more relevant to the solution of practical problems than it is to the solution of academic problems, at least as we are defining these terms. Conversely, fluid abilities, such as those required to solve letter series and figural analogy problems, are more relevant to the solution of academic problems than to the solution of practical problems. It follows that the growth in practical abilities that older participants report may reflect the greater contribution of maintained abilities—specifically, crystallized intelligence—in the solution of practical, everyday problems.

Empirical Studies of Practical Intelligence

The idea that practical and academic abilities follow different courses in adult development finds support in a variety of studies. For example, Denney and Palmer (1981) gave 84 adults between the ages of 20 and 79 years two types of reasoning problems: a traditional cognitive measure, the Twenty Questions Task (Mosher & Hornsby, 1966); and a problem-solving task involving real-life situations such as, "If you were traveling by car and got stranded out on an interstate highway during a blizzard, what would you do?" or, "Now let's assume that you lived in an apartment that didn't have any windows on the same side as the front door. Let's say that at 2:00 a.m. you heard a loud knock on the door and someone yelled, 'Open up. It's the police.' What would you do?" The most interesting result of the Denney and Palmer study for the purposes of this article is a difference in the shape of the developmental function for performance on the two types of problems. Performance on the traditional problem-solving task or cognitive measure decreased linearly after age 20. Performance on the practical problem-solving task increased to a peak in the 40 and 50 year-old groups, then declined.

Cornelius and Caspi (1987) obtained similar results in a study of 126 adults between the ages of 20 and 78. They examined the relations between fluid intelligence, crystallized intelligence, and everyday problem solving. Cornelius and Caspi gave their participants traditional measures of fluid ability (Letter Series) and crystallized ability (Verbal Meanings), as well as an everyday problem-solving inventory that sampled the domains of consumer problems (a landlord who won't make repairs), information seeking (additional data is needed to fill out a complicated form), personal concerns (you want to attend a concert but are unsure whether it is safe to go), family problems (responding to criticism from a parent or child), problems with friends (getting a friend to visit you more often), and work problems (you were passed over for a promotion).

The measure of crystallized ability was given to determine whether the development of everyday problem solving was more similar to the development of crystallized ability than to the development of fluid ability. Performance on the measure of fluid ability increased from age 20 to 30, remained stable from age 30 to 50, and then declined. Performance on the everyday problem-solving task and the measures of crystallized ability increased through age 70. Although Cornelius and Caspi's (1987) participants showed peak performance later in life than did Denney and Palmer's (1981), the pattern of traditional cognitive task performance peaking sooner than practical task performance was consistent across the studies. In addition to the developmental function of task performance, Cornelius and Caspi also examined the relation between performance on the fluid-ability and everyday problem-solving tasks and reported a modest correlation between the tasks ($r = .29$, $p < .01$). The correlation between everyday problem-solving ability and crystallized ability was not higher ($r = .27, p < .01$), leading Cornelius and Caspi to conclude that everyday problem solving was not reducible to crystallized ability, despite their similar developmental functions.

In summary, there is reason to believe that, whereas the ability to solve strictly academic problems declines from early to late adulthood, the ability to solve problems of a practical nature is maintained or even increased through late adulthood. The available evidence suggests that older individuals compensate for declining fluid abilities by restricting their domains of activity to those they know well (Baltes & Baltes, 1990) and by applying specialized procedural and declarative knowledge. For example, Salthouse (1984) has shown that age-related decrements at the "molecular" level (e.g., speed in the elementary components of typing skill) produce no observable effects at the "molar" level (i.e., the speed and accuracy with which work is completed).

These findings imply that, because fluid abilities are weaker determinants of performance on practical problems than they are of performance on academic problems, the use of scores on traditional cognitive ability tests to predict real-world performance should be problematic. In the past decade, a number of studies have addressed this and related issues. These studies, carried out in a wide range of settings and cultures, have been summarized and reviewed by Ceci (1990), Rogoff and Lave (1984), Scribner and Cole (1981), Sternberg (1985a), Sternberg and Frensch (1991), Sternberg and Wagner (1986, 1994), Sternberg, Wagner, and Okagaki (1993), and Voss, Perkins, and Segal (1991). It may help to convey the general nature of these studies with four examples from the single domain of everyday mathematics.

Scribner (1984, 1986) studied the strategies used by milk processing plant workers to fill orders. Workers who assemble orders for cases of various quantities (e.g., gallons, quarts, or pints) and products (e.g., whole milk, two percent milk, or buttermilk) are called assemblers. Rather than employing typical mathematical algorithms learned in the classroom, Scribner found that experienced assemblers used complex strategies for combining partially filled cases in a manner that minimized the number of moves required to complete an order. Although the assemblers were the least educated workers in the plant, they were able to calculate in their heads quantities expressed in different base number systems, and they routinely out-performed the more highly educated white collar workers who substituted when assemblers were absent. Scribner found that the order-filling performance of the assemblers was unrelated to measures of school performance, including intelligence test scores, arithmetic test scores, and grades.

Ceci and Liker (1986, 1988) carried out a study of expert racetrack handicappers. They studied strategies used by handicappers to predict post time odds at the racetrack. Expert handicappers used a highly complex algorithm for predicting post time odds that involved interactions among seven kinds of information. One obvious piece of useful information was a horse's speed on a previous outing. By applying the complex algorithm, handicappers adjusted times posted for each quarter mile on a previous outing by factors such as whether the horse was attempting to pass other horses, and if so, the speed of other horses passed and where the attempted passes took place. These adjustments are important because they affect how much of the race is run away from the rail. By adjusting posted times for these factors, a better measure of a horse's speed is obtained. Use of the complex interaction in prediction would seem to require considerable cognitive ability (at least as it is traditionally measured). However, Ceci and Liker reported that the degree to which a handicapper used the interaction (determined by the regression weight for this term in a multiple regression of the handicappers' predicted odds) was unrelated to the handicapper's IQ, ($M = 97$, $r = -.07$, $p > .05$).

Another series of studies of everyday mathematics involved shoppers in California grocery stores who sought to buy at the cheapest cost when the same products were available in different-sized containers (Lave, Murtaugh, & de la Roche, 1984; Murtaugh, 1985). (These studies were performed before cost per unit quantity information was routinely posted). For example, oatmeal may come in two sizes, 10 ounces for $.98 or 24 ounces for $2.29. One might adopt the strategy of always buying the largest size, assuming that the largest size is always the most economical. However, the researchers (and savvy shoppers) learned that the largest size did not represent the least cost per unit quantity for about a third of the items purchased. The findings of these studies were that effective shoppers used mental shortcuts to get an easily obtained answer, accurate (though not completely accurate) enough to determine which size to buy. As for the oatmeal example, the kind of strategy used by effective shoppers was to recognize that 10 ounces for $.98 is about 10 cents per ounce, and at that price, 24 ounces would be about $2.40, as opposed to the actual price of $2.29. Another common strategy involved mentally changing a size and price to make it more comparable with the other size available. For example, one might mentally double the smaller size, thereby comparing 20 ounces at $1.96 versus 24 ounces at $2.29. The difference of 4 ounces for about 35 cents, or about 9 cents per ounce, seems to favor the 24-ounce size, given that the smaller size of 10 ounces for $.98 is about 10 cents per ounce. These mathematical shortcuts yield approximations that are as useful as the actual values of 9.80 and 9.33 cents per ounce for the smaller and larger sizes, respectively, but that are much more easily computed in the absence of a calculator.

Another result of interest was that when the shoppers were given the M.I.T. mental arithmetic test, no relation was found between test performance and accuracy in picking the best values (Lave, Murtaugh, & de la Roche, 1984; Murtaugh, 1985). The same principle that applies to adults appears also to apply to children: Carraher, Carraher, and Schliemann (1985) found that Brazilian street children who could apply sophisticated mathematical strategies in their street vending were unable to do the same in a classroom setting.

One more example of a study of everyday mathematics was provided by individuals asked to play the role of city managers for the computer-simulated city of Lohhausen (Dörner & Kreuzig, 1983; Dörner, Kreuzig, Reither, & Staudel, 1983). A variety of problems were presented to these individuals, such as how to best raise revenue to build roads. The simulation involved more than one thousand variables. Performance was quantified in terms of a hierarchy of strategies, ranging from the simplest (trial and error) to the most complex (hypothesis testing with multiple feedback loops). No relation was found between IQ and complexity of strategies used. A second problem was created to cross-validate these results. This problem, called the Sahara problem, required participants to determine the number of camels that could be kept alive by a small oasis. Once again, no relation was found between IQ and complexity of strategies employed.

Tacit Knowledge

The distinction between academic and practical kinds of intelligence is paralleled by a similar distinction between two types of knowledge (Sternberg & Caruso, 1985; Wagner, 1987; Wagner & Sternberg, 1985, 1986). An academically intelligent individual is characterized by their facile acquisition of *formal academic knowledge,* the knowledge sampled by the ubiquitous intelligence tests and related aptitude tests. Conversely, the hallmark of the practically intelligent individual is their facile acquisition and use of *tacit knowledge.* Tacit knowledge refers to action-oriented knowledge, acquired without direct help from others, that allows individuals to achieve goals they personally value (Horvath et al., 1994). The acquisition and use of such knowledge appears to be uniquely important to competent performance in real-world endeavors. In this section we discuss the characteristic features of tacit knowledge, describe methods used in the testing of tacit knowledge, and review empirical support for the tacit knowledge construct.

What Is Tacit Knowledge?

There are three characteristic features of tacit knowledge. These features address, respectively, the structure of tacit knowledge, the conditions of its use, and the conditions under which it is acquired. First, tacit knowledge is procedural in nature. Second, tacit knowledge is relevant to the attainment of goals people value. Third, tacit knowledge is acquired with little help from others. Knowledge containing these three properties is called tacit because it often must be inferred from actions or statements. Please note, however, that although we have used the term *tacit* to refer to this type of knowledge, the intention or content of the tacit knowledge concept is not fully captured by the meaning of the lexical item *tacit*. Tacit knowledge is typically implied rather than stated explicitly—but there is more to the tacit knowledge concept than this most salient feature.

Tacit knowledge is procedural. Tacit knowledge is intimately related to action. It takes the form of "knowing how" rather than "knowing that" (Ryle, 1949). This sort of knowledge (knowing how) is called *procedural knowledge*, and it is contrasted with *declarative knowledge* (knowing that). More precisely, procedural knowledge is knowledge represented in a way that commits it to a particular use or set of uses (Winograd, 1975). Procedural knowledge can be represented, formally, as condition-action pairs of the general form

IF <antecedent condition> THEN <consequent action>

For example, the knowledge of how to respond to a red traffic light could be represented as

IF <light is red> THEN <stop>

Of course, the specification of the conditions and actions that make up proceduralized knowledge can be quite complex. In fact, much of the tacit knowledge that we have observed seems to take the form of complex, multiconditional rules for how to pursue particular goals in particular situations. For example, knowledge about getting along with one's superior might be represented in a form with a compound condition:

IF <you need to deliver bad news>
AND
IF <it is Monday morning>
AND
IF <the boss's golf game was rained out the day before>
AND
IF <the staff seems to be "walking on eggs">
THEN <wait until later>

As this example suggests, tacit knowledge is always wedded to particular uses in particular situations or in classes of situations. Individuals who are queried about their knowledge will often begin by articulating general rules in roughly declarative form (e.g., "a good leader needs to know people"). When such general statements are probed, however, they often reveal themselves to be abstract or summary representations for a family of complex specified procedural rules (e.g., rules about how to judge people accurately for a variety of purposes and under a variety of circumstances). Thus, procedural structure is characteristic of tacit knowledge.

Tacit knowledge is practically useful. Tacit knowledge is instrumental to the attainment of goals people value. The more highly valued a goal is, and the more directly the knowledge supports the attainment of the goal, the more useful is the knowledge. For example, knowledge about how to make subordinates feel valued is practically useful for managers or leaders who value that outcome, but is not practically useful for those who are unconcerned with making their subordinates feel valued. Thus, tacit knowledge is distinguished from knowledge, even "how to" knowledge, that is irrelevant to goals that people care about personally.

Tacit knowledge is acquired without direct help from others. Tacit knowledge is usually acquired on one's own. It is knowledge that is unspoken, underemphasized, or poorly conveyed relative to its importance for practical success. Thus, tacit knowledge is acquired under conditions of minimal environmental support. Environmental support refers to either people or media that help the individual acquire knowledge. When people or media support the acquisition of knowledge, they facilitate three knowledge acquisition components: selective encoding, selective combination, and selective comparison (Sternberg, 1985a, 1988). That is, when an individual is helped to distinguish more from less important information, is helped to combine elements of knowledge in useful ways, and is helped to identify knowledge in memory that may be useful in the present, then the individual has been supported in acquiring new knowledge. To the extent that this help is absent, the individual has not been supported.

To review, there are three characteristic features of tacit knowledge: (a) procedural structure, (b) high usefulness, and (c) low environmental support for acquisition. An important part of what makes the tacit knowledge concept a coherent one is the fact that these features are related to one another in nonarbitrary ways. In other words, we can explain why these features go together in the specification of a natural category of knowledge. We believe that this explanation strengthens the argument that tacit knowledge should be considered a well-formed concept.

First, it makes sense that procedural structure and high usefulness should both characterize a natural category of knowledge. Proceduralized knowledge also tends to be practically useful because it contains within it the specification of how it is used. Declarative knowledge, by contrast, is nonspecific with respect to use and, as a consequence, may remain unused or inert. Thus, procedural knowledge is more likely (than knowledge otherwise structured) to be instrumentally relevant in the pursuit of personally valued goals.

It also makes sense that high usefulness and low environmental support should both characterize a natural category of knowledge. Knowledge acquired in the face of low environmental support often confers a comparative advantage and thus tends to be practically useful in a competitive environment. When knowledge must be acquired in the face of low environmental support, the probability that some individuals will fail to acquire it increases. When some individuals fail to acquire knowledge, others who succeed in acquiring the knowledge may gain a competitive advantage over those who fail to acquire it. Note that the magnitude of this advantage would be lower if the knowledge in question was highly supported by the environment (i.e., explicitly and effectively taught), because more people would be expected to acquire and use it. Because many of the goals that individuals personally value are pursued in competition with other people, one may speculate that knowledge acquired under conditions of low environmental support is often particularly useful. This knowledge is more likely to differentiate individuals than is highly supported knowledge.

Finally, it makes sense that low environmental support and procedural structure should both characterize a natural category of knowledge. Proceduralized knowledge is often difficult to articulate and, thus, is more likely to be omitted from discussion or poorly conveyed. People know more than they can easily tell, and procedural knowledge is often especially difficult to articulate. Furthermore, procedural knowledge may become so highly automatized that people lose access to it completely. For these reasons, procedural knowledge is more likely than declarative knowledge to be acquired under conditions of low environmental support.

This discussion suggests that there is more to the tacit knowledge concept than a set of features assembled ad hoc to explain regularities in correlational data. Rather, the tacit knowledge concept is a coherent one, described not simply by a set of characteristic features but also by a set of nonarbitrary relations among those features.

Testing Tacit Knowledge

Instruments

Researchers have shown that tacit knowledge can be effectively measured (Sternberg, Wagner, & Okagaki, 1993; Wagner, 1987; Wagner & Sternberg, 1985, 1991; Williams & Sternberg, in press). The measurement instruments typically used consist of a set of work-related situations, each with between 5 and 20 response items. Each situation poses a problem for the participant to solve, and the participant indicates how he or she would solve the problem by rating the various response items. For example, in a hypothetical situation presented to a business manager, a subordinate whom the manager does not know well has come to him for advice on how to succeed in business. The manager is asked to rate each of several factors (usually on a 1 = *low* to 9 = *high* scale), according to their importance for succeeding in the company. Examples of factors might include (a) setting priorities that reflect the importance of each task, (b) trying always to work on what one is in the mood to do, and (c) doing routine tasks early in the day to make sure they are completed. Additional examples of work-related situations and associated response items are given in the Appendix [which appears in Sternberg et al., 1995].

Similarly, the tacit knowledge measurement instrument developed by Williams and Sternberg (in press) contains statements describing actions taken in the work-place, which participants rate for how characteristic the actions are of their behavior. In addition, complex open-ended problem situations are described, and participants are asked to write plans of action that show how they would handle the situations.

Scoring

The procedure for scoring a tacit knowledge test has evolved across several studies, and various scoring approaches are briefly described here. In Wagner and Sternberg's (1985b) study, the tacit knowledge test was scored by correlating ratings on each response item with a dummy variable representing group membership (e.g., 3 = *experienced manager,* 2 = *business school student,* 1 = *undergraduate*). A positive correlation between item and group membership indicated that higher ratings were associated with greater levels of expertise in the domain, whereas a negative correlation indicated that higher ratings were associated with lower levels of expertise in the domain. Items showing significant item-group correlations were retained for further analysis. Ratings for these items were summed across items in a given subscale, and these summed values served as predictor variables in analyzing the relationship, within groups, between tacit knowledge and job performance.

A second procedure for scoring tacit knowledge tests was employed by Wagner (1987). A sample of practically intelligent individuals (this time, academic psychologists) was obtained through a nomination process. The tacit knowledge test was administered to these individuals, and an expert profile was generated that represented the central tendency of their responses. Tacit knowledge tests for participants were scored, separately for each item subscale, as the sum of their squared deviations from this expert profile. Note that this scoring method, unlike that described previously, allows for meaningful comparisons between groups.

A third procedure for scoring tacit knowledge tests was that of Wagner, Rashotte, and Sternberg (1992). In a study of tacit knowledge for sales, they collected *rules of thumb* through reading and interviews. According to its dictionary definition, a rule of thumb is "a useful principle with wide application, not intended to be strictly accurate" (Morris, 1987, p. 1134). Examples of rules of thumb that differentiated expert from novice salespersons included, "Penetrate smokescreens by asking 'what if...?' questions," and "In evaluating your success, think in terms of tasks accomplished rather than hours spent working." These rules of thumb were grouped into categories and used to generate a set of work-related situations. Response items were constructed so that some items represented correct application of the rules of thumb, whereas other items represented incorrect or distorted application of the rules of thumb. The tacit knowledge test was scored for the degree to which participants preferred response items that represented correct applications of the rules of thumb.

Findings From the
Tacit Knowledge Research Program

Earlier we described several studies in which participants of different ages were given measures of everyday problem solving and measures of traditional cognitive abilities (Cornelius & Caspi, 1987; Denney & Palmer, 1981). The results suggested different developmental functions for the two kinds of abilities: Performance on traditional cognitive ability measures peaked in early adulthood, but performance on everyday problem-solving measures continued to improve through later adulthood. Which of these two functions better characterizes the development of tacit knowledge?

In a cross-sectional study, we administered a tacit knowledge inventory to three groups of participants, totaling 127 individuals, who differed in their breadth of experience and formal training in business management (Wagner & Sternberg, 1985, Experiment 2). One group consisted of 54 business managers, another group consisted of 51 business school graduate students, and a third group consisted of 22 Yale undergraduates. The means and standard deviations for amount of managerial experience were 16.6 (9.9) years for the business manager group; 2.2 (2.5) for the business graduate student group; and 0.0 (0.0) for the undergraduate group. Group differences were found on 39 of the response item ratings, with a binomial test of the probability of finding this many significant differences by chance yielding $p < .0001$. We conclude from this study that there were genuine differences in the ratings for the groups. We obtained comparable results for academic psychologists (Wagner & Sternberg, 1985a, Experiment 1). In a second cross-sectional study, we obtained tacit knowledge scores from three new groups of 64 managers, 25 business graduate students, and 60 Yale undergraduates (Wagner, 1987), and we used a prototype-based scoring system that allowed direct comparisons of the performance of the three groups. In this study, the business managers group, whose average age was 50, outperformed the business graduate students and the undergraduates. The business graduate students in turn outperformed the undergraduates. Again, comparable results were obtained for psychology professors, psychology graduate students, and undergraduates. Although these studies did not sample different age ranges as exhaustively as in the studies previously described (Cornelius & Caspi, 1987; Denney & Palmer, 1981), the results suggested that the development of tacit knowledge more closely resembles the development of everyday problem solving than that of cognitive ability as traditionally measured.

In a later study that focused on the development of tacit knowledge over the managerial career, Williams and Sternberg (in press) used extensive interviews and observations to construct both a general and a level-specific tacit knowledge measure. We administered this measure to all executives in four high technology manufacturing companies. We also obtained nominations from managers' superiors for "outstanding" and "underperforming" managers at the lower, middle, and upper levels. This approach enabled us to delineate the specific content of tacit knowledge for each level of management (lower, middle, and upper) by examining what experts at each level knew that their poorly performing colleagues did not.

Our results showed that there was indeed specialized tacit knowledge for each of the three management levels and that this knowledge was differentially related to success. We derived these results by comparing responses of outstanding and underperforming managers within each management level on level-specific tacit knowledge inventories. Within the domain of intrapersonal tacit knowledge, knowledge about how to seek out, create, and enjoy challenges was substantially more important to upper-level executives than to middle- or lower-level executives. Knowledge about maintaining appropriate levels of control became progressively more significant at higher levels of management. Knowledge about self-motivation, self-direction, self-awareness, and personal organization was roughly comparable in importance at the lower and middle levels, and became somewhat more important at the upper level. Finally, knowledge about completing tasks and working effectively within the business environment was substantially more important for upper-level managers than for middle-level managers, and substantially more important for middle-level managers than for lower-level managers. Within the domain of interpersonal tacit knowledge, knowledge about influencing and controlling others was essential for all managers, but especially for those in the upper level. Knowledge about supporting, cooperating with, and understanding others was extremely important for upper-level executives, very important for middle-level executives, and somewhat important for lower-level executives.

Questions About the
Tacit Knowledge Construct

We have argued elsewhere that the "g-ocentric view" of intelligence and job performance is wrong—that there is more to successfully predicting job performance than just measuring the general factor from conventional psychometric tests of intelligence (see Sternberg & Wagner, 1993). We suggested an aspect of practical intelligence, tacit knowledge, as a key ingredient to job success. Not everyone has agreed with this point of view. Jensen (1993), Schmidt and Hunter (1993), and Ree and Earles (1993) have presented various arguments against this position. This section addresses questions raised by critics of the tacit knowledge research program.

Are individual differences in tacit knowledge domain-general? Are measures of tacit knowledge highly domain-specific tests of job knowledge, analogous to a test for mechanics that requires identifying a crescent wrench, or do they represent some more general construct? The evidence to date is more compatible with the view that measures of tacit knowledge assess a relatively general construct.

Two kinds of factor analysis were performed on the tacit knowledge scores of a sample of 64 business managers (Wagner, 1987). A principal components analysis yielded a first principal component that accounted for 44% of the total variance, and for 76% of total variance after the correlations among scores were disattenuated for unreliability. The residual matrix was not significant after extracting the first principal component. A first principal component accounting for about 40% of total variance is typical of analyses carried out on traditional cognitive ability subtests. A confirmatory factor analysis was performed to test alternative models of the factor structure of the tacit knowledge inventory more formally. The results supported the generality of tacit knowledge. A model consisting of a single general factor provided the best fit to the data and yielded small and nonsignificant differences between predicted and observed covariances. The root mean square residual was .08 ($N = 64$, $X^2(9) = 12.13$, $p > .05$).

The domain generality of tacit knowledge was given additional support when the identical tacit knowledge framework was used to construct a new measure of tacit knowledge for the domain of academic psychology. A parallel study that included samples of psychology professors, graduate students, and undergraduates yielded a pattern of results nearly identical to that found in business samples. More important, a group of 60 undergraduates was given tacit knowledge measures for both domains—business management and academic psychology—in counterbalanced order. After determining that order of administration did not affect the latent structure of the two tacit knowledge measures, we calculated correlations between scores across measures. The magnitude of these cross-domain correlations was .58 for total score, .52 for managing oneself, .47 for managing tasks, and .52 for managing others (components of our tacit knowledge construct), all significant at the $p < .001$ level. These results support the domain generality of individual differences in tacit knowledge.

Are tacit knowledge inventories just intelligence tests in disguise? If individual differences in tacit knowledge appear to have some domain generality, has this accidentally reinvented the concept of "g," or general ability, that can be extracted from an intelligence test? Results from several studies of tacit knowledge, in which participants have been given a traditional measure of cognitive ability in addition to a tacit knowledge inventory, suggest that this is not the case.

For example, Wagner and Sternberg (1985) gave the Verbal Reasoning subtest of the Differential Aptitude Tests (Form T) to a sample of 22 undergraduates. The correlation between tacit knowledge and verbal reasoning was .16 ($p > .05$). In subsequent studies, a deviation scoring system, in which lower scores indicated better performance than higher scores, was used to quantify tacit knowledge. Thus, a positive relation between tacit knowledge and cognitive ability would be represented by a negative correlation. For a sample of 60 undergraduates, the correlation between tacit knowledge and verbal reasoning was $-.12$ ($p > .05$).

One important limitation of these results is that the participants were Yale undergraduates and thus represented a restricted range of verbal ability. In addition, undergraduates have relatively little tacit knowledge compared with experienced managers. Rather different correlations between tacit knowledge and IQ might therefore be expected for other groups, such as business managers. We administered the Tacit Knowledge Inventory for Managers to a sample of 45 managers who participated in a leadership development program at the Center for Creative Leadership in Greensboro, North Carolina (Wagner & Sternberg, 1990). Participants routinely completed a battery of tests, including an intelligence test. For this sample, the correlation between tacit knowledge and IQ was $-.14$ ($p > .05$).

But even business managers represent a restricted range in IQ, and perhaps in tacit knowledge as well. What would be the relation between tacit knowledge and IQ in a more general sample? In a study at the Human Resources Laboratory at Brooks Air Force Base that was supervised by Malcolm Ree, Eddy (1988) examined relations between the Tacit Knowledge Inventory for Managers and the Armed Services Vocational Aptitude Battery (ASVAB) for a sample of 631 Air Force recruits, 29% of whom were women, and 19% of whom were members of a minority group. The ASVAB is a multiple-aptitude battery used for the selection of candidates into all branches of the United States Armed Forces. Prior studies of the ASVAB suggested that it is a typical measure of cognitive ability, with correlations between ASVAB scores and other cognitive ability measures of about .7. Factor analytic studies have also suggested that the ASVAB appears to measure the same verbal, quantitative, and mechanical abilities as the Differential Aptitude Tests, and measures the same verbal and mathematical knowledge as the California Achievement Tests.

Eddy's (1988) study showed small correlations between tacit knowledge and ASVAB subtests. The median correlation was −.07, with a range from .06 to −.15. Of the 10 correlations, only 2 correlations were significantly different from 0, despite the large sample size of 631 recruits. A factor analysis of all the test data, followed by oblique rotations, yielded the usual four ASVAB factors (vocational-technical information, clerical speed, verbal ability, and mathematics) and a distinct tacit knowledge factor. The factor loading for the Tacit Knowledge Inventory for Managers score on the tacit knowledge factor was .99, with a maximum loading for the score on the four ASVAB factors of only .06. Upon oblique rotation, the four ASVAB factors were moderately intercorrelated, but the correlations between the tacit knowledge factor and the four ASVAB factors were near 0 (.075, .003, .096, and .082).

One final point about these results concerns the possibility that measures of tacit knowledge might identify potential managers from nontraditional and minority backgrounds whose practical knowledge suggests that they would be effective managers, although their performance on traditional selection measures, such as intelligence tests, does not. Eddy (1988) did not report scores separately by race and sex, but did report correlations between scores and dummy variables that indicated race and sex. Significant correlations in the .2–4 range between ASVAB subtest scores and both race and sex indicated that on the ASVAB, minority group members had poorer scores than majority group members, and women scored lower than men. However, nonsignificant correlations between tacit knowledge and both race (.03) and sex (.02) indicated comparable levels of performance on the tacit knowledge measures between minority and majority group members and between women and men.

Does performance on measures of tacit knowledge uniquely predict performance in management? In several early studies, we gave our tacit knowledge measure to samples of business managers and examined correlations between tacit knowledge scores and criterion reference measures of performance in business. For example, in samples of 54 (Wagner & Sternberg, 1985) and 64 (Wagner, 1987) business managers, we found correlations ranging from .2 to .4 between tacit knowledge score and criteria such as salary, years of management experience, and whether the manager worked for a company at the top of the *Fortune* 500 list. These uncorrected correlations were in the range of the average correlation between cognitive ability test scores and job performance of .2 (Wigdor & Garner, 1982).

In these studies, the managers were from a wide range of companies, and only global criterion measures—such as salary and years of management experience—were available for study. When more precise criterion measures have been available, higher correlations between tacit knowledge and performance have been found. For example, in a study of bank branch managers (Wagner & Sternberg, 1985), the correlation between tacit knowledge and average percentage of merit-based salary increase was .48 ($p < .05$). The correlation between tacit knowledge and average performance rating for the category of "generating new business for the bank" was 56 ($p < .05$).

Further support for the predictive validity of tacit knowledge measures was provided by the previously mentioned study of business managers who participated in the Leadership Development Program at the Center for Creative Leadership (Wagner & Sternberg, 1990). In this study, we were able to examine correlations among a variety of measures, including the Tacit Knowledge Inventory for Managers. The appropriate statistic to determine what will be gained by adding a test to existing selection procedures, or conversely, what will be lost by deleting a test, is the squared semipartial correlation coefficient, or change in R^2 from hierarchical regression analyses. We were able to provide an empirical demonstration of this type of validity assessment in the Center for Creative Leadership study.

Every manager who participated in the Leadership Development Program at the Center for Creative Leadership completed a battery of tests. By adding the Tacit Knowledge Inventory for Managers to the battery, we were able to determine the unique predictive power of the inventory in the context of other measures commonly used in managerial selection. These measures included the Shipley Institute for Living Scale, an intelligence test; 17 subtest scores from the California Psychological Inventory, a self-report personality inventory; 6 subtest scores from the Fundamental Interpersonal Relations Orientation—Behavior (FIRO—B), a measure of desired ways of relating to others; the Hidden Figures Test, a measure of field independence; 4 subtest scores from the Myers-Briggs Type Indicator, a measure of cognitive style; the Kirton Adaptation Innovation Inventory, a measure of preference for innovation; and 5 subtest scores from the Managerial Job Satisfaction Questionnaire, a measure of job satisfaction.

The criterion measure of managerial performance was behavioral assessment data ratings in two small-group managerial simulations called Earth II and Energy International. The managers worked in groups of five to solve realistic business problems. Trained observers rated the performance of the managers in eight categories: activity level, discussion leading, influencing others, problem analysis, task orientation, motivating others, verbal effectiveness, and interpersonal skills. To obtain a criterion measure with sufficient reliability, the ratings were averaged and summed across the two simulations. The Spearman-Brown corrected split-half reliability of this total score was .59.

Beginning with zero-order correlations, the best predictors of the criterion score of managerial performance were tacit knowledge ($r = -.61$, $p < .001$) and IQ ($r = .38$, $p < .001$). (The negative correlation for tacit knowledge was expected because of the deviation scoring system used, in which better performance corresponds to less deviation from the expert prototype and thus to lower scores.) The correlation between tacit knowledge and IQ was not significantly different from 0 ($r = -.14$, $p > .05$). We carried out a series of hierarchical regressions to examine the unique predictive value of tacit knowledge when used in conjunction with existing measures. For each hierarchical regression analysis, the unique prediction of the Tacit Knowledge Inventory for Managers was represented by the change in R^2 from a restricted model to a full model. In each case, the restricted model contained various measures, and the full model was created by adding the Tacit Knowledge Inventory for Managers as another predictor. If adding the tacit knowledge score resulted in a significant and substantial change in R^2, one could conclude that the predictive relation between tacit knowledge and the criterion measure was not subsumed by the set of predictors in the restricted model. The results are presented in Table 5.1.

In Table 5.1, the measures listed in the column titled "Measures in Restricted Model" were the predictors that already had been entered in the regression before entering the tacit knowledge score. In the first example, the sole predictor used in the restricted model was IQ. The values reported in the column titled "R^2 Change When Tacit Knowledge Is Added" are the increases in variance accounted for in criterion when tacit knowledge was added to the prediction equation. For the first example, tacit knowledge accounts for an additional 32% of criterion variance that is not accounted for by IQ. The values reported in the column titled "R^2 for Full Model" indicate the proportions of variance in

TABLE 5.1 Hierarchical Regression Results From the Center for Creative
Leadership Study

Measures in restricted model	R^2change when tacit knowledge is added	R for full model
IQ	.32***	.46***
Seventeen CPI subtests, IQ	.22**	.66*
6 FIRO-B subtests, IQ	.32***	.65***
Field Independence, IQ	.28***	.47***
Kirton innovation, IQ	.33***	.50***
Four Myers-Briggs subtests, IQ	.35***	.56***
Five Job Satisfaction subtests, IQ	.32**	.57***

NOTE: CPI = California Psychological Inventory; FIRO-B = Fundamental Interpersonal Relations Orientation-B.
*$p < .05$; **$p < .01$; ***$p < .001$.

the criterion that is accounted for by tacit knowledge and the other measures when used in conjunction.

In every case, tacit knowledge accounted for substantial and significant increases in variance. In addition, when tacit knowledge, IQ, and selected subtests from the personality inventories were combined as predictors, we accounted for nearly all of the reliable variance in the criterion. These results support the strategy of enhancing validity and utility by supplementing existing selection procedures with additional ones. They also suggest that the construct of tacit knowledge cannot readily be subsumed by the existing constructs of cognitive ability and personality represented by the other measures used in the study.

Williams and Sternberg (in press) also studied the interrelationship of tacit knowledge for management with demographic and experiential variables. (In this research, tacit knowledge was defined as the sum of squared deviation of participants' ratings from nominated experts' score arrays on a tacit knowledge measure.) We found that tacit knowledge was related to the following measures of managerial success: compensation ($r = .39, p < .001$), age-controlled compensation ($r = .38, p < .001$), and level of position ($r = .36, p < .001$). Note that these correlations were computed after controlling for background and educational experience. Tacit knowledge was also weakly associated with enhanced job satisfaction ($r = .23, p < .05$). Demographic and education variables unrelated to tacit knowledge included age, years of management experience, years in current position, degrees received, mother's and father's occupations, mother's and father's educational level attained, and mother's and father's degrees received. (The lack of a correlation of tacit knowledge with years of management experience suggests that it is not simply experience that matters, but perhaps what a manager learns from experience.) A manager's years with current company was negatively related to tacit knowledge ($r = -.29$, $p < .01$), perhaps suggesting the possibility that "deadwood" managers often stayed around a long time. The number of companies that a manager had worked for was positively correlated with tacit knowledge scores ($r = .35$, $p < .001$). Years of higher education was highly related to tacit knowledge ($r = .37$, $p < .001$), as was self-reported school performance ($r = .26$, $p < .01$). Similarly, college quality was related to tacit knowledge ($r = .34$, $p < .01$). These results, in conjunction with the independence of tacit knowledge and IQ, suggest that tacit knowledge overlaps with the portion of these measures that is not predicted by IQ.

This pattern of interrelationships between tacit knowledge scores and demographic and background variables prompted us to examine the prediction of our success measures, through hierarchical regression. These analyses showed whether tacit knowledge contained independent information related to success—information distinct from that provided by background and experience. The pattern of results was similar across analyses. In the regression analysis predicting maximum compensation, the first variable to enter the regression equation was years of education, accounting for 19% of the variance ($p < .001$). The second variable was years of management experience, accounting for an additional 13% of the variance ($p < .001$). The third and final variable to enter was tacit knowledge, accounting for an additional 4% of the variance ($p = .04$), raising the total explained variance to 36%. In the regression predicting maximum compensation controlled for age, years of education entered the equation first, accounting for 27% of the variance ($p < .001$). Finally, tacit knowledge entered, explaining an additional 5% of the variance ($p = .03$). This regression may be viewed as the most significant, insofar as it demonstrated the value of tacit knowledge to managers who were relatively successful for their age.

The general conclusions to be drawn from all of the regression analyses are, first, that it is difficult to predict success measures, such as salary and maximum compensation, presumably because of the myriad effects upon such variables that were outside the focus of this study. Nonetheless, approximately 40% of the variance in the success measures used in this study was explicable. For all four success measures, the educational variable was the most important, followed—in the case of salary and maximum compensation—by an experiential variable (years of management experience). After education and experience were included in the equations, tacit knowledge still explained a signifi-cant proportion of the variance in success. Thus, tacit knowledge con-tains information relevant to the prediction of success that is inde-pendent of that represented by the background and demographic variables.

Is tacit knowledge only important in business? Although our focus has been on the tacit knowledge of business mangers, there is evidence that the construct also explains performance in other domains. In two studies of the tacit knowledge of academic psychology professors, correlations in the .4 to .5 range were found between tacit knowledge and criterion measures such as number of citations reported in the Social Science Citation Index and the rated scholarly quality of an individual's departmental faculty (Wagner, 1987; Wagner & Sternberg, 1985). More recently, we have begun to investigate the role of tacit knowledge in the domain of sales (Wagner, Rashotte, & Sternberg, 1992). We have found correlations in the .3 to .4 range between measures of tacit knowledge about sales and criterion measures such as sales volume and sales awards received for a sample of life insurance salespersons. In this work, we also have been able to express the tacit knowledge of salespersons in terms of sets of rules of thumb that serve as rough guides to action in sales situations. Expressing tacit knowledge in terms of rules of thumb may permit explicit training of at least some aspect of tacit knowledge. A preliminary training study in which undergraduates were trained in tacit knowledge relevant to the profession of sales found greater pretest-post-test differences in tacit knowledge for groups whose training identified relevant rules of thumb than for those whose training did not make any such identifications (Sternberg, Wagner, & Okagaki, 1993).

We have also studied the role of tacit knowledge in school perfor-mance (Sternberg, Okagaki, & Jackson, 1990; Williams et al., in press). A six-year program of research, called the Practical Intelligence for Schools Project, involved intensive observations and interviews of stu-dents and teachers to determine the tacit knowledge necessary for success in school. Curricula designed to train the essential tacit knowl-edge were developed and evaluated in matched-group controlled studies in schools across Connecticut. This work was undertaken in collaboration with Howard Gardner and with other researchers at Harvard University, who also developed and evaluated curricular materials in Massachusetts schools. A final composite Practical Intelligence for School (PIFS) curricu-lum has been created by the Yale and Harvard teams (Williams et al., 1995) and is now being used in hundreds of classrooms across the United States and abroad.

The results of PIFS curriculum evaluations have been uniformly positive. In 1992-1993, Connecticut-area students receiving PIFS showed significantly greater increases in reading, writing, homework, and test-tak-ing ability over the school year, compared with students in the same schools not receiving the curriculum (ANCOVA F for PIFS variable = 60.89, $p < .0001$). Furthermore, teachers, students, and administrators reported fewer behavioral problems in PIFS classes. This research dem-onstrated that tacit knowledge is instrumental to school success and, significantly, that it can be effectively and efficiently taught.

Conclusions

Approximately 20 years ago, McClelland (1973) questioned the validity of cognitive ability testing for predicting real-world criteria such as job performance, arguing in favor of competency tests that more closely reflect job performance itself. Subsequent reviews of the literature on the predictive validity of intelligence tests suggest that McClelland may have been pessimistic about the validity of intelligence tests: Individual differences in intelligence-test performance account for between 4% and 25% of the variance in real-world criteria such as job performance (Barrett & Depinet, 1991; Hunter & Hunter, 1984; Schmidt & Hunter, 1981; Wigdor & Garner, 1982). Nevertheless, between 75% and 96% of the variance in real-world criteria such as job performance cannot be accounted for by individual differences in intelligence test scores. We view the emerging literature on practical intelligence, or common sense, as a belated response to McClelland's call for new methods to assess practical abilities. This literature provides three sources of evidence to support a distinction between academic and practical intelligence.

First, the distinction between academic and practical intelligence is entrenched in the conception of intelligence held by laypeople and researchers alike. In addition to evidence provided by studies of implicit theories of intelligence (Sternberg, 1985b; Sternberg, Conway, Ketron, & Bernstein, 1981), analyses of researchers' descriptions of the nature of intelligence suggest a prominent role for practical intelligence. Seventy years ago, the editors of the *Journal of Educational Psychology* convened a symposium at which prominent psychological theorists of the day were asked to describe what they imagined intelligence to be and what they considered the most crucial "next steps" in research. In a replication, Sternberg and Detterman (1986) posed these same questions to contemporary prominent theorists. An analysis of the responses of both cohorts of intelligence theorists revealed concern about practical aspects of intelligence (Sternberg & Berg, 1986). For example, among the 42 crucial next steps that were mentioned by one or more theorists from either cohort, studying real-life manifestations of intelligence was among the most frequently mentioned next steps of both the contemporary researchers and the original respondents. A distinction between academic and practical aspects of intelligence is also supported by older adults' perception of age-related changes in their ability to think and to solve problems (Williams, Denney, & Schadler, 1983). Three fourths of the older adults sampled believed that their ability to solve practical problems increased over the years, despite the fact that performance on academic tasks begins to decline upon completion of formal schooling.

A second source of evidence to support a distinction between academic and practical intelligence is the result of empirical studies of age-related changes in adults' performance on academic and practical tasks. The results suggest different developmental functions for changes in performance on the two kinds of tasks across the adult life span. Whereas performance on intelligence tests, particularly those that measure fluid ability, begins to decline in middle adulthood, performance on measures of everyday problem solving continues to improve until old age (Cornelius & Caspi, 1987; Denney & Palmer, 1981; Horn & Cattell, 1966). Our own studies of tacit knowledge in the domains of business management, sales, and academic psychology showed increases in tacit knowledge with age and experience across groups of undergraduates, graduate students, and professionals (Sternberg, Wagner, & Okagaki, 1993; Wagner, 1987; Wagner, Rashotte, & Sternberg, 1992; Wagner & Sternberg, 1985; Williams & Sternberg, in press). These increases emerged despite probable decreases in intelligence test performance across groups, particularly for the manager studies.

The third source of evidence to support a distinction between academic and practical intelligence is the result of studies in which participants were assessed on both academic and practical tasks. The consistent result is little or no correlation between performance on the two kinds of tasks. IQ is unrelated to (a) the order-filling performance of milk-processing plant workers (Scribner, 1986); (b) the degree to which racetrack handicappers employ a complex and effective algorithm (Ceci & Liker, 1986, 1988); (c) the complexity of strategies used in computer-simulated roles, such as city manager (Dörner & Kreuzig, 1983; Dörner, Kreuzig, Reither, & Staudel, 1983); and (d) the tacit knowledge of undergraduates (Wagner, 1987; Wagner & Sternberg, 1985), business managers (Wagner & Sternberg, 1990), salespersons (Wagner, Rashotte, & Sternberg, 1992), and U.S. Air Force recruits (Eddy, 1988). In addition, the accuracy with which grocery shoppers identified quantities that provided the best value was unrelated to their performance on the M.I.T. mental arithmetic test (Lave, Murtaugh, & de la Roche, 1984; Murtaugh, 1985).

Our conclusions about the value of measures of academic and practical intelligence for predicting real-world performance differ from those of previous reviews of literature by McClelland (1973) and by Barrett and Depinet (1971). McClelland argued that measures of academic abilities are of little value in predicting real-world criteria such as job performance. Barrett and Depinet (1991) argued that there was little in measures of practical abilities for predicting job performance. Our view is that there is complementary value in both kinds of measures. We believe that differences between our conclusions and those of both McClelland and Barrett and Depinet derive from differences in the studies that were included in the reviews.

McClelland's (1973) landmark article was published years before the emergence of meta-analysis, a methodology for cumulating results across studies. The results of meta-analytic studies, particularly when corrections for measurement error and restriction of range were used, provided larger estimates of the correlation between IQ and real-world criteria, such as job performance, than those apparent from inspection of the individual studies that were available to McClelland at the time of his review.

Although we agree with Barrett and Depinet's (1991) conclusion that cognitive ability tests have some value for selection, we are at odds with their dismissal of measures of practical performance. In what they described as a comprehensive review of the relevant literature (p. 1012), Barrett and Depinet considered, among other issues, McClelland's (1973) claim that practical tasks are necessary for predicting practical outcomes. In a section titled "Practical Tasks," we were surprised that Barrett and Depinet reported the results of only a single recent study, by Willis and Schaie (1986), concluding that it demonstrated that an "extremely high relationship existed between intelligence and performance on real-life tasks" (p. 1015). Barrett and Depinet ignored studies that did not support their thesis, even though the omitted studies (some of which we have discussed here) were described in chapters of the same book, *Practical Intelligence* (Sternberg & Wagner, 1986), from which they extracted Willis and Schaie's study. In fact, the study they included in their review was the sole study reported in *Practical Intelligence* that supported their thesis. Furthermore from their description of the Willis and Schaie study, one would not know that the criterion measure of performance on real-life tasks used in the study was, in fact, a paper-and-pencil psychometric test (the ETS Basic Skill Test; Educational Testing Service, 1977), with tasks such as reading paragraphs and describing the main theme, interpreting written guarantees for devices such as calculators, reading letters and determining on which point the authors are in agreement, and interpreting maps and charts. This test may measure basic skills relevant to real world performance, but it is decidedly more academic than changing a flat tire or convincing your superiors to spend a million dollars on your idea.

Our concern about selective inclusion of studies is twofold. Obviously, selective inclusion of studies can result in biased conclusions. But it also discourages researchers from seeking generalizations that incorporate ostensibly disparate results. For example, by comparing the characteristics of the measures used by Willis and Schaie (1986) with those used by other contributors, the following generalization emerged:

> Looking across the studies reported in this volume, the correlation between measures of practical and academic intelligence varies as a function of the format of practical intelligence measure: Correlations

are large when the practical intelligence measure is test-like, and virtually nonexistent when the practical intelligence measure is based on simulation. (Wagner, 1986, p. 372)

For the present and foreseeable future, we believe that the most viable approach to increasing the variance accounted for in real-world criteria (e.g., job performance) is to supplement existing intelligence and aptitude tests with selection of additional measures based on new constructs, such as practical intelligence. Although we are excited by the promise of a new generation of measures of practical intelligence, we are the first to admit that existing evidence for the new measures does not yet match that available for traditional cognitive-academic ability tests. However, a substantial amount of evidence indicates that performance on measures of practical intelligence is related to a wide variety of criterion measures of real world performance, but relatively unrelated to traditional measures of academic intelligence. Consequently, the use of both kinds of measures results in more effective prediction than reliance on either kind alone.

References

Baltes, P. B., & Baltes, M. M. (1990). Psychological perspectives on successful aging: A model of selective optimization with compensation. In P. B. Baltes & M. M. Baltes (Eds.), *Successful aging: Perspectives from the behavioral sciences.* Cambridge, England: Cambridge University Press.

Barrett, G. V., & Depinet, R. L. (1991). A reconsideration for testing for competence rather than for intelligence. *American Psychologist, 46,* 1012-1024.

Carraher, T. N., Carraher, D., & Schliemann, A. D. (1985). Mathematics in the streets and in schools. *British Journal of Development Psychology, 3,* 21-29.

Ceci, S. J. (1990). *On intelligence . . . more or less: A bio-ecological treatise on intellectual development.* Englewood Cliffs, NJ: Prentice Hall.

Ceci, S. J., & Liker, J. (1986). Academic and nonacademic intelligence: An experimental separation. In R. J. Sternberg & R. K. Wagner (Eds.), *Practical intelligence: Nature and origins of competence in the everyday world.* New York: Cambridge University Press.

Ceci, S. J., & Liker, J. (1988). Stalking the IQ-expertise relationship: When the critics go fishing. *Journal of Experimental Psychology: General, 117,* 96-100.

Cornelius, S. W., & Caspi, A. (1987). Everyday problem solving in adulthood and old age. *Psychology and Aging, 2,* 144-153.

Denney, N. W., & Palmer, A. M. (1981). Adult age differences on traditional and practical problem-solving measures. *Journal of Gerontology, 36,* 323-328.

Dixon, R. A., & Baltes, P. B. (1986). Toward life-span research on the functions and pragmatics of intelligence. In R. J. Sternberg & R. K. Wagner (Eds.), *Practical intelligence: Nature and origins of competence in the everyday world* (pp. 203-235). New York: Cambridge University Press.

Dörner, D., & Kreuzig, H. (1983). Problemlosefahigkeit und intelligenz [Problem solving and intelligence]. *Psychologische Rundschaus, 34,* 185-192.

Dörner, D., Kreuzig, H., Reither, F., & Staudel, T. (1983). *Lohhausen: Vom Umgang mit Unbestimmtheir und Komplexitat.* Bern, Switzerland: Huber.

Eddy, A. S. (1988). *The relationship between the Tacit Knowledge Inventory for Managers and the Armed Services Vocational Aptitude Battery.* Unpublished master's thesis, St. Mary's University, San Antonio, TX.

Educational Testing Service. (1977). *Basic Skills Assessment Test: Reading.* Princeton, NJ: Author.

Gottfredson, L. S. (1986). Societal consequences of the g factor. *Journal of Vocational Behavior, 29,* 379-410.

Hawk, J. (1986). Real world implications of g. *Journal of Vocational Behavior, 29,* 411-414.

Horn, J. L. (1982). The theory of fluid and crystallized intelligence in relation to concepts of cognitive psychology and aging in adulthood. In F. I. M. Craik & A. Trehub (Eds.), *Aging and cognitive processes* (pp. 237-278). New York: Plenum.

Horn, J. L., & Cattell, R. B. (1966). Refinement and test of the theory of fluid and crystallized intelligence. *Journal of Educational Psychology, 57,* 253-270.

Horvath, J. A., Forsythe, G. B., Sweeney, P. J., McNally, J. A., Wattendorf, J. M., Williams, W. M., & Sternberg, R. J. (1994, October). *Tacit knowledge in military leadership: Evidence from officer interviews* (Technical Report No. ADA289840). Alexandria, VA: U.S. Army Research Institute for the Behavioral and Social Sciences.

Hunter, J. E., & Hunter, R. F. (1984). Validity and utility of alternative predictors of job performance. *Psychological Bulletin, 96,* 72-98.

Jensen, A. R. (1993). Test validity: g versus "tacit knowledge." *Current Directions in Psychological Science, 1,* 9-10.

Labouvie-Vief, G. (1982). Dynamic development and nature autonomy: A theoretical prologue. *Human Development, 25,* 161-191.

Lave, J., Murtaugh, M., & de la Roche, O. (1984). The dialectic of arithmetic in grocery shopping. In B. Rogoff & J. Lace (Eds.), *Everyday cognition: Its development in social context* (pp. 67-94). Cambridge, MA: Harvard University Press.

McClelland, D. C. (1973). Testing for competence rather than for "intelligence." *American Psychologist, 28,* 1-14.

Morris, W. (Ed.). (1987). *The American heritage dictionary of the English language.* Boston: Houghton Mifflin.

Mosher, F. A., & Hornsby, J. R. (1966). On asking questions. In J. S. Bruner, R. R. Oliver, & P. M. Greenfield (Eds.), *Studies in cognitive growth.* New York: Wiley.

Murtaugh, M. (1985, Fall). The practice of arithmetic by American grocery shoppers. *Anthropology and Education Quarterly.*

Neisser, U. (1976). General, academic, and artificial intelligence. In L. Resnick (Ed.), *Human intelligence: Perspective on its theory and measurement* (pp. 179-189). Norwood, NJ: Ablex.

Oxford English Dictionary. (1933). Oxford: Clarendon Press.

Polanyi, M. (1976). Tacit knowledge. In M. Marx & F. Goodson (Eds.), *Theories in contemporary psychology* (pp. 330-344). New York: Macmillan.

Ree, M. J., & Earles, J. A. (1993). g is to psychology what carbon is to chemistry: A reply to Sternberg and Wagner, McClelland, and Calfee. *Current Directions in Psychological Science, 1,* 11-12.

Rogoff, B., & Lave, J. (Eds.). (1984). *Everyday cognition: Its development in social context.* Cambridge, MA: Harvard University Press.

Ryle, G. (1949). *The concept of mind.* London: Hutchinson.

Salthouse, T. A. (1984). Effects of age and skill in typing. *Journal of Experimental Psychology: General, 113,* 345-371.

Schaie, K. W. (1977/1978). Toward a stage theory of adult cognitive development. *International Journal of Aging and Human Development, 8,* 129-138.

Schmidt, F. L., & Hunter, J. E. (1981). Employment testing: Old theories and new research findings. *American Psychologist, 36,* 1128-1137.

Schmidt, F. L., & Hunter, J. E. (1993). Tacit knowledge, practical intelligence, general mental ability, and job knowledge. *Current Directions in Psychological Science, 1,* 8-9.

Scribner, S. (1984). Studying working intelligence. In B. Rogoff & J. Lave (Eds.), *Everyday cognition: Its development in social context* (pp. 9-40). Cambridge, MA: Harvard University Press.

Scribner, S. (1986). Thinking in action: Some characteristics of practical thought. In R. J. Sternberg & R. K. Wagner (Eds.), *Practical intelligence: Nature and origins of competence in the everyday world* (pp. 13-30). New York: Cambridge University Press.

Scribner, S., & Cole, M. (1981). *The psychology of literacy.* Cambridge, MA: Harvard University Press.

Sternberg, R. J. (1985a). *Beyond IQ: A triarchic theory of human intelligence.* New York: Cambridge University Press.

Sternberg, R. J. (1985b). Implicit theories of intelligence, creativity, and wisdom. *Journal of Personality and Social Psychology, 49,* 607-627.

Sternberg, R. J. (1988). *The triarchic mind: A new theory of human intelligence.* New York: Viking.

Sternberg, R. J., & Berg, C. A. (1986). Quantitative integration: Definitions of intelligence: A comparison of the 1921 and 1986 symposia. In R. J. Sternberg & D. K. Detterman (Eds.), *What is intelligence? Contemporary viewpoints on its nature and definition* (pp. 155-162). Norwood, NJ: Ablex.

Sternberg, R. J., & Caruso, D. (1985). Practical modes of knowing. In E. Eisner (Ed.), *Learning the ways of knowing* (pp. 133-158). Chicago: University of Chicago Press.

Sternberg, R. J., Conway, B. E., Ketron, J. L., & Bernstein, M. (1981). People's conception of intelligence. *Journal of Personality and Social Psychology, 41,* 37-55.

Sternberg, R. J., & Detterman, D. K. (Eds.). (1986). *What is intelligence? Contemporary viewpoints on its nature and definition.* Norwood, NJ: Ablex.

Sternberg, R. J., & Frensch, P. A. (Eds.). (1991). *Complex problem solving: Principles and mechanisms.* Hillsdale, NJ: Lawrence Erlbaum.

Sternberg, R. J., Okagaki, L., & Jackson, A. (1990). Practical intelligence for success in school. *Educational Leadership, 48,* 35-39.

Sternberg, R. J., & Wagner, R. K. (Eds.). (1986). *Practical intelligence: Nature and origins of competence in the everyday world.* New York: Cambridge University Press.

Sternberg, R. J., & Wagner, R. K. (1993). The g-ocentric view of intelligence and job performance is wrong. *Current Directions in Psychological Science, 2,* 1-5.

Sternberg, R. J., & Wagner, R. K. (Eds.). (1994). *Mind in context.* New York: Cambridge University Press.

Sternberg, R. J., Wagner, R. K., & Okagaki, L. (1993). Practical intelligence: The nature and role of tacit knowledge in work and at school. In H. Reese & J. Puckett (Eds.), *Advances in lifespan development* (pp. 205-227). Hillsdale, NJ: Lawrence Erlbaum.

Voss, J. F., Perkins, D. N., & Segal, J. W. (Eds.). (1991). *Informal reasoning and education.* Hillsdale, NJ: Lawrence Earlbaum.

Wagner, R. K. (1987). Tacit knowledge in everyday intelligent behavior. *Journal of Personality and Social Psychology, 52,* 1236-1247.

Wagner, R. K., Rashotte, C. A., & Sternberg, R. J. (1992). *Tacit knowledge in sales: Rules of thumb for selling anything to anyone.* Unpublished manuscript.

Wagner, R. K., & Sternberg, R. J. (1985). Practical intelligence in real-world pursuits: The role of tacit knowledge. *Journal of Personality and Social Psychology, 49,* 436-458.

Wagner, R. K., & Sternberg, R. J. (1986). Tacit knowledge and intelligence in the everyday world. In R. J. Sternberg & R. K. Wagner (Eds.), *Practical intelligence: Nature and origins of competence in the everyday world* (pp. 51-83). New York: Cambridge University Press.

Wagner, R. K., & Sternberg, R. J. (1990). Street smarts. In K. E. Clark & M. B. Clark (Eds.), *Measures of leadership* (pp. 493-504). West Orange, NJ: Leadership Library of America.

Wagner, R. K., & Sternberg, R. J. (1991). *Tacit knowledge inventory for managers.* San Antonio, TX: Psychological Corporation.

Wigdor, A. K., & Garner, W. R. (Eds.). (1982). *Ability testing: Uses, consequences, and controversies.* Washington, DC: National Academy Press.

Williams, S. A., Denney, N. W., & Schadler, M. (1983). Elderly adults' perception of their own cognitive development during the adult years. *International Journal of Aging and Human Development, 16,* 147-158.

Williams, W. M., Blythe, T., White, N., Li, J., Sternberg, R. J., & Gardner, H. I. (1995). *Practical intelligence for school.* New York: Harper Collins.

Williams, W. M., & Sternberg, R. J. (in press). *Success acts for managers.* Orlando, FL: Harcourt Brace.

Willis, S. L., & Schaie, K. W. (1991). Everyday cognition: Taxonomic and methodological considerations. In J. M. Puckett & H. W. Reese (Eds.), *Life-span developmental psychology: Mechanisms of everyday cognition.* Hillsdale, NJ: Lawrence Earlbaum.

Winograd, T. (1975). Frame representations and the declarative/procedural controversy. In D. G. Bobrow & A. Collins (Eds.), *Representation and understanding: Studies in cognitive science.* New York: Academic Press.

IMPLICATIONS FOR HUMAN RESOURCE DEVELOPMENT PROFESSIONALS

As with the Rowe and Cooke article (Chapter 4), the study by Sternberg et al. suggests that differences exist between experts and novices. Rowe and Cooke pointed to differences in mental models whereas Sternberg et al. focused on differences in tacit knowledge. Through interviews with experts, Sternberg et al. indicated that researchers were able to identify tacit knowledge or "rules of thumb." In some instances these rules of thumb may have been mental models, according to Rowe and Cooke's definition. By making this tacit knowledge (or mental model) explicit through specific training and development activities, the HRD professional can transform novice performance into expert performance. Doing so will ensure that workers have the knowledge needed to perform at high levels.

IMPLICATIONS FOR RESEARCH DESIGN AND METHODOLOGY

The approach used by Sternberg et al. provides a model for further development of a theoretical position using previous theory and research. Human resource development researchers in theory development need to examine other theoretical positions and to attempt to show how those positions connect with the theory being proposed. Of even greater value, however, is the review of previous research, including both qualitative and quantitative studies that lend support to the proposed theory.

IMPLICATIONS FOR FUTURE INQUIRY

One interesting line of inquiry would be an examination of the similarities and differences between tacit knowledge and mental models. Are these similar or dissimilar concepts? If they are related, how are they similar? If they are not related, how are they distinguished? Such research might examine the similarities and differences between the tacit knowledge (as defined by the "rules of thumb") and the mental models of experts.

As with the Rowe and Cooke work on mental models, HRD researchers should examine the quality of the "rules of thumb" using different measurement methods. In addition, HRD researchers could determine whether the "rules of thumb" of intermediate performers are more predictive of novice performance. This would suggest, as does the work on mental models, that there is a discontinuity between experts and novices that can best be bridged by the tacit knowledge or mental models of intermediate performers.

Finally, the Sternberg et al. article provides a model for advancing the measurement of competencies rather than intelligence. HRD researchers should examine this model and apply the approach to developing measures for other workplace competencies.

OTHER RESOURCES

McClelland, D. A. (1973). Testing for competence rather than for intelligence. *American Psychologist, 28,* 1-14.

Neisser, U., Boodoo, G., Bouchard, T. J., Jr., Boykin, A. W., Brody, N., Ceci, S. J., Halpern, D. F., Loehlin, J. C., Perloff, R., Sternberg, R. J., & Urbina, S. (1996, February). Intelligence: Knowns and unknowns. *American Psychologist, 51,* 77-101.

Russ-Eft, D. (1995). Defining competencies. *Human Resource Development Quarterly, 6*(4), 329-335.

Spencer, L. M., & Spencer, S. M. (1993). *Competence at work: Models for superior performance.* New York: Wiley.

PART

II

TEAM LEARNING AND PERFORMANCE

E xperts argue that the demands of current organizational tasks frequently require capabilities and resources that are beyond the means of any one individual. In addition, companies are increasingly organizing work so that tasks are accomplished by teams. These teams range from traditional face-to-face groups to computer-supported collaborative work teams (Morgan, Salas, & Glickman, 1992).

Most organization decision makers are tantalized by the prospect of connecting the energy of employee teamwork and team spirit with business goals. The possibility of securing and guiding the energy generated when people work together to accomplish tasks, solve problems, and achieve organization purposes is a siren call. The popular press contains many stories that dramatically illustrate the use of teams to revitalize businesses and achieve marketplace success. For example, Peters (1996) described how Oticon, a world leader in hearing-aid production, eliminated its formal organizational structure. Instead of a desk, each employee has a cart. Project teams form on their own initiative, gather where they wish, and get down to work.

How do Human Resource Development (HRD) professionals contribute to team performance within organizations? According to McClernon and Swanson (Chapter 9), HRD professionals focus on the methods and processes for increasing overall team effectiveness and for overcoming problems associated with team performance. Furthermore, HRD professionals "prepare team members to use effective team skills, develop lists of characteristics to differentiate high- and low-performance teams, and design team-building interventions to develop more successful teams" (p. 224).

Because organization decision makers are increasingly using teams to achieve business goals, HRD practitioners need to understand clearly the research basis for practices related to team performance, learning, and development. However, performance measurement research has characteristically focused on individuals, and understanding individual performance is not sufficient for understanding team performance (Baker & Salas, 1992).

The following chapters profile five research studies that contribute to our understanding of teams. The following section summarizes some key definitions that provide a framework for our examination of these and other research studies. The terms *team, team performance, team learning,* and *team development* provide boundaries for these chapters. Not surprisingly, the literature contains multiple definitions and perspectives for each term.

Definitions of Team, Team Performance, Team Learning and Team Development

The definitions of *team* that are found in the literature delimit the term conceptually and concretely. Conceptually, a team can be viewed as a socially constructed phenomenon or linking mechanism that integrates individuals and organizations (Horvath, Callahan, Croswell, & Mukri, 1996).

Definitions that contribute to more concrete understanding tend to identify specific *team* characteristics. Some definitions focus on attributes internal to the team. For example, Dyer (1984) defined a team as having the following characteristics: two or more people with a common goal, specific role assignments, and interdependence. Orasanu and Salas (1993) identified additional characteristics: Teams make decisions in the context of a larger task, team members have specialized knowledge and skills relevant to the task or decision, and task conditions under which teams operate often include high workloads and time pressures.

Some definitions recognize that work teams function within a larger organizational context. Sundstrom, DeMeuse, and Futrell (1990) defined work teams as interdependent collections of individuals who share responsibility for specific outcomes for their organizations. Similarly, Guzzo and Dickson (1996) defined a work group as made up of individuals who see themselves and who are seen by others as a social entity, who are interdependent because of the tasks they perform as members of a group, who are embedded in one or more larger social systems (e.g., community, organization), and who perform tasks that affect others (such as customers or co-workers). (pp. 308-309)

Druckman and Bjork (1994) characterized teams as dynamic entities. They noted the inevitability of change within a team. Members may develop new skills and relationships, individuals may modify their assignments, and team roles and norms gradually develop. In addition, teams adapt to inputs from larger social systems. Examples of inputs include feedback from the customers who receive the team product(s) (Druckman & Bjork, 1994) and external support and recognition (Larson & LaFasto, 1989).

Some researchers differentiate among teams. For example, Hackman (1990) studied 27 diverse teams and identified seven types of work groups that had special issues and opportunities: (a) top management groups, (b) task forces, (c) professional support groups, (d) performing groups, (e) human service teams, (f) customer service teams, and (g) production teams.

Teams can also be differentiated by the level of team involvement required. Orsburn, Moran, Musselwhite, and Zenger (1990) identified eight increasing levels of employee involvement and the expected actions at each level (see Table II.a).

Orsburn et al. (1990) observed that employee involvement for levels 1 through 6 is "an adjunct to the formal operating structure, not an integral part of it. . . . In contrast, levels 7 and 8 require a partial or full restructuring of organizational systems to support full-time self-management by the teams" (pp. 33-34).

In summary, the definitions of a work team delimit the term conceptually and concretely. Conceptually, teams link individuals and organizations. A team's concrete characteristics include its internal dynamics and its relationship to the external environment. Internal team dynamics include common goals, team roles, the interactions and the interdependencies of members as they share resources and competencies, and the use of feedback to adapt to changes. The team's relationship to the larger organizational environment includes external support and recognition, workload, and time pressure. These characteristics emphasize in fact that teams function in a dynamic environment and are themselves dynamic. Differences between teams include the type of work team and the level of involvement. In this chapter, the terms *team*, *work team*, and *work group* are used interchangeably.

TABLE II.a Eight Levels of Involvement as Identified by Orsburn, Moran, Musselwhite, and Zenger

Levels of Involvement	Expected Actions
1. Information sharing	Managers decide
2. Dialogue	Managers get employee input, then decide
3. Special problem solving	Managers assign a one-time problem to selected employees
4. Intragroup problem solving	Intact group meets weekly to solve local problems
5. Intergroup problem solving	Cross-functional group meets to solve mutual problems
6. Focused problem solving	Intact group deepens daily involvement in a specific issue
7. Limited self-direction	Teams at selected sites function full time with minimal supervision
8. Total self-direction	Executives facilitate self-management in an all-team company

NOTE: Adapted from Orsburn, Moran, Musselwhite, & Zenger, 1990.

TABLE II.b Definitions of Criteria for Performance

Criterion	Definition
Effectiveness	Doing the right things on time and in the right manner in terms of goals, objectives, activities, goods, products, services, etc.
Efficiency	The ratio of resources expected to be consumed in doing the right things to resources actually consumed.
Quality	Conformance to specifications, fitness for use.
Productivity	The ratio of quantities of output (goods and services) from an organizational system over a period of time to quantities of input resources consumed by that organizational system for that period of time; or, the ratio of quantity at the desired quality level to resources actually consumed.
Quality of work life	Human beings' affective response/reaction to working and living in organizational systems.
Innovation	The creative process of adaptation of product, service, process, structure, etc., in response to internal and external pressures, demands, changes, needs, etc.
Profitability/ budgetability	A measure or set of measures that assess attributes of financial resource utilization.

NOTE: Adapted from Sink, Tuttle, & DeVries, 1984, pp. 267-268.

Definitions of Team Performance

To effectively help teams make work contributions, HRD professionals must understand what is meant by performance. As Shea and Guzzo (1987) pointed out, "how effectively groups are used has a decided impact on organizational performance" (p. 25).

For both work teams and organizations, performance can be measured by at least seven causally related criteria: effectiveness, efficiency, quality, productivity, quality of work life, innovation, and profitability/budgetability (Sink, Tuttle, & DeVries, 1984). The authors' definition for each criterion provides a foundation for measuring team performance within a specific organizational system (see Table II.b).

Team performance is usually defined in terms of outcome criteria, although process measures are sometimes used. Guzzo and Dickson (1996) stated that there is no single, uniform measure of performance effectiveness for groups. Instead, they identified three indicators: (a) group-produced outputs (quantity or quality, speed, customer satisfaction, etc.), (b) the consequences a group has for its members, and (c) the enhancement of a team's capability to perform effectively in the future.

These two approaches for considering teams—the performance criteria identified by Sink et al. (1984) and the indicators identified by Guzzo and Dickson (1996)—can be related. Four performance criteria—effectiveness, efficiency, quality, and productivity—can be used to measure group-produced outputs. One performance criterion—quality of work life—can be used to measure the consequences a group has for its members. Finally, two performance criteria—profitability/budgetability and innovation—can be used to measure enhancement of the team's capability to perform effectively in the future.

In spite of the need for HRD expertise in measuring team performance, related theory and research has been limited. Dyer (1984) noted that models of team performance tend to focus only on limited factors that might influence performance and to exclude some potentially important factors. Further, most studies (a) examined group dynamics that were unrelated to performance or (b) were conducted in a laboratory (Shea & Guzzo, 1987). As a result, team studies have not greatly advanced our understanding of how naturally forming teams in the workplace interact over time to produce outputs that contribute to organization. In fact, as Campion, Medsker, and Higgs (Chapter 6) pointed out, it is not absolutely certain that inferences can be made about natural groups based on laboratory research.

Another limitation of team performance research is that the psychometric properties of measuring teamwork are not well addressed (Baker & Salas, 1992). A key question is, "Who assesses the team's performance?" Different outcomes may result, depending on whether team members, on-site observers, or off-site observers assess a team's performance. A second key question is, "What is the basis for the assessment?" Team performance measures based on member satisfaction, their alignment to predetermined process steps, or the quality and quantity of their output, can produce different outcomes (Baker & Salas, 1992).

In summary, work team performance can be measured in many ways. Early research on teams tended to focus on team dynamics that were not related to organization performance or on studies conducted within laboratory settings. Because an important goal of work teams is to contribute to performance, systematic studies that focus on naturally occurring work teams will make an important contribution to our understanding. Also, studies that examine the relationships among the identities of those who assess team performance, the basis or purpose for their assessment, and the assessment outcomes will make a strong contribution to HRD expertise.

Definitions of Team Learning

Team learning has been defined as "the construction of collective new knowledge by a team" (Brooks, Chapter 7, p. 181). Senge (1990) focuses on the process of aligning and developing the capacity of a team to create the results its members truly desire. Horvath, Callahan, Croswell, and Mukri (1996) view team learning as a collective endeavor to make sense of actions and experiences.

Jeris, May, and Redding (1996) view team learning as a component of organizational learning. Team members learn and accomplish their performance goals through interaction with multiple systems, including the organization, the team itself, and the individual members. Members of successful teams find ways to meet the needs of a dynamic organization system while they simultaneously interact to meet dynamic team and individual needs. During the process, they learn to share information, work collaboratively, and produce new knowledge. The output of team learning can be useful new knowledge (Brooks, Chapter 7) or the application of knowledge to achieve organization, team, and individual goals.

How does team learning occur? Team members can monitor their collective processes and outputs over time and use these observations to influence subsequent team performance. Also, team members can use shared mental models. Orasanu and Salas (1993) (cited in Druckman &

Bjork, 1994, p. 124) described how team members who have worked together over relatively long periods of time develop "shared mental models" that organize their knowledge. Shared models allow team members to carry out their roles in a timely and coordinated fashion and help the team work as a single unit.

Yet research on team learning is limited (Horvath et al., 1996). One study that has contributed to our understanding is a work by Watkins and Marsick (1993) on team learning as part of organizational learning. As a result of their research at two *Fortune* 100 companies, Watkins and Marsick identified five team learning processes: framing, reframing, experimenting, crossing boundaries, and creating an integrative perspective.

In summary, team learning is a continuous process by which team members acquire knowledge about the larger organization, the team, and the individual team members. Because the process by which people learn to work together collaboratively is important to team and organization performance, additional research in this area is vital to the practice of HRD.

Definitions of Team Development

The concept of team development reflects the premise that teams change and develop new ways of working as they adapt to their contexts (Sundstrom, DeMeuse, & Futrell, 1990). "Teams can evolve through different levels, from an initially fragmented state to the creation of pooled activities to synergistic effort and finally to an ongoing, continuous capacity to work collectively" (Watkins & Marsick, 1993, p. 14). Through team development, work groups can acquire team identification, enhanced cohesion, and new concepts that contribute to problem solving or to performance of their tasks. Further, *team development* can be defined to include interpersonal processes and group structures such as norms and roles (Sundstrom, DeMeuse, & Futrell, 1990).

Morgan, Salas, and Glickman (1992) described two general views of team development that are embraced in the literature. The traditional view is based primarily on studies of group therapy, human relations (T-group) training, or the communication patterns of problem-solving or decision-making groups. The models of team development resulting from this research suggest that teams exhibit fairly consistent phases of interaction over time, progress in a mostly linear fashion through a sequence of developmental phases, and must complete one phase before entering the next one.

A more recent view of team development has focused on naturally occurring, task-driven organizational work groups. Morgan et al. (1992) stated that "in contrast to the traditional view, these latter findings indicate that team development does not necessarily progress gradually in linear, lock-step fashion through clearly demarcated phases" (p. 280).

The traditional HRD prescription for developing work team effectiveness has been labeled *team development* or *team building*. Such efforts generally involve training and consulting on team tasks and interpersonal processes. The literature identifies four general approaches to team-building interventions: goal setting, interpersonal relations, role clarification, and problem solving (Druckman & Bjork, 1994; Sundstrom, DeMeuse, & Futrell, 1990).

From a scholarly perspective, how effective are currently accepted team-building efforts? Druckman and Bjork (1994) stated, "there is much enthusiasm for these approaches among practitioners and consultants, but it is not matched by strong empirical support for their effect on team performance" (p. 125). Buller (1986) noted that the results of team-building research have been ambiguous for two primary reasons: Team building as a concept has not been well defined and the research has generally been methodologically poor. Specifically, much of the team-building research has failed to adequately specify relationships between independent variables and performance criteria.

In summary, team-development research includes two perspectives on teams' transition through phases: a fixed sequence that teams follow and a variety of patterns based on the organizational context.

The research of team development, learning, and performance needs additional, methodologically sound studies. The five chapters in this part contribute to our knowledge of teams and to our understanding of how to better study teams. Campion, Medsker, and Higgs (Chapter 6) focus on team performance. They identified group characteristics and themes from the literature and evaluated them against both objective and subjective criteria of effectiveness for work groups in a financial organization. Driskell and Salas (Chapter 7) and Brooks (Chapter 8) provide insights into the individual and organizational characteristics that influence team learning. McClernon and Swanson (Chapter 9) and Cooley (Chapter 10) provide new knowledge about team development interventions. McClernon and Swanson investigated the effects of team building with two variations—facilitation and group decision support—on team process and outputs. Cooley examined the effects of a three-part training intervention in communication and decision making on team meeting behavior. The following section highlights their studies in greater detail.

Overview

Campion, Medsker, and Higgs (Chapter 6) focus on team performance. They examined the relationships between work group characteristics and effectiveness. The authors searched the literature to identify group themes and characteristics related to team effectiveness, developed a questionnaire to assess the identified characteristics, and, for work groups in a financial organization, examined the relationship between the characteristics and the objective and subjective effectiveness criteria.

Following are the five work group themes and the group characteristics for each:

work groups characteristics

1. Job Design—self-management, participation, task variety, task significance, task identity
2. Interdependence—task interdependence, goal interdependence, interdependent feedback/rewards
3. Composition—heterogeneity, flexibility, relative size, preference for group work
4. Context—training, managerial support, communication/cooperation between groups
5. Process—potency, social support, workload sharing, communication/cooperation within groups

The study examined 80 formal employee work groups from five geographic units of a large financial services company. Group size ranged from 6 to 30 individuals, but each work group performed the same set of tasks. Researchers sampled five employees from each group and the managers for 77 of the 80 groups. Results indicated that three effectiveness criteria—productivity, satisfaction, and manager judgments—were related to the group characteristics. Further, almost all the group characteristics were related to some of the effectiveness criteria.

Defining an interdisciplinary team's success or failure in accomplishing its purpose(s) is a prerequisite to delineating the factors that contribute to team success or failure (Cooley, Chapter 10). Knowing the relationship between specific team characteristics and effectiveness criteria provides a basis for a more meaningful study of team processes and inputs. For example, it makes little sense to observe teams and recommend improvements without first knowing whether a characteristic such as flexibility really contributes to team effectiveness.

The Campion et al. study contributed to team research because it linked the literature to practice, used natural work groups, and relied on multiple measures of effectiveness. As noted earlier, much team research has focused on groups of artificial populations (e.g., college students) rather than on natural work groups. Shea and Guzzo (1987) pointed out that inferences based on studies of artificial populations may not generalize to natural groups. The research design for this study used groups as the level of analysis and relied on random selection of participants. Many team studies have examined group effectiveness only in terms of affective responses. This study examined work group effectiveness in terms of measures of group productivity, managerial judgments of effectiveness, and employee satisfaction.

Brooks (Chapter 7) focuses on team learning. The initial question of the study asked why some teams learn and some do not. An exploratory study suggested that power differences between team members affected their ability to contribute to the specific tasks required for team learning. The researcher relied on a qualitative, multiple-case-study methodology to obtain new knowledge about the complex relationship between the distribution of power in teams and the outcomes of collective team learning. The remainder of the study focused on three research questions: (a) "What is the team learning process?" (b) "How do differences in the distribution of formal power to individual team members affect the collective team learning outcome?" and (c) "How do organizational structures and policies affect the team learning process?" (p. 182).

Answering these research questions involved examining four problem-solving teams from a research and development unit of a large high-technology manufacturing company. The researcher identified team learning tasks, examined how the differences in the distribution of formal power to team members affected the team learning outcome, and considered how organizational structures and policies affected the team learning process.

A strength of the Brooks article is the researcher's description of qualitative data collection and analysis. Data collection took place intensively over a 4-month period, with intermittent contact occurring over a longer time. The process included the researcher's personal narratives pertaining to the team learning experience, observations of team meetings, and records and documents relevant to the teams. Trustworthiness of the study was strengthened by using multiple data collection techniques, sources of data, and investigators; negative case analysis; and critical reflection on the research process. Further, Brooks narrated the story of each case as a whole before subjecting it to the fragmentation of analysis.

Based on the data, Brooks identified the distribution of formal power as a critical lever in the successful production of team knowledge. She generated four grounded propositions that provide a useful

p. 197

basis for future research and practice. In addition, Brooks's individual case studies detail specific links between participation and team effectiveness and describe how power and team learning shape those links. Her study findings can be linked to the Campion et al. correlational study, which identified a significant relationship between participation and five measures of team effectiveness.

In Chapter 8, Driskell and Salas, like Brooks, recognized that teams have an obvious advantage over individuals: groups have greater available knowledge and skills from which to draw. They also recognized that teams do not always use this advantage.

Driskell and Salas argued that attending to task inputs from other members in an interdependent manner is critical to effective team performance. To test this argument, the researchers used a two-phase experimental design that examined how team learning and performance were influenced by team composition based on a single characteristic: either collectively oriented members or egocentric members. By definition, collectively oriented members exhibit more interdependent behavior in task groups and egocentric members tend to reject task input from others.

The subjects for the study were 60 male naval technical school students who volunteered to participate. In phase one, the researchers differentiated collectively oriented and egocentric team members. Artificially created, two-person teams had no direct contact with one another. Instead they communicated via a computer network to complete a task that had no objective basis for making a decision. Driskell and Salas measured the proportion (P) of task resolutions that each subject resolved in favor of self. Subjects with the highest Ps were identified as egocentric team members and subjects with median Ps were identified as collectively oriented team members.

In phase two of the study, teams composed of entirely collectively oriented members, egocentric members, or controls performed a task. The researchers examined the effects of member behavior on team task performance. At the conclusion of the study, subjects completed a questionnaire assessing their preference for working as a group member and their general satisfaction with the group.

The results showed that egocentric team members saw their partners' inputs as less valuable and believed that it was less useful to work as a team than did the collectively oriented team members. The results also confirmed that collectively oriented team members were more likely to attend to inputs from other team members relative to the task. They were also more likely to improve their performance during team interactions.

Chapters 9 and 10 increase our understanding about interventions that are designed to improve team processes and performance.

McClernon and Swanson (Chapter 9) examine a team-building process using intact work groups in a nonprofit organization. Team building is a popular HRD practice that often employs two kinds of process aids: facilitators and computer decision support systems. Many articles in practitioner journals and many vendor advertisements explain in rational, easy-to-understand language that implementing team building with one or both of these process aids will improve team performance. But do such interventions have a lasting effect? This study provides some initial answers. It also makes important methodological contributions to the study of teams.

The experimental study investigated the effects of two approaches to team building, (1) facilitation alone and (2) facilitation coupled with group decision support systems (GDSS), on team processes and outputs and compared them with control groups. The subjects were 24 naturally occurring work groups in a nonprofit organization. McClernon and Swanson administered a self-report questionnaire to team participants immediately following the team-building session and readministered it following the next normally scheduled group meeting. This data measured the immediate and the delayed effects of the treatments.

Results showed that both the facilitated alone and the facilitated with GDSS team-building processes resulted in higher ratings on short-term measures of group process than did the treatment with no outside facilitation. However, "on most measures, the positive immediate effects did not last over time, indicating that the three-hour team-building session was not effective" (McClernon & Swanson, Chapter 9, p. 223).

McClernon and Swanson's research design addressed two of the traditional limitations of research on the effects of team interventions: the use of groups formed from artificial populations (e.g., college students) and the lack of experimental control due to the difficulty of providing for randomization and control groups in functioning organizations (Cooley, Chapter 10).

Cooley also studied the effects of a team intervention on intact work groups. Her study used a single-subject research design to examine the effects of a three-part training intervention in communication and decision making on team meeting behavior. Each part of the training emphasized one specific set of skills: (a) mapping skills, (b) mirroring skills, and (c) mining and refining skills. Teaching the skills involved "conceptual presentation, modeling, observational training using examples from their own videotaped meetings, written practice and role playing" (p. 255). The study used a multiple baseline design across behaviors that "involved collecting data continuously on all of the targeted behaviors at once and intervening in a staggered fashion on one specific set of behaviors at a time" (p. 252).

The study participants were 25 staff members of a rehabilitation clinic who participated in fluctuating, interdisciplinary teams. Data collection included administering an intake questionnaire, directly observing the videotaped meetings, and administering a social validation questionnaire after each of the three training sessions. Cooley also measured the distribution of participation among members during the meetings. Participants' subjective evaluations revealed that they found the workshops to be "useful, enjoyable, and practical, and that they considered the targeted skills to be relevant and worth integrating into their day-to-day work routines" (pp. 260-261). However, videotaped observations following the training sessions revealed that the intervention did not powerfully affect team dynamics. Although many targeted behaviors showed initial increases, behaviors returned to baseline levels later in the study.

References

Baker, D. P., & Salas, E. (1992). Principles for measuring teamwork skills. *Human Factors, 34*(4), 469-475.

Buller, P. F. (1986). The team building-task performance relation: Some conceptual and methodological refinements. *Group & Organization Studies, 11*(3), 147-168.

Druckman, D., & Bjork, R. A. (Eds.). (1994). *Learning, remembering, believing: Enhancing human performance*. Washington, DC: National Academy Press.

Dyer, J. L. (1984). Team research and team training: A state-of-the-art review. *Human Factors Review*, pp. 285-319.

Guzzo, R. A., & Dickson, M. W. (1996). Teams in organizations: Recent research on performance and effectiveness. *Annual Review of Psychology, 47*, 307-338.

Hackman, J. R. (1990). *Groups that work (and those that don't)*. San Francisco: Jossey-Bass.

Horvath, L., Callahan, J. L., Croswell, C., & Mukri, G. (1996). Team sensemaking: An imperative for individual and organizational learning (pp. 415-421). In E. Holton (Ed.), *Proceedings of the Academy of Human Resource Development*.

Jeris, L. S., May, S. C., Redding, J. C. (1996). Team learning: Processes, interventions and assessment (pp. 139-144). In E. Holton (Ed.), *Proceedings of the Academy of Human Resource Development*.

Larson, C. E., & LaFasto, F. M. J. (1989). *Teamwork: What miust go right/what can go wrong*. Newbury Park, CA: Sage.

Morgan, B. B., Jr., Salas, E., & Glickman, A. S. (1992). An analysis of team evolution and maturation. *Journal of General Psychology, 120*(3), 277-291.

Orsburn, J. D., Moran, L., Musselwhite, E., & Zenger, J. H. (1990). *Self-directed work teams: The new American challenge*. Homewood, IL: Business One Irwin.

Orasanu, J., & Salas, E. (1993). Team decision making in complex environments. In G. A. Klein, J. Orasanu, R. Calderwood, & C. E. Zsambok (Eds.), *Decision making in action: Models and methods*. Norwood, NJ: Ablex.

Peters, T. (1996, February). No halfway. *Office Systems, 96*, 54.

Salas, E., Bowers, C. A., & Cannon-Bowers, J. A. (1995). Military team research: 10 years of progress. *Military Psychology, 7*(2), 55-75.

Senge, P. M. (1990). *The fifth discipline: The art and practice of the learning organization.* New York: Doubleday.

Shea, G. P., & Guzzo, R. A. (1987). Group effectiveness: What really matters? *Sloan Management Review, 28*(3), 25-31.

Sink, D. S., Tuttle, T. C., & DeVries, S. J. (1984). Productivity measurement and evaluation: What is available? *National Productivity Review, 3*(3), 265-287.

Sundstrom, E., DeMeuse, K. P., & Futrell, D. (1990). Work teams: Applications and effectiveness. *American Psychologist, 45*(2), 120-133.

Watkins, K. E., & Marsick, V. J. (1993). *Sculpting the learning organization: Lessons in the art and science of systemic change.* San Francisco: Jossey-Bass.

6

Relations Between Work Group Characteristics and Effectiveness

Implications for Designing Effective Work Groups

Michael A. Campion, Gina J. Medsker
Purdue University

A. Catherine Higgs
Allstate Research and Planning Center

FIVE COMMON THEMES WERE DERIVED FROM THE LITERATURE ON EFFECTIVE work groups, and then characteristics representing the themes were related to effectiveness criteria. Themes included job design, interdependence, composition, context, and process. They contained 19 group characteristics which were assessed by employees and managers. Effectiveness criteria included productivity, employee satisfaction, and manager judgments. Data were collected from 391 employees, 70 managers, and archival records for 80 work groups in a financial

Source: Campion, M. A., Medsker, G. J., & Higgs, A. C. (1993). Relations between work group characteristics and effectiveness: Implications for designing effective work groups. *Personnel Psychology, 46*(4), 823-850. Used by permission.

Authors' Note: Paul R. Sackett acted as editor for this manuscript. Special thanks to the many operations managers and employees of Allstate Insurance Co. who participated in the study, and to Carol L. McClelland and the staff at Allstate Research and Planning Center for their support and guidance. Thanks to Richard A. Guzzo for his advice on conceptualizing the study within the literature. Thanks also to Kenneth P. DeMeuse, Patricia J. Holahan, John R. Hollenbeck, Karen May, Eduardo Salas, Larry J. Williams, and three anonymous reviewers for their constructive comments on an earlier version of this manuscript.

organization. Results showed that all three effectiveness criteria were predicted by the characteristics, and nearly all characteristics predicted some of the effectiveness criteria. The job design and process themes were slightly more predictive than the interdependence, composition, and context themes. Implications for designing effective work groups were discussed, and a 54-item measure of the 19 characteristics was presented for future research.

The use of work groups in organizations is gaining substantial popularity (e.g., Banas, 1988; Goodman, Ravlin, & Schminke, 1987; Guzzo & Shea, 1992; Magjuka & Baldwin, 1991; Majchrzak, 1988). The difficulty with groups is that sometimes they lead to negative outcomes, such as low productivity (Whyte, 1955), poor decisions (Janis, 1972), and conflict (Alderfer, 1977). However, according to some current models (e.g., Gladstein, 1984; Hackman, 1987) and reviews (e.g., Goodman, Devadas, & Hughson, 1988; Katzell & Guzzo, 1983), groups hold the potential for simultaneously increasing both productivity and employee satisfaction. This is very important. From a work design point of view, the establishment of groups is consistent with a psychological approach, and is thus intended to increase satisfaction and related outcomes. But psychological approaches to work design have been historically, theoretically, and empirically in conflict with traditional engineering approaches (e.g., specialization, assembly lines, etc.) which are intended to increase efficiency and related outcomes (Campion, 1988; Campion & McClelland, 1991; Campion & Thayer, 1985). Therefore, if work groups are truly related to both productivity and satisfaction, they may be the key to avoiding the production-satisfaction trade-off previously presumed to be inherent in work design. In summary, work groups are gaining importance in many organizations and they present many potential risks and opportunities, so there is a need to understand the characteristics of effective work groups.

The Present Study

This study adopts a work design perspective on groups. In that tradition, it attempts to examine relationships between design characteristics and various outcomes. It is recognized that other perspectives on groups exist (e.g., organizational design perspective), and that they might conceptualize the issues differently (e.g., regarding trade-offs) and examine different variables (e.g., centralization, formalization, etc.).

Specifically, the study tries to make three contributions. First, it reviews a wide range of literature and derives five common themes or clusters of work group characteristics that may be related to effectiveness. The review includes social psychology (e.g., McGrath, 1984; Steiner, 1972), socio-technical theory (e.g., Cummings, 1978; Pasmore, Francis, & Haldeman, 1982), industrial engineering (e.g., Davis & Wacker, 1987; Majchrzak, 1988), and, in particular, organizational psychology (e.g., Gladstein, 1984; Guzzo & Shea, 1992; Hackman, 1987; Sundstrom, DeMeuse, & Futrell, 1990). It also delineates an extensive set of 19 characteristics within these themes, and then develops a measure.

Second, this study relates these characteristics to effectiveness criteria in a field setting with natural work groups. Most group research has involved concocted groups in the laboratory, and it is not absolutely certain that inferences can be made about natural groups based on this research (Guzzo & Shea, 1992). More empirical research is needed to confirm the generalizability of findings from laboratory studies to actual work settings. This study answers the frequent call in recent reviews for more field research on groups (e.g., Levine & Moreland, 1990; McGrath, 1986; Shea & Guzzo, 1987).

Third, this study is more methodologically rigorous than many previous efforts. Consistent with most theories (e.g., Gladstein, 1984; Hackman, 1987; Sundstrom et al., 1990) and some previous studies (e.g., Gladstein, 1984; Goodman, 1979; Wall, Kemp, Jackson, & Clegg, 1986; Walton, 1972), work group effectiveness is defined in terms of both productivity and employee satisfaction. The inclusion of productivity criteria enhances the objectivity of the effectiveness evaluation, and it avoids the sole reliance on affective outcomes which typifies much of the research in the area. The other criteria examined in this study—employee satisfaction and manager judgments of effectiveness—are measured using methods which minimize common method variance. Finally, large samples and multiple sources of respondents are also used to enhance the rigor of the empirical evaluation.

Work Group Characteristics Related to Effectiveness

The five themes below are summaries of key components of previous theories. Together, the themes depict a hybrid conceptual framework (Fig. 6.1) based on the models of Gladstein (1984); Hackman (1987); Guzzo and Shea (1992); and Tannenbaum, Beard, and Salas (1992).

Job Design

This theme is most closely linked to the work of Hackman (1987), but is also reflected in the group structure component of Gladstein's (1984) model, the group task school of thought in Guzzo and Shea's

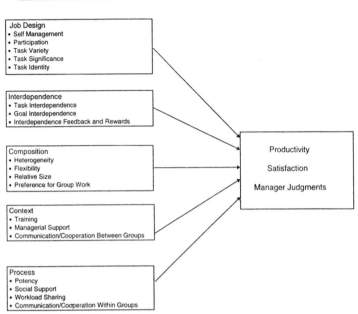

Figure 6.1. Themes and Characteristics Related to Work Group Effectiveness

(1992) review, and the task characteristics and work structure components of Tannenbaum et al.'s (1992) model. This theme contains work
group characteristics that derive directly from theories of motivational
job design. The main distinction is in terms of level of application rather
than content (Campion & Medsker, 1992; Shea & Guzzo, 1987; Wall
et al., 1986). All the job characteristics of Hackman and colleagues (e.g.,
Hackman & Lawler, 1971; Hackman & Oldham, 1980) can be applied
to groups, even though there have been few tests at the group level.

One characteristic in this theme is *self-management*, which is the
group level analogy to autonomy at the individual job level. It is central
to many definitions of effective work groups (e.g., Cummings, 1978,
1981; Hackman, 1987; Pearce & Ravlin, 1987) and part of most interventions (e.g., Cordery, Mueller, & Smith, 1991; Goodman, 1979; Goodman et al., 1988; Pasmore et al., 1982; Wall et al., 1986; Walton, 1972).
A related characteristic is *participation*. Regardless of management involvement in decision making, work groups can still be distinguished
in terms of the degree to which all members are allowed to participate
in decisions (McGrath, 1984; Porter, Lawler, & Hackman, 1987). Self-
management and participation are presumed to enhance group effectiveness by increasing members' sense of responsibility and ownership
of the work. These characteristics may also enhance decision quality by

increasing relevant information and by putting decisions as near as possible to the point of operational problems and uncertainties.

Another characteristic is *task variety,* or giving each member the chance to perform a number of the group's tasks. Variety motivates by allowing members to use different skills (Hackman, 1987) and by allowing both interesting and dull tasks to be shared among members (Davis & Wacker, 1987; Walton, 1972). *Task significance* is also applicable. Members should believe that their group's work has significant consequences, either for others inside the organization or its customers (Hackman, 1987). Finally, group work should have *task identity* (Hackman, 1987) or task differentiation (Cummings, 1978), which is the degree to which the group completes a whole and separate piece of work. Identity may increase motivation because it increases a group's sense of responsibility for a meaningful piece of work (Hackman, 1987), and it may facilitate cooperation within a group and increase control over sources of disturbance from goal attainment (i.e., technical variances) by keeping those sources within group boundaries (Cummings, 1978).

Interdependence

This theme comes primarily from the work of Guzzo and Shea (1992; Shea & Guzzo, 1987), although it is implicit in all the models. Interdependence is often the reason groups are formed in the first place (Mintzberg, 1979), and it is a defining characteristic of groups (Salas, Dickinson, Converse, & Tannenbaum, 1992; Tannenbaum et al., 1992; Wall et al., 1986). Interdependence may increase the motivational properties of work or the efficiencies with which the work is done, and thus may be related to effectiveness.

One form of interdependence is *task interdependence.* Group members interact and depend on one another to accomplish the work. Interdependence may vary across groups, increasing as work flow goes from pooled to sequential to reciprocal (Thompson, 1967). There has been little research at the group level, but interdependence among tasks in the same job (Wong & Campion, 1991) or between jobs (Kiggundu, 1983) has been related to increased motivation. It may also increase group effectiveness because it enhances the sense of responsibility for others' work (Kiggundu, 1983) or because it enhances the reward value of group accomplishments (Shea & Guzzo, 1987).

Another form of interdependence is *goal interdependence.* Goal setting is a well documented individual level performance improvement technique (Locke & Latham, 1990). There is less evidence at the group level, but a clearly defined mission or purpose is thought to be critical to group effectiveness (Davis & Wacker, 1987; Gladstein, 1984; Guzzo & Shea, 1992; Hackman, 1987; Hackman & Walton, 1986; Sundstrom et al., 1990). Its importance has also been shown in some empirical studies on groups (e.g., Buller & Bell, 1986; Koch, 1979; Pearson, 1987; Pritchard, Jones, Roth, Stuebing, & Ekeberg, 1988; Woodman & Sherwood, 1980). Not only should goals exist for groups, but individual members' goals must be linked to the groups' goals to be maximally effective.

Finally, *interdependent feedback and rewards,* or what Guzzo and Shea (1992) call outcome interdependence, is also important to group effectiveness. Individual feedback and rewards should be linked to the group's performance in order to motivate group-oriented behavior. This characteristic is recognized in many other theoretical treatments (e.g., Gladstein, 1984; Hackman, 1987; Hackman & Walton, 1986; Kolodny & Kiggundu, 1980; Leventhal, 1976; Pearce & Ravlin, 1987; Steiner, 1972; Sundstrom et al., 1990) and some research studies (e.g., Koch, 1979; Pasmore et al., 1982; Pritchard et al., 1988; Wall et al., 1986). Most of what is known about the effects of feedback and rewards on performance has been from research at the individual level, however, and it is uncertain how well the findings generalize to the group level (Shea & Guzzo, 1987). Feedback is one of the motivating job characteristics discussed by Hackman (Hackman & Oldman, 1980), but it is included here because of the need for interdependence of feedback for group members.

Composition

The composition of the work group is a theme in all the models of effectiveness. Gladstein (1984) and Guzzo and Shea (1992) refer to it directly as group composition, while Hackman (1987) refers to it under group design, and Tannenbaum et al. (1992) refer to it under team characteristics. The importance of composition has not been widely investigated for its impact on task performance, however, and the evidence has been mixed when it has been investigated (Guzzo & Shea, 1992).

Several aspects of composition may influence effectiveness. For one, membership *heterogeneity* in terms of abilities and experiences has been found to have a positive effect on performance. This is especially the case when tasks assigned to the group are diverse, because a wide range of competencies are needed (Gladstein, 1984; Goodman, Ravlin, & Argote, 1986; Hackman, 1987; Pearce & Ravlin, 1987; Shaw, 1983; Wall et al., 1986), and when tasks are disjunctive, because performance is determined by the most competent member (Steiner, 1972). Heterogeneity may also increase effectiveness because employees can learn from each other. On the other hand, the beneficial effects are unclear because most data are based on problem solving and creativity outcomes. Homogeneity may lead to better outcomes when satisfaction, conflict, communication (Pearce & Ravlin, 1987), and turnover (Jackson et al., 1991) are considered. Thus, heterogeneity is expected to have a positive effect in the present study, but the prediction is made with caution.

Another composition characteristic of effective groups is whether members have *flexibility* in terms of job assignments (Goodman, 1979; Poza & Markus, 1980; Sundstrom et al., 1990; Walton, 1972). If members can perform each other's jobs, effectiveness is enhanced because they can fill in as needed. *Relative size* is another aspect of composition. Groups need to be large enough to accomplish work assigned to them, but when too large, groups may be dysfunctional due to heightened coordination needs (Gladstein, 1984; O'Reilly & Roberts, 1977; Steiner, 1972) or reduced involvement (McGrath, 1984; Wicker, Kirmeyer, Hanson, & Alexander, 1976). Thus, groups should be staffed to the smallest number needed to do the work (Goodman et al., 1986; Hackman, 1987; Hackman & Walton, 1986; Sundstrom et al., 1990). However, most previous research on size has been in the laboratory (Sundstrom et al., 1990), so it is unclear if these findings generalize to actual work groups.

A final characteristic is employee *preference for group work.* Employees who prefer to work in groups may be more satisfied and effective in groups (Cummings, 1981; Hackman & Oldham, 1980). This preference is somewhat similar to cohesiveness (Cartwright, 1968; Goodman et al., 1987; Zander, 1979). It differs in that cohesiveness refers to attraction to and the desire to remain in a particular group, while preference for group work is not specific to a particular group, but refers to a general preference for working in groups. Research supports the notion that employee preferences may influence their reactions to their jobs (Fried & Ferris, 1987; Hackman & Oldham, 1980; Hulin & Blood, 1968), but little research has focused on this issue at the group level.

Context

Organizational context and resources are considered in all recent models of work group effectiveness. Gladstein (1984) considers organizational level resources, Hackman (1987) considers organizational context, Guzzo and Shea (1992) consider contextual influences, and Tannenbaum et al. (1992) consider organizational and situational characteristics.

One resource that groups need is adequate *training.* Training is an extensively researched determinant of group performance (for reviews see Dyer, 1984; Salas et al., 1992), and training is included in most interventions (e.g., Cordery et al., 1991; Goodman, 1979; Pasmore et al., 1982; Tannenbaum et al., 1992; Wall et al., 1986; Walton, 1972). Training content often includes team philosophy, group decision making, and interpersonal skills, as well as technical knowledge. It was recently shown that group member familiarity with the work and environment is related to productivity (Goodman & Leyden, 1991). Yet, the overall evidence in support of team training is mixed, methodologies of most studies have been weak, and most studies have focused on process outcomes rather than effectiveness (Baker, Dickinson, & Salas, 1991; DeMeuse & Liebowitz, 1981; Shea & Guzzo, 1987).

Managerial support is another contextual characteristic. Management controls resources (e.g., material and information) required to make group functioning possible (Shea & Guzzo, 1987), and an organization's culture and top management must support the use of groups (Sundstrom et al., 1990). Teaching facilitative leadership to management is often a feature of work group interventions (Pasmore et al., 1982). Although managerial support seems logically related to group effectiveness, there has been little prior research examining its influence.

Finally, *communication and cooperation between groups* is a contextual characteristic because it is often the responsibility of the management. Supervising group boundaries (Brett & Rognes, 1986; Cummings, 1978) and externally integrating the group with the rest of the organization (Sundstrom et al., 1990) enhance effectiveness. However, research has not extensively tested this, and there is little data on the link between intergroup relations and group effectiveness (Guzzo & Shea, 1992).

Process

Originally proposed by McGrath (1964), an input-process-output perspective is probably the dominant view of groups historically (Guzzo & Shea, 1992). The four themes above deal with the inputs to the group. Process describes those things that go on in the group that influence effectiveness. Gladstein's (1984) and Tannenbaum et al.'s (1992) models refer directly to group process, while Hackman (1987) refers to process criteria of effectiveness, and Guzzo and Shea (1992) refer to the social interaction process.

One process characteristic is *potency,* or the belief by a group that it can be effective (Guzzo & Shea, 1992; Guzzo, Yost, Campbell, & Shea, 1993; Shea & Guzzo, 1987). It is similar to the lay-term of "team spirit" and the notions of self-efficacy (Bandura, 1982) and high expectancy (Vroom, 1964). Hackman (1987) argues that groups with team spirit (potency) are more committed and willing to work hard for the group, but there has been little research on potency thus far (Guzzo et al., 1993).

Another process characteristic is *social support.* Effectiveness may be enhanced when members help each other and have positive social interactions. Gladstein (1984) describes supportiveness as a group maintenance behavior. Like social facilitation (Harkins, 1987; Zajonc, 1965), social support is arousing and may enhance effectiveness by sustaining effort on mundane tasks.

Another process characteristic is *workload sharing,* which enhances effectiveness by preventing social-loafing or free-riding (Albanese & Van Fleet, 1985; Harkins, 1987; Latané, Williams, & Harkins, 1979). To enhance sharing, group members should believe their individual performance can be distinguished from the group's, and that there is a link between their performance and outcomes. Most research has been conducted in laboratory settings, however (Sundstrom et al., 1990). It is assumed to relate to greater productivity, but the actual connection to productivity has not been tested.

Finally, *communication and cooperation within the work group* is also important to effectiveness. They have long been shown to influence effectiveness in laboratory studies (Deutsch, 1949; Leavitt, 1951), and they are considered in many current models (e.g., Gladstein, 1984; Pearce & Ravlin, 1987), but they have not been extensively field tested.

In the sections below, these characteristics are examined empirically in terms of their ability to predict several effectiveness criteria.

Method

Setting

The study was conducted in 5 geographic units of a large financial services company. Each unit supported 1 to 3 geographic territories ($M = 1.80$, $SD = .84$), for a total of 9 territories. Each territory was divided into 5 to 14 subterritories ($M = 8.89$, $SD = 2.67$), for a total of 80 subterritories. Each subterritory was staffed with a single work group and manager. The groups ranged in size from 6 to 30 ($M = 14.93$, $SD = 4.88$), but were more comparable in size within a territory. They were formal groups in that employees were permanently assigned; viewed themselves and were seen by others as groups; and interacted and shared resources to accomplish mutual tasks, responsibilities, and goals (Shea & Guzzo, 1987; Sundstrom et al., 1990).

Jobs were clerical and involved processing paperwork for other units that sold the products. Tasks included sorting, coding, computer keying, quality checking, answering customer inquiries, and related activities. Each group performed the same set of tasks. Jobs were interdependent in several ways. In addition to shared resources and responsibilities, work was often sequentially interdependent in that products flowed from some employees to others, and it was often reciprocally interdependent in that products flowed back and forth between employees. They were also interdependent in that members depended on each other for their knowledge of different products. Thus, the groups were teams and were referred to as such by the organization; they were not simply collections of individual workers (Salas et al., 1992).

Aside from performing the same work, the groups were similar in many other ways. Because they were in the same division of the same company, they were managed under the same policies and practices. Physical settings were very similar; furniture was identical and buildings were very comparable. Employees were similar in many ways (e.g., sex, education) as were managers (e.g., education, tenure) as described below. As a check, the measures were correlated with the demographics (e.g., age, tenure, sex, and education), and only trivial or nonsignificant relationships were observed.

Sample

Because the unit of analysis in group research is the group (McGrath, 1986; Shea & Guzzo, 1987), a sufficiently large and randomly selected sample of employees had to be included from each group so that the data accurately estimated the population parameters (i.e., values that would have been obtained had all the employees in each group been included). Using standard sampling accuracy formulas (e.g., Warwick & Lininger, 1975) and assuming an average variance on the measures of .50 ($SD = .71$; based on previous research and confirmed post hoc), an average 95% confidence interval of plus or minus 15% on the measures (i.e., .6 on the 1-5 scales) would require sampling no more than 5 members per group for the range of group sizes.

Thus, 5 employees were sampled from each of the 80 groups for a total of approximately 400 (usable sample = 391). Managers were also included for 77 of the 80 groups (7 managed two groups and provided data on both). Sample sizes below vary from 75 to 79 groups due to incomplete data and are indicated in the tables. Statistical power was 93% to detect an $r = .30$ and 70% for an $r = .20$ ($p < .10$, one-tailed; Cohen, 1977). To balance Type I and II errors, both the $p < .05$ and $p < .10$ significance levels were interpreted.

Employees were nearly all female (96.1%). Average age was 32.9 years ($SD = 9.9$), with half being 30 years old or younger. Average tenure was 6.0 years ($SD = 6.3$), with half having 3 years or less. Almost half (44.2%) had a high school education only, 51.9% had some additional education, but only 1.6% had a 4-year degree or more. Half the managers were female (51.5%). Average age was 29.3 years ($SD = 3.6$), with 69.1% under 30 years. Average tenure was 3.9 years ($SD = 2.5$), with 63.2% having 2 or 3 years. Nearly all had a 4-year college degree or more (92.6%).

Measurement Overview

Three objectives guided measurement based on McGrath's (1986) recommendations for studying work groups. First, multiple constructs of both characteristics and effectiveness were assessed, and data were collected from multiple sources for each. Characteristics were obtained from employees and managers; effectiveness was obtained from employees, managers, and records. Thus, self-perceptions, observer perceptions, and objective measures were used.

Second, common method variance between characteristics and effectiveness measures was minimized. Methodological separation was accomplished by using different data sources or time frames, by including respondents who only provided one set of measures but not both, or by using objective records.

Third, the group was the level of analysis. For some measures, data were collected at the group level; for others, data were collected from individuals and aggregated to the group level. Aggregation is a controversial issue, but several recommendations have emerged (e.g., Goodman et al., 1987; James, 1982; Roberts, Hulin, & Rousseau, 1978; Van de Ven & Ferry, 1980).

One recommendation is that there should be a strong rationale or "composition" theory to justify aggregation (Roberts et al., 1978, p. 84). As in aggregation in climate research (James, 1982, p. 219), this study views the characteristics as "macro perceptions" or shared views of the group. Another rationale (Van de Ven & Ferry, 1980) is that the meaning of the characteristics do not change from the individual to the group perspective. Further, in the work design literature it is not unusual to conceptualize and measure design at the incumbent level when examining individual positions, and then aggregate to the job level when examining positions held by multiple people (e.g., Algera, 1983; Campion, 1988; Campion & McClelland, 1991).

Another recommendation is that measures refer to the level of interest (Van de Ven & Ferry, 1980). In this study, most items refer to the group. Those referring to the individual are in the context of group membership. Lastly, the study performs the recommended check of demonstrating that the ratio of within- to between-group variance is statistically significant before aggregation (Goodman et al., 1987; James, 1982; Roberts et al., 1978).

Measures of Work Group Design

A questionnaire was developed to assess the 19 characteristics. It was completed individually by five randomly selected employees and the manager of each group. Based on the literature, three items were written for nearly all characteristics to obtain minimally adequate internal consistency yet limit length. Each characteristic's items were grouped under a descriptive label to help respondents clearly understand their meaning (with minor changes to labels to clarify meanings to laypersons). "Team" was used to refer to the group. A 5-point response format was used ranging from 5 = "strongly agree" to 1 = "strongly disagree." Items were averaged to form a scale for each characteristic. A copy of the 54-item questionnaire is in the Appendix.[1]

The 54 items were too many to use in confirmatory factor analysis (Bentler & Chou, 1987), so exploratory factor analysis was used to examine the acceptability of maintaining the 19 characteristics as separate scales ($n = 8.7$ per item). Common factor analysis was used because the factors were presumed to represent underlying attributes (Ford, MacCallum, & Tait, 1986). Although simpler solutions could be derived, it is noteworthy that each of the 19 characteristics loaded on its own factor when a 19-factor solution was imposed. That is, all items for each characteristic had their highest loadings on the same factor, separate from items of other characteristics. And there were only a few cross-loadings of .30 or above. This was found with both orthogonal and oblique rotations. Principal components analysis produced fairly similar results. The 19 factors explained 73% of the total variance, and 17 of the 19 characteristics loaded on their own factors with either orthogonal or oblique rotations. As an additional assessment of the independence of characteristics, intercorrelations among scales were examined (Table 6.1). With exceptions, intercorrelations were generally low (average r using z transformation = .22). Based mainly on conceptual distinctions between characteristics, but bolstered by these analyses, the 19 characteristics are kept separate in analyses below.

Several types of reliability were examined (Table 6.1). First, internal consistency reliabilities assessed unidimensionality. Only one was much below .60. Second, intraclass correlations assessed interrater reliability of the aggregate responses across the five employees in each group (Cronbach, Gleser, Nanda, & Rajaratnam, 1972). With five exceptions, all were significant although some were modest in size. Third, interrater agreement was assessed using the James, Demaree, and Wolf (1984) procedure (see Kozlowski & Hattrup, 1992), which compares observed variance of the ratings with the null variance expected with slight positive leniency. With three exceptions, agreement was moderate (.50) to high. Fourth, manager ratings were correlated with average employee ratings. Only 11 of 19 were significant, and most were small. In summary, each analysis showed some scales had low reliability. But each analysis suggested the scales were reliable as a set, all 19 scales showed reliability in one or more analyses, and 15 of 19 showed reliability in two or more analyses. All scales are tested below, but results for scales with low

TABLE 6.1 Means, Standard Deviations, Reliabilities, and Intercorrelations Among the Work Group Characteristics

Themes/Characteristics	M^a	SD	^{b}	^{c}	^{d}	^{e}	1^f	2	3	4	5	6	7	8	9	10	11	12	13	14	15	16	17	18
Job design																								
1) Self-management	3.33	.79	.76	.41**	.58	.24**																		
2) Participation	3.44	.81	.88	.54**	.66	.20*	.55																	
3) Task variety	3.14	.76	.71	.43**	.58	-.03	.34	.44																
4) Task significance	4.24	.56	.74	.26*	.55	.07	.21	.33	.27															
5) Task identity	4.03	.56	.71	.24*	.83	-.03	.20	.24	.25	.35														
Interdependence																								
6) Task interdependence	3.54	.66	.61	.04	.68	.05	.06	.17	.19	.15	.09													
7) Goal interdependence	3.37	.77	.68	.03	.56	.12	.28	.33	.31	.34	.23	.12												
8) Inter. feedback & rewards	3.05	.75	.59	.16	.50	.11	.20	.26	.28	.14	.10	.11	.29											
Composition																								
9) Heterogeneity	4.05	.51	.74	.04	.87	.15*	.09	.08	.04	.24	.14	.11	.04	.09										
10) Flexibility	3.05	.79	.66	.33**	.46	.18	.21	.25	.37	.17	.21	.04	.14	.16	.05									
11) Relative size	2.82	1.05	—	.42**	.18	.15*	.13	.11	.14	.10	.07	.00	.03	-.01	-.07	.15								
12) Preference for group work	3.84	.78	.90	.53**	.71	.30**	.12	.37	.32	.40	.24	.21	.29	.19	.16	.22	.03							
Context																								
13) Training	3.39	.81	.81	.39**	.59	.30**	.19	.28	.29	.27	.24	.07	.18	.11	.03	.28	.18	.32						
14) Managerial support	4.00	.62	.74	.14	.78	.18*	.27	.30	.21	.42	.30	.07	.26	.16	.27	.19	.07	.29	.34					
15) Comm./Coop. bet. groups	3.46	.67	.47	.21*	.57	.15*	.13	.13	.14	.20	.08	.03	.10	.08	.05	.20	.09	.16	.25	.17				
Process																								
16) Potency	3.67	.77	.80	.66**	.65	.53**	.27	.39	.38	.43	.23	.10	.22	.18	.05	.35	.16	.50	.34	.28	.18			
17) Social support	3.85	.64	.78	.44**	.79	.14	.22	.45	.37	.50	.25	.20	.25	.14	.21	.28	.10	.51	.34	.38	.22	.55		
18) Workload sharing	3.22	.92	.84	.58**	.36	.37**	.19	.26	.24	.23	.10	.05	.16	.17	-.04	.32	.05	.29	.34	.23	.14	.45	.38	
19) Comm./Coop. within group	3.87	.65	.81	.57**	.80	.20*	.18	.40	.29	.42	.18	.16	.28	.15	.15	.28	.07	.46	.32	.35	.20	.57	.62	.48

a. n = 391 employees and 77 managers.
b. Internal consistency reliability.
c. Interrater reliability (intraclass correlation).
d. Interrater agreement (James et al., 1984).
e. Correlation between employees and managers.
f. Intercorrelations of .08 significant at p <.05, one-tailed.
*p < .10; **p < .05, one-tailed.

reliabilities should be interpreted cautiously. Further, employees and managers converged only moderately, and thus are tested separately.

Measures of Work Group Effectiveness

Three measures of work group effectiveness were collected.

Productivity. Interviews with managers and employees were conducted to determine the productivity measures collected, the degree to which they were contaminated or deficient as criteria, and the extent to which they were used to evaluate effectiveness. Indications were that the measures most carefully collected and closely monitored were indicators of the amount of work not finished on a weekly basis which was received by the group from the subterritory it supported. That is, the groups' goals were not to reach the highest productivity per se, but to complete all the work that came in each week. Most territories did not even record the amount of work completed, but they did record most of these six measures related to unfinished work per week: (1) New Work Unfinished—number of new pieces of work not finished, (2) Percentage of New Work Unfinished—amount of new work unfinished as a percentage of new work received, (3) Revisions Unfinished—number of revisions to existing pieces of work not finished, (4) Percentage of Revisions Unfinished—number of revisions unfinished as a percentage of revisions received, (5) Calls Not Answered—number of phone calls to members of the group not answered, and (6) Percentage of Calls Not Answered—number of calls not answered as a percentage of calls received.

Each piece of work required the same set of tasks (e.g., coding, computer keying, quality checking, etc.). Although pieces of work varied somewhat in difficulty, distribution of difficulty was considered equivalent across groups in a given territory. Group size was used to adjust for differences in workload generated by the subterritories or skills among employees. Groups with higher workloads or fewer trained employees were assigned more employees. Group size did not change frequently because workload was fairly stable. Thus, groups were comparable *within* a territory, even though they differed in number of employees, and there was no need to standardize productivity data based on group size. There were differences across territories, however, such as complexity of the work and average group size. Therefore, productivity measures were standardized across territories using z-scores.

Although productivity is often stable (e.g., Deadrick & Madigan, 1990), the range of jobs studied has been limited. Thus, productivity data were collected and aggregated for each group over a long period

(*M* = *27.89 weeks per group, SD* = 3.88). To avoid temporal influences, the time period was the same for each group, from 3 months before to 3 months after the collection of the characteristics data. Intraclass correlations were used to assess reliability, or the degree of variance in productivity across weeks within a group compared to between groups. They can be interpreted as the correlations between the mean of this 30 weeks of productivity and the mean of another (hypothetical) 30 weeks. Average intraclass correlations ranged from .77 to .95 ($p < .05$), thus suggesting substantial reliability.

The six measures were intercorrelated, so they were averaged into a composite (*M* = .00, *SD* = .42, internal consistency = .74). All measures were not available for all groups (range from 46-79), so the composite was based on the available data for each group. Analyses with measures having the least missing data were similar, so only data for the composite are presented.[2] The signs on the correlations were reversed so that positive numbers indicate relationships with *higher* productivity (i.e., less work not finished).

Employee satisfaction. To avoid common method variance, the organization's opinion survey was used as the measure of satisfaction rather than adding a scale to the questionnaire. That is, it was administered at a different point in time (3 months earlier) and for an unrelated purpose, thus mitigating any consistency or priming effects. Data were obtained from all employees (total *n* = 1,175), not just the 5 who provided other measures. This gave the maximum data for each group (*M* = 14.87 employees per group, *SD* = 5.52), enhanced interrater reliability, and further reduced common method variance because satisfaction data were included from many additional employees who did not provide characteristics data.

The aggregate data from all employees in each group were used as the satisfaction measure. Such aggregation of satisfaction data is common, and may be somewhat justified by the definition of morale as referring to either the individual or group (*Webster's,* 1965), even though the practice is not without criticism (Roberts et al., 1978).

The survey consisted of 71 items on a range of topics. Five-point response formats were used, usually ranging from 5 = "very satisfied" or "strongly agree" to 1 = "very dissatisfied" or "strongly disagree." A principal components analysis revealed 12 factors explaining 61% of total variance: supervision, job, quality of service, upper management, career development, rewards, management's commitment to quality, employee relations, communications, co-workers, recognition, and workload. Scales were formed for each factor. They showed good reliability and a pattern of relationships very similar to a single average composite combining all items (*M* = 3.54, *SD* = .55). Thus, only results for the composite are presented.[3] Internal consistency was .97, interrater reliability was .79 ($p < .05$), and interrater agreement was .96. Satisfaction was fairly independent of productivity ($r = .15$, $p < .10$).

Manager judgments of effectiveness. Managers evaluated all groups in their territories on four items in their questionnaire: (1) Quality of Work, (2) Customer Service, (3) Satisfaction of the Members, and (4) Productivity. These items reflected the company's definition of effectiveness. Having both productivity and satisfaction is also consistent with effectiveness definitions in the literature (Gladstein, 1984; Hackman, 1987; Sundstrom et al., 1990). A 5-point response format was used ranging from 5 = "well above" to 1 = "well below" the average in the territory. Reliability was increased, and common method variance decreased, by collecting judgments on each group from all managers in each territory ($M = 6.18$ managers judging each group, $SD = 1.52$) as opposed to just collecting judgments from the manager providing characteristics data.

Principal components analysis revealed one factor (explaining 64% of total variance), thus items were averaged into a composite ($M = 3.31$, $SD = .46$). Relationships with characteristics were highly comparable between items and the composite.[4] Internal consistency was .82, interrater reliability was .75 ($p < .05$), and interrater agreement was .77. Judgments were related to productivity ($r = .56$, $p < .05$), but more independent of satisfaction ($r = .29$, $p < .05$).

Procedures

Researchers visited two sites prior to data collection to qualitatively evaluate the conceptual framework and degree to which the characteristics would capture the differences between groups (cf. Strauss & Corbin, 1990), as well as to identify effectiveness criteria. Discussions were held with intact work groups and the managers at each site.

Selection of employees began by including those involved in a study of job design 2 years before (Campion & McClelland, 1991) who were still with the company and assigned to a group ($n = 126$). Additional employees were randomly sampled using a random number table and alphabetical listings so that 5 employees were included from each group (additional $n = 265$). Using employees who were in the prior study did not substantially decrease randomness because they were originally randomly sampled. All employees agreed to participate if available. Those unable to do so due to absenteeism or scheduling problems ($n = 51$) were replaced by randomly chosen alternates. Questionnaires were completed at individual work stations on company time.

Managers of all 80 groups agreed to participate, but 3 were unavailable. They were instructed to respond to group characteristics questions based on their perceptions of employees' views of the group. Productivity, opinion survey, and demographic data were obtained from records. Productivity data required considerable study and communication with personnel from each site to ensure comparability across sites and minimize contamination and deficiency.

Results

Primary Analyses

Primary analyses correlated the five sets of work group characteristics with the three effectiveness criteria (Table 6.2). Job design characteristics were related to all criteria, with half the relationships significant and in the positive direction. Self-management and participation related to effectiveness in five of six analyses. Variety and significance showed three positive relationships each. Task identity was unrelated to any of the criteria.

To examine the predictiveness of all job design characteristics together, and control for experiment-wise error rate, characteristics were averaged to a composite and correlated with the criteria. Unit-weighted averages were more robust than differentially weighted regressions (Wainer, 1976), and unlike regressions, unit-weighted averages did not lose statistical power. Five of the six correlations were significant (Table 6.2), although modest in size.

Interdependence characteristics were related to all three criteria, but proportionately fewer of the correlations were significant. Each characteristic showed one or two positive significant relationships, but the composite was significantly related to effectiveness in four of six analyses.

Composition characteristics were related to all three criteria, especially manager judgments. A third of the correlations were positive and significant. Relative size was related to effectiveness in all six analyses, flexibility had two positive relationships, preference for group work had one positive relationship, but heterogeneity only showed a reversal. The composite was significant in five of six analyses.

Context characteristics related mostly to satisfaction and manager judgments criteria, with a third of the correlations positive and significant. Managerial support had four relationships, training had three, and communication/cooperation between groups had none. Two of six correlations with the composite were significant.

Finally, process characteristics related mostly to productivity and manager judgments criteria, with over half the correlations positive and significant. Potency was related in all six analyses. Workload sharing had four relationships, communication/cooperation within the group

TABLE 6.2 Correlations of Work Group Characteristics Reported by Employees and Managers with Productivity, Employee Satisfaction, and Manager Judgments of Effectiveness

Themes/ Characteristics	Productivity		Employee satisfac.		Manager judg.	
	Empl. data (n = 78)	Manag. data (n = 75)	Empl. data (n = 78)	Manag. data (n = 75)	Empl. data (n = 79)	Manag. data (n = 76)
Job design						
Self-management	.23**	.18*	.13	.16*	.28**	.16*
Participation	.15*	.22*	.34**	.11	.16*	.16*
Task variety	.10	.20**	.23**	.09	.19**	.12
Task significance	.14	.10	.20**	-.22**	.21**	.19**
Task identity	.06	.07	.07	-.06	.06	.12
Composite	.19**	.25**	.28**	.07	.25**	.25**
Interdependence						
Task interdep.	.14*	.06	.01	.06	.05	-.14
Goal interdep.	.13	.01	.11	.10	.18*	-.02
Inter. feedback and rewards	.13	.08	.27**	.16*	.13	.06
Composite	.20**	.08	.20**	.18*	.18*	-.04
Composition						
Heterogeneity	-.05	-.15*	-.05	-.04	.03	-.14
Flexibility	.12	-.02	-.02	-.01	.35**	.19**
Relative size	.23**	.19**	.23**	.25**	.29**	.24**
Preference for group work	.10	.01	.18*	.05	.13	-.10
Composite	.21**	.08	.19**	.17*	.36**	.20**
Context						
Training	.11	.08	.18**	.08	.19**	.15*
Managerial support	.14	.16*	.28**	.20**	.09	.18*
Comm./Coop. between groups	.04	-.06	-.03	-.12	-.01	.02
Composite	.13	.08	.20**	.06	.14	.16*
Process						
Potency	.29**	.22**	.20**	.27**	.38**	.28**
Social support	.20**	.12	.03	-.06	.13	.14
Workload sharing	.21**	.22**	.06	.07	.20**	.23**
Comm./Coop. within the group	.18**	.20**	.08	-.01	.18*	.13
Composite	.26**	.25**	.11	.11	.27**	.27**

* $p < .10$; ** $p < .05$

had three, and social support had one. The composite was significant in four of six analyses.

In summary, many relationships were observed between group characteristics and effectiveness, even though small in size. The manager judgments criterion was most predictable, followed by productivity, and then satisfaction. All five themes predicted some of the effectiveness criteria. Job design and process characteristics were slightly more predictive than interdependence, composition, and context characteristics. Characteristics data provided by employees and managers were somewhat similar (i.e., both significant in about a third of the cases, both non-significant in about a third, and one significant and the other not in about a third), thus modestly strengthening the findings.

Supplementary Analysis

The practical significance of the findings was examined because results in Table 6.2 suggested small effects. Based on the average of the 19 characteristics, the best (top ranked one third) and worst (bottom ranked one third) groups were identified and compared on two effect size indicators: standard deviation differences and differences expressed as percentages of the means. For employee data, the standard deviation (percentage of mean) differences were .66 (33%) for productivity, .52 (5%) for satisfaction, and .70 (12%) for manager judgments. Differences for manager data were slightly smaller, with differences of .26 (12%) for productivity, .22 (2%) for satisfaction, and .43 (7%) for manager judgments. Thus, differences between best and worst groups were practically important, especially in terms of productivity.

Discussion

Summary and Conclusions

Based on a review of the work group effectiveness literature, 5 themes and 19 characteristics were delineated. They were then evaluated against both objective and subjective criteria of effectiveness for 80 work groups.

Job design characteristics were very useful in predicting effectiveness. They related to all three criteria. Except for task identity, all the characteristics showed positive relationships with most criteria. Self-management and participation were the most predictive, perhaps partly because they were the more readily observable characteristics of effective work groups (cf. higher correlations between employees and managers in Table 6.1).

Theoretically, the findings suggest that the model validated so many times at the job level may also be valid at the group level. The motivational value of group work may come in part because such work designs, especially self-managed groups, enhance the motivational quality of members' jobs.

Interdependence characteristics, which are much more recent in the literature (Shea & Guzzo, 1987) and relatively untested, may also have some value. They showed several relationships with effectiveness criteria. In particular, interdependent feedback and rewards were related to employee satisfaction in both samples.

Composition characteristics showed relationships with all three criteria, but mainly with manager judgments. This may be because composition is determined by staffing, which is an important responsibility of managers. Relative size was related to all criteria in both samples, with larger groups more effective. Relationships were also observed for flexibility, with groups having flexible members viewed as more effective by managers. And preference for group work also showed one positive relationship with satisfaction.

Heterogeneity showed no positive relationships with effectiveness. This could have been partly due to the lack of heterogeneity in the sample (e.g., nearly all female and similar levels of education), but this may have also been due to improper construct operationalization. The literature may have recommended that a variety of different skills be present in the group (Cordery et al., 1991; Gladstein, 1984; Goodman et al., 1986; Pearce & Ravlin, 1987; Shaw, 1983; Wall et al., 1986). That is, all members must be skilled, but in different areas. Whereas, the measures in this study assessed the variation of skill levels in the group, perhaps implying that some members were skilled and others were not. The scale in the Appendix has been modified for future research to be more consistent with the former meaning of heterogeneity.

Context characteristics related mainly to satisfaction and manager judgments, but characteristics relevant to each were different. Management support was more predictive of employee satisfaction, while training was more predictive of manager judgments. This may represent the inputs to the group perceived as most valuable by each party. Employees view manager support as most critical, while managers view observable contributions like training as most critical. Communication and cooperation between groups was not related to effectiveness probably because the groups were very independent in this sample.

It is a recent trend to recognize the importance of context and resources (Guzzo & Shea, 1992). These characteristics showed somewhat fewer relationships than some others, but the results suggest they do add to our understanding of potential determinants of effectiveness.

Process characteristics related mainly to productivity and manager judgments. Potency related to all three criteria in both samples. It was the strongest predictor of all characteristics, thus supporting assertions as to the importance of the construct (Shea & Guzzo, 1987; Guzzo et al., 1993). Workload sharing was also very predictive, and social support and communication and cooperation within the group showed several relationships. These results highlight the importance of proper group processes to the functioning of effective work groups (Gladstein, 1984; Hackman, 1987; McGrath, 1964).

Implications for Work Group Design

The implication of relating work group characteristics to effectiveness is that such information might be used to design more effective work groups. As such, this study may make practical contributions. First, it focuses attention on characteristics management can influence. The degree to which they can be controlled or designed into groups by management varies, however. Input characteristics (i.e., job design, interdependence, composition, and context) are more directly controllable than process characteristics. Process may be only indirectly affected by management through encouragement, modeling, and reinforcement. Nevertheless, identifying and validating these characteristics is a first step in learning how to design effective work groups. Second, the study provides 19 characteristics and a 54-item measure (Appendix) as practical tools for designing work groups. Each characteristic can be viewed as a group design recommendation. With due consideration of the limits of the study, it is cautiously recommended that groups be designed to have higher levels of each characteristic (e.g., higher levels of self-management, interdependence, managerial support, etc.). The Appendix could even be converted into a work design checklist for enhancing team effectiveness. Third, it illustrates the potential importance of proper design in terms of productivity and satisfaction differences associated with groups that are high or low on the characteristics.

Practical implications could also be recognized by conceptualizing these work group characteristics within a human resources (HR) management framework. That is, many characteristics related to HR activities line managers perform (e.g., staffing, training, assigning work, appraising performance, allocating rewards, etc.). Linking characteristics to HR activities has several advantages. First, it helps line managers understand how they can create and maintain effective work groups as part of their HR responsibilities. Second, by linking to HR activities organizations understand, it provides focal points for work group interventions. Note that reviews of interventions by Katzell and Guzzo (1983) and Guzzo, Jette, and Katzell (1985) were also organized by HR activities. Third, it might enhance awareness in HR departments of their responsibilities regarding work groups (e.g., advising management how to staff, train, appraise, and reward groups), in addition to traditional concerns for individual employees (Shea & Guzzo, 1987). Finally, integration of work group design with HR activities may identify important interactions not recognized previously (e.g., between job design and compensation, Campion & Berger, 1990).

Limitations and Future Research

The implications of the study should perhaps be viewed as propositions for future research given the study's limitations. Some ideas for future research derive from methodological limitations. First, statistical power was only moderate for small effect sizes. Group research is susceptible to this problem because of the group level of analysis. Objective criteria like productivity exacerbate the problem because of smaller effect sizes than subjective measures with common method variance. Second, reliabilities of some scales were low. Future studies might lengthen or purify some scales, include more than five employees per group, and examine perceptual differences between employees and managers. Third, some data were collected from individuals and then aggregated to the group. Future research might use a group level of measurement (e.g., have groups give consensus ratings). Fourth, passive observation research does not allow causal inferences, and thus causation could be reversed (e.g., employees were aware of their effectiveness and described the groups accordingly). However, there is substantial laboratory experimental evidence that many of these characteristics cause the outcomes (e.g., Cartwright & Zander, 1968; Levine & Moreland, 1990; McGrath, 1984; Steiner, 1972; Zander, 1979), and the present study complements this research by assessing generalizability to the field. Nevertheless, field experiments should be conducted. Fifth, static research does not allow an examination of change over time, as is likely with work design (Campion & McClelland, 1993; Campion & Medsker, 1992; Griffin, 1991).

Other ideas for future research are more theoretical. First, tasks and technologies may be moderators of design-outcome relationships (Fry & Slocum, 1984; Gladstein, 1984). For example, heterogeneity may relate to productivity in creative tasks, and communication between groups might relate to productivity in groups with highly interdependent tasks. Second, future research might combine and test the themes in an integrated input-process-output model. It would be useful to know which inputs enhance key process variables, like potency, and whether these process variables mediate the influence of input variables on the outcomes. Third, other potentially important design characteristics could be examined in future research. For example, leadership and employee abilities have been shown to be highly influential in other areas of personnel research and most certainly play a role in determining group effectiveness. Finally, from a practical perspective, more needs to be known about how managers can actually affect these design characteristics when implementing group work design in organizations.

Notes

1. The heterogeneity scale was slightly modified. See the Discussion for explanation. Original items are available from the authors.

2. Results for relationships between the characteristics and individual productivity measures are available from the authors.

3. Results for relationships between the characteristics and individual satisfaction subscales are available from the authors.

4. Results for relationships between the characteristics and individual items of the managers' effectiveness judgments are available from the authors.

References

Albanese, R., & Van Fleet, D. D. (1985). Rational behavior in groups: The free-riding tendency. *Academy of Management Review, 10,* 244-255.

Alderfer, C. P. (1977). Group and intergroup relations. In J. R. Hackman & J. L. Suttle (Eds.), *Improving life at work: Behavioral science approaches to organizational change* (pp. 227-246). Santa Monica, CA: Goodyear.

Algera, J. A. (1983). Objective and perceived task characteristics as a determinant of reactions by task performers. *Journal of Occupational Psychology, 56,* 95-107.

Baker, T. A., Dickinson, T. L., & Salas, E. (1991, April). *The influence of team and individual training in interdependent tasks.* Paper presented at the Annual Conference of the Society of Industrial and Organizational Psychology, St. Louis, MO.

Banas, P. A. (1988). Employee involvement: A sustained labor/management initiative at the Ford Motor Company. In J. P. Campbell, R. J. Campbell, & Associates (Eds.), *Productivity in organizations* (pp. 255-294). San Francisco: Jossey-Bass.

Bandura, A. (1982). Self-efficacy mechanism in human agency. *American Psychologist, 37,* 122-147.

Bentler, P. M., & Chou, C. P. (1987). Practical issues in structural modeling. *Sociological Methods & Research, 15,* 78-117.

Brett, J., & Rognes, J. (1986). Intergroup relations in organizations. In P. S. Goodman (Ed.), *Designing effective work groups* (pp. 202-236). San Francisco: Jossey-Bass.

Buller, P. F., & Bell, C. H., Jr. (1986). Effects of team building and goal setting on productivity: A field experiment. *Academy of Management Journal, 29,* 305-328.

Campion, M. A. (1988). Interdisciplinary approaches to job design: A constructive replication with extensions. *Journal of Applied Psychology, 73,* 464-481.

Campion, M. A, & Berger, C. J. (1990). Conceptual integration and empirical test of job design and compensation relationships. *Personnel Psychology, 43,* 525-554.

Campion, M. A., & McClelland, C. L. (1991). Interdisciplinary examination of the costs and benefits of enlarged jobs: A job design quasi-experiment. *Journal of Applied Psychology, 76,* 186-198.

Campion, M. A., & McClelland, C. L. (1993). Follow-up and extension of the interdisciplinary costs and benefits of enlarged jobs. *Journal of Applied Psychology, 78,* 339-351.

Campion, M. A., & Medsker, G. J. (1992). Job design. In G. Salvendy (Ed.), *Handbook of industrial engineering* (2nd ed., pp. 845-881). New York: Wiley.

Campion, M. A., & Thayer, P. W. (1985). Development and field evaluation of an interdisciplinary measure of job design. *Journal of Applied Psychology, 70,* 29-43.

Cartwright, D. (1968). The nature of group cohesiveness. In D. Cartwright & A. Zander (Eds.), *Group dynamics: Research and theory.* New York: Harper & Row.

Cartwright, D., & Zander, A. (Eds.). (1968). *Group dynamics: Research and theory.* New York: Academic Press.

Cohen, J. (1977). *Statistical power analysis for the behavioral sciences* (rev. ed.). New York: Academic Press.

Cordery, J. L., Mueller, W. S., & Smith, L. M. (1991). Attitudinal and behavioral effects of autonomous group working: A longitudinal field study. *Academy of Management Journal, 34,* 464-476.

Cronbach, L. J., Gleser G. C., Nanda, H., & Rajaratnam, N. (1972). *The dependability of behavioral measurements: Theory of generalizability for scores and profiles.* New York: Wiley.

Cummings, T. G. (1978). Self-regulating work groups: A socio-technical synthesis. *Academy of Management Review, 3,* 625-634.

Cummings, T. G. (1981). Designing effective work groups. In P. C. Nystrom, & W. H. Starbuck (Eds.), *Handbook of organization design* (Vol. 2, pp. 250-271). New York: Oxford University Press.

Davis, L. E., & Wacker, G. L. (1987). Job design. In G. Salvendy (Ed.), *Handbook of human factors* (pp. 431-452). New York: Wiley.

Deadrick, D. L., & Madigan, R. M. (1990). Dynamic criteria revisited: A longitudinal study of performance stability and predictive validity. *Personnel Psychology, 43,* 717-744.

DeMeuse, K. P., & Liebowitz, S. J. (1981). An empirical analysis of team building research. *Group & Organization Studies, 6,* 357-378.

Deutsch, M. (1949). An experimental study of the effects of cooperation and competition upon group process. *Human Relations, 2,* 199-231.

Dyer, J. (1984). Team research and team training: A state-of-the-art review. In F. A. Muckler (Ed.), *Human factors review* (pp. 285-323). Santa Monica, CA: Human Factors Society.

Ford, J. K., MacCallum, R. C., & Tait, M. (1986). The application of exploratory factor analysis in applied psychology: A critical review and analysis. *Personnel Psychology, 39,* 291-314.

Fried, Y., & Ferris, G. R. (1987). The validity of the job characteristics model. *Personnel Psychology, 40,* 287-322.

Fry, L. W., & Slocum, J. W. (1984). Technology, structure, and workgroup effectiveness: A test of a contingency model. *Academy of Management Journal, 27,* 221-246.

Gladstein, D. L. (1984). Groups in context: A model of task group effectiveness. *Administrative Science Quarterly, 29,* 499-517.

Goodman, P. S. (1979). *Assessing organizational change: The Rushion quality of work experiment.* New York: Wiley.

Goodman, P. S., Devadas, R., & Hughson, T. L. G. (1988). Groups and productivity: Analyzing the effectiveness of self-managing teams. In J. P. Campbell & R. J. Campbell (Eds.), *Productivity in organizations* (pp. 295-327). San Francisco: Jossey-Bass.

Goodman, P. S., & Leyden, D. P. (1991). Familiarity and group productivity. *Journal of Applied Psychology, 76,* 578-586.

Goodman, P. S., Ravlin, E. C., & Argote, L. (1986). Current thinking about groups: Setting the stage for new ideas. In P. S. Goodman (Ed.), *Designing effective work groups* (pp. 1-27). San Francisco: Jossey-Bass.

Goodman, P.S., Ravlin, E. C., & Schminke, M. (1987). Understanding groups in organizations. In B. M. Staw & L. L. Cummings (Eds.), *Research in organizational behavior* (Vol. 9, pp. 121-173). Greenwich, CT: JAI Press.

Griffin, R. W. (1991). Effects of work redesign on employee perceptions, attitudes, and behaviors: A long-term investigation. *Academy of Management Journal, 34,* 425-435.

Guzzo, R. A., Jette, R. D., & Katzell, R. A. (1985). The effects of psychologically based intervention programs on work productivity: A meta-analysis. *Personnel Psychology, 38,* 275-291.

Guzzo, R. A., & Shea, G. P. (1992). Group performance and intergroup relations in organizations. In M. D. Dunnette & L. M. Hough (Eds.), *Handbook of industrial and organizational psychology* (Vol. 3, pp. 269-313). Palo Alto: Consulting Psychologists Press.

Guzzo, R. A., Yost, P. R., Campbell, R. J., & Shea, G. P. (1993). Potency in groups: Articulating a construct. *British Journal of Social Psychology, 32,* 87-106.

Hackman, J. R. (1987). The design of work teams. In J. W. Lorsch (Ed.), *Handbook of organizational behavior* (pp. 315-342). Englewood Cliffs, NJ: Prentice Hall.

Hackman, J. R., & Lawler, E. E., III. (1971). Employee reactions to job characteristics [Monograph]. *Journal of Applied Psychology, 55,* 259-286.

Hackman, J. R., & Oldham, G. R. (1980). *Work redesign.* Reading, MA: Addison-Wesley.

Hackman, J. R., & Walton, R. E. (1986). Leading groups in organizations. In P. S. Goodman (Ed.), *Designing effective work groups* (pp. 72-119). San Francisco: Jossey-Bass.

Harkins, S. G. (1987). Social loafing and social facilitation. *Journal of Experimental Social Psychology, 23,* 1-18.

Hulin, C. L., & Blood, M. R. (1968). Job enlargement, individual differences, and worker responses. *Psychological Bulletin, 69,* 41-55.

Jackson, S. E., Brett, J. F., Sessa, V. I., Cooper, D. M., Julin, J. A., & Peyronnin, K. (1991). Some differences make a difference: Individual dissimilarity and group heterogeneity as correlates of recruitment, promotions, and turnover. *Journal of Applied Psychology, 76,* 675-689.

James, L. R. (1982). Aggregation bias in estimates of perceptual agreement. *Journal of Applied Psychology, 67,* 219-229.

James, L. R., Demaree, R. G., & Wolf, G. (1984). Estimating within-group interrater reliability with and without response bias. *Journal of Applied Psychology, 69,* 85-98.

Janis, I. L. (1972). *Victims of groupthink: A psychological study of foreign-policy decisions and fiascos.* Boston: Houghton Mifflin.

Katzell, R. A., & Guzzo, R. A. (1983). Psychological approaches to productivity improvement. *American Psychologist, 38,* 468-472.

Kiggundu, M. N. (1983). Task interdependence and job design: Test of a theory. *Organizational Behavior and Human Performance, 31,* 145-172.

Koch, J. L. (1979). Effects of goal specificity and performance feedback to work groups on peer leadership, performance, and attitudes. *Human Relations, 33,* 819-840.

Kolodny, H. F., & Kiggundu, M. N. (1980). Towards the development of a sociotechnical systems model in woodlands mechanical harvesting. *Human Relations, 33,* 623-645.

Kozlowski, S. W. J., & Hattrup, K. (1992). A disagreement about within-group agreement: Disentangling issues of consistency versus consensus. *Journal of Applied Psychology, 77,* 161-167.

Latané, B., Williams, K., & Harkins, S. (1979). Many hands make light the work: The causes and consequences of social loafing. *Journal of Personality and Social Psychology, 37,* 822-832.

Leavitt, H. J. (1951). Some effects of certain communication patterns on group performance. *Journal of Abnormal and Social Psychology, 46,* 38-50.

Leventhal, G. S. (1976). The distribution of rewards and resources in groups and organizations. In L. Berkowitz & E. Walster (Eds.), *Advances in experimental social psychology* (Vol. 9, pp. 91-131). New York: Academic Press.

Levine, J. M., & Moreland, R. L. (1990). Progress in small group research. *Annual Review of Psychology, 41,* 585-634.

Locke, E. A., & Latham, G. P. (1990). *A theory of goal setting and task performance.* Englewood Cliffs, NJ: Prentice Hall.

Magjuka, R. J., & Baldwin, T. T. (1991). Team-based employee involvement programs for continuous organizational improvement: Effects of design and administration. *Personnel Psychology, 44,* 793-812.

Majchrzak, A. (1988). *The human side of factory automation.* San Francisco: Jossey-Bass.

McGrath, J. E. (1964). *Social psychology: A brief introduction.* New York: Holt, Rinehart, and Winston.

McGrath, J. E. (1984). *Groups: Interaction and performance.* Englewood Cliffs, NJ: Prentice Hall.

McGrath, J. E. (1986). Studying groups at work: Ten critical needs. In P. S. Goodman (Ed.), *Designing effective work groups* (pp. 362-391). San Francisco: Jossey-Bass.

Mintzberg, H. (1979). *The structuring of organizations: A synthesis of the research.* Englewood Cliffs, NJ: Prentice Hall.

O'Reilly, C. A., & Roberts, K. H. (1977). Task group structure, communication, and effectiveness. *Journal of Applied Psychology, 62,* 674-681.

Pasmore, W., Francis, C., & Haldeman, J. (1982). Sociotechnical systems: A North American reflection on empirical studies of the seventies. *Human Relations, 35,* 1179-1204.

Pearce, J. A., & Ravlin, E. C. (1987). The design and activation of self-regulating work groups. *Human Relations, 40,* 751-782.

Pearson, C. A. L. (1987). Participative goal setting as a strategy for improving performance and job satisfaction: A longitudinal evaluation with railway track maintenance gangs. *Human Relations, 40,* 473-488.

Porter, L. W., Lawler, E. E., III, & Hackman, J. R. (1987). Ways groups influence individual work effectiveness. In R. M. Steers & L. W. Porter (Eds.), *Motivation and work behavior* (4th ed., pp. 271-279). New York: McGraw-Hill.

Poza, E. J., & Markus, M. L. (1980). Success story: The team approach to work restructuring. *Organizational Dynamics, 8*(4), 3-25.

Pritchard, R. D., Jones, S., Roth, P., Stuebing, K., & Ekeberg, S. (1988). Effects of group feedback, goal setting, and incentives on organizational productivity [Monograph]. *Journal of Applied Psychology, 73,* 337-358.

Roberts, K. H., Hulin, C. L., & Rousseau, D. M. (1978). *Developing an interdisciplinary science of organizations.* San Francisco: Jossey-Bass.

Salas, E., Dickinson, T. L., Converse, S. A., & Tannenbaum, S. I. (1992). Toward an understanding of team performance and training. In R. W. Swezey & E. Salas (Eds.), *Teams: Their training and performance* (pp. 3-29). Norwood, NJ: ABLEX.

Shaw, M. E. (1983). Group composition. In H. H. Blumberg, A. P. Hare, V. Kent, & M. Davies (Eds.), *Small groups and social interaction* (Vol. 1, pp. 89-96). New York: Wiley.

Shea, G. P., & Guzzo, R. A. (1987). Groups as human resources. In K. M. Rowland & G. R. Ferris (Eds.), *Research in human resources and personnel management* (Vol. 5, pp. 323-356). Greenwich, CT: JAI Press.

Steiner, I. D. (1972). *Group process and productivity.* New York: Academic Press.

Strauss, A., & Corbin, J. (1990). *Basics of qualitative research: Grounded theory procedures and techniques.* Newbury Park, CA: Sage.

Sundstrom, E., De Meuse, K. P., & Futrell, D. (1990). Work teams: Applications and effectiveness. *American Psychologist, 45,* 120-133.

Tannenbaum, S. I., Beard, R. L., & Salas, E. (1992). Team building and its influence on team effectiveness: An examination of conceptual and empirical developments. In K. Kelley (Ed.), *Issues, theory, and research in industrial/organizational psychology* (pp. 117-153). Amsterdam, Holland: Elsevier.

Thompson, J. D. (1967). *Organizations in action.* New York: McGraw-Hill.

Van de Ven, A. H., & Ferry, D. L. (1980). *Measuring and assessing organizations.* New York: Wiley.

Vroom, V. H. (1964). *Work and motivation.* New York: Wiley.

Wainer, H. (1976). Estimating coefficients in linear models: It don't make no nevermind. *Psychological Bulletin, 83,* 213-217.

Wall, T. D., Kemp, N. J., Jackson, P. R., & Clegg, C. W. (1986). Outcomes of autonomous workgroups: A long-term field experiment. *Academy of Management Journal, 29,* 281-304.

Walton, R. E. (1972). How to counter alienation in the plant. *Harvard Business Review, 50*(6), 70-81.

Warwick, D. P., & Lininger, C. A. (1975). *The sample survey: Theory and practice.* New York: McGraw-Hill.

Webster's Seventh New Collegiate Dictionary. (1965). Springfield, MA: G. C. Merriam.

Whyte, W. F. (1955). *Money and motivation: An analysis of incentives in industry.* New York: Harper.

Wicker, A., Kirmeyer, S. L., Hanson, L., & Alexander, D. (1976). Effects of manning levels on subjective experiences, performance, and verbal interaction in groups. *Organizational Behavior and Human Performance, 17,* 251-274.

Wong, C. S., & Campion, M. A. (1991). Development and test of a task level model of motivational job design. *Journal of Applied Psychology, 76,* 825-837.

Woodman, R. W., & Sherwood, J. J. (1980). The role of team development in organizational effectiveness: A critical review. *Psychological Bulletin, 88,* 166-186.

Zajonc, R. B. (1965). Social facilitation. *Science, 149,* 269-274.

Zander, A. (1979). The psychology of group processes. In M. R. Rosenzweig & L. W. Porter (Eds.), *Annual Review of Psychology, 30,* 417-451.

APPENDIX
Work Group Characteristics Measure

Self-Management

1. The members of my team are responsible for determining the methods, procedures, and schedules with which the work gets done.

2. My team rather than my manager decides who does what tasks within the team.

3. Most work-related decisions are made by the members of my team rather than by my manager.

Participation

4. As a member of a team, I have a real say in how the team carries out its work.

5. Most members of my team get a chance to participate in decision making.

6. My team is designed to let everyone participate in decision making.

Task Variety

7. Most members of my team get a chance to learn the different tasks the team performs.
8. Most everyone on my team gets a chance to do the more interesting tasks.
9. Task assignments often change from day to day to meet the work load needs of the team.

Task Significance (Importance)

10. The work performed by my team is important to the customers in my area.
11. My team makes an important contribution to serving the company's customers.
12. My team helps me feel that my work is important to the company.

Task Identity (Mission)

13. The team concept allows all the work on a given product to be completed by the same set of people.
14. My team is responsible for all aspects of a product for its area.
15. My team is responsible for its own unique area or segment of the business.

Task Interdependence (Interdependence)

16. I cannot accomplish my tasks without information or materials from other members of my team.
17. Other members of my team depend on me for information or materials needed to perform their tasks.
18. Within my team, jobs performed by team members are related to one another.

Goal Interdependence (Goals)

19. My work goals come directly from the goals of my team.
20. My work activities on any given day are determined by my team's goals for that day.
21. I do very few activities on my job that are not related to the goals of my team.

Interdependent Feedback and Rewards (Feedback and Rewards)

22. Feedback about how well I am doing my job comes primarily from information about how well the entire team is doing.

23. My performance evaluation is strongly influenced by how well my team performs.
24. Many rewards from my job (e.g., pay, promotion, etc.) are determined in large part by my contributions as a team member.

Heterogeneity (Membership)

25. The members of my team vary widely in their areas of expertise.
26. The members of my team have a variety of different backgrounds and experiences.
27. The members of my team have skills and abilities that complement each other.

Flexibility (Member Flexibility)

28. Most members of my team know each other's jobs.
29. It is easy for the members of my team to fill in for one another.
30. My team is very flexible in terms of changes in membership.

Relative Size (Size)

31. The number of people in my team is too small for the work to be accomplished. (Reverse scored)

Preference for Group Work (Team Work Preferences)

32. If given the choice, I would prefer to work as part of a team rather than work alone.
33. I find that working as a member of a team increases my ability to perform effectively.
34. I generally prefer to work as part of a team.

Training

35. The company provides adequate technical training for my team.
36. The company provides adequate quality and customer service training for my team.
37. The company provides adequate team skills training for my team (e.g., communication, organization, interpersonal, etc.).

Managerial Support

38. Higher management in the company supports the concept of teams.
39. My manager supports the concept of teams.

Communication/Cooperation Between Work Groups

40. I frequently talk to other people in the company besides the people on my team.

41. There is little competition between my team and other teams in the company.

42. Teams in the company cooperate to get the work done.

Potency (Spirit)

43. Members of my team have great confidence that the team can perform effectively.

44. My team can take on nearly any task and complete it.

45. My team has a lot of team spirit.

Social Support

46. Being in my team gives me the opportunity to work in a team and provide support to other team members.

47. My team increases my opportunities for positive social interaction.

48. Members of my team help each other out at work when needed.

Workload Sharing (Sharing the Work)

49. Everyone on my team does their fair share of the work.

50. No one in my team depends on other team members to do the work for them.

51. Nearly all the members on my team contribute equally to the work.

Communication/Cooperation Within the Work Group

52. Members of my team are very willing to share information with other team members about our work.

53. Teams enhance the communication among people working on the same product.

54. Members of my team cooperate to get the work done.

Note: Headings in parentheses are the labels in the questionnaire if they were different from the headings in Table 6.1. Heterogeneity items have been modified (see Discussion). Instructions: "This questionnaire consists of statements about your team, and how your team functions as a group. Please indicate the extent to which each statement describes your team." Common response scale: "(5) Strongly agree, (4) Agree, (3) Neither agree nor disagree, (2) Disagree, or (1) Strongly disagree. (Leave blank if you don't know or the statement is not applicable)."

IMPLICATIONS FOR HUMAN RESOURCE DEVELOPMENT PROFESSIONALS

HRD practices can directly and indirectly influence the characteristics and effectiveness of work groups. This chapter provides two useful references for HRD professionals who are engaged in such practices: (1) the section titled "Work Group Characteristics Related to Effectiveness" and (2) the instrument contained in the Appendix. Both sections provide HRD practitioners who are working with teams with valuable information from the literature on team characteristics.

IMPLICATIONS FOR RESEARCH DESIGN AND METHODOLOGY

In structuring this study, the researchers developed a questionnaire to assess 19 group characteristics. However, they did not describe the process used to validate the data-collection instrument or to pilot test it. Because the instrument provided a key link between the literature and study results, instrument validation is an area for additional study.

Because this study used a correlational design, the results provide information on the relationships between the team characteristics and the effectiveness criteria. To make predictions about the effects of team characteristics on the criteria of productivity, employee satisfaction, and manager judgments, additional studies are needed that use experimental and causal-comparative design.

IMPLICATIONS FOR FUTURE INQUIRY

The results of this study should be synthesized with other research on work teams. For example, Larson and LaFasto (1989) interviewed individuals from different kinds of high-performing teams, including executive management and project teams. As a result of their interviews, the researchers identified eight characteristics of effectively functioning teams: a clear and elevating goal, a results-driven structure, competent members, unified commitment, collaborative climate, standards of excellence, external support and recognition, and principled leadership. Larson and LaFasto used the characteristics to analyze 32 management teams. Three interrelated factors were perceived to be team strengths: a clear and elevating goal, competent team members, and standards of excellence.

OTHER RESOURCES

Brooks, A. K. (1994). Power and the production of knowledge: Collective team learning in work organizations. *Human Resource Development Quarterly, 5*(3), 213-235.

Katz, R. (1994). Managing high performance R&D teams. *European Management Journal, 12*(3), 243-252.

Larson, C. E., & LaFasto, F. M. J. (1989). *Teamwork: What must go right/what can go wrong.* Newbury Park, CA: Sage.

Russ-Eft, D. (1993). Predicting organizational orientation toward teams. *Human Resource Development Quarterly, 4*(2), 125-134.

Power and the Production of Knowledge

Collective Team Learning in Work Organizations

Ann K. Brooks
University of Texas, Austin

EXTENDED AND COMPLEX WORK ENVIRONMENTS HAVE MADE IT DIFFICULT FOR individuals to single-handedly conceptualize and solve organizational problems. Recognizing the limited information and knowledge available to a single person and the potential creative power of teams, organizations have increasingly used teams to take on learning tasks such as product development, improvement of work processes, and strategic planning. In spite of the extensive research on groups and teams, little research has been conducted on how teams learn.

This article draws on a qualitative multiple case study to identify team-learning tasks, and then to examine how organizational structures make it difficult for low-power members to carry out those learning tasks. It proposes that unequal formal power among employees is a "critical level" influencing the success or failure of learning teams and links the difficulties teams encounter to the culture and history of the United States.

When work and work organizations become more complex, the consequences of individual decisions and actions become less clear. As they

Source: Brooks, A. K. (1994). Power and the production of knowledge: Collective team learning in work organizations. *Human Resource Development Quarterly, 5*(3), 213-235. Used by permission.

are joined with the decisions and actions of others to extend across the organization and into the future, individual experience becomes a less reliable basis for learning. Therefore, increasingly, such learning tasks as developing new products, improving work processes, planning organizational strategy, and developing or improving services are being taken on by teams (Gray, 1989; Parker, 1990; Brooks, 1992).

Although an extensive body of research exists on teams, particularly in the areas of work-group effectiveness, group dynamics, and adult learning, little has been reported on learning as a collective team activity. From the few studies that have been reported, it seems that aspects of the adult learning process such as framing and reframing, experimenting, crossing boundaries, and integrating perspectives also characterize the collective team-learning process (Dechant, Marsick, & Kasl, 1993). Information transfer also seems to be uniquely important to collective team learning (Ancona & Caldwell, 1990; Allen, 1984; Kraut, Egido, & Galegher, 1990; Pelz & Andrews, 1966; Cicourel, 1987, 1990; Austin & Baldwin, 1991). Much of the research in this vein has addressed information transfer as an instrumental process without much attention being given to the barriers that inhibit it, and only recently have researchers begun to address these barriers by integrating insights from the research on group dynamics.

Most recently, researchers have developed the notion of dialogue to capture the open and interactive climate that seems essential to collective group learning (Cicourel, 1990; Dixon, 1995). Cicourel (1990), for example, observes that because individuals in collaborative work relationships are likely to vary in the knowledge they have, they must engage in dialogue in order to pool resources and negotiate their differences to accomplish tasks. In a similar vein, Purser, Pasmore, and Tenkasi (1992) introduce the idea of deliberation to capture the reflective and communicative behavior that appears to be characteristic of team learning. Forces that affect reflective and communicative behavior are small, informal forums versus large, formal forums; knowledge sharing versus interdisciplinary competition; active inquiry versus advocacy without inquiry; appreciation of the product system versus a lack of product systems knowledge; and participative management versus a fear of challenging positional authority.

The contribution of the present study to our understanding of team learning is to propose an explicit link between the distribution of formal power to individual team members and the collective team-learning outcome of producing useful new knowledge. Specifically, based on research conducted with teams over a one-year period, I identify two domains in which new knowledge is produced: the technical and the social. I also suggest four grounded propositions to explain how the collective team-learning process interacts with organizational authority structures. I propose that (1) the collective production of new knowledge by teams requires them to engage in both active and reflective work, (2) members with insufficient formal power have difficulty in carrying out either the active or the reflective work, (3) the production of knowledge in the technical domain occurs only when power differences among team members are controlled, and (4) the production of knowledge in the social domain occurs only when no power differences exist among team members. Finally, I explore the barriers to collective team learning implicit in the cultural and historical themes of technical rationality and competitive individualism that are characteristic of the United States in the late twentieth century.

Research Methods

I have approached this study from a critical perspective. It has followed an emergent design and relied on qualitative case-study data. In the following sections, I will tell the story of how I carried out this research.

Definitions

This study drew on the reflective-learning literature to define learning as the transformation of experience into knowledge (Kolb, 1984). It drew on the work of Schutz (1964) and Berger and Luckmann (1967) to understand knowledge as socially distributed and socially constructed. Although learning was often taken to mean either the acquisition of expert knowledge or socialization, for the purpose of this study, learning was defined as the construction of new knowledge. Thus, collective team learning was defined as the construction of collective new knowledge by a team. Similarly, useful new knowledge was taken to be the successful output of learning.

Theoretical Perspective

I began the exploratory phase of this project influenced by the idea that knowledge is socially distributed and constructed. However, early in the study, I began to notice that the notion of contributing was brought up repeatedly by study participants. Because the job of the teams was to produce knowledge, for team members to contribute seemed to mean contributing knowledge to the team or company. As the study progressed, it became increasingly clear that for many of the team members, the ability to contribute was related to the amount of formal power they had relative to others on the team and to whether they had enough power to collect data and attend team meetings. Following this line of thought, as I continued my study I began to seek theorists who had written about the relationship between power and knowledge. Poststructuralists, race-based theorists, and feminists such as Foucault (1980), hooks (1989), Lather (1991), and Lazega (1992) seemed to have developed an understanding of this relationship that contributed to what I was beginning to see occurring in the knowledge-production process of the teams I was studying. For example, Foucault (1980) writes explicitly, "Knowledge derives not from some subject of knowledge, but from the power relations that invest it. . . . All knowledge is political" (p. 220). In other words, to contribute knowledge means to participate in defining how a social group or culture will understand reality. These writers view power as being embedded in existing social structures and discourse, rather than as being the possession of individuals or groups who then use it to dominate and control others in the way conceptualized by such writers as Max Weber or Karl Marx.

Research Questions

The research began with the general question of why some teams learn and some do not. An exploratory study suggested that the team-learning process included specific tasks and that power differences among individual team members affected their ability to contribute to carrying out these tasks. Using these insights, the remainder of the study addressed the following three questions: (1) What is the team-learning process? (2) How do differences in the distribution of formal power to individual team members affect the collective team-learning outcome? and (3) How do organizational structures and policies affect the team-learning process?

Context and Study Participants

The study took place in the research-and-development unit of a large high-technology manufacturing company. The research and development unit was responsible for designing the manufacturing processes for new products. Four teams whose general task was to improve the production process were recruited for the study by the unit's team coordinator. Three of the four teams considered themselves successful, and one did not. The teams indicated their opinion of their own success by their decision about whether to compete on the basis of their accomplishments in an international, company-wide competition for teams. The teams' goal was to contribute to the reduction in the time it took to move a product from design to market. Employees became members of teams by volunteering, and membership ranged from ten to fifteen people, with the exact number and composition changing over time. Teams selected their own leaders. Each team was assigned a "godfather," or person with managerial authority, to support and help secure resources. None of the teams had been formally trained together in group process or inquiry skills, although some individual members had been trained in the past as members of other teams. For the most part, teams structured their own learning, with only occasional reference to guidelines that had been remembered by individual members about how to work together as a team.

Research Design

Because of the extensive research literature currently existing on groups, I paid special attention to the scholarly critique of this extant literature. Several suggestions for future research on groups emerged from these critiques: (1) it needs to be carried out with groups in their natural context rather than with artificially constructed groups in laboratories (Goodman, Ravlin, & Schminke, 1990; Hackman, 1987; Schwartzman, 1986); (2) it needs to distinguish between groups that are doing different kinds of tasks (McGrath, 1984); (3) it should link group process to outcome rather than simply describing the process (Hackman, 1987); and (4) it should attempt to identify critical "levers" that can influence group performance (Goodman, 1986).

This study addressed these research design concerns in several ways: (1) it was carried out on teams in the research-and-development unit of a large high-technology manufacturing firm in an organizational rather than a laboratory setting; (2) it explicitly examined the interaction between teams and their organizational context; (3) it looked only at teams that had the task of constructing useful new knowledge; (4) it considered useful new knowledge to be the teams' output; (5) it used organizational and team assessments of this output to determine whether or not a team was successful; and (6) it identified the distribution of formal power as a "critical lever" in the successful production of knowledge in both the technical and social domains.

Procedures

The specific research methodology and procedures were influenced by Denzin's (1989) interpretive interactionist approach to data collection and analysis, in which an attempt is made to understand "how this historical moment universalizes itself in the lives of interacting individuals" (p. 139). According to Denzin, what we often take to be individual and personal troubles in fact are rooted in structural problems at the societal level. Thus, my interviews and observations focused on identifying the difficulties these teams encountered in producing new knowledge collectively and on finding out how these difficulties might be related to organizational structures and policies. If difficulty was pervasive across individuals and teams, I inferred that it reflected an organizational or social pattern. If a difficulty was idiosyncratic, I reserved judgment, since the difficulty might be specific to an individual or team.

The research included the following tasks: (1) identifying the research questions; (2) critically reviewing the literature on adult learning and group effectiveness; (3) collecting data, especially personal narrative pertaining to the team-learning experience, but also observation of team meetings and records and documents relevant to the teams; (4) describing each team and closely examining the data in order to identify recurring features and key elements for each team; (5) determining how each individual and team are alike yet unlike each other; (6) coding the data and identifying key themes; (7) assembling and comparing data in order to gain insight into the theme's meaning in relation to the research questions; (8) reassembling the team-learning experience in order to understand it again empathetically and in context rather than analytically and without context; (9) locating the team-learning experience within the historical moment and the social structures of the work organization and the nation; and (10) constructing the narrative. Although the tasks are listed sequentially, in fact, they occurred recurrently and even at times simultaneously.

Intensive data collection took place over a four-month period, although intermittent contact occurred over a longer period as a result of the continued presence on-site of a doctoral student research assistant who, although not a team member, was also employed by the company in the research and development unit. Team members who participated in formal interviews were selected to achieve a broad variation in hierarchical rank, gender, age, and ethnic and racial background. Eleven team members were interviewed formally, with additional informal discussions occurring over the four-month period with various team and organizational members. In addition, eight formal observations of team meetings were held. I undertook repeated rounds of data selection and analysis in order to refine my understanding of what was taking place on the teams. The recurrent interviews, the observations, and the participation of the on-site research assistant ensured an ongoing exchange of information and opportunities for the validation of data.

To help ensure trustworthiness, the data for this study came from multiple sources (Lincoln and Guba, 1985). I kept field notes in order to record encounters with members of the organization, as well as maintaining field journals in which I recorded methodological decisions, reflections on personal interaction with the research process, and emerging hypotheses about the meaning of the data (Goetz and LeCompte, 1984). Data were sorted, coded and interpreted in an ongoing process that continued throughout the study. Additional measures employed to strengthen trustworthiness were the use of two investigators, multiple data sources, and multiple data collection techniques; negative-case analysis; and critical reflection on the research process.

The Stories of the Four Teams

It is important in a qualitative case study to narrate the story of the case as a whole before subjecting it to the fragmenting process of analysis. This helps to ensure that the essence of the case is not lost in the process of analysis. In this study, I considered each team as a separate case although they all share the same organizational setting. What follows is the story of each of the teams at the time I studied them.

The Empowered Team

The Empowered Team, a team of about twelve members, was area-specific and included approximately equal numbers of engineers, operators, technicians, and clerks, as well as an auditor. It included eight men and four women. Of those, five were Hispanic, three were black, one was Asian, and the rest were white European Americans. The chair, Hal, was an engineer in the area and was guided by a clear vision of worker empowerment. He described himself as giving the workers encouragement and helping them value themselves: "I want them to see that their position can make a difference—that what they do is important. Leading this team is all contact and relationship building. If I care and they can tell I care, they do better." For Hal, the way in which he led this team was an expression of a personal mission and set of facilitation skills he had developed through his volunteer work with church youth groups. In fact, if he didn't have to work, Hal would have been happy to volunteer full-time with these youth groups.

Participants on this team spoke warmly of their leader and the way in which he expressed the value he placed on them and their contribution. One operator noted, "Everyone has something to do and contributes." A technician described his experience: "I do a lot of computer analytical work for the team. Hal imposed that on me—not in a bad way—I love it. I had thought I should drop out. I didn't feel I was a contributor. But Hal said, 'No, I won't let you.' He made me feel I was needed. He might not have gone that far with me if I had only been an operator."

Hal encouraged members' contributions by the way he facilitated the meetings. The following interchange illustrates such concrete skills as restatement, open-ended requests for help, inclusion of all team members with the pronoun "we," enthusiasm, and reference to the importance of skills and knowledge of people who were not present but who would be able to make a contribution. Team members responded by offering their own knowledge and ideas:

HAL: What else can we do?

DAVE (technician): (Makes a suggestion.)

HAL: (Restates Dave's suggestion for clarification.)

DAVE: (Explains what he meant.)

BRIGIT (operator): (Adds more information.)

HAL: Maybe we could get Bruce (not a team member) to really see what is happening. If we could get Bruce, that would really be great!

JAMILLA (operator): How about I bring in another overhead next week to show data?

Both team and individual learning were fostered on this team. Team learning was facilitated in several ways. First, an atmosphere of collaboration was fostered in which "everyone is friends here. They help each other." Second, the team leader was concerned that each member be enabled to participate. One operator said, "When I came back from maternity leave, Hal made a big issue out of explaining to me what was going on at the meeting. He came by where I was working and gave me a book about what we were working on on the team. He even got me into a class about it." According to one technician, "Since our team has both engineers and operators, things are done so everyone can understand. Participants are all collecting data. Everyone participates directly in the team. Operators have specific knowledge about parts of our area. We want everyone involved and able to contribute." He went on to give specific examples of the knowledge each team member brought. Third, the team works on tasks they find interesting, difficult, and relevant. A team member explained, "People didn't contribute on the other team I was on because they were not interested in the task. It was too cut-and-dried and operators had a hard time understanding all of the technical stuff. We dealt with things that weren't important. Now we look at the process and decide what needs help the most and choose that. The task is actually in process. We also work on harder issues than the other team did. We set our standards higher than the other team did. We work harder. If the task is too easy, I lose interest."

The team also provided opportunities to learn for many individual team members. On the Empowered Team, one member talked about getting insight about her job from the team: "I learn about 'specs' and maintenance. I learned to work on a computer and how to present graphs in different ways." Hal structured this individual team member's learning in several ways: by his skilled facilitation of team meetings; by working closely with individual team members to see that they were able to collect data, come to team meetings, and understand what was going on; by monitoring and intervening when individuals seemed to be losing their connection to the team; and by bringing in information from beyond the boundaries of the members' jobs and the team. In many ways, Hal played the role of a teacher. However, his handling of this role appeared to have both a liberating and a constraining dimension. In my field notes, I jotted down that "Hal seems like a teacher. He seems to already know the answers he wants from the team members to a lot of the questions he's asking."

The "A" Team

The "A" Team had a reputation as "a winner," and the operator and technician I interviewed both attributed this to the large number of engineers. The engineer interviewed attributed the team's success to a new interpersonally oriented management style that had been brought into their area and shared with the engineers. He believed that what the engineers learned about this new management style would trickle down to the technicians and operators.

The "A" Team was an all-male team and was made up of five engineers and six operators or technicians. It included one Hispanic, one Asian, and the rest white European Americans. Team meetings were heavily dominated by the engineers, with input from the operators and technicians only on nontechnical issues like costuming for their presentation at the company's international teams' competition. A technician described his team in this way: "This team is engineering-heavy. It's experienced a lot of success because of the engineers, but there's not enough operator input. The operators need to get organized so they can get their input heard. Maybe have a premeeting of five minutes in order to get organized. Actually, operators should chair these meetings because it is the only time for them to get their problems addressed. I've seen engineer leaders brush operators' problems aside."

The "A" Team's leader, Barry, functioned very differently from Hal. According to one technician, "He doesn't educate operators because it distracts from the conversation." An engineer described his experience on the team: "We have several enthusiastic members who each assume leadership roles at different times. We have temporary leaders who lead around specific tasks. We have good chemistry on this team. There are no rivals among members." This engineer went on to describe the positive qualities he saw in Barry's leadership: not heavy-handed, patient, easygoing, allowing leadership to change hands, and tolerant. As an example of this final attribute, he cited incidents in which operators talked at length about what engineers considered to be a small matter, "but Barry listened anyway."

Motivation to participate in teamwork seemed to vary among members. For example, the engineer interviewed said he had joined the team because it had a reputation as being enthusiastic, and it had a large impact. In addition, he anticipated a career advantage from the visibility he gained from being on the team and from interacting with people other than engineers. The technician interviewed explained his reasons by saying, "It's exciting to be on a winning team. The winning feeling is unaffected by whether operators contribute or not. Just winning makes it good to be on the team." Finally, the operator interviewed cited the opportunity to learn and develop and to help the company "do something better." He said he had no expectation of career advancement as a result of team participation.

The Lost Team

The Lost Team was the only team I studied that did not consider its accomplishments significant enough for it to enter the international teams' competition. The team included five engineers and five technicians. Four members were women and six were men. One was Hispanic, one was black, and the rest were white European Americans. The team was dominated by its engineer leader, Dave, and by another engineer with whom Dave frequently talked at length during team meetings. My field notes document multiple instances in which the leader argued down or belittled contributions by various team members and dominated the meeting time as he talked with the other engineer. A typical interchange on this team was as follows:

> DAVE: What other ideas are there? John. Are you awake?
>
> JOHN (an engineer): (with embarrassment) Yeah. I'm awake
>
> DAVE: Carlos. Do you have any ideas?
>
> CARLOS (a technician): (After a long pause Carlos asks a technical question which the chair answers.)
>
> DAVE: Do you have any ideas, Bettina, of what we can do?
>
> BETTINA (technician): (Responds with silence.)
>
> DAVE: Shall we . . . ? (Makes a suggestion that is met by silence. Maria, a technician, is the only one shaking her head.)
>
> MARTHA (an engineer): (Offers some information that the chair argues down.)

This team was not consistent on setting action items from week to week Often, the only item addressed was who was going to bring the donuts. When data collection tasks were assigned, they were frequently not followed up on at the next meeting because the responsible person was not present or had not collected the data. Learning on this team appeared to be perceived as the dissemination of expert knowledge by the engineers to other team members. This attitude was symbolized by a "Far Side" cartoon printed on each week's minutes in which a student in a classroom raises his hand and asks to be excused because his head is full.

There was no consistent perception about the source of the team's difficulties. One engineer on the team believed that it was lack of operator input and another thought that there was a conflict over whether the operators' primary task was to raise production rates or help conduct research to improve the production process. Another engineer suggested that operators perceived themselves as being exploited in the meetings by the engineers for their own benefit. Dave believed the problem was that the departmental area the team focused on had no problems that weren't shared by the rest of the department so they lacked the control to implement solutions. Two former team members attributed the team's problems to a lack of enthusiasm on the part of the leader and a disregard for operators.

The People's Team

The People's Team was unique among the teams that participated in this study. Its uniqueness originated in the fact that its membership consisted entirely of operators and technicians rather than including engineers and represented multiple areas in the department rather than a single area. It included eight men and four women, of whom one was black, one East Indian, one East Asian, one Hispanic, and the rest white European Americans. The team leader, Chris, had been elected by his teammates. A technician studying at the local university to be an engineer, Chris was described by other team members as aggressive, tactless, and at times not well liked. But in the words of one operator, "He is very gung ho. He expects a lot out of people, and he gets the job done." From Chris's perspective, "People want to do a good job, so I give them a plan." The team members perceived their team as very successful and pointed to several innovations they had made that had won them recognition in the company.

Chris believed that management did not put aggressive enough expectations on the teams and underestimated their capabilities. Like Chris, other operators and technicians also thought that management underestimated their abilities, and this caused them to become bored with and cynical about their job. However, belonging to a team afforded many of them the opportunity to extend their understanding and experience beyond the confines of their particular job. One team member described how being on the team had given her a better overview of the whole operation: "Before, if I had an inspector coming—look out! Now I'm wondering what's coming in from other areas. Now I know what the inspection is for. I'm more involved in the process." She gave the specific example of how her group had worked with a slump after lunch, and they never thought about how their slump might affect the work of some other group. By being on the team, she began to see that other groups needed her group to work more evenly throughout the shift so that work didn't pile up in the last hour.

Members of the People's Team viewed the purpose of the teams very differently than did the engineers and managers I interviewed on other teams. Whereas the engineers and managers on other teams frequently expressed the belief that the purpose of the teams was to make operators feel that they were participating in the company and to provide information to engineers, the members of the People's Team saw the purpose as helping the company gain a competitive edge in order to "reduce cycle time." Thus, they believed that their team's accomplishments were important to the company. It did not seem to occur to them that the purpose of the teams was to make them feel that they were participating.

Analysis of the Data

This analysis addresses the four research questions: (1) What was the team-learning process? (2) How did the differences in the distribution of formal power to individual team members affect the collective team learning outcome? (3) How did organizational structures and policies affect the team-learning process? and (4) What historical and cultural patterns were implied by the barriers to successful collective team learning? First, I will describe the team-learning process and how the different availability of power to individual team members affected the collective team-learning outcome. Next, I will address the question of how organizational structures and policies affected the process.

The Collective Team-Learning Process

Collective team learning appeared to require team members to carry out both active and reflective work. Essential to doing the reflective work was the team members' ability to communicate among themselves. This was enhanced when they controlled the ways in which power differences among individual team members affected their ability to contribute what they knew and their own time, movement, and work. Essential to doing the active work was the team members' ability to carry out team tasks and interact with individuals beyond the teams' boundaries. The team members' ability to successfully carry out this active work was also predicated on the degree of control they had over their own time, movement, and work.

The Reflective Work. Team members carried out the reflective work of team learning during team meetings. This work consisted of the tasks of problem-posing, sharing knowledge and information, and integrating the shared knowledge. In order to carry out these tasks, team members needed to be able to contribute their ideas without fear of intimidation, embarrassment, or belittlement. The major inhibitor to contributing ideas consisted of power differences among team members. In fact, one of the strongest themes to emerge from the comments of team members, regardless of their position in the company, was that low-power members' contributions during meetings were often constrained. Unless power differences among team members were controlled or simply did not exist, low-power team members described the climate at the team meetings as "stifling," "intimidating," and "damaging." Team members described behaviors such as treating members differently if an action item was not completed and publicly ridiculing them if they did not sit quietly during team meetings.

In this organization, a hierarchical authority structure and supporting policies institutionalized these differences. For example, the Lost Team described having difficulties defining a problem. Dave complained that it was "hard to get the right project, one with a visible contribution and a reasonable amount of work. . . . Our area doesn't have a local problem. All problems are 'lab' wide." Nevertheless, technicians and operators on the team described themselves as reticent to identify problems because they were afraid that their superiors would then associate them with the problem. They were also worried that the auditors who were on the team would expect the workers to have fixed the problems on their own by the next audit.

The reflective work was also constrained by the fact that some team members had insufficient formal power to control their own time, movement, and work. The first requirement essential to either sharing or integrating knowledge in team meetings was attendance. This presented a major obstacle for operators who, according to one engineer, were rewarded for high production rates rather than for carrying out experiments. He explained, "The work of operators is to run lots, not experiments. The team takes away from their main job. There's a conflict of responsibilities." Operators were often unable to attend team meetings because their supervisors wanted them to remain at their workplace. Another constraint was that since operators work shifts, for some of them, the team meetings were held outside of their work hours. Thus, as one operator explained, "When someone doesn't do what they're asked or doesn't show up, sometimes they're just tired and so go home. The meeting is at 7:15 A.M. The night shift has to stay for the team meeting." Managers and engineers did not face these limitations since they had more autonomy and control over how they apportioned their time.

The Active Work. The active work of team learning included the tasks of gathering data from outside team boundaries and disseminating new team knowledge to the organization. In order to carry out these tasks, team members needed sufficient formal power to control their own time, movement, and work so that they could gather data and interact with employees and work areas beyond their own. For operators, time, movement, and work were controlled by their supervisors. They were hourly workers who carried out a specific task, at a specific time, in a specific place. In fact, although the company encouraged and supported teams officially, the support of the operators' supervisors was needed before they could gather data. Supervisors, it seemed, were rewarded for placing production output before improvement of the manufacturing process. Thus, this conflict in organizational priorities often meant that although operators were encouraged to join teams, their supervisors constrained their participation by not allowing them to carry out their data collection tasks or attend team meetings.

Dissemination of new knowledge was also difficult for operators and technicians since they had little ability to cross boundaries within the organization. As one technician noted, "There's no communication between shifts. I've tried to get to know people on other shifts, but it has been almost impossible." This constraint also limited their understanding of what work their organization did, where their own work fit into the larger organization, how systems within the company operated, and how to get things done so that they could assess the practicality of their projects and develop strategies for disseminating their new knowledge. Although their low-power position limited them, operators spoke repeatedly about how being on the teams had given them a broader picture of their work and the organization. This was true for operators on all four teams and not just the successful teams.

Team Learning in the Technical and Social Domains

Team-learning output affected both the technical and the social systems of the organization. However, most of the team learning evidenced occurred in the technical domain. The "A" Team, the Empowered Team, and the People's Team all gave evidence of having produced knowledge within the technical domain. However, three incidents of collective team learning occurred within the social domain: two on the People's Team and one on the "A" Team. It is important to note that on both teams, those who participated in the learning process were team members at the same hierarchical level.

In one incident, the People's Team became frustrated by the lack of regular attendance at team meetings and the spotty collection and reporting of data between meetings. Since the experiments that yielded the data were part of a larger team inquiry, team members' absence frustrated the team-learning process. Out of this frustration, Chris finally asked the team what they could do to solve the problem. Chris described the results: "We wound up dividing members into the areas they work in. They each elect their own leader. Then action items can go to the groups, not to individuals. The groups delegate and someone from each group comes to the meeting prepared. We brainstormed this idea." Thus, the People's Team moved beyond the technical domain of learning to produce new knowledge in the social domain. Because their technical learning was frustrated by formal and cultural structures in the organization that constrained their attendance at meetings and their ability to collect data, they focused their attention on developing new structures that would enable them to continue their technical learning. With the creation of area subteams, operators as members of groups could exercise the power to attend meetings and run experiments, a power they were not formally entitled to as individuals. At the same time they found a way to meet their responsibility to carry out the work assigned to them by their supervisors.

A second incident of team learning in the social domain also took place on the People's Team. Having a limited ability to cross organizational boundaries in order to disseminate their knowledge, the People's Team developed a team newspaper in which they disseminated not only their new technical knowledge but also their team ideology, which seemed to embody at its heart an ethic of mutual respect.

On the "A" Team, team members inspired by a new management style and discouraged by what one of them termed "poor personal interactions" structured their team learning so that "each project has a strong champion. Champions have the expertise to lead a project, so they lead the team then. Many different members rise to take leadership. Leadership is allowed to change hands." It is important to note, however, that this norm of "changing leadership" did not typically include moving nonengineers into the leadership position. This was probably true because formal and informal power in this organization was accrued through technical expertise. Not only did operators and technicians not lead this team, they participated very little in the learning process.

Both of these incidents of learning went beyond collective team learning in the technical domain to team learning in the social domain, which generated new possibilities for social structuring within the organization. They also seemed to reflect the teams' attempts to overcome barriers to the active work of the team-learning process. It is worth noting a few unique characteristics of these teams. First, all members, including the leaders who engaged in the team learning process, were at roughly the same hierarchical level. Second, in contrast to Hal, who also encouraged participation, both Chris and Barry seemed to truly believe that

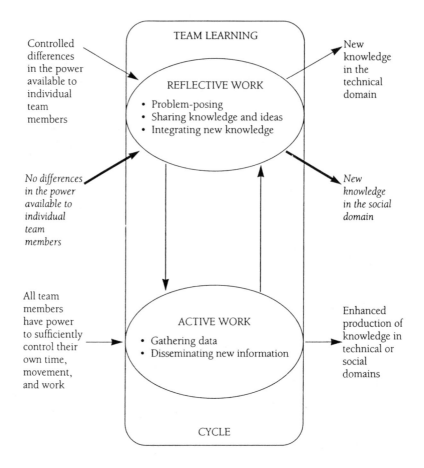

Figure 7.1. The Team-Learning Process

each team member included in the learning process had something important to contribute. Third, both leaders believed that the purpose of the teams was to contribute to the company, not to make employees feel as though they were participating. Thus, although it appears that learning can occur in the technical domain when the authority structure is controlled, as in the case of the Empowered Team, for it to occur in the social domain there must be no significant hierarchical differences between the team members who engage in the learning process. This parity in rank must include the team leader as well. Figure 7.1 provides a simple model to illustrate the proposed relationship of formal power distribution to team learning.

Organizational Authority Structure and the
Distribution of Formal Power

Within the company, employees perceived and interacted with each other according to where they were placed within the company's authority structure. Authority was accrued first by formal position and second through technical knowledge, so that managers and engineers stood above technicians and operators. Employees seemed to interact with each other in ways that were consonant with the distribution of power by the authority structure. Thus, employees' positions in the authority structure determined whether or not their problems were addressed, their knowledge was solicited or given attention, or their attempts at meaning-making were taken seriously. Similarly, the authority structure determined whether or not they had any control over the team-learning process. The following statements, contributed by members of all of the teams and including the perceptions of operators, technicians, and supervisors, depict an environment in which power based on authority is used to control the process of producing knowledge:

"I've seen engineer leaders brush operators' problems aside."

"The fact that operators don't talk is management's fault. They let engineers run the show."

"Operators are told not to be on the team because they're needed on-line."

"On some teams it's more stifling. There's the attitude that 'your opinion is not as good as mine.' "

"On the other teams, managers and engineers would get on a roll. Then it was all over."

"Women are not on the team. If they are, they keep quiet rather than be identified with problems."

"There's different treatment depending on the person if the action item is not complete. These things build in reluctance on the teams."

It is important to note that members of the Empowered Team and the People's Team made these statements in regard to teams they had been members of previously rather than currently. Thus, the power differences that seemed to constrain participation on some of the other teams were not doing so on these two teams. The following discussion of the collective team learning process explains how constraints on participation interfered with tasks that were an essential part of the team-learning process.

Role of Team Leadership

Leadership style and the power a leader could claim in relation to other team members was important on all four teams. Leadership style varied most noticeably on the dimension of inclusion or exclusion in the team-learning process. Dave, from the Lost Team, could claim relatively high power in the context of the team because he was an engineer. He made little effort to include low-power members and communicated in a way that discouraged their participation. Barry, from the "A" Team, could also claim high power because he was an engineer. He focused on the contributions of engineers and allowed low power employees to play only minimal supporting roles. Hal, from the Empowered Team, also claimed high power because he was an engineer. He used it to impose a culture of empowerment in which each team member's contribution was treated as valuable, and he persistently advocated for low-power team members to collect data and attend team meetings. Chris, from the People's Team, could claim only marginally more power than the other team members. Like Hal, he treated each team member's contribution as valuable. However, unlike Hal, who apparently did so to help low-power employees feel as if they were important to the company. Chris, having relatively little power himself, seemed to truly believe that low-power employees really did have something important to contribute.

Discussion and Research Implications

This study explored the process of team learning and identified ways in which the organizational context of four teams interacted with this process. An analysis and comparison of the four teams provided several potential insights into the collective team-learning process. First, collective team learning appears to encompass a process of alternating between reflective and active work. Each kind of work requires team members to enact specific learning tasks. The reflective work includes posing problems, sharing knowledge, and combining and recombining knowledge, and the active work includes gathering data from outside team boundaries and disseminating new team knowledge to the organization.

However, the organization's authority structure and supporting policies make it difficult for team members to carry out either the reflective or the active work of team learning by structuring power differences among team members, and they provide insufficient formal power for some team members to control their own time, movement, and work. Collective team learning occurs only when power differences are either controlled or not present.

Thus, according to the data from this study, the differences in power among employees are a critical lever affecting the output of knowledge by teams. The way in which formal power is distributed to employees affects who may contribute to the production of knowledge and whose contributions others take seriously. It also determines who has sufficient power to control her or his own time, movement, and work, thus affecting who can gather data and distribute new knowledge.

Grounded Propositions

While this research was not intended to result in the identification of universal laws, I have used the data to generate four grounded propositions regarding collective team learning in work organizations. The intent of these propositions is to serve as a heuristic device to enable scholars and practitioners to view teams from a potentially unfamiliar perspective. The following four propositions are grounded in the data I gathered about the four teams:

1. The collective production of new knowledge by teams requires them to engage in both active and reflective work.
2. Members with insufficient formal power have difficulty in carrying out either the active or the reflective work.
3. The production of knowledge in the technical domain occurs only when power differences among team members are controlled.
4. The production of knowledge in the social domain occurs only when no power differences exist among team members.

Knowledge and Power

This study suggests that differences in power among team members and insufficient formal power for some team members to control their own time, movement, and work constrain the production of knowledge. Although employee empowerment has long been recognized in practice as being important to employee commitment, productivity, and production of high-quality goods and services, there has been no attempt to link it with the more recently recognized competitive need for companies to produce new knowledge.

Although there is little in the literature on human resource development about the link between power and the production of knowledge, it has been explored by philosophers (Foucault, 1980; Habermas, 1973), educators (Apple, 1982; Freire, 1972; Giroux, 1988), feminists (Lather, 1991; Minnich, 1991; Smith, 1975), and ethnic and racial scholars (hooks, 1989; Ogbu, 1982), among others. The argument put forth by many of these writers is that existing power relations are embedded in our institutions, and that these institutions perpetuate themselves. Those with sufficient power to participate in the ongoing production of knowledge, unwittingly or not, usually reproduce knowledge that supports the existing distribution of formal power. Lazega (1992) helps explain this by pointing out that part of formal power usually includes a formal authority to know and the right and duty to define the situation for others (p. 68). This formal power enables individuals to further their own interests.

This literature speaks primarily from a moral vantage point, arguing that justice in a democratic society is not served by excluding particular groups from participating in the production of knowledge. However, a different argument, and the one made in this article, is that work organizations are seriously disadvantaged by relying predominantly on the limited knowledge and information of high power individuals. A more diverse and broad-based knowledge and information base is needed to ground decisions, planning, and such things as the development of new products and services. Employees from all levels and functions within the organization must be able to contribute their unique knowledge about the work of the organization.

If the unequal distribution of formal power inhibits broad-based participation in the production of knowledge, then it is to these differences that we must address ourselves if we are to maximize our ability to produce new knowledge. Although this argument may seem to point to the need for flat and nonhierarchical organizations, the actions of the teams in this study suggest that there are many alternatives for controlling or eliminating differences in the distribution of formal power. For example, two of the successful teams were constructed to include only members at the same hierarchical level in the process of producing knowledge. This left the organization's hierarchy intact while establishing an environment for producing knowledge that did not reproduce this hierarchy. However, it is also important to remember that in the case of the People's Team, even though knowledge was produced in both the technical and the social domains, the major barriers the team had to address grew out of their lack of sufficient formal power to control their own time, movement, and work and their inability to move easily across organizational boundaries. Without ongoing and focused intervention to alleviate these problems, members with little power available to them had difficulty breaking free from their jobs to gather data, attend team meetings, and distribute new knowledge back to the organization. The lack of power to move outside of team boundaries was not resolved by controlling power differences within team boundaries.

The fact that organizations have tried a succession of change initiatives directed at altering power differences suggests that although such changes are sought, they are not easily implemented. Such initiatives have included attempts to institute workplace democracy, employee empowerment, self-directed work teams, total quality improvement, and flatter organizational hierarchies. Similarly, the tendency of top management to endorse such initiatives while at the same time failing to support them on a daily basis and to retain authority while at the same time redistributing responsibility downward (Dickens, 1993; Lewis,

1993) suggests that organizational structures and patterns of interaction have deeper roots than most change programs can easily alter. These structures and patterns appear to be historically and culturally situated. Since both history and culture are collective constructions and have for the most part become taken for granted as part of our daily reality, they are difficult to identify and resistant to change.

Historical and Cultural Perspectives

From a historical perspective, although such innovations as the attempt to work more as teams may indicate a transition to an era in which the dominant metaphors are those of change and uncertainty rather than rational order and predictability, much of life in today's institutions is still imbued with the ideal of technical rationality. This ideal is expressed in the way we enact learning and share knowledge. In work organizations, scientific knowledge is applied to problem solving by professional experts such as engineers and managers. A professional education acquired at a university, particularly a research university, seems to uniquely qualify managers and engineers to address the work and technical problems of high-technology manufacturing companies like the one in this study. Engineers and managers bring knowledge to the work setting and use workers with less knowledge, such as operators and technicians, to enact it. From this perspective, the work of less knowledgeable employees should be routine and require no problem solving. Furthermore, any learning about improving the practice of the organization should be done by engineers or managers. In a rational hierarchy such as this, scientists create knowledge, engineers and man-agers solve problems in the application of that knowledge, and semi-skilled and unskilled workers enact the knowledge. This hierarchy effec-tively concentrates learning in the hands of scientists and professional practitioner while the learning of workers is tightly controlled and prescribed by those above them. From a critical perspective, knowledge actually belongs to the community, not high-power individuals, and the act of critical self-reflection or attention to and skepticism regarding one's own suppositions, is central learning.

From a cultural perspective, the cultural ideal for achieving main-stream success in the United States appears to be through competitive individualism (Tocqueville, 1836/1963). This contrasts with some other national culture in which the ideal is to distinguish oneself because of membership in a work group or to reflect well upon one's family or work group, as is more the case in Japan and India (Roland, 1988). The success of teams in work organization in Japan, for example, is not just an industrial innovation but is rooted in the Meiji Restoration, in which modern Western institutions were assimilated while retaining "traditional patterns of familial hierarchical relationships with their associated values of emotional interdependence, reciprocal loyalties and obligations, and high levels of performance" (Roland, 1988, p. 129). These values reward teamwork by enhancing personal identity for successful participation in and support of group and team efforts.

In contrast, the United States has a culture rooted in the political, economic, and religious persecution of many of its people before their immigration to this country. Our right as individuals to do what we want as long as we do not interfere with the rights of someone else is enshrined in our nation's constitution. We frequently view ourselves as self-made and our success having been won in competition with others. According to Bellah and others (1985, p. 185), the dream of many Americans is "often a very private dream of being a star, the uniquely successful and admirable one, the one who stands out from the crowd of ordinary folk who don't know." Thus, the shift to working in teams in many U.S. work organizations represents not just a structural change in how work is done, but a significant historical and cultural shift that affects the way many individuals identify themselves and attempt to establish their social worth. By identifying and analyzing the difficulties teams encounter in carrying out their tasks, it is possible to see what specific aspects our history, society, and culture are in conflict with our intentions to enact exchange.

Power, Knowledge, and Team Learning in Organizations

The exclusion of low-power employees from the team-learning process, although reflective of cultural patterns in the United States, has serious implications for organizations that are attempting to transform or adapt in order to function or compete better in a diverse, technologically complex, and quickly changing global environment. Alfred Schutz (1964) writes that knowledge is socially distributed. Following in that same tradition, Berger and Luckmann (1967) write that knowledge of an object is negotiated in the interaction between actors. Building on this theoretical understanding of knowledge, the study reported here suggests that dialogue among team members as well as between team members and others in the organization is central to the production of new knowledge. This supports the work of Cicourel (1990); Purser, Pasmore, and Tenkasi (1992); and Dixon (1995), who also name dialogue as central to the production of knowledge.

However, this study goes on to draw on the insights of feminist, racial and ethnic, critical, and postmodern scholars to explicitly point to the existence of differences in the amount of power available to team members as a critical lever in determining team-learning success. Team-learning processes that include the unique bodies of knowledge and information distributed among employees throughout the organization are severely inhibited by differences in the power available to individual employees. Team leaders can address these differences and enhance team learning in the technical domain by controlling power differences in ways similar to Hal's use of empowerment ideology. However, in order to enhance team learning in the social domain, power differences must be eliminated. In other words, in order to remake the culture of the organization, power differences among team members must not simply be controlled; they must be eliminated. Such power differences result in the exclusion rather than the integration of multiple and divergent perspectives and thus severely limit the learning that is possible by teams in work organizations.

Research Implications

In the future, to better understand how power differences among team members interact with collective team learning, research should be conducted that examines team learning within different contexts. Although the four teams reported here varied substantially, the organization within which they functioned represented only a small portion of the spectrum of organizations within which learning teams are being utilized. In particular, teams within organizations with different purposes, in different places within their life cycle, and with various configurations of structured authority need to be studied. Teams within large and small, new and declining, government and private, and hierarchical and flat organizations all need to be examined.

Studies might also be conducted on teams that have as their explicit goal the production of knowledge within the social domain of the organization. Teams that reflect on, critique, and develop strategies to change organizational structures and policies should be explored to see what happens when they are explicitly charged with remaking social structures within the organization.

On the whole, as the move toward team-based organizations is coupled with the intention to change unproductive ways of organizing ourselves for work in organizations, more research needs to be done on team learning. In particular, we need to design research that takes into account the ways in which our patterns of thought and behavior that are taken for granted are culturally and historically structured. Collective team learning cannot be understood outside of its cultural and historical context.

Conclusion

Based on an analysis of the study reported here, I have identified the distribution of formal power as a critical lever in the successful collective production of knowledge by teams. I have also explored how the context of the particular organization and the current cultural and historical context in the United States interact to produce the team-learning experiences described in this study. Although I propose that power differences among team members and the insufficient power of some team members to control their own time, movement, and work are critical levers influencing the successful production of knowledge by teams in a variety of organizations, I make no claims of generalizability. In similar studies in the future, the way in which the distribution of formal power interacts with the collective production of knowledge is likely to be influenced by the organization's type, its size, the racial and gender makeup of its members, and its place in an organizational life cycle. The influence of these and other contextual factors will influence how power is distributed and used by individual employees. Similarly, I acknowledge that the interaction will probably be influenced by the composition of individuals on a team, the type of knowledge the team is trying to produce, and the norms and values of the organization.

In the United States, team learning is likely to be profoundly affected by deep-rooted assumptions about the superiority of technical rationality as a way of knowing and competitive individualism as a way of relating. Even if we personally find these particular qualities of our national culture at odds with our gender of local cultural experiences, the institutions that dominate much of public life are structured so that it is difficult to live out and express a different cultural pattern. Similarly, many of the institutions to which we work reflect these deeply rooted assumptions about technical rationality and competitive individualism. Even if we can see the limitations of this worldview, and this is often very difficult, we may be stymied in our efforts to envision or create more appropriate ones. The appearance of more and more teams with the goal of producing new and useful knowledge for work organizations is an example of our attempt to transcend the limitations of our own history and culture. Although collective team learning is problematic to implement in current organizations, it stands as an important example of our ability to imagine and enact alternative ways of relating and knowing.

References

Allen, N. (1984). *Managing the flow of technology. Technology transfer and the dissemination of technological information within the R & D organization.* Cambridge, MA: MIT Press.

Ancona, D. G., & Caldwell, D. F. (1990). Information technology and work groups. The case of new product teams. In J. Galegher, R. E. Kraut, & C. Egido (eds), *Intellectual teamwork* (pp. 173-190). Hillsdale, NJ: Lawrence Erlbaum.

Apple, M. (1982). *Cultural and economic reproduction in education.* New York: Routledge & Kegan Paul.

Austin, A. E., & Baldwin, R. G. (1991). *Faculty collaboration: Enhancing the quality of scholarship and teaching* (Ashe-Eric Report No. 7). Washington, DC: George Washington University.

Bellah, R., Madsen, R., Sullivan, W., Swidler, A., & Lipton, S. (1985). *Habits of the heart.* New York: HarperCollins.

Berger, P. L., & Luckmann, I. (1967). *The social construction of reality.* London: Allen Lane.

Brooks, A. (1992). Building learning organizations. The individual culture interaction. *Human Resource Development Quarterly, 3*(3), 323-335.

Cicourel, A. V. (1987). Cognitive and organizational aspects of medical diagnostic reasoning. *Discourse Processes, 10,* 347-367.

Cicourel, A. V. (1990). The integration of distributed knowledge in collaborative medical diagnosis. In J. Galegher, R. E. Kraut, & C. Egido (eds), *Intellectual teamwork* (pp. 221-242). Hillsdale, NJ: Lawrence Erlbaum.

Dechant, K., Marsick, V., & Kasl, E. (1993). Toward a model of team learning. *Studies in Continuing Education, 15*(1), 1-14.

Denzin, N. (1989). *Interpretive interactionism.* Newbury Park, CA: Sage.

Dickens, L. (1993). [Action research in a high technology company A case study]. Unpublished raw data.

Dixon, N. (1995). *Organizational learn cycle.* New York: McGraw-Hill.

Foucault, M. (1980). *Power and knowledge: Selected interviews and other writings 1972-1977.* New York: Pantheon Books.

Freire, P. (1972). *Cultural action for freedom.* Harmondsworth, England: Penguin Books.

Giroux, H. A. (1988). *Schooling and the struggle for public life. Critical pedagogy in the modern age.* Minneapolis: University of Minnesota Press.

Goetz, J. P., & LeCompte, M. D. (1984). *Ethnography and qualitative design in educational research.* San Diego, CA: Academic Press.

Goodman, P. S. (1986). Impact of task and technology on group performance. In P. S. Goodman & Associates (eds.), *Designing effective work groups* (pp. 120-167). San Francisco: Jossey-Bass.

Goodman, P. S., Ravlin, E. & Schminke, M. (1990). Understanding groups in organizations. In C. Cummings & B. M. Staw (eds), *Leadership, participation, and group behavior* (pp. 333-385). Greenwich, CT: JAI Press.

Gray, B. (1989). *Collaborating: Finding common ground for multiparty problems.* San Francisco: Jossey-Bass.

Habermas, J. (1973). *Knowledge and human interest.* Boston: Beacon Press.

Hackman, R. J. (1987). The design of work teams. In J. W. Borsch (ed), *Handbook of organizational behavior* (pp. 315-340). Englewood Cliffs, NJ: Prentice Hall.

hooks, b. (1989). *Talking back. Thinking feminist, thinking black.* Boston: South End Press.

Kolb, D. (1984). *Experiential learning.* Englewood Cliffs, NJ: Prentice Hall.

Kraut, R. E., Egido, C., & Galegher, J. (1990). Patterns of contact and communication in scientific research collaborations. In J. Galegher, R. E. Kraut, & C. Egado (eds), *Intellectual team-work* (pp. 149-172). Hillsdale, NJ: Lawrence Erlbaum.

Lather, P. (1991). *Getting smart. Feminist research and pedagogy with/in the postmodern.* New York: Routledge & Kegan Paul.

Lazega, F. (1992). *The micropolitics of knowledge.* New York: Aldine de Gruyter.

Lewis, K. (1993). *Why leaders support common principles of Total Quality Management.* Unpublished doctoral dissertation, University of Texas, Austin.

Lincoln, Y. S., & Guba, E. G. (1985). *Naturalistic inquiry.* Newbury Park, CA: Sage.

McGrath, J. E. (1984). *Groups: Interaction and performance.* Englewood Cliffs, NJ: Prentice Hall.

Minnich, F. K. (1991). *Transforming knowledge*. Philadelphia: Temple University Press.

Ogbu, J. (1982). *Minority education and caste: The American system in cross cultural perspective*. San Diego, CA: Academic Press.

Parker, G. M. (1990). *Team players and teamwork: The new competitive business strategy*. San Francisco: Jossey-Bass.

Pelz, D. C. & Andrews, E. M. (1966). *Scientists in organizations*. New York: Wiley.

Purser, R. E., Pasmore, W. A., & Tenkasi, R. V. (1992). The influence of deliberations on learning in new product development teams. *Journal of Engineering and Technology Management, 9*(1), 1-28.

Roland, A. (1988). *In search of the self in India and Japan*. Princeton, NJ: Princeton University Press.

Schon, D. (1983). *The reflective practitioner*. New York: Basic Books.

Schutz, A. (1964). *Collected papers II: Studies in social theory*. The Hague: Nijhoff.

Schwartzman, H. (1986). Research on work group effectiveness: An anthropological critique. In P. S. Goodman & Associates (eds.), *Designing effective work groups* (pp. 237-276). San Francisco: Jossey-Bass.

Smith, D. E. (1975). An analysis of ideological structures and how women are excluded: Consideration for academic women. *Canadian Review of Sociology and Anthropology, 12*, 353-369.

Tocqueville, A. de (1963). *Democracy in America*. (G. Lawrence, trans.). New York: Doubleday Anchor. (Original work published 1836)

IMPLICATIONS FOR HUMAN RESOURCE DEVELOPMENT PROFESSIONALS

The Brooks study links employee empowerment and the competitive need of today's companies to produce new knowledge. The researcher's propositions could serve as heuristics, encouraging HRD practitioners to explore further how member empowerment and participation shape team learning and effectiveness in organizations. Further, practitioners could use the case studies when explaining empowerment because the individual cases in the study provide specific examples of how organizational structures make it difficult for low-power members to carry out team learning tasks.

IMPLICATIONS FOR RESEARCH DESIGN AND METHODOLOGY

This study shows how qualitative case-study research can provide unique insights into complex situations. Further, it serves as a model for reporting qualitative research. Qualitative researchers sometimes have the following difficulties in publishing their studies: (a) explaining the methodology and the rigor of the study, (b) reducing enormous amounts of written data, and (c) bounding the work to fit a refereed journal article. For example, a qualitative research design may employ language that is unfamiliar to quantitative researchers (e. g., trustworthiness). Also, qualitative researchers often tell in depth the stories found in the situation. As a consequence, qualitative research reports may contain many pages of detailed context-specific information. Reporting such a study in a refereed journal that has set a page limit challenges the researcher to adequately explain the methodology and the findings while simultaneously reducing the data. This study also provides an excellent example of how to report a case study that uses emergent design to examine complex organizational issues.

IMPLICATIONS FOR FUTURE INQUIRY

Brooks generated four grounded propositions regarding team learning in work organizations. Additional research is needed to examine each proposition for teams engaged in various types of tasks, employed in various types of organizations, or influenced by various contextual factors. Also, research is needed to explore the existence of other critical levers for team learning.

OTHER RESOURCES

Barker, J. R. (1993). Tightening the iron cage: Concertive control in self-managing teams. *Administrative Science Quarterly, 38,* 408-437.

Jaeger, R. M. (1988). *Complementary methods for research in education.* Washington, DC: American Educational Research Association.

Magjuka, R. J., & Baldwin, T. T. (1991). Team-based employee involvement programs: Effects of design and administration. *Personnel Psychology, 44*(4), 793-812.

Collective Behavior
and Team Performance

James E. Driskell
Florida Maxima Corporation, Winter Park, Florida

Eduardo Salas
Naval Training Systems Center, Orlando, Florida

MODERN COMPLEX SYSTEMS REQUIRE EFFECTIVE TEAM PERFORMANCE, YET THE question of which factors determine effective teams remains to be answered. Group researchers suggest that collective or interdependent behavior is a critical component of team interaction. Furthermore, anecdotal evidence suggests that some team members are less collectively oriented than others and that the tendency to ignore task inputs from others is one factor that contributes to poor team performance. In this study we develop a procedure for differentiating collectively oriented versus egocentric team members. Experimental results confirm that collectively oriented team members were more likely to attend to the task inputs of other team members and to improve their performance during team interaction than were egocentric team members.

Modern complex systems, such as military combat information centers, space shuttles, and commercial airliners, require effective team interaction and coordination. Traditionally, however, selection, training, and human factors efforts have focused almost exclusively on individual skills

Source: Driskell, J. E., & Salas, E. (1992). Collective behavior and team performance. *Human Factors, 34*(3), 277-288. Used by permission.

Authors' Note: The views expressed herein are those of the authors and do not reflect the official position of the U.S. Navy or Department of Defense. We wish to acknowledge the valuable input provided by Brian Mullen and two anonymous reviewers.

and technical proficiency. More recently, Foushee (1984), Foushee and Helmreich (1988), Driskell and Salas (1991), and others noted an increased recognition of the importance of team performance. In fact, a review of worldwide jet transport accidents from 1968 to 1970 documented more than 60 in which breakdown of crew coordination played a significant part (Cooper, White, and Lauber, 1979). Nevertheless, group researchers such as Hoffman (1965), Hackman and Morris (1975), and Driskell, Hogan, and Salas (1987) have lamented the fact that despite decades of research, very little is known about the factors that determine effective team performance.

One of the most obvious advantages of teams is that they offer a greater amount and variety of knowledge and skills on which to draw. Perhaps more important to team success, however, is the interdependent nature of team dynamics: team members are able to pool information, share resources, and check errors in accomplishing a task. One of the earliest studies of group performance attributed the effectiveness of groups to the ability of group members to exchange and coordinate information (Shaw, 1932). Lanzetta and Roby (1960) also recognized the importance of coordination in team performance, observing that the way in which skills were utilized was as important to team success as whether those skills were present or absent. These and other studies suggest that the ability of team members to exchange information in an interdependent manner is critical to effective group performance. Indeed, many have argued that the interdependence or collective behavior of group members—what Allport (1962) called *reciprocal give-and-take behaviors*— is the critical essence that constitutes a functioning group (see Lewin, 1948; McGrath, 1984; Steiner, 1986).

Furthermore, a lack of collective behavior is often evident in real-world descriptions of poor team performance. Foushee (1982) reported one flight crew incident in which, after ignoring repeated flight advisories from a copilot, the captain responded "just look out the damn window" (p. 1063). Other studies of real-world teams have shown that the failure to exchange information and coordinate interaction is one factor that differentiates good teams from bad ones (Foushee, Lauber, Baetge, and Acomb, 1986; Foushee and Manos, 1981). We argue that the tendency to attend to task inputs from others in an interdependent manner, which we term *collective behavior,* is a critical factor in effective team performance. We conducted an empirical study to distinguish collectively oriented team members from egocentric ones and to examine the effect of collective behavior on team task performance.

Team Coordination and Collective Behavior

One of the central features of a team (and usually one of the most obvious in terms of applied work groups) is that it is a group of people

working together. Although group tasks differ in the degree of cooperation required (see Shaw, 1981), an essential feature that differentiates a
group from an aggregate of individuals is that they interact—that is, one
person's behavior forms the basis for the other's response. In fact,
McGrath (1984) concluded that "the central feature, the 'essence' of a
group lies in the interaction of its members—the *behaving together* . . . of
two or more people" (p. 12).

Well-functioning teams are often described intuitively in terms of
coordinated behavior; we distinguish between the well-coordinated and
interdependent behavior of a set of individuals who embody the team
concept and that of a set of disparate individuals in a group context who
are perhaps more properly termed an aggregate. Sports that require high
levels of teamwork, such as basketball, illustrate this concept vividly: the
top teams that end up competing for the national championship usually
display a high level of team coordination, whereas teams that fare more
poorly often contain one or more equally talented but self-centered
ballplayers who are usually tagged as "poor team players." A more critical
example of the need for effective team member coordination is aircrew
performance. In 1982, an Air Florida B-737 rolled on takeoff and crashed
at Washington National Airport. The National Transportation Safety
Board recovered cockpit transcripts that clearly showed that the first
officer advised the captain several times of his concerns over instrument
readouts but that the captain ignored this input and continued to take
off (National Transportation Safety Board, 1982).

This concept of behavioral interdependence, which we term *collective behavior*, refers to the tendency to coordinate, evaluate, and utilize
task inputs from other group members in an interdependent manner in
performing a group task. Collective behavior is in fact one of the criteria
that define group performance; Golembiewski (1962) defined a group
as a system of "coordinated behavior" (p. 97), Shaw (1981) defined a
group as requiring "mutual influence" (p. 8), McGrath and Kravitz (1982)
defined a group as including members who are "mutually aware and take
one another into account" (p. 199), and Steiner (1986) referred to a
group's "mutual responsiveness" (p. 257).

There is some empirical evidence that collective behavior makes a
difference in how well teams perform. Davis (1969) found that the
preference for working alone versus working with a group was related
to both the amount of group discussion and group effectiveness. In
examining problem-solving groups composed of those who preferred to
work without a partner or those who preferred teamwork, he found that
the team preference groups interacted more, solved problems faster, and
were more accurate. Thomas (1957) found that groups whose members
performed a task interdependently (i.e., behavior was structured so that

subjects had to work together in an interactive manner to solve the task) were more productive. In fact, Thomas found that group performance was affected more by behavioral interdependence than by whether the task was structured by competitive or cooperative goals. Even those who worked interactively but were told to strive for individual goals said that they worked harder for the group than for themselves. Finally, studies of flight crew interaction have found that ineffective crews are characterized by a relative lack of communication and failure to exchange information effectively (Foushee et al., 1986; Foushee & Manos, 1981).

In sum, the concept of mutual interdependence pervades the literature on team interaction. Furthermore, research suggests that some team members are more collectively oriented than are others—that is, they exhibit more interdependent behavior in task groups—and this may affect team performance. Specifically, we argue that collectively oriented team members benefit from group interaction: they are able to enhance their own performance (and that of the team) by attending to others' task inputs. In effect, they benefit from the opportunity to pool information, share resources, and check errors that is afforded by the team environment. We also argue that egocentric team members, who tend to reject task input from others, will not benefit from being in a team setting.

The following research examines the influence of collective behavior on team performance. The research was carried out in two phases. Phase 1 was conducted to identify collectively oriented team players and egocentric or nonteam players. In Phase 2 teams were composed of either collectively oriented or egocentric members, and data were gathered to examine the effects of collective behavior on team task performance.

Phase 1

Overview

Consider a prototype team situation in which two persons are engaged in a collective task and must make a series of task decisions. For each decision, each person makes an initial decision, the two exchange this information, and then each offers a final team decision. Furthermore, they are in a *no-information* task environment—that is, they know nothing about their partner, the task, or their relative abilities at the task. The team members know only that they are to work together as a team. In such a situation, when team members initially disagree, we may expect them to resolve the disagreement according to an approximate 50/50 decision rule. In other words, half the time I may be right, so I will reject my partner's input; half the time my partner may be right, so I will accept my partner's input. This behavior reflects a mutual interdependence, or collective behavior, in this idealized two-person team environment.

However, some members may exhibit less team behavior—that is, they are less likely to attend to their partner's task inputs during group decision making. This type of behavior is evident in what Foushee and Helmreich (1988) call the *wrong stuff* for flight crew members: a tendency toward self-sufficiency and rejection of influence from others. For example, a team member may exhibit a more egocentric decision style by not attending to the partner's input and resolving most disagreements in his or her own favor. The first type of behavior we term *collective behavior,* and the second we term *egocentric.* The purpose of the Phase 1 study was to isolate these types of behaviors.

Method

Subjects. Participants in this study were 60 male naval technical school students who volunteered to take part in a study examining team performance. (Because some were undoubtedly "volunteered" by their commanding officer, all were given the opportunity to decline privately and anonymously when they arrived to take part in the study. One did, but the rest seemed to view this as an interesting break from normal activities.)

Procedure. Subjects were seated alone in separate laboratory rooms, where they were told that the nature of the study concerned team problem solving and that they would be working together as a team making a series of task decisions. Subjects worked in two-person teams on a task developed to operationalize relevant aspects of the group decision-making process. Each team was confronted with a series of binary choice problems: a series of slides was shown depicting two checkerboard patterns, and the subjects' task was to choose which of the two patterns in each slide contained the greater area of white. For each slide, each team member made an initial choice as to the correct answer (either the top or the bottom pattern). The two then exchanged this information (after making an initial choice, each subject saw his partner's choice), and then, after restudying the task and considering his partner's choice, each member made a final choice. The subjects were told that only final choices would be counted in determining final team scores. Initial scores were only for exchanging information, and the subjects were to take their partner's initial choice as their own final choice if they thought this would help them make a correct final team decision. To reinforce the team nature of the task, subjects were told that their final team score would be compared with that of other teams.

Initial choice feedback was controlled by computer, so that for 20 of 25 trials, subjects were faced with initial choice disagreements (that is, if they chose the top checkerboard, they saw that their partner chose the bottom one). Therefore, when initial choices disagreed, a team member could either accept his partner's initial choice as his own final choice (accepting his partner's influence) or keep his own initial choice as his final choice (rejecting his partner's input). The measure $P(s)$ is the proportion of resolutions resolved in favor of self, a measure of rejection of the partner's task input.

Phase 1 constituted a baseline, no-information task condition. This was achieved through several means. First, each subject was seated alone in a laboratory room and had no direct contact with his partner; this was done to ensure that subjects did not form initial task expectations based on their partner's status, which could have been communicated by nonverbal or other social cues. Team members were linked and communicated task choices via a computer network. Second, the subjects were told the task was unrelated to traditional skills such as math or reading, in order to dissociate performance on this task from their previous experience. Third, the task was ambiguous. Pretesting ensured that the probability of choosing either answer on any one problem trial was approximately 0.50; therefore there was no objective basis for making a decision. In this type of no-information team environment, $P(s)$ reflects a baseline propensity to reject others' influence.

Data from Driskell (1982) and others show that in such an idealized task situation, when one has no information on the task or on one's partner, $P(s)$ approximates 0.60 (this reflects a slight baseline tendency to stay with one's own choices when resolving task disagreements). Thus in an ambiguous task situation, knowing only that they are working together with a partner as a team, group members tend to reject their partners' task inputs about 60% of the time. However, in any particular subject population, this figure will range from 0.0 (representing a team member who accepts his or her partner's initial task decisions on every trial) to 1.0 (representing a team member who rejects information provided by the partner on every trial).

The purpose of Phase 1 was to establish this $P(s)$ metric for the subject population and to trisect this population into three subgroups based on $P(s)$ scores: (a) those in the highest range who constituted the egocentric group, rejecting their partners' opinions most of the time; (b) the group around the mean who constituted the collectively oriented group, and (c) those in the lowest tripartition who represented the altercentric group, accepting their partners' decisions on most all occasions.

Results

Sixty subjects took part in the baseline study. Data for four subjects were excluded from analysis because of equipment failure ($n = 2$) and failure to follow instructions ($n = 2$). The $P(s)$ measure for the subjects ranged from 0.0 to 1.0, with a mean of 0.66. On the basis of the $P(s)$ score, subjects were partitioned into three groups: (1) egocentric—19 subjects with the highest $P(s)$ (range = 1.0-0.75, mean = 0.82); (2) collectively oriented—the 21 subjects in a median $P(s)$ group (range = 0.70-0.60, mean = 0.65); and (3) altercentric—the group of 16 subjects with a lower $P(s)$ (range = 0.55-0.0, mean = 0.43). Because the purpose of this study was to identify and examine the effects of collectively oriented versus egocentric team members on team performance, the altercentric group members were dropped from further analysis. The question of how to deal with the altercentric team member, who abdicates almost every decision to other team members, was not examined in this study.

Phase 2

Overview

In Phase 2, egocentric teams, collectively oriented teams, and a control group of individuals who had not participated in Phase 1 performed a team task similar to that in Phase 1. However, there were two critical differences on this task: (a) it was not ambiguous but contained items that had correct answers, so that performance on the task could be evaluated; and (b) team members received actual rather than controlled initial choice feedback from their partners. Because team members made initial choices, received team member input, and then made final choices, Phase 2 allowed us to examine the gain in performance from initial choice to final choice for each team and to test the hypothesis that collectively oriented team members are more likely than egocentric team members to improve their performance by attending to their team member's task inputs.

Method

Subjects. Participants in Phase 2 were those subjects identified in Phase 1 as either collectively oriented or egocentric, in addition to a separate group of new participants from the same initial subject pool, who were selected to perform the Phase 2 task as individuals.

Procedure. In Phase 2 new two-person teams were composed according to *P*(s) scores from Phase 1. Condition 1 comprised egocentric teams, Condition 2 comprised collectively oriented teams, and Condition 3 comprised the group of subjects who worked on the task as individuals, making initial and final choices as in Conditions 1 and 2 but without another team member's input.

As in Phase 1, team members were seated alone in laboratory rooms. They again performed a team task, making initial choices, receiving their partner's initial choice feedback, and then making final choices on a series of checkerboard-patterned problems. However, in Phase 2 there were two changes in procedure as previously noted. First, the problems contained correct answers; slides were chosen on the basis of pretesting that yielded an average correct response of 66%, representing a task of intermediate difficulty. Second, each subject received information on his partner's initial choice prior to making a final choice.

Initial and final choices and response latency were recorded for each subject over 25 trials. At the conclusion of this task, subjects completed a questionnaire, which contained items assessing subjects' preference for working as a team member and general satisfaction with the group. After completing the questionnaire, each subject was interviewed individually, fully debriefed, and thanked for his participation.

Results

Table 8.1 presents task performance data for each of the three conditions for the 25 task trials.

Performance Scores. Performance scores (the number of correct responses out of the 25 trials) were derived for both initial choices and final choices for each subject in each of the three conditions. The primary analysis applied to the performance scores was a 3 (Condition) × 2 (Scores: initial and final) repeated-measures analysis of variance (ANOVA). This analysis revealed no significant main effect for condition, $F(2,60) = 0.38$, $p = 0.69$. There was a significant main effect for scores, $F(1,60) = 20.25$, $p < 0.0001$. Finally, there was a significant Condition × Scores interaction, $F(2,60) = 5.92$, $p < 0.005$.

An analysis of simple effects was carried out using a priori contrasts within the complete design (Kirk, 1982). First, results indicate that there was no significant change from initial score to final score for the egocentric team members of Condition 1, $F(1,60) = 1.17$, $p > 0.1$; the mean gain in performance score from initial to final choice for the 25 trials was 0.36.

Second, for the collectively oriented team members (Condition 2), there was a significant gain in performance from initial to final score,

TABLE 8.1 Performance Scores by Condition

Condition	n	P(s) Phase 2	Mean Initial Score (SD)		Mean Final Score (SD)		Mean Gain
1. Egocentric	19	0.84	16.32	(2.68)	16.68	(2.21)	0.36
2. Collectively oriented	21	0.60	15.62	(2.31)	17.33	(2.18)	1.71
3. Individuals	23	—	15.78	(2.35)	16.17	(2.37)	0.39

$F(1,60) = 29.20$, $p < 0.001$, with a mean performance gain of 1.71. The improvement in performance for collectively oriented team members was almost five times that of the egocentric team members.

Third, there was no significant performance gain for the individual performers (Condition 3), $F(1,60) = 1.66$, $p > 0.1$; the mean gain in performance scores for this condition was 0.39. Furthermore, the mean gain score for the individual task performers did not differ from that of the egocentric teams, $F(1,40) = 0.002$, $p = 0.96$. This indicates that the egocentric teams, given the opportunity to work in a team setting, benefited no more than did those who performed the task alone (see Appendix).

Finally, analysis of the $P(s)$ data for Phase 2 reveals that the subjects retained their pattern of attending or not attending to partners' input demonstrated in Phase 1. The egocentric team members rejected their partners' input when initial choices disagreed an average of 84% of the time, compared with 60% for the collectively oriented performers. A simple ANOVA indicates that this difference is statistically significant, $F(1,38) = 18.59$, $p = 0.0001$.

Response Latency. Coordinated team behavior involves the pooling of information—an information-processing function whereby team members evaluate others' input, reevaluate their own choice, and gather all available information to make a task decision. Indeed, one of the factors that allow teams to outperform individuals in certain instances is this ability to pool information and check errors (see Hill, 1982; Shaw, 1981). To assess this process, data were gathered on the latency or interval between initial and final choices for both agreement trials and disagreement trials. Following an initial choice, each subject was presented with his partner's initial choice. Subjects were instructed to look at their partner's choice, look again at the slide, and then make a final choice. Response latency was computed as the interval between initial choice and final choice.

A repeated-measures ANOVA produced a significant main effect for agreement/ disagreement trials on response latency, $F(1,38) = 8.08$, $p = 0.007$, with disagreement trials resulting in a longer response latency than agreement trials. Thus, in general it takes longer to make a task decision when team members disagree than when they agree. Of more interest is that the data also indicate a marginally significant interaction between type of group (collectively oriented vs. egocentric) and type of trial (agreement vs. disagreement), $F(1,38) = 3.56$, $p = 0.07$. The collectively oriented team members took significantly more time to make a final choice on a disagreement trial ($M = 6.04$ s) than on a trial in which initial choices agreed ($M = 5.40$), $F(1,20) = 8.83$, $p = 0.008$, reflecting the additional cognitive processing necessary to evaluate contradictory team member information and make a task resolution.

For the egocentric team members, there was no difference in response latency between agreement ($M = 5.56$) and disagreement trials ($M = 5.69$), $F(1,18) = 0.69$, $p = 0.42$. In other words, when team members' initial choices agreed, no task resolution was necessary. However, when initial choices disagreed, subjects faced the cognitive task of pooling discrepant information, evaluating partners' input, and making a team decision. These data suggest that only the collectively oriented team members were making this effort.

The latency data suggest that the egocentric team members were ignoring their partner's input—or, perhaps more specifically, simply ignoring the disagreements. This possibility can be evaluated by examining performance scores for both egocentric and collective groups on agreement trials versus disagreement trials. For collectively oriented team members, the improvement in performance from initial score to final score on disagreement trials ($M = 1.67$) was significantly greater than the improvement on agreement trials ($M = 0.05$); $F(1,20) = 28.26$, $p < 0.001$. In other words, the response of collectively oriented team members to disagreement was different from their response to agreement. This suggests that collectively oriented team members were attending to their partner's inputs and were more likely to reevaluate their initial choices when they found that they disagreed.

For egocentric team members, the improvement in performance on disagreement trials was much smaller ($M = 0.4$) but still significantly greater than the improvement on agreement trials ($M = -0.05$); $F(1,18) = 7.15$, $p = 0.015$. If egocentric team members were simply ignoring their partners, we would expect no difference in performance improvement between disagreement trials and agreement trials. However, these results suggest that the egocentric team members at least distinguished between when their partner disagreed with them and when they agreed, and thus they were not completely oblivious to their partner's actions.

These data provide a bit more insight into egocentric behavior. Although egocentric team members do not show a reliable *overall* improvement in performance during team interaction, they do show more of an improvement on disagreement trials than on agreement trials.

This analysis suggests that egocentric team members do not completely ignore their partners, but they may be less likely to use or act on the information provided by their partners when they disagree. The critical difference seems to be *not* that egocentric individuals ignore their partners and collectively oriented team members don't but that when collectively oriented team members disagree, they attend to that information and improve their performance, and when egocentric members disagree, they do not.

One further analysis of these data supports this general profile. There was no difference in the extent of initial choice disagreements between the egocentric teams ($M = 10.4$) and the collectively oriented teams ($M = 9.4$); $F(1,38) = 1.50, p > 0.1$. However, there was a significant difference on final choice disagreements between egocentric teams ($M = 8.2$) and collectively oriented teams ($M = 5.1$); $F(1,38) = 26.32, p < 0.001$. In other words, the collectively oriented teams were more likely to agree or converge on final choices than were egocentric teams.

Questionnaire Data. The postexperimental questionnaire included two items presented on a 6-point scale that asked each subject how valuable he felt his partner's input was on the task (where 1 = *extremely valuable* and 6 = *not at all valuable*) and how useful he thought it was to work on the task as a team (1 = *extremely useful*, 6 = *not at all useful*). A simple ANOVA was performed to examine differences between egocentric and collectively oriented team member responses to these items. The implication that egocentric team members are poor team players is bolstered by the fact that egocentric team members saw their partners' input as less valuable ($M = 3.84$) than did collectively oriented team members ($M = 3.15$), $F(1,37) = 4.29, p < 0.05$. Furthermore, egocentric team members believed that it was less useful to work as a team ($M = 3.63$) than did collectively oriented team members ($M = 2.65$), $F(1,37) = 7.4, p = 0.01$.

Finally, subjects were asked how satisfied they were with the group (this was assessed on a 7-point scale, where 1 = *extremely satisfied* and 7 = *extremely dissatisfied*). There was no significant difference between egocentric ($M = 2.6$) and collectively oriented team members ($M = 2.6$), $F(1,38) = 0.002, p > 0.1$. This suggests that the collective behavior construct is distinct from cohesiveness and other affective measures that assess attraction to the group.

Discussion

The pattern of decision behavior in egocentric teams reflected what Meeker (1983) has termed *mutual noncooperation* (p. 228). Results indicated that the performance of egocentric teams could be no more accurate than the initial individual inputs. In other words, egocentric team members showed no improvement in performance through the opportunity to work as a team. Further analysis suggested that egocentric team members were less likely to use the information provided by their partner and that they viewed the opportunity to work as a team, as well as their partner's input, as less valuable than did collectively oriented team members.

By contrast, collectively oriented teams were shown to outperform the initial individual scores of their members. In collectively oriented teams group members benefit from the advantages of teamwork, such as the opportunity to pool resources and correct errors—factors that make teamwork effective. In this sense these teams were more than simply an aggregate of two individual performers, and the increase in team scores reflects this fact. The increase in performance in collectively oriented teams is a measure of this *process gain*—that is, performance stemming from team interaction beyond that expected on the basis of individual input or initial ability alone.

The present results indicate that collective behavior is one factor that determines performance in a team setting. However, it is likely that the effects of collective orientation on group effectiveness will vary according to the task at hand. Tasks differ in the degree to which they require interdependence among group members, a fact recognized in the task typologies of Shaw (1973), Steiner (1972), and Herold (1978). Tasks that can be accomplished with little exchange of resources are likely to be unaffected by the collective behavior of group members. It is also likely that collective behavior is less relevant to tasks with simple technical and social demands (see Herold, 1978). However, for tasks that require interdependency of team members, transfer of information, and coordination of member activities to achieve a group product, the interdependent behavior of group members should be a significant determinant of group success. Therefore we would expect to find a greater effect of collective behavior on difficult tasks and on tasks that require a high level of interdependence.

A second factor that may moderate the effect of collective behavior on group performance is the ambiguity of the task. Van de Ven, Delbecq, and Koenig (1976) argued that one way in which groups coordinate activities to accomplish a task is through mutual adjustments among members in response to new task information. In a study of organizational work groups, they found that as task uncertainty increased, a greater amount of mutual adjustments, or coordination among group members, was required. Therefore it is likely that collective behavior is particularly important for tasks marked by high levels of uncertainty or unpredictability, such as those encountered by teams performing under stressful conditions.

Third, whereas the egocentric group member is shown to be a bad team player, he or she is likely to be an even worse team leader. When the egocentric individual is placed in the position of coordinating group activities, the group is less likely to capitalize on the heterogeneous skills and viewpoints available to the group to accomplish tasks.

Finally, it is important to note limitations of the present research, which was conducted in an experimental laboratory setting. This setting was chosen because of increased control and precision in isolating collective behavior and in testing the effects of collective behavior on team member performance. However, this setting was devoid of factors that may affect collective behavior in more natural settings. Certainly these real-world factors, such as experience with one's teammates or confidence in one's own ability, will affect the degree of mutual interdependence in decision making. Further research is required to examine the effects of collective behavior in real-world settings.

Goldstein (1986) noted the scarcity of information of a prescriptive nature to offer for training effective teams. The present research suggests that collective behavior is one critical factor in effective team performance. However, in order to propose interventions to enhance collective behavior in teams, one must first consider the nature of egocentric behavior. What impelled the egocentric individuals in this study to disregard the experimenter's instructions to work together as a team and to interact more as individuals than as team members?

Foushee and Helmreich (1988) noted that pilot selection has traditionally been based on the "wrong stuff" as far as group performance is concerned: the selected individuals are self-sufficient, somewhat egotistic, and less prone to sharing responsibility with others. This may have been the "right stuff" for a single-seat test pilot, but this approach is less likely to produce the good team players required by modern multipiloted aircraft. Furthermore, they noted that most pilots, who were selected on the basis of individual proficiency, have little real experience in situations that require teamwork. This supports our supposition that egocentric team members may have little experience as effective team players. Sampson (1977) noted that although humans are socialized from birth to be autonomous and self-sufficient, they receive little training at any time in interdependence. Indeed, team researchers have noted that when teams receive training, they invariably receive training in individual skills to the neglect of team skills (Swezey & Salas, 1992). Therefore it is likely that egocentric team members have not developed the proper schema for effective team interaction. Simulations that emphasize team coordination may be one effective means for building collective team behavior. Further research is needed examining whether relatively simple interventions focused on training team members to coordinate task inputs in a more effective manner will be successful in promoting collective behavior in teams.

APPENDIX

It should be noted that the collectively oriented group differed significantly from the other two groups in final score performance $F(1,60)$ = 10.89, p = 0.0008. However it should also be recognized that the collectively oriented group was marginally significantly different from the other two groups in initial score performance, $F(1,60)$ = 2.46 p 0.061. This suggests the possibility that the improvement in performance reported for the collectively oriented group is attributable to the fact that they were, by happenstance, lower on initial scores. If this argument were true, then when we remove the lower-scoring performers in Condition 2, there should no longer be a significant improvement in performance from initial to final score. However, this plausibility receives no support from additional analyses.

To assess this possibility, we first derived frequency ranking of all scores within Condition 2, from low to high. We then eliminate the data for the three subjects who performed most poorly on initial score in Condition 2 (approximately 15% of this sample). This resulted in an overall mean initial score for Condition 2 of 16.28 and a mean final score of 17.78. Results of a repeated-measures 3 × 2 ANOVA indicate no main effect for condition, $F(2,57)$ = 1.22, p = 0.304, a significant main effect for scores, $F(1,57)$ = 15.35, p = 0.0002 and a significant Condition × Scores interaction, $F(2,57)$ = 3.93, p = 0.025.

Next, an a priori comparison of initial scores for Condition 2 (the collectively oriented group) versus the combined egocentric and individual groups indicates that Condition 2 is equivalent to the other two conditions on initial score performance, $F(1,57)$ = 0.67, p = 0.21. Finally, an a priori comparison of initial and final scores for the collectively oriented group shows that the improvement in performance for this group is *still* significant, $F(1,57)$ = 20.25, p < 0.0001. Therefore this more fine-grained analysis, eliminating the extreme low performers so that the collectively oriented group was in fact equivalent to the other two groups in initial score performance, still shows a significant improvement in performance for the collectively oriented group. Therefore the overall improvement from initial to final score, and the significant difference from the other two conditions at the final measurement, cannot be attributed to the fact that collectively oriented subjects were lower in initial performance.

References

Allport, F. H. (1962). A structuronomic conception of behavior: Individual and collective. *Journal of Abnormal and Social Psychology, 64,* 3-30.

Cooper, G. E., White, M. D., & Lauber, J. K. (Eds.). (1979). *Resource management on the flight deck* (NASA Conference Publication 2120). Moffett Field, CA: NASA-Ames Research Center.

Davis, J. H. (1969). Individual-group problem solving, subject preference, and problem type. *Journal of Personality and Social Psychology, 13,* 362-374.

Driskell, J. E. (1982). Personal characteristics and performance expectations. *Social Psychology Quarterly, 45,* 229-237.

Driskell, J. E., Hogan, R., & Salas, E. (1987). Personality and group performance. In C. Hendrick (Ed.), *Review of personality and social psychology* (Vol. 9, pp. 91-112). Newbury Park, CA: Sage.

Driskell, J. E., & Salas, E. (1991). Group decision-making under stress. *Journal of Applied Psychology, 76,* 473-478.

Foushee, H. C. (1982). The role of communications, socio-psychological, and personality factors in the maintenance of crew coordination. *Aviation, Space, and Environmental Medicine, 53,* 1062-1066.

Foushee, H. C. (1984). Dyads and triads at 35,000 feet: Factors affecting group process and aircrew performance. *American Psychologist, 39,* 885-893.

Foushee, H. C., & Helmreich, R. L. (1988). Group interaction and flight crew performance. In E. L. Weiner & D. C. Nagel (Eds.), *Human factors in aviation* (pp. 189-228). San Diego, CA: Academic.

Foushee, H. C., Lauber, J. K., Baetge, M. M., & Acomb, D. B. (1986). *Crew performance as a function of exposure to high-density, short-haul duty cycles* (NASA Tech. Memorandum 88322). Moffett Field, CA: NASA-Ames Research Center.

Foushee, H. C., & Manos, K. L. (1981). Information transfer within the cockpit: Problems in intracockpit communications. In C. E. Billings & E. S. Cheaney (Eds.), *Information transfer problems in the aviation system* (NASA Tech. Paper 1875, pp. 63-71). Moffett Field, CA: NASA-Ames Research Center.

Goldstein, I. I. (1986). *Training on organizations: Needs assessment, development, and evaluation.* Monterey, CA: Brooks/Cole.

Golembiewski, R. T. (1962). *The small group: An analysis of research concepts and operations.* Chicago: University of Chicago Press.

Hackman, J. R., & Morris, C. G. (1975). Group tasks, group interaction process, and group performance effectiveness: A review and proposed integration. In L. Berkowitz (Ed.), *Advances in experimental social psychology* (Vol. 8, pp. 45-99). New York: Academic.

Herold, D. M. (1978). Improving the performance effectiveness of groups through a task-contingent selection of intervention strategies. *Academy of Management Review, 3,* 315-325.

Hill, G. W. (1982). Group versus individual performance: Are N + 1 heads better than one? *Psychological Bulletin, 91,* 517-539.

Hoffman, I. R. (1965). Group problem solving. In L. Berkowitz (Ed.), *Advances in experimental social psychology* (Vol. 2, pp. 99-132). New York: Academic.

Kirk, R. E. (1982). *Experimental design: Procedures for the behavioral sciences.* Monterey, CA: Brooks/Cole.

Lanzetta, J. T., & Ruby, T. B. (1960). The relationship between certain group process variables and group problem-solving efficiency. *Journal of Social Psychology, 52,* 135-148.

Lewin, K. (1948). *Resolving social conflicts.* New York: Harper.

McGrath, J. E. (1984). *Groups: Interaction and performance.* Englewood Cliffs, NJ: Prentice Hall.

McGrath, J. E., & Kravitz, D. A. (1982). Group research. *Annual Review of Psychology, 33,* 195-230.

Meeker, B. F. (1983). Cooperative orientation, trust, and reciprocity. *Human Relations, 37,* 225-243.

National Transportation Safety Board. (1982). *Aircraft accident report—Air Florida, Inc., Boeing 737-222, N62AF, collision with 14th Street Bridge, near Washington National Airport, Washington, DC, January 13, 1982* (NTSB-AAR-82-8). Washington, DC: Author.

Sampson, E. E. (1977). Psychology and the American ideal. *Journal of Personality and Social Psychology, 35,* 767-782.

Shaw, Marjorie E. (1932). A comparison of individuals and small groups in the rational solution of complex problems. *American Journal of Psychology, 44,* 491-504.

Shaw, Marvin E. (1973). Scaling group tasks: A method for dimensional analysis. *JSAS Catalog of Selected Documents in Psychology, 3,* 8 (Ms. 294).

Shaw, Marvin E. (1981). *Group dynamics: The psychology of small group behavior.* New York: McGraw-Hill.

Steiner, I. D. (1972). *Group process and productivity.* New York: Academic.

Steiner, I. D. (1986). Paradigms and groups. In L. Berkowitz. (Ed.), *Advances in experimental social psychology* (Vol. 19, pp. 251-289). Orlando, FL: Academic.

Swezey, R., & Salas, E. (Eds.). (1992). *Teams: Their training and performance.* Norwood, NJ: Ablex.

Thomas, E. J. (1957). Effects of facilitative role interdependence in group functioning. *Human Relations, 10,* 347-366.

Van de Ven, A. H., Delbecq, A. L., & Koenig, R. (1976). Determinants of coordination modes within organizations. *American Sociological Review, 41,* 322-338.

IMPLICATIONS FOR HUMAN RESOURCE DEVELOPMENT PROFESSIONALS

Because team effectiveness is related to the participation of all members in team decisions and to the interdependence of the group (Campion et al., Chapter 6), this study has important implications for HRD practitioners who are diagnosing team performance within their organizations. On synthesis, Driskell and Salas, Campion et al., and Brooks (Chapter 7) provide insight into barriers to team performance. Member empowerment and participation aid information exchange among team members and shape team learning and effectiveness. But structural barriers to information exchange exist (see Brooks). Another barrier to information exchange is the tendency of egocentric team members to ignore task inputs from others (see Driskell and Salas). HRD practitioners should consider barriers when diagnosing poor work group performance.

IMPLICATIONS FOR RESEARCH DESIGN AND METHODOLOGY

This study was conducted in an experimental laboratory setting. The research method involved first collecting baseline data related to collectively oriented and egocentric team members. The researchers then collected data related to the performance, the satisfaction, and the perceived value for collectively oriented and egocentric teams.

IMPLICATIONS FOR FUTURE INQUIRY

Driskell and Salas pointed out that real-world factors such as experience with other team members or confidence in one's own abilities could affect the degree of mutual interdependence in decision making. Future research should examine the effects of these factors. Further, as Driskell and Salas noted, research should examine how these effects vary based on the amount of interdependence required by the task or the extent of task ambiguity.

OTHER RESOURCES

Druckman, D., & Bjork, R. A. (Eds.). (1994). *Learning, remembering, believing: Enhancing human performance.* Washington, DC: National Academy Press.

Team Building

An Experimental Investigation of the Effects of Computer-Based and Facilitator-Based Interventions on Work Groups

Timothy R. McClernon
CIGNA Corporation, Hartford, CT

Richard A. Swanson
University of Minnesota, St. Paul

THIS STUDY EXAMINED THE EFFECTS OF USING A GROUP DECISION SUPPORT *System (GDSS) and outside facilitation support in a three-hour team-building process on the attainment of "team." Twenty-four preexisting work groups (N = 186) were randomly assigned to three treatments: (1) a facilitated team-building process without computer support, (2) a facilitated team-building process with computer support, and (3) normally scheduled meetings without a facilitation or computer support. Twelve dependent "team" measures were assessed using a self-report questionnaire following the team-building session (immediate effect) and following the next normally scheduled group meeting (delayed effect).*

On immediate-effect measures, both facilitated team building processes resulted in higher member ratings of group process than ratings for meetings with no outside facilitation. On most measures, the

Source: McClernon, T. R., & Swanson, R. A. (1995). Team building: An experimental investigation of the effects of computer-based and facilitator-based interventions on work groups. *Human Resource Development Quarterly,* 6(1), 39-48. Used by permission.

positive immediate effects did not last over time, indicating that the three-hour team-building session was not effective. The implications for practice are severe in that both team building and GDSS technology are often implemented as one-time interventions. It is common practice to use these techniques and/or methods as a three- to four-hour component of a development session or as part of a specific task-related meeting.

HRD professionals, along with behavioral scientists, leaders, and technologists, have been focusing on methods and processes for increasing overall team effectiveness and overcoming problems associated with team performance. HRD professionals prepare team members to use effective team skills, develop lists of characteristics to differentiate high- and low-performance teams, and design team-building interventions to develop more successful teams. These all share a focus on accomplishing interdependent objectives through a group process.

However, accomplishing work through teams has not always been more effective or more efficient than accomplishing work through individuals. While teams may outperform individuals at certain times, researchers have found that at other times the collaborative effort of the team does not exceed or equal the performance of the best individual on the team (Shaw, 1978). Teams can make notoriously bad decisions in myriad ways (Janis, 1982; Harvey, 1988). Process losses result from the additional problems created when people work together (Steiner, 1966). Norms, the hidden rules that build high performance levels, can also work to reinforce patterns of low productivity (Whyte, 1955).

Many structured techniques and procedures have been developed to improve group performance, but more are needed (Hackman, 1987). Traditional procedures for overcoming process losses include parliamentary procedure and Robert's Rules of Order. Newer procedures include the Delphi method (Dalkey, 1969; Dalkey and Halmer, 1963) and the nominal group technique (Van De Ven and Delbecq, 1974). The newest procedures include the application of computer technologies in the form of group decision support systems (GDSSs) (DeSanctis and Gallupe, 1987; Gray, 1983; Huber, 1982, 1984). Kraemer and King (1988) identified six types of GDSS: electric boardroom, information center, teleconferencing facility, decision conference, local area group network, and collaboration laboratory.

Solutions to team performance problems have centered around the use of procedures and facilitation to increase group performance. Group procedures of almost any type have been shown to increase group outcomes (Poole, 1991). For example, the use of procedures such as the nominal group technique and the Delphi process have been shown to generate a greater quantity and quality of ideas (Delbecq, Van De Ven, and Gustafson, 1975). In addition, the use of a facilitator has been shown to increase process and content performance (Anson, 1990). An additional answer to this group performance problem may be the application of GDSS technologies as a mode to incorporate procedural management into groups.

Poole (1991) suggests four benefits of GDSS: (1) it presents procedures consistently and competently, (2) it makes procedures more convenient, (3) it makes the beneficial effects of procedures obvious, and (4) it provides new methods of meeting. Using GDSS features such as modeling tools, data bases, and group authoring support, groups may be able to perform tasks they normally would not attempt as a group.

Advances in information technology systems have created GDSSs that may be adapted by HRD professionals for use in team-building applications. If these computer-based systems can increase the benefits or decrease the costs associated with team performance, they could be an important tool for improving team effectiveness. Researchers have identified a number of structural features in GDSSs that affect team outcomes: anonymity, parallel processing or simultaneous input, public display, meeting structure, electronic display and recording, and an information-processing capability (Bostrom and Anson, 1988; DeSanctis and Gallupe, 1987; Nunamaker, Applegate, and Konsynski, 1987; Poole and DeSanctis, 1987; Zigurs, 1987). Three classes of benefits based on these features have been identified by Kraemer and Pinsonneault (1989): affective benefits from the introduction of new ways of running meetings and enlisting cooperation, protocol facilitation benefits from structuring and streamlining processes, and information-quality benefits from using mathematical models and data sources. These features—particularly anonymity, full member participation, and democratic decision making— are seen as important elements of team building.

Research Question and Hypotheses

The purpose of the study was to determine the work effects a GDSS has on ongoing managerial and nonmanagerial groups during a three-hour team-building process. The general research question was: What are the effects of computer-based and facilitator-based team-building interventions on a team task among intact work groups?

The framework for this research consisted of three treatments. Two used team building, one each without computer support (T_1) and with computer support (T_2). The third group was a control (T_3). The measures administered at the end of each meeting assessed team performance and process outcomes. The basic hypothesis was that none of the groups would differ in any way on any of the dependent variables. The specific null hypotheses were as follows:

HYPOTHESIS 1: *Cohesion will not significantly differ between T_1, T_2, and T_3.*

HYPOTHESIS 2: *Quality of group process will not significantly differ between T_1, T_2, and T_3.*

HYPOTHESIS 3: *Participants' behaviors will not significantly differ between T_1, T_2, and T_3.*

HYPOTHESIS 4: *Solution satisfaction* (performance) *will not significantly differ between T_1, T_2, and T_3.*

HYPOTHESIS 5: *Socioemotional behavior will not significantly differ between T_1, T_2, and T_3.*

HYPOTHESIS 6: *Decision-scheme satisfaction will not significantly differ between T_1, T_2, and T_3.*

HYPOTHESIS 7: *Personal task participation will not significantly differ between T_1, T_2, and T_3.*

HYPOTHESIS 8: *Informal leadership will not significantly differ between T_1, T_2, and T_3.*

HYPOTHESIS 9: *Confidence in conclusion will not significantly differ between T_1, T_2, and T_3.*

HYPOTHESIS 10: *Depth of evaluation will not significantly differ between T_1, T_2, and T_3.*

HYPOTHESIS 11: *Perceived change in understanding will not significantly differ between T_1, T_2, and T_3.*

HYPOTHESIS 12: *Commitment to implement results will not significantly differ between T_1, T_2, and T_3.*

Summary of the Literature

This summary is divided into three areas: small-group research, team building, and computer-based support for groups (GDSS). Each of these areas was extensively reviewed.

Small-Group Research

McGrath's conceptual framework for the study of groups (1984) has been proposed as a theoretical model for research on a group process involving the GDSS (DeSanctis & Gallupe, 1987; Zigurs, Poole, & DeSanctis, 1988). McGrath's taxonomy distinguishes the relatively stable characteristics of the standing group (existing relationships between group members) as distinct from the dynamic processes of the acting group (the behavior created between members in relation to a specific task or situation and environment) (Miranda, 1991). This model provides a taxonomy of four classes of variables and relationships that must be accounted for in systematic group research. The influence of the four classes of variables—standing (preexisting) group characteristics, task characteristics, individual differences, and environmental variables—can be monitored or manipulated to determine their effects on the acting group processes and outcomes.

To measure the effects of differences in treatment, this study adapted an available instrument from a leading training-and-development-resources firm that addressed the areas of goals and objectives, utilization of resources, trust and conflict, leadership, control and procedures, interpersonal communication, problem solving and decision making, experimentation and creativity, evaluation, roles and responsibilities, and organizational context (Alexander, 1985; Phillips & Elledge, 1989).

Team Building

A number of criteria have been identified as important to an effective team (Likert, 1961; McGregor 1960, 1967). Measures of team effectiveness can be considered in terms of both performance and process outcomes.

The research on team-building interventions shows mixed results. A review of thirteen published studies conducted between 1980 and 1990 yielded nine that considered ultimate team performance. Of these nine, only four showed performance improvement. Ten of the studies used some form of interpersonal intervention in conjunction with another type of intervention. The conclusion of the review was that "in some circumstances team development interventions may have enhanced work group effectiveness" (Sundstrom, DeMeuse, & Futrell, 1990, p. 128).

Traditional team-building interventions generally focus on a performance improvement cycle consisting of problem recognition, data gathering, data analysis (diagnosis), feedback and action-planning sessions, implementation, and follow up and evaluation (Dyer, 1987). The team work performance improvement process for the present study followed a simplified version of this model, consisting of data collection, data analysis, feedback, and action planning (Nadler, 1977).

Computer-Based Support for Groups

Experimental research has shown inconsistent results concerning differences in decision quality between GDSS and non-GDSS groups, while field studies have shown increased decision quality. Readers are directed to a number of well-written reviews of GDSS research (Anson, 1990; Dennis et al., 1988; George, Easton, Nunamaker, & Northcraft, 1990; Kraemer & King, 1988).

Anson (1990) suggests that a primary reason for the differences between GDSS laboratory and field study findings may be the key differences in facilitation, a position supported by Dennis, Nunamaker, and Vogel (1989). They showed that groups with facilitator support and computer support outperformed groups without support or groups with only computer support. Process perceptions were significantly improved in groups that received facilitator support over computer support (Anson, 1990).

Significant differences in decision making exist based on the degree of human support provided to the group. Facilitated use of the GDSS showed benefits over user-driven use of the GDSS (Anson, 1990; Dickson, Lee, Robinson, and Heath, 1989). Increased experience on the system showed a higher degree of comfort (Miranda, 1991). Many of the studies may show different results as groups develop greater expertise and understanding of how to use or manipulate the GDSS. Many of the initial research results may not remain valid when group learning occurs and participants' ability to use and understand the GDSS increases (Gallupe, DeSanctis, & Dickson, 1988).

This study used a GDSS called DISCOURSE. Each participant has a keypad, networked to the facilitator's computer. The facilitator uses the DISCOURSE software to control how participant responses are collected, displayed, reported, scored, and used as a basis for discussion. DISCOURSE has more tools than keypad-based GDSSs, but it does not have the higher-level tools used in systems based on networked computers.

Research Methodology

A number of group performance and process outcome measures were used to assess and compare the three treatment groups; they are displayed in Figure 9.1.

Experimental Design

A three-hour team-building session was facilitated for the experimental treatments. Treatment 1 (T_1) teams consisted of a team-building session without the assistance of computer support. Treatment 2 (T_2) teams consisted of a similar team-building session that used GDSS technology for computer support. The teams in T_1 and T_2 then held their next regularly scheduled meeting, which became part of the experiment. A control treatment (T_3) team assessed their own two regularly scheduled meeting without a team-building intervention (see Figure 9.2).

At the beginning of the first meeting, participants completed a background questionnaire and measure of group cohesion. At the end of the first meeting, they completed a postmeeting questionnaire that addressed dependent measures of group cohesion, performance, and processes. An identical questionnaire was completed at the end of their

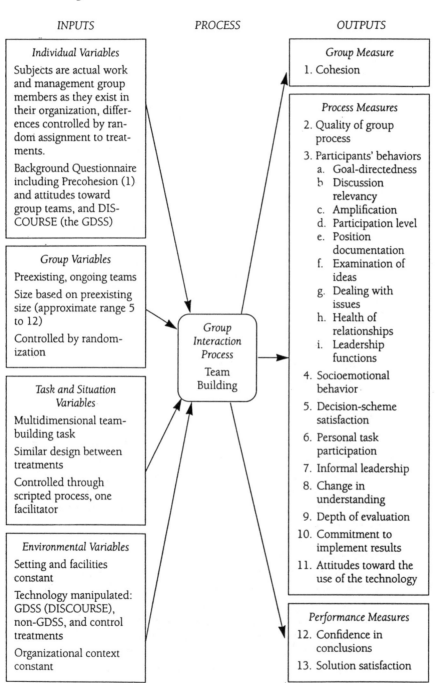

Figure 9.1. Overview of Research Design Showing Research Variables in the Context of an Input, Process, and Output Model of Group Process

Groups	Time 1 Pretreatment	Time 2 Immediate	Time 3 Delayed
1. Team Building	M_1 T Team Building	M_{1-13} T Team Meeting	M_{1-13}
2. Team Building plus Computer Support	M_1 T Team Building	M_{1-13} T Team Meeting	M_{1-13}
3. Control, Meetings Only	M_1 T Team Meeting	M_{1-13} T Team Meeting	M_{1-13}

Key: T = Treatment   M= Measurement
M_1 = Team cohesion
M_{2-11} = Team-process measures
M_{12-13} = Team-performance measures

Figure 9.2. Experimental Research Design Displaying Treatments and Measures Over Time

next regularly scheduled meeting as a team, assessing that meeting's group-process and group performance outcomes.

Properties of the Team Task

A unique aspect of this study is the team-building focus of the task. A team-building task—or more technically, a team-building process—was developed specifically for this study. The task requirements of this team-building process benefited primarily from the information-processing, display, simultaneous-data-entry, and anonymity features of the GDSS. The nontechnology treatment benefited from the use of a facilitator and a data-based process (data collection, analysis, feedback, and action planning) to carry out the team-building task.

The team-building process started with a set of questions based on a group-effectiveness critique published in a leading team-building sourcebook (Alexander, 1985). These items address key dimensions of a group's effectiveness: goals and objectives, utilization of resources, trust and conflict, leadership, control and procedures, interpersonal communication, problem solving and decision making, experimentation and creativity, evaluation, and roles and responsibilities.

The team-building task consisted of several parts: (1) introduction to team building, which included rating the group on a seven-point degree-of-collaborative-work scale as they were working together at the time of the experiment and as they would ideally work together in the future; (2) data collection, analysis, and feedback, using a survey of twelve group dimensions; (3) discussion of the survey data; (4) brainstorming a list of group strengths; (5) brainstorming a list of areas to focus on to improve the group's functioning; and (6) creating an action plan of specific ways the group could improve their performance in the future, including prioritizing items and assigning specific members the responsibility to complete each item.

Subjects and Groups

This study focused on naturally occurring groups within the nonprofit organization. The groups were either intact work groups or long-term task forces. Differences were controlled by randomly assigning treatments to groups as well as by using a sufficient number of individuals to allow for a statistically insignificant chance that differences in individual group members would affect research outcomes. The pretreatment survey asked several questions concerning individual members' experiences and backgrounds, which were used to statistically verify randomization of individual differences and possible individual differences affecting outcomes. Questions concerning such issues as how long members had belonged to their group, attitudes toward team building, attitudes toward using the GDSS, work experience, familiarity with computers, and other demographic data were included.

Because the study was based on existing, ongoing groups, group size, by necessity, varied naturally according to the size of the groups in the organization. In this organization, the group size varied from five to twelve members. Randomization of treatments to groups controlled for confounding effects based on group size. There were a total of 186 subjects and 24 groups—8 groups for each treatment.

Another control variable was the perceived attitudes toward the use of the technology by the subjects who participated in the computer-supported team-building sessions. Sambamurthy's questionnaire (1989) to assess participants' attitudes toward the technology in GDSS sessions provided some indication of how the participants using GDSS support responded to the technology. Three factors were assessed with this questionnaire: level of challenge introduced into the task by the technology, level of respect for the technology, and users' comfort with the technology.

Properties of the Team-Building Environment

Two aspects of the environment were considered: setting and facilitation. In this study, variables associated with the setting and the procedures were controlled. Each group met in the same room at an off-site conference center operated by the larger organization. The room consisted of a U-shaped arrangement with small tables in front of the participants. At the front of the room were two flipcharts, a large-screen projection device and screen, and the computer used by the facilitator. Keyboards were situated in front of each participant. For the groups not using the technology, the same arrangement and room were used, but the GDSS equipment was removed.

Facilitation is a major factor in a GDSS group process. To control for facilitation in this study, key parts of the team-building process were scripted to increase the similarity of the facilitations among sessions. In addition, the same person facilitated all groups in the experiment, helping to control for possible differences in facilitation across groups.

Dependent Variables and Analysis

The dependent variables involved performance and process measures. The variables and the analysis of the resulting data follow.

Performance Measures. Two performance measures were assessed: solution satisfaction and confidence in conclusions. A set of five self-report questions was used concerning the participants' level of satisfaction with the solutions. Participants answered five questions on the Green and Taber questionnaire (1980) to arrive at a satisfaction-with-solution rating. A reliability coefficient of .88 was reported for this scale. Sambamurthy (1989) devised and validated an eight-item measure to assess the degree of certainty group members felt toward the group's conclusions.

Process Measures. The nature of this team-building task did not lend itself to common organizational performance measures. Thus, a focus on the processes occurring in the group became an alternate means of assessing group performance. In certain situations, such as decision making, where the link between process and outcomes is difficult to establish, researchers argue that the process by which an issue is considered may be more important than assessing the actual outcome (Rohrbaugh, 1988).

Process measures used in this study included the perceived quality of the group process, group behavioral measures, decision-scheme satisfaction, personal task participation, socioemotional behavior, confidence in conclusions, commitment to implement results, perceived change in understanding, perceived depth of evaluation, and attitudes toward the technology.

Analysis of the Data

The analysis of the data corresponds to the general research question and the twelve hypotheses. Testing of the hypotheses required a nested analysis of covariance. The model statement for the analysis considered the effects of treatments, groups within treatment, and individuals within groups. Assuming that groups were random, the appropriate *F* ratio for testing treatment differences was *F* equals means squared of treatments over means squared of groups within treatments.

A special *t*-test for multiple comparisons, Duncan's multiple-range test, was used when significant results appeared with any of the nested analysis of variance (ANOVA) procedures. Duncan's multiple-range test accounts for the variances of all the groups rather than only the variance of the two specific groups being compared. This minimizes the probability that significant differences between mean scores will occur simply because multiple comparisons are made on the same data (Borg and Gall, 1989). In the tables of statistical analysis results, the Duncan's test result is assumed to show that the means of T_1 = the means of T_2 = the means of T_3, unless shown otherwise. In the footnotes to the tables showing the results of the covariate analysis, the Duncan's test results did not change from the results reported in the table unless it is stated as such in the footnote.

The analysis was conducted in exactly the same way as the experiment. A straightforward ANOVA on the individual scores would have ignored the effect of the group on the individual scores. The individual scores are not necessarily independent measures. For example, if one person in a group rated cohesion high, it is probable that other members of the group would also rate the measure high. Because the ANOVA assumes independence of measures, using a straightforward ANOVA without accounting for group effect would not be appropriate for this study. Performing an ANOVA on the group-level data without nesting would fail to produce the appropriate *F* statistic based on the reduced-error term for groups within treatments.

Individual and Group Characteristics

Because groups were randomly assigned to treatments, it may be assumed that significant differences between the groups making up the samples for the three treatments have been statistically accounted for. In addition, an analysis of the treatment groups showed no significant difference ($p < .05$) on the variables of sex, age, employment status, amount of time spent in meetings, typing ability, previous team-building experience, attitudes toward teamwork and groups, and attitudes toward using the GDSS.

Another key variable that could have interacted with other variables was difference in group size. An ANOVA at the group level on differences in group size showed no significant difference (means squared = 3.88, $F = 1.16$, $df = (2, 21)$, $p = .3314$).

Task

At the end of each session, participants answered a series of eight questions based on McGrath's taxonomy (1984) to rate the tasks completed during the meeting. A multivariate analysis of variance of the scores for the eight questions that compared the team-building task meetings with the regular meetings did reveal the existence of significant differences (Wilks's Lambda = .79, $F = 2.24$, $df = (16,290)$, $p = .0045$). The team-building task meetings differed from regular meetings by being rated as requiring multiple solutions (versus a specific solution), having more intrinsic interest, requiring slightly more cooperation, being possibly less familiar, and being more important. The scores indicated that T_2 participants rated the computer-supported team-building process more like a regular meeting than did the T_1 participants who did not receive computer support. Comparisons of the differences between ratings of the task on the delayed measures were not significant (Wilks's Lambda = .86, $F = 1.37$, $df = (16,282)$, $p = .1573$).

Results

The results in relation to the research hypotheses, considering each of the dependent or output measures, are summarized in Table 9.1.

The cohesiveness of the groups did not significantly differ over time (H_1). While both team-building treatments showed an increase from when they started, the increase was not enough to be significant.

For the measures concerning group performance (H_{12}), solution satisfaction did not differ between the team-building treatments. The team-building groups in general were significantly better than the control groups in producing a higher level of solution satisfaction.

Process measures (H_2–H_{11}) showed considerable differences between team-building treatments and between the combined team-building treatments and the control. During team building with computer support, participants were significantly less likely to have one or two members dominate the meeting than in the other two treatments. Socioemotional behaviors in the team-building-with-computer-support treatment were significantly better than in the control treatment, but not significantly different from the team-building-without-computer-support treatment. In summary, computer support reduced member domination and, to a lesser degree, created more positive socioemotional behaviors.

TABLE 9.1 Summary of Results for the Null Hypotheses

Dependent Variable ($T_1 = T_2 = T_3$)	Unit of Analysis	Immediate Effect	Duncan's Test[a]	Delayed Effect	Duncan's Test[a]
H_1 Cohesion	Indiv.	Reject*	2 > 3	Accept	
	Group	Accept		Accept	
H_2 Quality of group process	Indiv.	Reject**	1 > 2 > 3	Reject*	3>2
	Group	Reject*	1 > 3	Accept	
H_3 Behavior scales (overall)	Indiv.	Reject**	1, 2 > 3	Accept	
	Group	Reject*	1, 2 > 3	Accept	
H_4 Solution satisfaction	Indiv.	Reject**	1, 2 > 3	Accept	
	Group	Accept		Accept	
H_5 Socioemotional behaviors	Indiv.	Reject*	2 > 3	Reject*	1, 3 > 2
	Group	Accept		Accept	
H_6 Decision-scheme satisfaction	Indiv.	Reject*	1, 2 > 3	Accept	
	Group	Accept		Accept	
H_7 Personal Task Participation	Indiv.	Accept		Accept	
	Group	Accept		Accept	
H_8 Informal leadership	Indiv.	Reject**	2 > 1 > 3	Reject*	2 > 3
	Group	Reject**	2, 1 > 3	Accept	
H_9 Confidence in conclusions[b]	Indiv.	Reject*	2 > 1, 3	Accept	
	Group	Accept		Accept	
H_{11} Change in understanding	Indiv.	Reject	1 > 3	Accept	
	Group	Accept		Accept	
H_{12} Commitment to implement results	Indiv.	Accept		Accept	
	Group	Accept		Accept	

a. Duncan's multiple-range-test results are reported if significant differences in means are detected, 1 = team-building treatment, 2 = team-building-with-computer-support treatment, 3 = control treatment.
b. H_{10}, "depth of evaluation," was eliminated due to an unacceptable reliability score.
*p <.05; **p <.01.

The team-building-without-computer-support treatment was perceived as providing a significantly higher quality group process, but the team-building-with-computer-support treatment equalized the amount of influence for each member in the group (informal leadership) better than the other treatments. Also, leadership functions and change in understanding were perceived as significantly better than in the control groups, but not significantly different from the other team-building treatment.

The facilitated team-building sessions, with and without computer support, differed significantly from the regular meetings on eight mea-

TABLE 9.2 Differences Between Treatment Groups on Measures
Immediately Following Treatment

Both Team-Building Treatments Over Control	Team-Building-With-Computer-Support Treatment	Team-Building-Without-Computer-Support Treatment	Control
1. Quality of group process	1. Cohesion (over the control)	1. Quality of group process (over team building with computer support and over the control[a])	None
2. Behavior scales[a] (overall)	2. Quality of group process (over the control and less than the other team-building treatment)		
3. Goal-directed behavior		2. Informal leadership (over the control)	
4. Relevancy of discussion	3. Socioemotional behaviors (over the control)	3. Change in understanding (over the control)	
5. Amplifications of contributions[a]			
6. Distribution of participation			
7. Documentation of positions[a]			
8. Dealing with issues			
9. Leadership functions			
10. Solution satisfaction			
11. Decision-scheme satisfaction			
12. Informal leadership[a]			

a. The significant difference was also found using the group as the unit of analysis.

sures: quality of group process, goal-directed behavior, relevancy of discussion, amplification of participants' contributions, even distribution of participation, documentation of positions, systematically dealing with issues, and solution satisfaction.

In summarizing the results over time, differences were detected on five process measures. The team-building-without-computer-support treatment was significantly higher than the team-building-with-computer-support treatment on these measures: goal-directed behavior, documentation of positions, healthier interpersonal relationships, leadership functions fulfilled, and more positive socioemotional behaviors. In addition, the team-building-without-computer-support treatment was significantly better than the control on the measure concerning documentation of positions.

The significant results for the immediate and delayed measurements are summarized in Tables 9.2 and 9.3. Table 9.4 provides a review of findings based on a comparison of the difference scores between groups and by treatment.

TABLE 9.3. Differences Between Treatment Groups on Delayed Measures

Both Team-Building Treatments Over Control	Team-Building-With-Computer-Support Treatment	Team-Building-Without-Computer-Support Treatment	Control
None	1. Informal leadership (over the control)	1. Goal-directed behavior (over team building with computer support)	1. Quality of group process (over team building with computer support)
		2. Documentation of positions (over team building with computer support and the control[a])	2. Goal-directed behavior (over team building with computer support)
		3. Leadership functions (over team building with computer support)	3. Interpersonal relationships (over team building with computer support)
		4. Socioemotional behaviors (over team building with computer support)	4. Leadership functions (over team building with computer support)
			5. Socioemotional behaviors (over team building with computer support)

a. The significant difference was also found using the group as the unit of analysis.

Both team-building treatments were consistently higher than the control on measures of immediate effects. Measures of team building with computer support did not greatly differ from measures of team building without computer support. The use of the technology apparently reduced the unequal influence of one or two people (informal leadership). Measures of team-building-without-computer-support groups were significantly higher in terms of perceived quality of group process. Measures of the delayed effects suggest that there may be some difference; the groups receiving the team-building-without-computer-support treatment outperformed the groups receiving the computer-supported treatment on four measures.

Considerable differences were found between the facilitated team-building sessions and the nonfacilitated control group meetings for the immediate measures. When the facilitation was removed, the delayed results showed that group processes and performance for groups going

TABLE 9.4. Significant Differences over Time for Each Team-Building Treatment (Based on *t*-Tests and Analysis of Variance on Differences)

Both Team-Building Treatments Over Control	Team-Building-With-Computer-Support Treatment	Team-Building-Without-Computer-Support Treatment	Control
1. Quality of group process (decreased)	1. Goal-directed behavior (decreased[a])	1. Relevancy of discussion (decreased[a])	1. Behavior measures (overall) (increased)
2. Behavior measures (overall) (decreased)	2. Amplification of contributions (decreased)	2. Socioemotional behaviors (increased more than other two treatments)	2. Distribution of participation (increased)
3. Documentation of positions (decreased[a])	3. Documentation of issues (decreased)	3. Change in understanding (decreased)	3. Leadership functions (increased)
4. Leadership functions (decreased[a])	4. Interpersonal relationships (decreased[a])	4. Solution satisfaction (decreased)	4. Solution satisfaction (increased)
5. Commitment to implement results (decreased[a])	5. Socioemotional behaviors (decreased)		5. Confidence in solutions (increased)
	6. Personal task participation (increased)		
	7. Informal leadership (decreased[a])		
	8. Confidence in conclusions (decreased[a])		

a. This measure showed a significant decrease compared with the control treatment.

through team building did not differ from those of the control groups. One reason for this lack of difference over time is noted in previous reports of a pattern in which groups respond to the GDSS with an initial lag followed by a jump above non-GDSS-supported groups (Chidambaram, 1989). It is possible that in this study, a similar pattern would have occurred if the treatment had been continued. The overall mean scores for the GDSS groups were slightly below those of the non-GDSS scores, which is consistent with the theory of an initial lag. Perhaps with additional sessions, the scores would have changed significantly.

Rather than indicating significant advantages or disadvantages to the use of technology in team building, this study implies that the use of GDSS technology did not interfere with the team-building process. Given the issues involved in using the technology, this may be a considerable accomplishment. Within the three-hour time constraint for the task, the computer-supported participants not only had to focus on the team-building process; they also had to learn how to use the GDSS. Most of the participants in the study had little or no experience with computers in general and with the GDSS in particular. When they entered the room, computer-supported participants saw the technology associated with the computers. In addition to having concerns about team building, participants reported that seeing the equipment in the room created fears about how the computers would be used. Some portion of the GDSS session agenda was spent helping people feel more comfortable with using the technology, creating another focus from the team-building task. With additional sessions, differences between the two treatments may have been detected as familiarity with the technology increased, reducing its direct influence on the outcome measures.

Group Outcome (Cohesion). The measure of group development used in this study was cohesion, or attraction to group. For this study, the initial cohesion levels of the two team-building treatments were not identical, with cohesion being slightly higher for the team-building-with-computer-support groups. They showed a significant increase immediately after the team-building session, when precohesion was used as a covariate. Given the direction of change for this variable, it may be that team building with or without computer support would have increased cohesion more significantly with more sessions.

The use of computer support had a slight effect on cohesiveness. The direction of change for the team-building sessions was positive and was sustained over time when compared with the direction or lack of change for control sessions.

Performance Outcomes. Two measures of performance were considered: solution satisfaction and confidence in group conclusions. Solution satisfaction was significantly higher for the team-building treatments over the control, indicating that the facilitated session with or without computer support resulted in a higher level of performance. Field study research has consistently supported the value of GDSS groups having increased solution satisfaction over non-GDSS groups. Experimental research has shown mixed results. This result does not support the field study research results, especially given the lack of significant difference for the measure of confidence in conclusions. The analysis infers no significant difference in solution quality between the GDSS and non-GDSS team building. It does infer that facilitation, with or without the GDSS, produces a higher level of perceived performance.

Process Outcomes. A number of process measures differed between treatments. As previous research has shown (Anson, 1990), facilitation with or without computer support created significant differences compared with groups not using a facilitator. In addition, two measures indicated significant differences between the two team-building treatments: quality of group process and informal leadership.

Why would participants in groups not receiving computer support rate quality of group process higher than participants in groups receiving computer support? Previous research has shown that the GDSS allows groups to focus more on issues where they differ. Where the normal group process focuses on areas of agreement to cover up areas of contention, a GDSS-supported group process may accentuate areas of contention. At least part of this result may be a consequence of using the GDSS's anonymity and forced simultaneous responses, which might serve to heighten differences and increase conflict.

This study showed that the non-GDSS participants rated their perceived changes in understanding higher than did control participants. Non-GDSS participants were more likely to feel that they better understood and could better predict the positions and opinions of other members. This may indicate that the technology interfered with the team-building session's ability to focus the group on issues in depth. Or perhaps the anonymity of the GDSS made it difficult to associate people with an opinion.

The other difference between the two team-building treatments concerned informal leadership. This difference showed that group decisions of GDSS-supported groups were significantly less likely to be strongly influenced by only one or two members, based on the immediate measure. Possibly the use of the technology moderated the amount of influence any one individual such as the leader could exert on the decision-making process. If the purpose of team building is to reduce the influence of one or two strong members, the technology could be a significant supporting factor for the goal.

Nonsignificant differences between the two team-building treatments were many. Compared to previous research, this study did not find significant differences in the areas of critical examination of ideas, healthiness of interpersonal relationships, decision-scheme satisfaction, depth of evaluation, or commitment to implement results (as referenced in Table 9.1). Part of the reason for this lack may be the additional time needed to explain, to practice, and to create comfort in using the technology at the beginning of the session. Measured results indicated factors that may only be reflective of the initial learning curve, and not use of the technology over time. However, the reported measures concerning comfort, challenge, and respect for the GDSS on the part of the participants indicated that they rated use of the GDSS at levels comparable to those of participants in other studies where the participants had more training and more experience using the GDSS.

Findings Concerning Team Building. Given the increased satisfaction with solution ratings for facilitated sessions over regular meetings, this study further substantiated the benefits of using an outside facilitator for group meetings if performance improvement is desired. Improvement was found on eleven of seventeen group-process measures for the facilitated sessions over the nonfacilitated sessions. Facilitation in this study, as in previous studies, was shown to increase group functioning.

These positive effects did not necessarily transfer to future performance. A one-time three-hour team-building session did not create measurable long-term changes in group outcomes. Delayed measures indicated a greater likelihood that groups will transfer the improved processes into their future meetings when they receive team building without computer support.

Conclusions and Suggestions for Future Research

Members of the groups receiving facilitated team building without computer support reported the highest rating for quality of group process on the *immediate-effect measures*. These members also reported a greater change in understanding compared with ratings by the members of the control group.

Members of the groups receiving facilitated team building with computer support reported that one or two members of the group were less likely to strongly affect the decision (informal leadership) and were more confident in the group's conclusions on the *immediate-effect measures*. To a lesser degree, these members reported increased cohesion and more positive socioemotional behaviors in the group process when compared with the ratings by members of the control groups.

Members of the groups receiving facilitated team building—with or without computer support—reported significantly higher ratings than members of the control groups on twelve out of twenty-one of the immediate-effect measures (including the nine participant-behavior subscores): quality of group process, overall behavior scales, goal-directed behavior, relevancy of discussion, amplification of contributions, distribution of participation, and documentation of positions, systematically dealing with issues, fulfilled leadership functions, solution satisfaction, decision-scheme satisfaction, and informal leadership.

Measures of critical examination of ideas, healthiness of interpersonal relationships, personal task participation, and commitment to implement results did not significantly differ between treatments for the immediate-effect measures.

Delayed-effect measures showed that members of the team-building-without-computer-support group rated their meetings significantly better than members of the team-building-with-computer-support group did for their meetings on four measures: goal-directed behavior, documentation of positions, leadership functions, and socioemotional behaviors. The members of the control groups rated their meetings higher than members of the groups receiving team building with computer support on the five delayed measures: quality of group process, goal-directed behavior, healthiness of interpersonal relationships, fulfilled leadership functions, and more positive socioemotional behaviors. Overall, the differences between control groups and treatment groups on the delayed measures were minimal.

On immediate-effect measures, the facilitated team-building process resulted in higher member ratings of group process than the nonfacilitated process. For the most part, the positive immediate effects did not last over time, indicating that the three-hour team-building session was not effective over time.

In conclusion, the implications for practice are severe in that both team building and GDSS technology are typically implemented as one-time interventions. It is common to have these techniques and/or methods as a three-to four-hour component of a management development session or used as part of a specific task-related meeting. This study demonstrates that one-time HRD interventions in team building are not effective and that GDSS technology as an aid to improving one-time team-building interventions has no lasting positive impact.

Three strengths of this experimental study are the use of intact work groups, controlled treatments, and measures over time. Suggestions for future research include the following:

- The effects of using the GDSS over an extended time period
- The cost-effectiveness of the GDSS compared to other team-building options
- The process learning of team members using the GDSS versus non-GDSS interventions
- Group willingness to use the GDSS as a part of team decision making over the long term
- The effects of the GDSS on long-term team functioning
- The effects of the GDSS on the validity and quality of team action plans
- The effects of the GDSS on business performance outcomes

References

Alexander, M. (1985). The team effectiveness critique. In I. D. Goodstem & J. W. Pfeiffer (Eds.), *The 1985 annual: Developing human resources.* San Diego: University Associates.

Anson, R. (1990). *Effects of computer support and facilitator support on group processes and outcomes. An experimental assessment.* Unpublished doctoral dissertation, Indiana University, Bloomington.

Borg, W. R., & Gall, M. D. (1989). *Educational research: An introduction* (5th ed.). New York: Longman.

Bostrom, R. P., & Anson, R. G. (1988). *A case for collaborative work support systems in a meeting environment.* Unpublished working paper, University of Georgia, Athens.

Chidambaram, I. (1989). An empirical investigation of the impact of computer support on group development and decision making performance (Doctoral dissertation, Indiana University). *Dissertation Abstracts International* (1990), *50*(8), 2561A-2562A.

Dalkey, N. C. (1969). *The Delphi method: An experimental study of group opinion.* Santa Monica, CA: The Rand Corporation.

Dalkey, N. C., & Halmer, O. (1963). An experimental application of the Delphi method to the use of experts. *Management Science, 6,* 458-467.

Delbecq, A. L., Van De Ven, A. H., & Gustafson, D. H. (1975). *Group techniques for program planning: A guide to nominal group and Delphi processes.* Glenview, IL: Scott, Foresman.

Dennis, A. R., George, J. F., Jessup, L. M., Nunamaker, J. F., Jr., & Vogel, D. R. (1988). Information technology to support electronic meetings. *MIS Quarterly, 12*(4), 591-624.

Dennis, A. R., Nunamaker, J. F., Jr., & Vogel, D. R. (1989). GDSS laboratory experiments and field studies. Closing the gap. In *Proceedings of the IEEE Twenty-Second Annual Hawaii International Conference on System Sciences* (pp. 300-309). Kona, HI.

DeSanctis, G., & Gallupe, R. B. (1987). A foundation for the study of group decision support systems. *Management Science, 33*(5), 589-609.

Dickson, G. W., Lee, J. E., Robinson, L., & Health, R. (1989). Observations on GDSS interaction: Chauffeured, facilitated, and user-driven systems. In *Proceedings of the IEEE Twenty-Second Annual Hawaii International Conference on System Sciences* (pp. 337-343). Kona, HI.

Dyer, W. G. (1987). *Team building* (2nd ed.). Reading, MA: Addison-Wesley.

Gallupe, R. B., DeSanctis, G., & Dickson, G. (1988). Computer-based support for group problem-finding: An experimental investigation. *MIS Quarterly, 12*(2), 277-296.

George, J. F. (1989). A comparison of four recent GDSS experiments. In *Proceedings of the IEEE Twenty-Second Annual Hawaii International Conference on System Sciences* (pp. 397-402). Kona, HI.

George, J. F., Easton, G. K., Nunamaker, J. F., Jr., & Northcraft, G. B. (1990). A study of collaborative group work with and without computer-based support. *Information Systems Research, 1*(4), 394-415.

Gray, P. (1983). Initial observations from the decision support room project. In *Proceedings of the Third International Conference on Decision Support Systems* (pp. 135-138). Boston, MA.

Green, S. G., & Taber, T. D. (1980). The effects of three decision schemes on decision group process. *Organizational Behavior and Human Performance, 25,* 97-106.

Hackman, J. R. (1987). The design of work teams. In J. Lorach (Ed.), *Handbook of organizational behavior* (pp. 315-342). Englewood Cliffs, NJ: Prentice Hall.

Harvey, J. B. (1988). *The Abeline paradox and other meditations on management.* Lexington, MA: Lexington Books; San Diego: University Associates.

Huber, G. P. (1982). Group decision support systems as aids in the use of structured group management techniques. In *Second International Conference on Decision Support Systems* (pp. 96-108).

Huber, G. P. (1984). Issues in the design of group decision support systems. *MIS Quarterly, 8*(3), 195-204.

Kraemer, K. L., & King, J. L. (1988). Computer-based systems for cooperative work and group decision making. *ACM Computing Surveys, 20*(2), 115-146.

Kraemer, K. L., & Pinsonneault, A. (1989). The implications of group support technologies: An evaluation of the empirical research. In *Proceedings of the IEEE Twenty-Second*

  Annual Hawaii International Conference on System Sciences (pp. 326-336). Kona, HI.

Likert, R. (1961). *New patterns of management.* New York: McGraw-Hill.

McGrath, J. E. (1984). *Groups: Interaction and performance.* Englewood Cliffs, NJ: Prentice Hall.

McGregor, D. (1960). *The human side of enterprise.* New York: McGraw-Hill.

McGregor, D. (1967). *The professional manager.* New York: McGraw-Hill.

Miranda, S. M. (1991). *The effect of group decision support systems on team development.* Unpublished doctoral dissertation, University of Georgia, Athens.

Nadler, D. A. (1977). *Feedback and organization development: Using data-based methods.* Reading, MA: Addison-Wesley.

Nunamaker, J. F., Applegate, L. M., & Konsynski, K. R. (1987). Facilitating group creativity with GDSS. *Journal of Management Information Systems, 3*(4), 5-19.

Phillips, S. L., & Elledge, R. I., (1989). *The team-building source book.* San Diego: University Associates.

Poole, M. S. (1991). Procedures for managing meetings: Social and technological innovation. In R. A. Swanson & B. O. Knapp (Eds.), *Innovative meeting management.* Austin, TX: 3M Meeting Management Institute.

Poole, M. S., & DeSanctis, G. (1987). *Group decision making and group decision support systems.* Unpublished working paper no. MISRC-WP-88-02. Minneapolis: University of Minnesota.

Rohrbaugh, J. (1988). Organizationally-based experiments: Looking at processes, not outcomes, of group decision making. In *Harvard Business School Colloquium on Experimental Methods in Information Systems,* University of British Columbia, Vancouver, Canada.

Sambamurthy, V. (1989). Supporting group performance during stakeholder analysis: The effects of alternative computer-based designs (Doctoral dissertation, University of Minnesota). *Dissertation Abstracts International* (1989), *50*(11), 3660A-3661A.

Shaw, M. E. (1978). *Group dynamics: The psychology of small group behavior* (2nd ed.). New York: McGraw-Hill.

Steiner, I. D. (1966). Models for inferring relationships between group size and potential group productivity. *Behavioral Science, 11,* 273-283.

Sundstrom, E., DeMeuse, D. P., & Futrell, D. (1990). Work teams: Applications and effectiveness review. *American Psychologist, 45*(2), 120-133.

Van De Ven, A. H., & Delbecq, A. L. (1974). The effect of nominal, Delphi and interacting group decision making processes. *Academy of Management Journal, 17*(4), 605-621.

Whyte, W. E. (1955). *Money and motivation: An analysis of incentives in industry.* New York: HarperCollins.

Zigurs, I. (1987). The effect of computer based support on influence attempts and patterns in small group decision-making (Doctoral dissertation, University of Minnesota). *Dissertation Abstracts International* (1988), *49*(3), 543A.

Zigurs, I., Poole, M. S., & DeSanctis, G. (1988). A study of influence in computer-mediated group decision making. *MIS Quarterly, 12*(4), 625-644.

IMPLICATIONS FOR HUMAN RESOURCE DEVELOPMENT PROFESSIONALS

This research has important implications for practitioners who are seeking strategies, methods, and processes for increasing overall team effectiveness within their organizations. Because team-building strategies such as facilitated team-building processes and group decision support systems (GDSS) can require considerable financial and human resources, these strategies should be used only if the benefits are forecast to exceed the costs. This study used immediate and delayed measures of team-building efforts and found that the facilitated team-building process resulted in higher member ratings. However, the positive effects of facilitation, for the most part, did not last over time.

Team facilitation and GDSS are often implemented as one-time interventions. Because this study demonstrated that the one-time HRD intervention in team building was not effective over the long term and, further, that GDSS technology as an aid to improving the one-time team-building intervention did not have a lasting effect, HRD practitioners who are investing in such efforts in their organizations should take a hard look at their actions.

IMPLICATIONS FOR RESEARCH DESIGN AND METHODOLOGY

This study provides a template for studying intact work groups. For example, in this study, groups were randomly assigned to treatments. Further, a pretreatment survey was used to assure randomization of possible individual differences that would affect the study outcomes. Also, the analysis reflected the importance of both group- and individual-level perceptions. In measuring individual members' perceptions of team activities, consideration must be given to the effect the team can have on individual team member's ratings.

A potential improvement for future research involves reporting the data. In their summary of results, McClernon and Swanson reported only the acceptance and rejection for the null hypotheses. Including the actual numerical data could contribute to greater understanding.

IMPLICATIONS FOR FUTURE INQUIRY

One interesting finding in this study is that the use of technology affected power within the group. McClernon and Swanson reported that "the group decisions of GDSS were significantly less likely to be strongly influenced by only one or two members" (p. 240). This finding relates to that of the other studies in this part that focus on group member participation. Because the technology allows all members to be included in a decision-making process, GDSS may provide a means to address some of the concerns expressed by Brooks (Chapter 7) related to power and decision making.

Another interesting finding relates to the lack of long-term success for the team-building activities. Demonstration that a one-time HRD intervention in team-building was not effective and, further, that GDSS technology did not have a lasting effect on improving the one-time team building intervention raises some larger questions: "What are the necessary and sufficient conditions for team building to be effective with naturally forming work groups?" and "How do one-time team-building efforts relate to the research presented in Part I of this book indicating that individual learning requires repetition and practice?"

OTHER RESOURCES

DeSanctis, G., & Gallupe, R. B. (1987). A foundation for the study of group decision support systems. *Management Science, 33*(5), 589-609.

Rebstock, S. E. (1995). *Group support systems and power and influence: A case study.* Unpublished doctoral thesis, Oklahoma State University.

Training an Interdisciplinary Team in Communication and Decision-Making Skills

Elizabeth Cooley
Far West Laboratory for Educational Research and Development

THE USE OF INTERDISCIPLINARY TEAMS TO ADDRESS HUMAN SERVICE DELIVERY issues is becoming increasingly common. Complicated problems require the expertise of a variety of specialists from different disciplines, and increased specialization brings with it a heightened need for interdisciplinary collaboration. While team meetings are expected to serve as the vehicle for successful collaboration among professionals, three barriers often stand in the way of effective team interactions: disorganization, misunderstandings, and problem-solving difficulties. These problems suggest a need for interventions aimed at improving team communication and decision-making processes, as well as a need for methods to observe and evaluate the effects of such interventions on a team's functioning. The purpose of this research was twofold: First, we sought to investigate the effects of an intervention that differentially targeted and trained three sets of group communication and decision-making skills aimed at addressing the three barriers mentioned above. A second goal was to develop new methods of observation that would overcome several serious limitations which have characterized the bulk of existing team intervention research. An interdisciplinary rehabilitation clinic's staff served as the subject of the study. Using a multiple

Source: Cooley, E. (1994). Training an interdisciplinary team in communication and decision-making skills. *Small Group Research, 25*(1), 5-25. Used by permission.

Author's Note: This research was funded in part by grant #H086P90023 between the Oregon Research Institute and the U.S. Dept. of Education. The views expressed herein do not necessarily reflect those of the funding agency.

baseline design across categories of behaviors, the effects of a three-part intervention on the team's day-to-day meeting behavior was assessed. While there was substantial variability and overlap in much of the data, videotaped observations revealed that following each training session, there were modest increases in the average frequency of use of most targeted behaviors. Social validation data indicated that team members found the training to be both useful and enjoyable. Implications for future research are discussed.

Interdisciplinary team practice has been gaining momentum in a wide variety of settings including hospitals, rehabilitation facilities, mental health centers, nursing homes, hospices, drug/alcohol treatment programs, and schools (Gaitz, 1987; Lecca & McNeil, 1985). Contributing to its rising prevalence is the fact that as medical technology advances and knowledge about human service delivery and educational issues burgeons, it becomes impossible for a single professional or discipline to possess all of the requisite information/ skills to adequately meet the needs of a given client or student (Gaitz, 1987; Giangreco, 1986; Lecca & McNeil, 1985). Complex problems often require the expertise of specialists from a variety of disciplines, and increased specialization brings with it a heightened need for interdisciplinary collaboration in order to avoid fragmented service delivery (Rothberg, 1985).

Interdisciplinary team meetings are expected to serve as the vehicle for this collaboration among professionals, and effective teamwork is vital to that collaboration. Figure 10.1 presents a conceptual framework for viewing team functioning. Essentially, an effective team meeting may be thought of as comprising at least three elements: organized presentation of material and use of time, interactive communication among members resulting in mutual understanding of group goals and decisions, and sufficient involvement of group members in constructive problem-solving efforts.

Unfortunately, however, simply bringing together a group of professionals does not necessarily ensure that they will function effectively as a team or make appropriate decisions. Effective teamwork does not occur automatically. Many problems related to the interdisciplinary team interaction process itself have been cited with respect to teams and work groups that run the gamut of service delivery settings, purposes, and compositions. Also shown in Figure 10.1, these process-related difficulties tend to cluster into three categories:

1. *Disorganization*: Interdisciplinary teams frequently operate in the absence of any well-defined procedures. The purpose and outcomes of meetings are often unclear to the members, and information may not

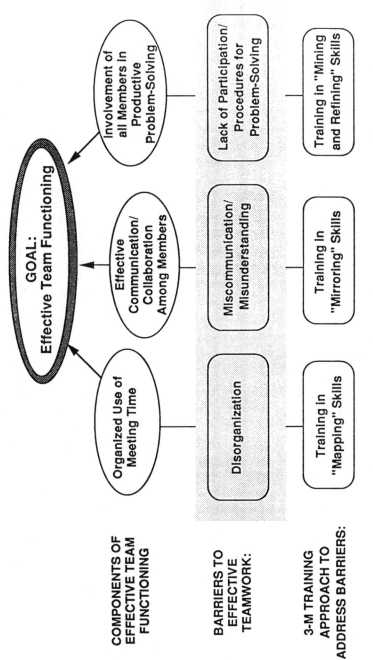

COMPONENTS OF EFFECTIVE TEAM FUNCTIONING

BARRIERS TO EFFECTIVE TEAMWORK:

3-M TRAINING APPROACH TO ADDRESS BARRIERS:

GOAL: Effective Team Functioning

Organized Use of Meeting Time

Effective Communication/ Collaboration Among Members

Involvement of all Members in Productive Problem-Solving

Disorganization

Miscommunication/ Misunderstanding

Lack of Participation/ Procedures for Problem-Solving

Training in "Mapping" Skills

Training in "Mirroring" Skills

Training in "Mining and Refining" Skills

Figure 10.1. A Conceptual Framework and Training Model for Addressing Common Barriers to Effective Team Functioning

be presented in a logical fashion (Bailey, 1984; Hackman & Walton, 1984).

2. *Miscommunication and misunderstanding*: Because interdisciplinary teams are by definition composed of individuals with diverse professional perspectives and languages, they are particularly prone to problems that stem from heterogeneity (Randolph & Blackburn, 1989). These problems include misunderstanding arising from members' varied use and interpretation of each others' jargon, conflicts and "turfism" (Golightly, 1987; McGonigel & Garland, 1988). Good communication skills would be helpful in preventing or alleviating such problems; unfortunately, members of interdisciplinary teams often lack training and proficiency in such skills (Moore, Fifield, Spira, & Scarlato, 1989).

3. *Inadequate participation in/procedures for problem solving*: To achieve the goal of bringing a variety of perspectives to bear on a particular problem, a team meeting would ideally be a situation in which every member's input is readily available and used. Unfortunately, members do not always participate optimally in group discussions; some are too reserved, while others may dominate the meeting by speaking disproportionately or inappropriately (Bailey, 1984). In addition, groups frequently lack a structured approach for group problem solving, making it difficult if not impossible for the group to address issues in anything but a haphazard fashion (Bulger, 1985; Moore et al., 1989).

All of the problems listed above concern the *internal processes* associated with a team's collaborative efforts to accomplish its goals. While effective team processes are not necessarily ends in themselves, they are the means to achieve effective service delivery to clients. Previous research has shown that problems in a team's interactional processes can hinder its accomplishment of its goals (Johnson & Johnson, 1987; Robbins, 1989).

Due to the relationship between the effectiveness of team processes and the quality of team outcomes, a line of research has emerged that aims to identify ways to improve team functioning. A wide variety of team-based interventions have been developed and evaluated, and Figure 10.1 outlines the training model employed and evaluated by this study. Before detailing the procedures of this study, however, we turn next to a discussion of previous team intervention research.

The difficulties associated with measuring the effects of team interventions have resulted in serious limitations in the research done to date in this area. For example, many of the experimental group studies of team development interventions lack validity because the groups consist of college students or other "artificial" populations (Schweiger & Sandberg, 1989). Conversely, studies of intact work groups operating in real-world settings have tended to lack experimental control due to the difficulty in arranging suitable randomized control groups in actual organizational settings (Spencer & Coye, 1988).

Furthermore, measurement of team communication processes has proven equally challenging, and most existing studies of team development interventions have not employed measures of observable behavior change in team members. Thus, while many team development interventions result in improvements in member satisfaction, one is usually left to wonder whether or not those interventions actually resulted in any behavioral change in the teams' day-to-day operations.

The purpose of this study was to investigate the behavioral effects of a team training model (depicted in Figure 10.1) that differentially targeted three categories of group communication and decision-making skills. The three skill areas related specifically to the three barriers to team functioning discussed earlier. This effort was intended to overcome the limitations described above by employing a controlled research design using an intact service delivery team as the subject of study. Moreover, the study operationally defined key communication and decision-making skills in such a way as to allow systematic assessment of the effects of the training on the team's day-to-day meeting behavior.

Method

Subjects and Setting

The subjects in this study were 25 staff members of a rehabilitation clinic specializing in the treatment of individuals with chronic pain. This clinic is located in a Pacific Northwest community of 150,000. Its staff consisted of 11 administrative members and 14 treatment professionals from a variety of disciplines including medicine, psychology, social work, physical therapy, and occupational therapy. There were 9 males and 16 females on the staff. The mean age was 37 years, with a range of 21 to 48 years. The entire staff participated in the training workshops, and the average number of staff members present during observed meetings was 9 (range = 5-17).

Ideally, a group under study would consist of stable membership. However, the staff of this treatment center met in different configurations depending on which client or issue was being discussed, making it impossible to target and observe one stable staff subgroup over time. The fact that members' attendance varied somewhat according to the purpose of a particular meeting created an instability in the unit of analysis that posed measurement challenges. And yet, since this kind of fluctuation in team membership is typical of so many intact human service delivery teams operating in real-world settings, it was seen as worthy of accommodation in the study's design. The primary challenge was to determine whether the intervention was powerful enough to produce changes in behavior over and above whatever variability was inherent to the team's fluctuating composition.

This study's accommodation of fluctuating team membership was accomplished in two ways. First, by delivering the intervention to the entire staff instead of only to certain staff members, it was ensured that no matter what the configuration of individuals present at any given staff meeting, the members had received equal exposure to the intervention. Second, the meeting itself (i.e., the summative rates of target behaviors that occurred in each one) as opposed to a particular configuration of team members, served as the unit of analysis. Measuring summative rates of target behaviors per 5-minute intervals during meetings allowed for the examination of the intervention's behavioral effects on the center's meetings. Given that the baseline occurrences of behavior remained fairly constant in level and variability, changes seen in targeted (but not control) behaviors following intervention could be attributed to intervention. In other words, this system of measurement enabled assessment of whether or not any changes in the rehabilitation center's overall meeting behavior (regardless of member configuration) occurred as a function of intervention.

To render the observations as representative as possible of interdisciplinary team experiences, only those meetings in which at least three disciplines were represented were observed. Therefore, meetings consisting solely of administrative support personnel, for example, were excluded because the homogeneity of membership in such meetings is not typical of interdisciplinary team meetings.

Design

Single subject research designs are well suited to the study of team-focused interventions because they provide a means of exercising experimental control while observing only a few or even a single team in its natural context (Kazdin & Tuma, 1982; Komaki & Zlotnick, 1985). This study employed a multiple baseline design across behaviors to investigate the effects of a behavioral skills training program for interdisciplinary team members. The rehabilitation staff's team meetings served as the unit of analysis. The effects of the three-part intervention targeting specific communication and decision-making skills were assessed by collecting data continuously on all of the targeted behaviors at once and intervening in staggered fashion on one specific set of behaviors at a time. Thus there were four phases of the study (three of them corresponding to the titles of the training components): baseline, mapping, mirroring, and mining and refining. In each phase the nontargeted behaviors served as experimental controls for the targeted ones. The Baseline condition refers to observed occurrences of targeted behaviors prior to intervention upon them.

Procedures

Access to Setting and Data Collection Procedures

The team under study was recruited via a flier describing the training program and offering it free of charge to interdisciplinary teams. Upon obtaining written consent from all staff members of the clinic to participate in the study, each participant completed an intake questionnaire which solicited demographics of the participants and information about the nature and content of the center's team meetings.

The data collection process included conducting direct observations of videotaped team meetings and administering a social validation questionnaire following each of three training sessions. Both are described further in the Measures section.

To collect videotaped observations of team meetings, a $\frac{1}{2}$ inch VHS video camera was positioned on a tripod in a corner of the treatment center's conference room which provided an adequate view of the team members and the immediate surroundings. The camera's built-in timer function allowed the running time to be displayed along the bottom of the screen. One of the staff members was instructed in how to operate the video equipment and was responsible for recording the meetings. Five videotaped observations of team meetings were conducted prior to any training. There were three training workshops; between each one five videotaped observations were made. Thus the total number of meetings videotaped was 20, and the total span of time covered by the study was roughly 3 months.

Training Content

All staff members participated in three 2-hour on-site training workshops that were held 3 to 4 weeks apart. Each of the three workshops was conducted by the author and was designed to teach a set of skills relevant to overcoming each of the three team process barriers mentioned earlier:

"3-M" TeamTraining Approach

1. Disorganization ⟶ Mapping skills workshop
2. Miscommunication ⟶ Mirroring skills workshop
3. Problem-solving difficulties ⟶ Mining and refining skills workshop

Each workshop targeted specific skills and employed teaching methods that have already in the literature been demonstrated or posited to be important elements of an effective work group. Following are brief rationales for and identification of the sets of skills targeted in the three training sessions, called respectively mapping, mirroring, and mining and refining. A more detailed description of training procedures and skill definitions may be found in Cooley (1991).

Session One: Mapping

This session focused on the development of skills that help a group track or map where it's going, where it is, and where it's been, thus reducing disorganization. Groups easily get sidetracked because of the natural tendency for individual members to be thinking different things at different times. Even when a group uses a written agenda, members may get lost in discussions and fail to progress in a logical fashion from one topic to the next. The three communication skills targeted in this session were previewing what will occur next in the meeting (Sugai & Colvin, 1990), consensus testing to determine group agreements (Schmuck & Runkel, 1985), and summarizing remarks (Schmuck & Runkel, 1985).

Session Two: Mirroring

This session targeted four skills designed to foster improved communication and understanding among team members. The mirroring analogy alludes to the right and responsibility of each team member to "see and be seen, to hear and be heard" during team meetings. Given the heterogeneity of interdisciplinary team membership, the potential for miscommunication to occur is great. Skills targeted in this workshop consisted of both listening and sending skills, including paraphrasing other members' remarks (Johnson & Johnson, 1987), probing for clarification of another's remarks (Bormann & Bormann, 1988), pinpointing specific behaviors and examples (Schmuck & Runkel, 1985), and personalizing via the use of "I statements" when describing a problem's impact (Johnson & Johnson, 1987).

Session Three: Mining and Refining

The third session was designed to teach processes and skills that facilitate more involvement and creativity on the part of members during problem solving, since a lack of participation may result in fewer contributions and options being considered. The mining and refining image refers to ways that a group can "mine" its raw material more effectively by eliciting every member's involvement and input, and then "refine" that material by using a structured problem-solving sequence. This session emphasized the importance of equalizing member participation and focused primarily on the introduction and practice of a structured problem-solving sequence called "SYNERGY." The sequence employed in this intervention drew upon a variety of group problem-solving strategies identified in the literature, all of which consist of a sequence similar to the following: Problem definition, problem analysis, generation of alternatives, selection of a solution, evaluation and follow-up (Aubrey & Felkins, 1988; Fox, 1987; Schmuck & Runkel, 1985; Ulschak, Nathanson, & Gillan, 1981). The SYNERGY acronym served as a mnemonic device for the seven problem-solving steps for facilitating broader involvement and creativity that were taught in the training session (See Cooley, 1991).

Training Format

All three of the workshops employed the following behavioral training procedures (Porras & Anderson, 1981; Zamanou & Glaser, 1989) for teaching team members the targeted skills: conceptual presentation, modeling, observational training using examples from their own video-taped meetings, written practice and role playing.

Measures

Videotaped Observations and Reliability Checks

The investigator observed videotapes of the team meetings and coded the frequency with which the various targeted behaviors occurred during every 5-minute interval of the meeting. That is, meetings were observed in their entirety—not sampled. Targeted skills were operationally defined, and a scoring grid was developed that listed the target behaviors along one dimension and 5-minute meeting intervals along the other. Tally marks were made to indicate the frequency with which the behaviors occurred in each meeting interval.

A mean rate (frequency per 5-minute interval) of each of the targeted behaviors was calculated for every observed meeting, regardless of meeting length or the number of members present, thus allowing comparison of skill use across different kinds of meetings. This observational procedure was followed for all of the targeted skills except the use of the problem-solving sequence.

The team's use of the problem-solving sequence was expressed as a percentage of the seven steps used during a given meeting as opposed to a rate per interval. For example, a meeting in which the group engaged in three of the seven steps would receive a score of .43, while a meeting in which six of the seven steps were used would receive a score of .86.

Also measured was the extent to which the participation during a given meeting was evenly distributed among the members. In arriving at a means of measuring this, the concepts of market share and industry concentration were borrowed from the field of economics. A statistic known as the Herfindahl Index (Martin, 1988) is used to compute the density of competition within an industry. That is, firms within a particular industry each possess a certain proportion or share of the market. By squaring the proportion of the market that each firm holds and then summing these figures, one arrives at a figure between 0 and 1 that serves as an index of industry concentration. The lower the index, the more evenly distributed the shares of the market.

Group participation can be usefully viewed in the same way by substituting the notion of "airtime" for market share. That is, each member, whenever she or he speaks, uses up a certain proportion of the available airtime. By squaring each person's total proportion of airtime and adding these figures, one arrives at a figure, herein referred to as the participation index, which measures the distribution of participation among members during the meeting. Participation indexes were calculated for all of the videotaped meetings to assess the effects of the intervention on the degree to which participation was equalized among the members. The procedure for obtaining these indexes is further detailed in Cooley (1991).

Twenty-five percent of the videotapes were randomly selected and coded by a second observer who was blind to the phases of the study. Interobserver reliability was calculated by dividing the total number of agreements by the total number of agreements plus disagreements across all behaviors observed.

Satisfaction Measures

Social validation data were collected via a one-page questionnaire that assessed participants' satisfaction with each of the three training workshops. Following each training workshop, participants responded anonymously to six items asking them to rate various aspects of the training using a 5-point, Likert-type scale (1 = *very disappointing*, 3 = *acceptable*, 5 = *extremely well done*). These items included: organization of the workshop, content, skill practice, handouts, presenter's delivery, and overall quality/usefulness. Open-ended written comments regarding the strengths and weaknesses of each session were solicited as well.

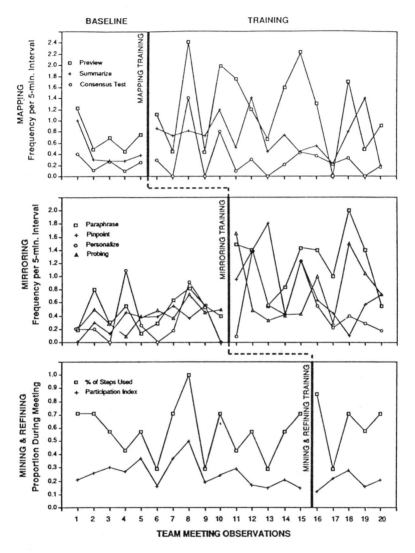

Figure 10.2. Behaviors Observed During Team Meetings

Results

Skill Use

Figure 10.2 depicts the degree to which team members used the various communication and decision-making skills in their meetings before and after each of the three training workshops, as well as the

TABLE 10.1 Pre- and Postintervention Means and Standard Deviations for Targeted Skills

	Pretraining		Post-Training	
	X	SD	X	SD
Mapping				
Previewing	.71	.30	1.21	.72
Summarizing	.44	.31	.73	.37
Consensus testing	.22	.13	.31	.37
Mirroring				
Paraphrasing	.47	.25	1.21	.46
Pinpointing	.31	.20	.83	.52
Personalizing	.34	.39	.54	.44
Probing	.40	.18	.79	.49
Mining and refining				
Percentage of steps	.57	.20	.63	.21
Distribution of participation	.26	.10	.20	.06
	.29[a]	.20[b]	.20[b]	.06[b]

a. Premirroring.
b. Postmirroring.

extent to which the distribution of meeting participation varied over the course of the entire study. Table 10.1 reports the pre-and postintervention means and standard deviations for these same skills.

The data for many of the measures were highly variable, and there was considerable overlap between pre-and post-training data points. Moreover, effects appear to be inconsistent across both behaviors and time. In light of these facts, the results need to be interpreted cautiously and viewed as merely suggestive at best. Nevertheless, there appear to be some changes occurring as a function of intervention, and these will be described next for each category of behavior.

While quite variable, the degree to which members initially used all three skills of previewing, summarizing, and consensus testing was relatively low during the baseline phase. After the 2-hour mapping workshop, there appeared to be somewhat of an increase in both the level and variability of members' use of all three of these targeted skills over subsequent meetings (see Figure 10.2 and Table 10.1). For example, the mean frequency of previewing per 5-minute interval across meetings increased from .71 during baseline to 1.21 for the 15 meetings following training. In other words, prior to the intervention, any one member of the team would preview an average of once every 7 minutes, whereas in postintervention meetings, the mean rate increased to roughly once every 4 minutes. The standard deviation of all three skills also increased following training (see Table 10.1) reflecting the fact that after training there were more high data points in spite of the considerable overlap between phases.

The baseline rates for all four mirroring skills were also quite variable, although there was no change in overall trend during this phase. Mean baseline rates for the four skills were .47, .31, .34 and .40 for paraphrasing, pinpointing, personalizing, and probing, respectively (see Table 10.1 and Figure 10.2). Subsequent to the mirroring workshop, the mean rates for the four skills increased to 1.21, .83, .54, and .79, and the variability also increased. For both the mapping and mirroring sets of skills, initial effects were modest and unsustained over time.

The third category of behaviors appears to have been unaffected by the third workshop which was designed to affect them. That is, the group's use of the seven problem-solving steps varied widely throughout the study, and there was no change in overall level following intervention. Thus the intervention appeared to have no effect on the group's use of the steps in the problem-solving sequence.

One unanticipated result was that following the second workshop (mirroring), there appeared a slight decrease in trend of the participation indexes (see Figure 10.2), suggesting that participation became somewhat more evenly distributed following the mirroring workshop. As can be seen from the numbers with superscripts in Table 10.1, the premirroring mean participation index was .29 as compared with a postmirroring mean of .20. Following the mining and refining workshop, the mean participation index remained unchanged at .20. Thus it appears that the mirroring portion of the intervention had a small effect on the degree to which members shared participation in the meeting, while the mining and refining workshop had no additional effect on the distribution of participation.

Reliability

Interobserver reliability checks were made on five randomly selected videotaped observations (25% of all observations). Reliability was calculated by dividing the number of agreements by the number of agreements plus disagreements on all communication and decision-making code categories and averaged 92% across the five observations (range = 86% to 96%).

Perceptions of the Intervention

Means and standard deviations for workshop evaluation questionnaire items are reported in Table 10.2. All questionnaire items asked participants to rate the particular workshop along several dimensions using a 5-point Likert-type scale (1 = *very disappointing*, 3 = *acceptable*, 5 = *extremely well done*). In addition to the quantitative items, there were

TABLE 10.2　Means and Standard Deviations of Workshop Evaluation Items[a]

		Mapping (n = 25)	Mirroring (n = 24)	Mining and Refining (n = 22)
Organization	$\overline{X}$	4.16	3.92	4.45
	SD	0.78	0.56	0.50
Content	$\overline{X}$	3.80	3.86	4.23
	SD	0.49	0.66	0.73
Skill practice	$\overline{X}$	3.76	3.68	4.36
	SD	0.86	0.88	0.57
Handouts	$\overline{X}$	3.92	4.25	4.41
	SD	0.69	0.66	0.49
Presenter's delivery	$\overline{X}$	4.12	4.12	4.33
	SD	0.59	0.52	0.47
Workshop overall	$\overline{X}$	3.92	3.81	4.33
	SD	0.69	0.47	0.56
Grand mean	$\overline{X}$	3.95	3.94	4.35
	SD	0.15	0.19	0.07

a. 1 = very disappointing; 5 = extremely well done.

two open-ended items soliciting likes, dislikes, and suggestions regarding the workshop.

The grand mean for all mapping workshop items was 3.95; for the mirroring workshop it was 3.94. The mining and refining workshop received the highest ratings of the three, with a grand mean of 4.35. Means on the individual items for all sessions ranged from 3.68 to 4.45. Open-ended comments indicated that participants found the workshops relevant, useful, and well-organized, but that they would have liked more time for the sessions. Several people commented on the usefulness of the SYNERGY problem-solving process in particular.

Discussion

This study investigated the effects of training an interdisciplinary team in communication and decision-making skills. Using a multiple baseline design across behaviors within one service delivery team, the degree to which a three-part intervention affected the group's behavior in applied work situations was assessed. In addition, subjective measures were used to ascertain participants' satisfaction with the intervention.

Participants' subjective evaluations of the three workshops indicated that they found all three to be useful, enjoyable, and practical, and that they considered the targeted skills to be relevant and worth integrating into their day-to-day work routines. The observations of team meeting behavior yielded data that was highly variable and in which there was considerable overlap between phases, indicating that the intervention did not powerfully affect team dynamics. While many of the targeted skills showed initial "spikes" following intervention in the desired directions, they also returned to baseline levels later in the study. Such results are not surprising given the difficulties associated with achieving transfer of skill use from the training environment to the work environment. Effects of training are often minimal and transient unless some type of ongoing consequences are provided for the newly acquired behaviors (Komaki, Heinzmann, & Lawson, 1980; Quilitch, 1975). Exactly what those consequences would need to be in the case of the skills targeted herein would be a possible avenue for further research. Interpretation of these results is complex, however, given the realities of studying a team with fluctuating membership in its natural context. "Clean" results (whereby the use of targeted skills is absent during baseline and frequent following training) are highly unlikely in a study such as this one because all of the targeted skills occurred to some extent during baseline observations. That is, at least some team members had these skills in their behavioral repertoire from the start. Increases in skill use following intervention could indicate either that some team members acquired new skills and began implementing them in team meetings or that the workshops functioned to call attention to skills already in members' repertoires and enabled members to use them more often as needed.

The latter interpretation may shed some light on the meaning of the observed increases in variability of skill use. While some variability surely stemmed from varying team composition, fluctuating membership alone would not account for observed increases in variability seen only in targeted behaviors following intervention. Instead, variability in skill use may serve as an indicator of a particular skill's consistency of usefulness. Rather than being uniformly useful in all situations and types of meetings, certain targeted skills may be more appropriate in some situations than in others. One interpretation of the observed increases in variability for two of the skill sets, then, is that the first two workshops perhaps served to add to the team members' repertoire of skills and/or to enhance their ability to draw more often on this repertoire as the need for certain skills arose.

A critical difficulty in interpreting this or any other observational data on communication skill use during meetings is that it is as yet unknown what constitutes an optimal level of skill usage. Clearly, all of the targeted skills are relatively low-rate behaviors even when used optimally. For example, if summarizing were to occur any more than once every couple of minutes, the result would be a meeting in which the group spent almost all of its time summarizing its progress while making none! Yet, if summarizing did not occur at all, the group might never succeed in deriving any conclusions from their discussions. Thus a potential avenue of future research might be to attempt to identify optimal skill use under various circumstances.

Similar questions remain unanswered with respect to distribution of participation as were evident for communication skill use. It is generally assumed that fairly equal participation among members will optimize team performance. Different distributions of participation may, however, be more appropriate under certain circumstances. The fact is that no one yet knows what constitutes a particularly high or low distribution of participation or under what circumstances a particular participation index is optimal.

Despite its limitations and modest results, the present investigation contributes to the research on interdisciplinary teams in a number of important ways. The problem of studying team interactions and interventions designed to affect them has always been a thorny one. It has in the past been assumed that a necessary tradeoff exists between scientific rigor and relevance of findings to intact, functioning teams, for the difficulties associated with performing randomized group studies using real-world teams are virtually insurmountable. Yet, by applying the single subject research methodology to the study of an intact team functioning in the community, this study did not sacrifice experimental control as many other studies of real-world teams have. Moreover, the current study identified and operationally defined specific, measurable behaviors as targets of intervention and observation. This kind of approach would seem to be at the heart of any empirical endeavor, yet it has been lacking in much of the existing team-related research. The coding scheme developed for tracking the use of targeted skills using the team meeting as the unit of analysis may be a useful contribution, as may be the creation of a new method for indexing the extent to which participation is distributed among team members during meetings.

A critical area unaddressed by this study and many others is the domain of team outcomes. Only when we are better able to define an interdisciplinary team's success or failure in accomplishing its purpose(s) can we most usefully employ methods such as those developed in this study to delineate the factors that contribute to team success or failure. When team outcomes can be better defined, future research may usefully link team processes to outcomes by asking such questions as: Under what circumstances are particular communication and decision-making behaviors associated with positive and negative team outcomes? What effect does the distribution of participation among team members have on team outcomes? If participation is skewed as opposed to equalized among members, are there particular configurations of participation that contribute toward more positive outcomes (i.e., whose participation matters most?). Is there a predictable relationship between team composition and type of outcome achieved?

Once team outcomes can be reliably defined and evaluated, the relationships between particular outcomes and the processes used to achieve them may be further clarified. The means of observation and intervention employed by this study may prove useful along the way toward that end.

References

Aubrey, C. A., & Felkins, P. K. (1988). *Teamwork: Involving people in quality and productivity improvement.* Milwaukee, WI: Quality Press.

Bailey, D. B. (1984). *Organization development: A total systems approach to positive change in any business organization.* Englewood Cliffs, NJ: Prentice Hall.

Bormann, E. G., & Bormann, N. C. (1988). *Effective small group communication.* Edina, MN: Burgess.

Bulger, R. J. (1985). Hospital team practice. In P. J. Lecca & J. S. McNeil (Eds.), *Interdisciplinary team practice: Issues and trends* (pp. 3-18). New York: Praeger.

Cooley, E. A. (1991, March). Investigating the effects of training an interdisciplinary team in communication and decision-making skills. *Dissertation Abstracts International, 52*(4).

Fox, W. M. (1987). *Effective group problem solving: How to broaden participation, improve decision making, and increase commitment to action.* San Francisco: Jossey-Bass.

Gaitz, C. M. (1987). Multidisciplinary team care of the elderly: The role of the psychiatrist. *The Gerontologist, 27*(5), 553-556.

Giangreco, M. F. (1986). Delivery of therapeutic services in special education programs for learners with severe handicaps. *Physical & Occupational Therapy in Pediatrics, 6*(2), 5-25.

Golightly, C. J. (1987). Transdisciplinary training: A step forward in special education teacher preparation. *Teacher Education and Special Education, 10*(3), 126-130.

Hackman, J. R., & Walton, R. E. (1984, September). *Leading groups in organizations.* Symposium conducted at the Groups in Organizations Conference, Carnegie-Mellon University, Baltimore, MD.

Johnson, D., & Johnson, F. (1987). *Joining together: Group theory and group skills.* Edina, MN: Interaction Book Company.

Kazdin, A. E., & Tuma, A. H. (Eds.). (1982). *Single-case research designs.* San Francisco: Jossey-Bass.

Komaki, J., Heinzmann, A. T., & Lawson, L. (1980). Effect of training and feedback: Component analysis of a behavioral safety program. *Journal of Applied Psychology, 65*, 261-270.

Komaki, J. L., & Zlotnick, S. (1985). Toward effective supervision in business and industry. In L. L'Abate & M. Milan (Eds.), *Handbook of social skills training and research* (pp. 539-554). New York: Wiley.

Lecca, P., & McNeil, J. (Eds.). (1985). *Interdisciplinary team practice: Issues and trends.*
New York: Praeger.
Martin, S. (1988). *Industrial economics: Economic analysis and public policy.* New York:
Macmillan.
McGonigel, M. J., & Garland, C. W. (1988). The individualized family service plan and the
early intervention team: Team and family issues and recommended practices. *Infants
and Young Children, I*(1), 10-21.
Moore, K. J., Fifield, M. B., Spira, D. A., & Scarlato, M. (1989). Child study team decision
making in special education: Improving the process. *Remedial and Special Education,
10*(4), 50-58.
Porras, J. I., & Anderson, B. (1981, Spring). Improving managerial effectiveness through
modeling-based training. *Organizational Dynamics.*
Quilitch, H. R. (1975). A comparison of three staff-management procedures. *Journal of
Applied Behavioral Analysis, 8,* 59-66.
Randolph, W. A., & Blackburn, R. S. (1989). *Managing organizational behavior.* Home-
wood, IL: Irwin.
Robbins, S. P. (1989). *Organizational behavior: Concepts, controversies, and applications.*
Englewood Cliffs, NJ: Prentice Hall.
Rothberg, J. S. (1985). Rehabilitating team practice. In P. Lecca & J. McNeil (Eds.),
Interdisciplinary team practice: Issues and trends. New York: Praeger.
Schmuck, R. A., & Runkel, P. J. (1985). *The handbook of organization development in
schools* (3rd ed.). Palo Alto, CA: Mayfield.
Schweiger, D. M., & Sandberg, W. R. (1989). The utilization of individual capabilities in
group approaches to strategic decision-making. *Strategic Management Journal, 10,*
31-43.
Spencer, P. E., & Coye, R. W. (1988). Project BRIDGE: A team approach to decision-making
for early services. *Infants & Young Children, I*(1), 82-92.
Sugai, G., & Colvin, G. (1990). *From assessment to development: Writing behavior IEPs*
(The Oregon Conference Monograph). Eugene, OR: University of Oregon.
Ulschak, F. L., Nathanson, L., & Gillan, P. G. (1981). *Small group problem solving: An aid
to organizational effectiveness.* Reading, MA: Addison-Wesley.
Zamanou, S., & Glaser, S. R. (1989). *Communication intervention in an organization:
Measuring the results through a triangulation approach.* Paper submitted to the
Applied Communication Section of the 1989 Speech Communication Association
Conference, San Francisco, CA.

IMPLICATIONS FOR HUMAN RESOURCE DEVELOPMENT PROFESSIONALS

The Cooley study has implications for practitioners that are similar to the implications of the McClernon and Swanson (Chapter 9) study. Given the evidence in this study that team-building training did not lead to long-term behavior changes but was perceived by the participants as effective, to what extent should HRD practitioners invest resources in one-time team-building training? Further, how can HRD practitioners manage the performance situation to elicit new behaviors?

IMPLICATIONS FOR RESEARCH DESIGN AND METHODOLOGY

Little effort has been devoted to investigating how team members interact with one another and how these interactions change over time (Baker & Salas, 1992). Clearly, additional research in this area is sorely needed. Single-subject research design is an appropriate methodology when the baseline can not be recovered (e.g., in this situation, knowledge of mapping skills could not be removed from the subjects once this information had been presented). Further, using video camera technology to document team behavior raises questions of its effects on behavior. Future research should consider the effect of the video camera on team member behaviors. An additional concern is the researcher bias that can occur when researchers actively participate in delivering the training that they are also measuring.

IMPLICATIONS FOR FUTURE INQUIRY

Additional research is needed to develop measures of teamwork that accurately judge performance. Baker and Salas (1992) described a study by Brannick et al. (1991) that addressed the issue of construct validity by evaluating multiple measures of teamwork. The study reported that "it appears that team members are limited in their ability to judge their own performance" (p. 473). Cooley's study provides additional support for that view.

Additional research is also needed to identify the long-term behavioral and performance effects of HRD programs. Druckman and Bjork (1994) noted that "the major contribution of team building is its effects on morale, cohesion, cooperation, and mutual trust. These effects do not translate into improved team performance in a simple or direct way. For example, a cohesive team may not improve its performance due to lack of resources, poor intergroup relations, technical problems, or adverse conditions in the environment" (p. 129).

Finally, the results of this study relate to Brooks's (Chapter 7) examination of individual power and team learning. If team participation is a function of formal power, structures, and policies, should HRD practitioners' intervention of choice for improving participation be short-term, nonstructure-changing, team-building interventions?

OTHER RESOURCES

Baker, D. P., & Salas, E. (1992). Principles for measuring teamwork skills. *Human Factors, 34*(4), 469-475.

Druckman, D., & Bjork, R. A. (Eds.). (1994). *Learning, remembering, believing: Enhancing human behavior.* Washington, DC: National Academy Press.

PART III

ORGANIZATIONAL LEARNING AND PERFORMANCE

The assumptions that underlie much of the thinking represented in this section of the book include the following: Learning and work are inherently intertwined, learning is about making meaning from individuals' experiences, organizational learning is more than the sum of individual learning, and as a collective, we are capable of solving difficult organizational challenges (Dixon, 1994).

Definition of Organizational Learning

Although many definitions of organizational learning exist, those offered by the authors of the articles reprinted in this section include the following: "the capacity or processes within an organization to maintain or improve performance based on experience" (Nevis, DiBella, & Gould, Chapter 11, p. 275), "the basic elements and processes of organizational development and growth" (Inkpen & Crossan, Chapter 12, p. 301), "a system that has embedded a continuous learning process and has an enhanced capacity to change or transform" (Watkins & Marsick, Chapter 15, p. 387), and "the process by which knowledge about action outcome relationships between the organization and the environment is developed" (Duncan & Weiss, 1979, p. 84, quoted in Dixon, Chapter 14, p. 350).

Whichever definition is used, organizational learning is typically characterized by ongoing processes and integrated systems that facilitate individuals' and teams' ability to learn, grow, and change as a result of organizational experiences.

Organizational Learning Processes as a Focus for the Articles

The articles in this part address several issues related to understanding the concept and processes of organizational learning. They were chosen for their ability to (a) explicate the characteristics of organizational learning, (b) ground current models of learning and organizational theory, (c) demonstrate the linkages between organizational learning and performance, and (d) address the role of HRD professionals in facilitating organizational learning.

After carefully reviewing various databases and searching for empirical research on organizational learning, we have observed that although the notion of organizational learning dates back more than 20 years to the work of Argyris and Schön (1978), Bateson (1971), and Simon (1969), contemporary scholarly work has been primarily concerned with theory and model building or philosophical forms of research. We see this phase of research as critical and indicative of the first step in a long-term research agenda.

Just as critics of organizational learning are increasingly asking for empirical evidence of the value of organizational learning (Jacobs, 1995; Kuchinke, 1995), we find ourselves on the cusp of the next phase of research. As we scan the horizon, we note that several HRD researchers are in the process of developing and validating survey instruments to diagnose and develop learning organizations, and they are conducting empirical studies that test models and describe the processes and outcomes of organizational learning (ASTD, 1996; Watkins & Marsick, Chapter 15). Because the timing of this book occurs during the transition from theory and model building to empirical research studies, the articles presented in the following pages illustrate this spectrum of scholarship.

The first two articles focus on two different but related conceptual frameworks for understanding organizational learning (Nevis, DiBella & Gould; Inkpen & Crossan). The third article, by Dixon, then reviews some of the theoretical and empirical research literature that underpins the first two articles' frameworks and relates these studies to the role of HRD professionals as facilitators of organizational learning. The fourth article, by Rouiller and Goldstein, is a specific example of the relationship between training transfer climate and the role of HRD professionals in facilitating a learning climate. Finally, the fifth and final article, by Watkins and Marsick, brings us back to a more general framework, but this time with the intent of encouraging HRD professionals to develop an integrated vision of how to build the learning organization.

Overview of the Articles

The first article in this part provides a model for thinking about the construct of the learning organization and offers a framework for examining a company based on its learning capacity. From qualitative case study research with upper-level managers and lower-level workers in two U.S. companies and two European firms, Nevis, DiBella, and Gould (Chapter 11) developed a three-stage model of organizations as learning systems. The stages they identified were (a) knowledge acquisition, (b) knowledge sharing, and (c) knowledge utilization. They acknowledged that most previous research had focused primarily on the acquisition of knowledge and less so on the other two stages, and they suggested that their schema filled this void.

The authors described their model as consisting of two parts. They called the first part *learning orientations*, which are "the values and practices that reflect where learning takes place and the nature of what is learned" (p. 280). These include knowledge source (internal/ external), product-process focus (what/how), documentation mode (personal/public), dissemination mode (formal/informal), learning focus (incremental/transformative), value-chain focus (design/deliver), and skill development focus (individual/group). In the second part of the model they focused on 10 facilitating factors within the organization, which "are the structures and processes that affect how easy or hard it is for learning to occur and the amount of effective learning that takes place" (p. 281). Some of these include scanning imperative, performance gap, concern for measurement, experimental mind-set, and climate of openness. "Helping organizations become better learning systems" (p. 275) was the stated goal of these authors, and they recommended guidelines for developing and implementing a chosen learning strategy.

The strength of this article lies in its comprehensive model and the attention to its theoretical underpinnings. As with all good theory (Hill,

1990), the article illustrates the researchers' point of view about what the independent and dependent variables are and how the construction of organizational learning should be studied. Second, the authors have attempted to summarize knowledge about the laws of learning in a brief, concise way that allows for breadth of understanding and simplicity. The authors further tested the model by gathering data from workshops on personnel from over 20 *Fortune* 500 companies. Finally, they creatively explained how organizational learning occurs and what prevents it from succeeding.

The next article, by Inkpen and Crossan (Chapter 12), is another attempt to develop a conceptual framework for studying organizational learning, but it focuses on the role of managers. The Inkpen and Crossan study examined four key elements of organizational learning: (a) the nature of managerial learning experiences, (b) the sharing and integration of managerial learning within an organization, (c) the institutionalization of learning, and (d) the relationship between organizational learning and performance. The authors further sought to understand (a) the extent to which learning occurs at the individual, group, and organizational levels; (b) the degree to which learning involves both behavioral and cognitive change; (c) the question of whether learning involves a process of change in the cognition and behavior that result in outputs or in content of learning; and (d) whether learning should be tied directly to performance enhancement.

To test out their framework, Inkpen and Crossan studied the learning opportunities of American joint-venture companies and their Japanese partners in the automotive industry. The authors' analysis of nearly 100 interviews uncovered several issues concerning the interrelationships between levels of learning, the cognitive-behavioral interface, and the complicated nature of the learning-performance relationship. Although the authors' research supported the premise that learning occurs at the individual, group, and organizational levels, their most important conclusion may be that the effectiveness of organizational learning practices and processes is largely determined by employees' willingness to "cast off or unlearn past practices" (p. 301). For example, the authors discovered that firms that were failing to compete effectively in the marketplace "often had managers with the most entrenched belief systems" (p. 322), which prevented them from being more flexible in their approach to learning. The authors strongly suggested that managers' beliefs and managerial interpretation systems must be recognized when studying individual and organizational learning. That learners experience interference from previously learned information has been documented in research on individual learning (e.g., Dempster, 1985; McGeoch, 1942; Russ-Eft, 1979; Whitely, 1927). Furthermore, some interference effects may remain even with substantial practice (Pirolli & Anderson, 1985). Such research implies that unlearning is critical but difficult.

The next article (Chapter 13) brings us closer to understanding how previous research on organizational learning might affect the role of HRD in organizations. In her review of the organizational learning literature, Nancy Dixon (1991, 1994) suggested that the changing nature of work, global competition, and consistent organizational change requires that HRD professionals focus on reframing their practice to facilitate organizational learning. Extending Huber's (1991) classification scheme, Dixon organized her findings into five areas: (a) information acquisition, (b) information distribution and interpretation, (c) making meaning, (d) organizational memory, and (e) information retrieval. She then explained what the extant literature contained for each of these areas and described the specific implications for HRD professionals as learning facilitators.

Dixon concluded that "HRD professionals are uniquely positioned to facilitate organizational learning because they are the recognized learning specialists" within an organization (p. 367). However, she warned that for HRD professionals to succeed in this effort, they must engage in learning new processes rather than stay with the more familiar and comfortable practices of the past. The challenges to HRD practitioners are to begin rethinking what it means to learn within organizations and how to provide these opportunities in new and innovative ways.

One way an HRD professional can facilitate organizational learning is by helping the organization develop a positive transfer-of-training climate. In the next article, Rouiller and Goldstein (Chapter 14) have described their investigation of the organizational transfer climate concept and discussed the degree to which climate influences trainees' transfer of the behaviors learned in a training program back to their jobs. The study was conducted with a large fast-food franchise in a metropolitan area. The subjects were 102 assistant managers who participated in an intensive 9-week training program that emphasized both classroom knowledge and hands-on performance improvement. After the training was completed, a variety of instruments were used to measure climate and transfer of training. These included a climate survey developed by the authors, a criterion-referenced knowledge test, a tool to measure transfer behavior through observations by the trainees' managers, a job performance measure completed by the trainees' managers, and the regional manager's rating of the unit's performance.

The authors' multiple regression analyses indicated several interesting findings. First, the study confirmed that "individuals who learn more in training also perform better in transferring those behaviors" (p. 344) and that transfer behaviors are related to job performance ratings. However, the study found that there was no "direct relationship between learning in training and job performance ratings" (p. 343). Nor did the authors find a relationship between unit performance and transfer behavior. Although the authors offered several possible explanations for these findings, they concluded that organizational transfer climate clearly affects the transfer of learned behavior.

The final article (Chapter 15) is included expressly to promote and stimulate a dialogue among HRD professionals regarding a future vision for HRD. This vision has at its core HRD's role in facilitating learning in organizations. Suggesting that the traditional definition of HRD and learning focuses more on outcomes than processes (which is echoed in the article by Inkpen and Crossan), Watkins and Marsick asked human resource developers "to increase individual learning as well as the overall learning capacity of the organization by enabling individuals to be more effective continuous learners, groups to identify and overcome barriers to collective learning, and organizations to create structures and a culture for continuous learning" (p. 373). Instead of looking solely at the learning outcomes of training, the authors have asked us to consider organizational learning as a product of HRD efforts. To explicate this concept, they described how organizational learning occurs. Building on the work of Argyris and Schön (1978), deGeus (1988), Shrivastava (1983), March and Olsen (1975), and Senge (1990), the authors defined and described three types of learning: (a) learning as error detection and correction, (b) learning as changing mental models, and (c) learning as capturing knowledge from experience. Watkins and Marsick; Nevis, DiBella and Gould; and Rouiller and Goldstein have reinforced the finding that learning is best facilitated by a supportive learning culture.

In their conclusion, Watkins and Marsick suggested that the learning organization construct "brings together the fields of training, career development, and organizational development into a single vision of the role of the human resource developer" (p. 386). They found this vision exciting because it expands the HRD professional's role beyond the training classroom and into key organizational change processes.

A sign of good research and scholarly inquiry is that each of the articles in this section leaves us with more questions than answers. In addition, the articles challenge us to think in new ways about the role of HRD professionals. Each article asks us to stop and consider how effective we've been as trainers, instructional designers, organization development consultants, performance technologists, and the like, in fostering organizational learning. The implications of these questions are addressed in each of the following articles.

References

Argyris C., & Schön, D. (1978). *Organizational learning: A theory of action perspective.* Reading, MA: Addison-Wesley.

ASTD. (1996, January). The learning organization: A workshop sponsored by The American Society for Training and Development. Alexandria, VA.

Bateson, G. (1971). *Steps to an ecology of mind.* New York: Ballantine.

DeGeus, S. P. (1988). Planning as learning. *Harvard Business Review, 66*(2), 70-74.

Dempster, F. N. (1985). Proactive interference in sentence recall: Topic-similarity effects and individual differences. *Memory and Cognition,* 81-89.

Dixon, N. (1991). Organizational learning. In R. Jacobs (Ed.), *Organizational issues and human resource development research questions* (pp. 23-31). Columbus, OH: University Council for Research in Human Resource Development. ED 334349.

Dixon, N. (1994). *The organizational learning cycle: How we can learn collectively.* London: McGraw-Hill.

Galagan, P. A. (Ed.). (1994, May). The past, present, and future of workplace learning. *Training & Development, 48*(5).

Hill, W. F. (1990). *Learning: A survey of psychological interpretation.* New York: Harper Collins.

Huber, G. (1991). Organizational learning: The contributing processes and the literatures. *Organizational Science, 2*(1), 88-115.

Jacobs, R. L. (1995). Impressions about the learning organization: Looking to see what is behind the curtain. *Human Resource Development Quarterly, 6*(2), 119-122.

Kuchinke, K. P. (1995). Managing learning for performance. *Human Resource Development Quarterly, 6*(3), 307-316.

Levinthal, D. A., & March, J. C. (1993). The myopia of learning. *Strategic Management Journal, 14,* 95-112.

March, J. G., & Olsen, J. P. (1975). The uncertainty of the past: Organizational learning under ambiguity. *European Journal of Political Research, 3,* 147-171.

McGeoch, J. A. (1942). *The psychology of human learning.* New York: Longmans, Green.

Pirolli, P. L., & Anderson, J. R. (1985). The role of practice in fact retrieval. *Journal of Experimental Psychology: Learning, Memory, and Cognition, 11,* 136-153.

Russ-Eft, D. (1979). Proactive interference: Buildup and release for individual words. *Journal of Experimental Psychology: Human Learning and Memory, 5,* 422-434.

Senge, P. (1990). *The fifth discipline: The art and practice of the learning organization.* New York: Random House.

Shrivastava, P. (1983). A typology of organizational learning systems. *Journal of Management Studies, 20*(1), 8-28.

Simon, H. A. (1969). *The sciences of the artificial.* Cambridge, MA: MIT Press.

Training and Development. (1994). *48*(5).

Whitely, P. L. (1927). The dependence of learning and recall upon prior intellectual activities. *Journal of Experimental Psychology, 10,* 489-508.

Understanding Organizations as Learning Systems

Edwin C. Nevis
MIT Sloan School of Management

Anthony J. DiBella
Boston College

Janet M. Gould
Organizational Learning Center

HOW CAN YOU TELL IF YOUR COMPANY IS, INDEED, A LEARNING ORGANIZATION? What is a learning organization anyway? And how can you improve the learning systems in your company? The authors provide a framework for examining a company, based on its "learning orientations," a set of critical dimensions to organizational learning, and "facilitating factors," the processes that affect how easy or hard it is for learning to occur. They illustrate their model with examples from four firms they studied —Motorola, Mutual Investment Corporation, Electricité de France, and Fiat—and conclude that all organizations have systems that support learning.

Source: Nevis, E. C., DiBella, A. J., & Gould, J. M. (1995, Winter). Understanding organizations as learning systems. *Sloan Management Review,* pp. 73-85. Used by permission.

Authors' Note: The research in this chapter was supported by a grant from the International Consortium for Executive Development Research, Lexington, Massachusetts, and by the MIT Organizational Learning Center. The authors would like to thank Joseph Reelin, Edgar Schein, Peter Senge, and Sandra Waddock for their helpful comments on an earlier version of this paper.

With the decline of some well-established firms, the diminishing competitive power of many companies in a burgeoning world market, and the need for organizational renewal and transformation, interest in organizational learning has grown. Senior managers in many organizations are convinced of the importance of improving learning in their organizations. This growth in awareness has raised many unanswered questions: What is a learning organization? What determines the characteristics of a good learning organization (or are all learning organizations good by definition)? How can organizations improve their learning? In the literature in this area, authors have used different definitions or models of organizational learning or have not defined their terms.[1] Executives have frequently greeted us with comments like these:

- "How would I know a learning organization if I stumbled over it?"
- "You academics have some great ideas, but what do I do with a mature, large organization on Monday morning?"
- "I'm not sure what a good learning organization is, but you should not study us because we are a bad learning organization."

Our research is dedicated to helping organizations become better learning systems. We define organizational learning as the capacity or processes within an organization to maintain or improve performance based on experience. Learning is a systems-level phenomenon because it stays within the organization, even if individuals change. One of our assumptions is that organizations learn as they produce. Learning is as much a task as the production and delivery of goods and services. We do not imply that organizations should sacrifice the speed and quality of production in order to learn, but, rather, that production systems be viewed as learning systems. While companies do not usually regard learning as a function of production, our research on successful firms indicates that three learning-related factors are important for their success:

1. Well-developed core competencies that serve as launch points for new products and services. (Canon has made significant investments over time in developing knowledge in eight core competencies applied in the creation of more than thirty products.)
2. An attitude that supports continuous improvement in the business's value-added chain. (Wal-Mart conducts ongoing experiments in its stores.)
3. The ability to fundamentally renew or revitalize. (Motorola has a long history of renewing itself through its products by periodically exiting old lines and entering new ones.)

These factors identify some of the qualities of an effective learning organization that diligently pursues a constantly enhanced knowledge base. This knowledge allows for the development of competencies and incremental or transformational change. In these instances, there is assimilation and utilization of knowledge and some kind of integrated learning system to support such "actionable learning." Indeed, an organization's ability to survive and grow is based on advantages that stem from core competencies that represent collective learning.[2]

As a corollary to this assumption, we assume that all organizations engage in some form of collective learning as part of their development.[3] The creation of culture and the socialization of members in the culture rely on learning processes to ensure an institutionalized reality.[4] In this sense, it may be redundant to talk of "learning organizations." On the other hand, all learning is not the same; some learning is dysfunctional, and some insights or skills that might lead to useful new actions are often hard to attain. The current concern with the learning organization focuses on the gaps in organizational learning capacity and does not negate the usefulness of those learning processes that organizations may do well, even though they have a learning disability. Thus Argyris and Schön emphasize double-loop learning (generative) as an important, often missing, level of learning in contrast with single-loop learning (corrective), which they have found to be more common.[5] Similarly, Senge makes a highly persuasive case for generative learning, "as contrasted with adaptive learning," which he sees as more prevalent.[6] The focus for these theorists is on the learning required to make transformational changes— changes in basic assumptions—that organizations need in today's fast-moving, often chaotic environment. Their approach does not negate the value of everyday incremental "fixes"; it provides a more complete model for observing and developing organizational learning. After periods of significant discontinuous change, incremental, adaptive learning may be just the thing to help consolidate transformational or generative learning.

Another assumption we make is that the value chain of any organization is a domain of integrated learning. To think of the value chain as an integrated learning system is to think of the work in each major step, beginning with strategic decisions through to customer service, as a sub-system for learning experiments. Structures and processes to achieve outcomes can be seen simultaneously as operational tasks and learning exercises; this holds for discrete functions and for cross-functional activities, such as new product development. The organization encompasses each value-added stage as a step in doing business, not as a fixed classification scheme. Most organizations do not think this way, but it is useful for handling complexity. With this "chunking," we are able to study learning better and to see how integration is achieved at the macro-organizational level. This viewpoint is consistent with a definition of organizations as *complex arrangements of people in which learning takes place.*

While we have not looked at organizations' full value-added chains, we selected our research sites so that we could examine learning in different organizational subsets. In addition, we gathered data indicating preferences or biases in investments in learning at different points of the chain and to understand how learning builds, maintains, improves, or shifts core competencies. Do organizations see certain stages of the chain where significant investment is more desirable than at others?

Our last assumption is that the learning process has identifiable stages. Following Huber, whose comprehensive review of the literature presented four steps in an organizational learning process, we arrived at a three-stage model:

1. Knowledge acquisition—The development or creation of skills, insights, relationships.
2. Knowledge sharing—The dissemination of what has been learned.
3. Knowledge utilization—The integration of learning so it is broadly available and can be generalized to new situations.[7]

Most studies of organizational learning have been concerned with the acquisition of knowledge and, to a lesser extent, with the sharing or dissemination of the acquired knowledge (knowledge transfer). Less is known about the assimilation process, the stage in which knowledge becomes institutionally available, as opposed to being the property of select individuals or groups. Huber refers to the assimilation and utilization process as "organizational memory." While this is an important aspect of knowledge utilization, it is limited and works better when discussing information, as distinct from knowledge. True knowledge is more than information; it includes the meaning or interpretation of the information, and a lot of intangibles such as the tacit knowledge of experienced people that is not well articulated but often determines collective organizational competence. Studies of organizational learning must be concerned with all three stages in the process.

Early in our research, it became clear that organizational learning does not always occur in the linear fashion implied by any stage model. Learning may take place in planned or informal, often unintended, ways. Moreover, knowledge and skill acquisition takes place in the sharing and utilization stages. It is not something that occurs simply by organizing an "acquisition effort." With this in mind, we shifted our emphasis to look for a more fluid and chaotic learning environment, seeking less-defined, more subtle embodiments.

The first phase of our research was based on intensive field observations in four companies, Motorola Corporation, Mutual Investment Corporation (MIC), Electricité de France (EDF), and Fiat Auto Company.[8] We wanted to have both service and manufacturing settings in U.S. and European environments. We chose two sites where we had access to very senior management and two where we were able to study lower levels. We selected Motorola as an example of a good learning organization; we were able to observe organizational learning during its fourteen-year quality improvement effort.

We did not attempt to study entire firms or to concentrate on any single work units in these four organizations. For example, at Motorola, we began by studying two senior management teams of twenty to twenty-five executives each from all parts of the corporation. Each team focuses on a critical issue defined by the CEO and COO, to whom the groups report. The teams' structures were designed as executive education interventions and vehicles for "real-time" problem solving. Our objective was to see how these teams reflected and utilized organizational learning at Motorola.

From our interview data, we identified what organizational members claimed they had learned and why. We wrote case descriptions of the learning processes in their organizations, which we shared with the organizations to ensure their accuracy. Using a grounded analysis, we identified categories that reflected learning orientations and then constructed a two-part model of the critical factors that describe organizations as learning systems. We have since tested this model in data-gathering workshops with personnel from more than twenty *Fortune* 500 companies. Our testing led us to revise some of the model's components, while retaining its overall framework.

Core Themes

Next we discuss the core themes that emerged from our research and provided a basis for our model.

All Organizations Are Learning Systems

All the sites we studied function as learning systems. All have formal and informal processes and structures for the acquisition, sharing, and utilization of knowledge and skills. Members communicated broadly and assimilated values, norms, procedures, and outcome data, starting with early socialization and continuing through group communications, both formal and informal. We talked with staff people in some firms who claimed that their companies were not good learning organizations, but, in each, we were able to identify one or more core competencies that could exist only if there were learning investments in those areas. Some type of structure or process would have to support the informed experience and formal educational interventions required for knowledge acquisition, sharing, and utilization. We found this in both our field sites and other firms. For example, one firm that considers itself to be a poor learning organization because of its difficulty in changing some dysfunction has a reputation in its industry for superior field marketing. It is clear that this group has well-developed recruiting, socialization, training and development, and rotating assignment policies that support its cadre of respected marketing people. Obviously, some learning has been assimilated at a fairly deep level.

Learning Conforms to Culture

The nature of learning and the way in which it occurs are determined by the organization's culture or subcultures. For example, the entrepreneurial style of MIC's investment funds group results in a learning approach in which information is made available to fund managers and analysts, but its use is at the managers' discretion. In addition, there is a good deal of leeway in how fund managers make their investments; some are intuitive, some rely heavily on past performance, and a few use sophisticated computer programs. Thus the fund managers' use or application of learning is largely informal, not dictated by formal, firm-wide programs. Meanwhile, the culture of MIC's marketing groups is more collaborative; learning is derived more from interaction within and between cross-functional work groups and from improved communication.

In contrast, there is no question that a great deal of organizational learning about quality has occurred at Motorola, but its emphasis on engineering and technical concerns resulted in an earlier, complete embrace of total quality by product manufacturing groups. In a culture that heavily rewards product group performance, total quality in products and processes that require integrated, intergroup action lags behind, particularly in the marketing of systems that cut across divisions.

Style Varies between Learning Systems

There are a variety of ways in which organizations create and maximize their learning. Basic assumptions about the culture lead to learning values and investments that produce a different learning style from a culture with another pattern of values and investments. These style variations are based on a series of learning orientations (dimensions of learning) that members of the organization may not see. We have identified seven learning orientations, which we see as bipolar variables.

For example, each of two distinct groups at both Motorola and MIC had different approaches to the way it accrued and utilized knowledge and skills. One Motorola group had great concern for specifying the metrics to define and measure the targeted learning. The other group was less concerned with very specific measures but, instead, stressed broad objectives. In the two groups at MIC, the methods for sharing and utilizing knowledge were very different; one was informal, and the other more formal and collaborative. From these variations, we concluded that the pattern of the learning orientations largely makes up an organizational learning system. The pattern may not tell us how *well* learning is promoted but tells a lot about what is learned and where it occurs.

Generic Processes Facilitate Learning

How well an organization maximizes learning within its chosen style does not occur haphazardly. Our data suggest that talking about "the learning organization" is partially effective; some policies, structures, and processes do seem to make a difference. The difference is in how easy or hard it is for useful learning to happen, and in how effective the organization is in "working its style." By analyzing why learning took place in the companies we studied, we identified ten facilitating factors that induced or supported learning. While we did not observe all the factors at each site, we saw most of them and at other sites as well. Thus we view them as generic factors that any organization can benefit from, regardless of its learning style. For example, scanning, in which benchmarking plays an important role, was so central to learning at Motorola that it is now an integral, ongoing aspect of every important initiative in the company. Although MIC tends to create knowledge and skill internally, it maintains an ongoing vigilance toward its external environment. On the negative side, the absence of solid, ongoing external scanning in other organizations is an important factor in their economic difficulties.

A Model of Organizations as Learning Systems

Our two-part model describes organizations as learning systems (see Figure 11.1). First, *learning orientations* are the values and practices that reflect where learning takes place and the nature of what is learned. These orientations form a pattern that defines a given organization's "learning style." In this sense, they are descriptive factors that help us to understand without making value judgments. Second, *facilitating factors*

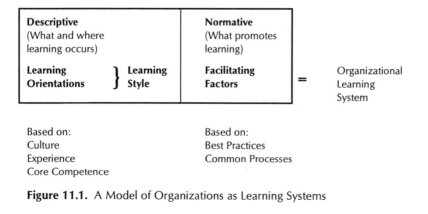

Figure 11.1. A Model of Organizations as Learning Systems

are the structures and processes that affect how easy or hard it is for learning to occur and the amount of effective learning that takes place. These are standards based on best practice in dealing with generic issues. (See the sidebar on page 292 for definitions of the learning orientations and facilitating factors we identified.)

Both parts of the model are required to understand an organization as a learning system; one without the other provides an incomplete picture. In addition, separating the parts enables organizations to see that they do indeed function as learning systems of some kind, and that their task is to understand better what they do well or poorly. (The idea of assessing what exists is more useful than the pejorative notion that there is only one good way to be a learning organization.) Finally, a refined, detailed list of factors related to organizational learning may help companies select areas for learning improvement that do not demand drastic culture change but, rather, can lead to incremental change over time.

Learning Orientations

In the next section, we expand on the definitions of the seven learning orientations and provide examples of each.

1. Knowledge Source. To what extent does the organization develop new knowledge internally or seek inspiration in external ideas? This distinction is seen as the difference between innovation and adaptation—or imitation. In the United States, there is a tendency to value innovativeness more highly and look down on "copiers." American critiques of Japanese businesses often mention that the Japanese are good imitators but not good innovators. In our opinion, both of these approaches have great merit as opposing styles rather than as normative or negative behaviors.

good imitators but not good innovators. In our opinion, both of these approaches have great merit as opposing styles rather than as normative or negative behaviors.

Although our data show a tendency in organizations to prefer one mode over the other, the distinction is not clear-cut. While MIC does scan its environment, it prefers to innovate in responding to customer needs and problems and has been a leader in developing new financial products and services. EDF modeled its nuclear power plants on U.S. technology. Motorola appears to be equally vigorous in innovation and in reflective imitation; it has been innovative in developing new products and adroit at adapting others' processes, such as benchmarking and TQM procedures. Among firms not in this study, American Airlines, Wal-Mart, Merck, and Rubbermaid appear to be innovative in producing knowledge. And American Home Products is a good example of a highly successful, reflective imitator, as are AT&T's Universal Credit Card, Tyco Toys (a Lego "copier"), and Lexus and Infiniti automobiles.

2. *Product-Process Focus.* Does the organization prefer to accumulate knowledge about product and service outcomes or about the basic processes underlying various products? Many observers have stated that one reason Japanese companies are so competitive is that they make considerably more investments in process technologies in comparison to U.S. companies. The difference is between interest in "getting product out the door" and curiosity about the steps in the processes. All organizations give some attention to each side; the issue is to organize for learning in both domains.

Motorola makes learning investments on both sides. The executives we observed spent roughly equal amounts of time in collaborative learning about processes and outcomes. They paid less attention to "people processes" than to "hard" or technical processes, but many of them accepted the importance of process issues. MIC, EDF, and Fiat have traditionally focused almost exclusively on product issues but are now making greater learning investments in process issues.

3. *Documentation Mode.* Do attitudes vary as to what constitutes knowledge and where knowledge resides? At one pole, knowledge is seen in personal terms, as something an individual possesses by virtue of education or experience. This kind of knowledge is lost when a long-time employee leaves an organization; processes and insights evaporate because they were not shared or made a part of collective memory. At the other pole, knowledge is defined in more objective, social terms, as being a consensually supported result of information processing. This attitude emphasizes organizational memory or a pub-licly documented body of knowledge.

MIC's investment funds group focuses on a personal documentation style, eschewing policy statements and procedure manuals. In keeping with its entrepreneurial orientation, MIC makes it possible for individuals to learn a great deal, but there is little pressure to codify this. Though engaged in a business that values "hard data," the group supports subjective, tacit knowledge in decision-making processes. And at Fiat's Direzione Technica, where the individual has historically been the repository of knowledge, efforts are being made to establish a *memoria technica,* or engineering knowledge bank. Motorola shows evidence of both approaches but works hard to make knowledge explicit and broadly available.

4. *Dissemination Mode.* Has the organization established an atmosphere in which learning evolves or in which a more structured, controlled approach induces learning? In the more structured approach, the company decides that valuable insights or methods should be shared and used by others across the organization. It uses written communication and formal educational methods or certifies learning through writing the procedures down. In the more informal approach, learning is spread through encounters between role models and gatekeepers who compellingly reinforce learning. In another approach, learning occurs when members of an occupational group or work team share their experiences in ongoing dialogue.[10]

MIC's investment funds group clearly prefers informal dissemination in which learning develops and is shared in loosely organized interactions. This method occurs in other MIC areas, although the marketing groups are becoming more structured in their dissemination. Motorola supports both approaches, though it invests heavily in structured, firmwide programs when senior management wants a basic value or method institutionalized. It considered quality so critical that it now includes vendors and customers in its dissemination. (Recently, some vendors were told that they had to compete for the Malcolm Baldrige Quality Award in order to be on the company's approved vendor list.) EDF prefers formal modes, emphasizing documented procedures that all share. Fiat's Direzione Technica formally spreads knowledge by accumulating it in specialist departments and then disseminating it to cross-functional design teams.

If a particular organization is "engineering focused" or "marketing driven," it is biased in favor of substantial learning investments in those areas.

5. *Learning Focus.* Is learning concentrated on methods and tools to improve what is already being done or on testing the assumptions underlying what is being done? Argyris and Schön call the former

"single-loop learning" and the latter "double-loop learning."[11] They have rightfully argued that organizational performance problems are more likely due to a lack of awareness and inability to articulate and check underlying assumptions than to a function of poor efficiency. In our opinion, these learning capabilities reinforce each other. Organizations may have a preference for one mode over the other, but a sound learning system can benefit from good work in both areas.

Our research sites displayed a range of behavior. EDF is primarily focused on incremental issues and does not question its basic assumptions. It prides itself on being the world's major nuclear power utility and devotes significant resources to being the most efficient, safe operator through small improvements rather than transformations. Though similar, Fiat's Direzione Technica is beginning to question assumptions about its new product development process. Since 1987, MIC has been in a transformational mode, particularly in the way that its marketing groups have focused on a questioning learning style. Motorola is fairly well balanced in its orientation; the founding family has historically accepted the concept of organizational renewal, which has led to far-reaching changes in the company's product lines through the years and to an inquisitive style. On the other hand, its strong dedication to efficiency learning often precludes questioning basic assumptions.

6. *Value-Chain Focus.* Which core competencies and learning investments does the organization value and support? By learning investments, we mean all allocations of personnel and money to develop knowledge and skill over time, including training and education, pilot projects, developmental assignments, available resources, and so on. If a particular organization is "engineering focused" or "marketing driven," it is biased in favor of substantial learning investments in those areas. We divided the value chain into two categories: internally directed activities of a "design and make" nature, and those more externally focused of a "sell and deliver" nature. The former include R&D, engineering, and manufacturing. The latter are sales, distribution, and service activities. Although this does some disservice to the value chain concept, the breakdown easily accounts for our observations.

At MIC, the investment funds group focuses on the design and make side. While this is balanced by learning investments on the deliver side in the MIC marketing groups, there is a strong boundary between these groups, and the fund management side is regarded as the organization's core. Motorola's total quality effort clearly recognizes the importance of value-added at both sides, but "design and make" is significantly ahead of "deliver" in learning investments in quality. Fiat's Direzione Technica is clearly oriented toward design and make, although its new system of simultaneous engineering is balancing its approach with increased sensitively to the deliver side. EDF nuclear operations focuses squarely on efficient production. While not in our study, Digital Equipment Corporation's learning investments traditionally were much more heavily focused on "design and make" than on "deliver."

7. Skill Development Focus. Does the organization develop both individual and group skills? We believe it helps to view this as a stylistic choice, as opposed to seeing it in normative terms. In this way, an organization can assess how it is doing and improve either one. It can also develop better ways of integrating individual learning programs with team needs by taking a harder look at the value of group development.

MIC designed the investment funds group to promote individual learning, which seems to fit with its culture and reward system. Heavy investment in team learning would probably improve its performance. On the other hand, MIC's marketing groups, more supportive of collective learning, are now investing in team development as one way to improve its total effectiveness. Fiat's Direzione Technica has been oriented toward more individual development, but, with its new reliance on cross-functional work teams, group development is increasingly more important. Recently, Motorola has become more team oriented and is making heavier investments in collaborative learning. It designed the two executive groups we observed to foster collective learning on two strategic issues affecting the entire company. EDF develops both individual and group skills, especially in control-room teams. All EDF employees follow individual training programs for certification or promotion. Control-room teams also learn, in groups, by using plant simulators. Some other firms that emphasize team learning are Federal Express, which invests heavily in teams for its quality effort, and Herman Miller, which stresses participative management and the Scanlon plan.

We view the seven learning orientations as a matrix. An organizational unit can be described by the pattern of its orientations in the matrix, which in turn provides a way to identify its learning style. Given the characteristics of the sites we studied and other sites we are familiar with, we believe it is possible to identify learning styles that represent a distinct pattern of orientations. Such styles may reflect the industry, size, or age of an organization, or the nature of its technology.

Facilitating Factors

The second part of our model is the facilitating factors that expedite learning. The ten factors are defined in the sidebar on page 292.

1. *Scanning Imperative.* Does the organization understand or comprehend the environment in which it functions? In recent years, researchers have emphasized the importance of environmental scanning and agreed that many organizations were in trouble because of limited or poor scanning efforts. Thus many firms have increased their scanning capacity. Five years into Motorola's quality program, a significant scanning effort showed it what others, particularly the Japanese, were doing. In reaction, Motorola substantially changed its approach and won the first Baldrige Award four years later. By contrast, the mainframe computer manufacturers (Cray, Unisys, IBM) and the U.S. auto companies in the 1970s failed to respond to developing changes that sound investigative work would have made painfully visible. Recent changes at Fiat result from a concerted scanning effort in which fifty senior managers visited the manufacturing facilities of world-class auto and other durable goods companies.

2. *Performance Gap.* First, how do managers, familiar with looking at the differences between targeted outcomes and actual performance, analyze variances? When feedback shows a gap, particularly if it implies failure, their analysis often leads to experimenting and developing new insights and skills. One reason that well-established, long-successful organizations are often not good learning systems is that they experience lengthy periods in which feedback is almost entirely positive; the lack of disconfirming evidence is a barrier to learning.

Secondly, is there a potential new vision that is not simply a quantitative extension of the old or goes well beyond the performance level seen as achievable in the old vision? One or more firm members may visualize something not previously noted. Awareness of a performance gap is important because it often leads the organization to recognize that learning needs to occur or that something already known may not be working. Even if a group cannot articulate exactly what that need might be, its awareness of ignorance can motivate learning, as occurred at Motorola after its 1984 benchmarking. Currently, this "humility" is driving Fiat's Direzione Technica to make a major study of what it needs to know.

In our findings, EDF provides perhaps the best instance of a performance gap leading to adaptive learning. Due to the nature of the nuclear power business, performance variations became the catalyst for a learning effort to again achieve the prescribed standard. We also found that future-oriented CEOs encouraged performance-gap considerations related to generative learning at Motorola and MIC (parent company).

3. *Concern for Measurement.* Does the organization develop and use metrics that support learning? Are measures internally or externally

focused, specific, and custom-built or standard measures? The importance of metrics in total quality programs has been well documented and is used in target-setting programs such as management by objectives.[12] Our interest is in how the discourse about measurements, and the search for the most appropriate ones, is a critical aspect of learning, almost as much as learning that evolves from responding to the feedback that metrics provide.

Motorola executives believe that concern for measurement was one of the most critical reasons for their quality program's success. At three or four critical junctures, reexamination of measurement issues helped propel a move to a new level of learning. They are applying this factor to new initiatives, a major concern of the executive groups we observed. At EDF, the value of metrics is clearly associated with the performance gap. Its nuclear power plants are authorized to operate at certain specifications that, if not met, may suggest or predict an unplanned event leading to shutdown. Each occasion becomes an opportunity for learning to take place.

4. Experimental Mind-Set. Does the organization emphasize experimentation on an ongoing basis? If learning comes through experience, it follows that the more one can plan guided experiences, the more one will learn. Until managers see organizing for production at any stage of the value chain as a learning experiment as well as a production activity, learning will come slowly. Managers need to learn to act like applied research scientists at the same time they deliver goods and services.[13]

We did not see significant evidence of experimental mind-sets at our research sites, with some notable exceptions at Motorola. At its paging products operation, we observed the current production line for one product, a blueprint and preparation for the new setup to replace the line, and a "white room" laboratory in which research is now underway for the line that will replace the one currently being installed. Motorola University constantly tries new learning approaches; the two executive groups we observed at Motorola were also part of an experiment in executive education.

We have seen evidence of experimental mind-sets in reports about other firms. For example, on any given day, Wal-Mart conducts about 250 tests in its stores, concentrated on sales promotion, display, and customer service. Although a traditional firm in many ways, 3M's attitude toward new product development and operational unit size suggests a strong experimental mind-set.

5. Climate of Openness. Are the boundaries around information flow permeable so people can make their own observations? Much informal learning is a function of daily, often unplanned interactions among people. In addition, the opportunity to meet with other groups and see higher levels of management in operation promotes learning.[14] People need freedom to express their views through legitimate disagreement and debate. Another critical aspect is the extent to which errors are shared and not hidden.[15]

Perhaps the most dramatic example of openness in our findings is EDF, where abnormalities or deviations are publicly reported throughout the entire system of fifty-seven nuclear power plants. The company treats such incidents as researchable events to see if the problem exists anywhere else and follows up with a learning-driven investigation to eliminate it. It then disseminates this knowledge throughout the company. While this openness may be explained by the critical nature of problems in a nuclear power plant, we can only speculate as to what would be gained if any organization functioned as though a mistake is potentially disastrous and also an opportunity to learn.

6. *Continuous Education.* Is there a commitment to lifelong education at all levels of the organization? This includes formal programs but goes well beyond that to more pervasive support of any kind of developmental experience. The mere presence of traditional training and development activities is not sufficient; it must be accompanied by a palpable sense that one is never finished learning and practicing (something akin to the Samurai tradition). The extent to which this commitment permeates the entire organization, and not just the training and development groups, is another indicator. In many ways, this factor is another way of expressing what Senge calls "personal mastery."

MIC does an excellent job of exposing its young analysts to developmental experiences. Its chairman also seeks knowledge in many areas, not just direct financial matters. Motorola has a policy in which every employee has some educational experience every year; it has joint ventures with several community colleges around the country, joint programs with the state of Illinois for software competence development and training of school superintendents, and on-the-job and classroom experiences for managers up to the senior level. The company spends 3.6 percent of its revenues on education and plans to double this amount.[16] Among firms not in our study, General Electric, Unilever, and Digital Equipment Corporation have valued continuous education at all levels for many years.

7. *Operational Variety.* Is there more than one way to accomplish work goals? An organization that supports variation in strategy, policy, process, structure, and personnel is more adaptable when unforeseen problems arise. It provides more options and, perhaps even more important, allows for rich stimulation and interpretation for all its mem-

bers. This factor helps enhance future learning in a way not possible with a singular approach.

We did not see a great deal of variety at our sites. EDF, perhaps due to the importance of total control over operations, shows little variation. Fiat's Direzione Technica follows similar response routines, although the change to a new structure should lead to greater variation because of its independent design teams. An exception is MIC investment funds group, where we identified at least three different methods that fund managers used in making investment decisions. Senior management, although a bit skeptical about one of the methods, seemed willing to support all three as legitimate approaches.

8. Multiple Advocates. Along with involved leadership, is there more than one "champion" who sets the stage for learning? This is particularly necessary in learning that is related to changing a basic value or a long-cherished method. The greater the number of advocates who promote a new idea, the more rapidly and extensively the learning will take place. Moreover, in an effective system, any member should be able to act as an awareness-enhancing agent or an advocate for new competence development. In this way, both top-down and bottom-up initiatives are possible.

The greater the number of advocates who promote a new idea, the more rapidly and extensively the learning will take place.

One of the authors participated in two significant change efforts that failed, largely because there was only one champion in each case. One highly frustrated CEO said, "It doesn't do me or the company any good if I'm the only champion of this new way of doing business." At Motorola, we found that a major factor in the quality effort's success was the early identification, empowerment, and encouragement of a significant number of advocates. In a current initiative we observed, Motorola is enlisting a minimum of 300 champions in strategic parts of the company. Digital Equipment Corporation has had learning initiators throughout the company since its early days. Digital's problem has been in assimilating and integrating the lessons of its myriad educational and experimental efforts, rather than in creating an environment that enables broad-scale initiation. MIC's investment funds group encourages many individuals to initiate their own learning but not to proselytize.

9. Involved Leadership. Is leadership at every organizational level engaged in hands-on implementation of the vision? This includes eliminating management layers, being visible in the bowels of the organization, and being an active, early participant in any learning effort. Only through direct involvement that reflects coordination, vision, and integration can leaders obtain important data and provide powerful role models.

At Motorola, CEO Bob Galvin not only drove the quality vision, he was a student in the first seminars on quality and made it the first item on the agenda at monthly meetings with his division executives. Much-admired Wal-Mart CEO David Glass spends two or three days each week at stores and warehouses; employees can call him at home and are often transferred to his hotel when he is in the field. Mike Walsh of Tenneco (formerly of Union Pacific Railroad) meets with groups of employees at all levels in what Tom Peters calls "conversation."[17]

10. Systems Perspective. Do the key actors think broadly about the interdependency of organizational variables? This involves the degree to which managers can look at their internal systems as a source of their difficulties, as opposed to blaming external factors. Research in the field of systems dynamics has demonstrated how managers elicit unintended consequences by taking action in one area without seeing its dynamic relationship to its effects.[18]

Despite its importance, this factor was relatively lacking at our research sites. MIC and Motorola are structured so that there are strong boundaries between groups and functions. Both have changed their perspectives recently, MIC as a consequence of unexpected internal problems related to the October 1987 stock market crash, and Motorola after experiencing difficulties in selling large-scale systems (as opposed to discrete products). In a 1992 survey of 3,000 Motorola employees that asked them to evaluate their unit based on Senge's five factors, they rated systems thinking the lowest and the one that required the most work to improve organizational learning. In contrast, Fiat's Direzione Technica took a systems approach to understanding the consequences of its structure on new product development. As a result, it changed the structure to establish mechanisms for simultaneous engineering. To reduce the new products' time to market, functions now work in parallel rather than sequentially.

General Directions for Enhancing Learning

We have divided the seven learning orientations and ten facilitating factors into three stages—knowledge acquisition, dissemination, and utilization. Figure 11.2 shows the orientations and factors within this framework. Within our two-part model, there are two general directions for enhancing learning in an organizational unit. One is to embrace the existing style and improve its effectiveness. This strategy develops a fundamental part of the culture to its fullest extent. For example, a firm that is a reflective imitator more than an innovator could adopt this strategy with heightened awareness of its value. A company that has

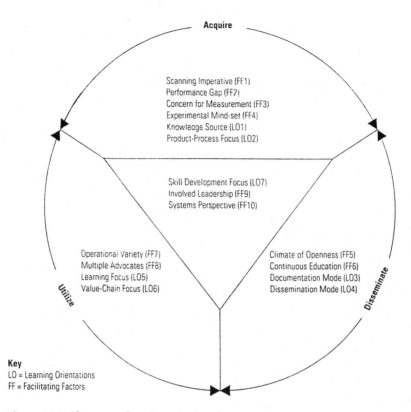

Acquire

Scanning Imperative (FF1)
Performance Gap (FF2)
Concern for Measurement (FF3)
Experimental Mind-set (FF4)
Knowledge Source (LO1)
Product-Process Focus (LO2)

Skill Development Focus (LO7)
Involved Leadership (FF9)
Systems Perspective (FF10)

Operational Variety (FF7)
Multiple Advocates (FF8)
Learning Focus (LO5)
Value-Chain Focus (LO6)

Climate of Openness (FF5)
Continuous Education (FF6)
Documentation Mode (LO3)
Dissemination Mode (LO4)

Utilize

Disseminate

Key
LO = Learning Orientations
FF = Facilitating Factors

Figure 11.2. Elements of an Organizational Learning System

benefited from heavy learning investments on the "make" side of the value chain would see the value of those investments and decide to build further on them. This approach builds on the notion that full acceptance of what has been accomplished is validating and energizing for those involved. It is similar to the appreciative inquiry numerous organizational change consultants advocate.[19] The task is to select two or three facilitating factors to improve on.

The second direction is to change learning orientations. The organizational group would make more learning investments at a different part of the value chain, try to be an innovator if it is now more of an imitator, and so on. These are different changes from those involved in enhancing the facilitative factors, and the tactics will be different. Some changes will be seen as an attack on the organization's basic values, and it may be possible to avoid this by moving toward balance between the two poles, so members of the organization will support the existing style and advocate the "new look" as a supplementary measure.

Definitions of the Orientations and Factors

Seven Learning Orientations

1. **Knowledge Source: Internal—External.** Preference for developing knowledge internally versus preference for acquiring knowledge developed externally.

2. **Product-Process Focus: What?—How?** Emphasis on accumulation of knowledge about what products/services are versus how organization develops, makes, and delivers its products/services.

3. **Documentation Mode: Personal—Public.** Knowledge is something individuals possess versus publicly available know-how.

4. **Dissemination Mode: Formal—Informal.** Formal, prescribed, organization-wide methods of sharing learning versus informal methods, such as role modeling and casual daily interaction.

5. **Learning Focus: Incremental—Transformative.** Incremental or corrective learning versus transformative or radical learning.

6. **Value-Chain Focus: Design—Deliver.** Emphasis on learning investments in engineering/production activities ("design and make" functions) versus sales/service activities ("market and deliver" functions).

7. **Skill Development Focus: Individual—Group.** Development of individuals' skills versus team or group skills.

Ten Facilitating Factors

1. **Scanning Imperative.** Information gathering about conditions and practices outside the unit awareness of the environment; curiosity about the external environment in contrast to the internal environment.

2. **Performance Gap.** Shared perception of a gap between actual and desired state of performance; performance shortfalls seen as opportunities for learning.

3. **Concern for Measurement.** Considerable effort spent on defining and measuring key factors when venturing into new areas; striving for specific, quantifiable measures; discussion of metrics as a learning activity.

4. **Experimental Mind-set.** Support for trying new things; curiosity about how things work; ability to "play" with things: "failures" are accepted, not punished; changes in work processes, policies, and structures are a continuous series of learning opportunities.

5. **Climate of Openness.** Accessibility of information; open communications within the organization; problems/errors/lessons are shared, not hidden; debate and conflict are acceptable ways to solve problems.

6. **Continuous Education.** Ongoing commitment to education at all levels of the organization; clear support for all members' growth and development.

7. **Operational Variety.** Variety of methods, procedures, and systems, appreciation of diversity, pluralistic rather than singular definition of valued competencies.

8. **Multiple Advocates.** New ideas and methods advanced by employees at all levels; more than one champion.

9. **Involved Leadership.** Leaders articulate vision, are engaged in its implementation; frequently interact with members; become actively involved in educational programs.

10. **Systems Perspective.** Interdependence of organizational units; problems and solutions seen in terms of systemic relationships among processes; connection between the unit's needs and goals and the company's.

Supporting the Learning Orientations

In the second phase of our research, in which we worked closely with personnel from more than thirty *Fortune* 500 companies to identify their learning orientations, we validated our notion that organizations learn in varied ways. The singular "learning organization" should be a pluralistic model.

Looking at "what is" in a descriptive rather than normative way has another advantage in that you see better what you are *not* by examining better what you *are*. In the gestalt approach to dealing with resistance to organizational change, it has been well documented that change comes more readily if the targets of change first become more aware of and more accepting of their resistance.[20] In other words, it is important to gain full knowledge and appreciation of your organizational assumptions about learning whether you want to build on them or alter them.

This model may also be used to identify the complementarity of styles between coordinating organizations and to recognize that circumstances may dictate conditions and orientations in particular settings. For example, EDF's nuclear operations are constrained from transforming real-time operations due to the potentially dire consequences (e.g., the Chernobyl disaster) of operating under novel assumptions. However, at EDF, testing system assumptions is characteristic of its R&D division, which uses new technologies in the design of new plants. Thus changing one's style needs to be considered from a systems perspective; it may also be associated with the stage of organizational development.[21]

Strategies for Improving Organizational Learning Capability

When starting to improve its learning capabilities, an organization may decide to focus on any stage of the learning cycle—knowledge acquisition, dissemination, or utilization. While it may be possible or necessary to look at all three phases simultaneously, focusing on a single area is more manageable. The next task is to select an option for focus:

1. Improve on learning orientations. There are two reasons for selecting this option. First, the organization may decide to shift its position on one or more learning orientations. Second, the current pattern of learning orientations has resulted in identifiable strong competencies, so improving or expanding them may be the best way to enhance the unit's learning capabilities. This focus assumes that facilitating factors meet an acceptable standard and that more can be accomplished by adding to the strong base established by the learning orientations.

2. Improve on facilitating factors. In this option, the organization accepts its pattern of learning orientations as adequate or appropriate to its culture and decides that improving the systems and structures of the facilitating factors is the most useful course. This option assumes that maximizing the facilitating factors would add more to the organization's learning capabilities than enhancing or changing the current learning orientations.

3. Change both learning orientations and facilitating factors. An organization should select this option when it sees the other variables as inadequate. This option assumes that large-scale change is necessary and that changing one group of variables without changing the other will be only partially successful.

Each organizational unit or firm must make the decision to pursue one strategy or another for itself. While there are no rules for making this decision, the three options are incrementally more difficult to implement (i.e., one is the easiest to implement; three is the hardest). From the first to the third options, the resistance to change within the organization increases significantly. It is one thing to develop a plan for improving what is already done reasonably well; it is another to engage in nothing less than near-total transformation. It is one thing to stay within accepted, assimilated paradigms; it is another to replace institutionalized models.

Whatever the organization's choice, we offer three guidelines for developing and implementing a chosen strategy:

1. Before deciding to become something new, study and evaluate what you are now. Without full awareness and appreciation of current assumptions about management, organization, and learning, it is not possible to grasp what is being done well and what might be improved or changed.

2. Though the systemic issues and relationships in organizational life require that change be approached from multiple directions and at several points, organizations can change in major ways if people experience success with more modest, focused, and specific changes. As with many skills, there is a learning curve for the skill of managing and surviving transitions. Large-scale change requires that many initiatives be put into place in a carefully designed, integrated sequence.

3. Organizations must consider cultural factors in choosing and implementing any strategy, particularly when considering how it does specific things. For example, in a highly individualistic society like the United States or the United Kingdom, skill development focuses on

individual skills; in comparison, more communitarian societies such as Japan or Korea have traditionally focused on group skill development. Moving from one pole to the other is a major cultural change; to simply improve on the existing orientation is much easier.

To help managers better understand the learning capabilities in their own organizations, we have developed and are testing an "organizational learning inventory." This diagnostic tool will enable an organization's members to produce a learning profile based on our model. The profile can guide managers to their choices for improving learning capability. Through further research, we intend to show how learning profiles vary within and across different companies and industries.

Notes

1. C. Argyris, "Double Loop Learning in Organizations," *Harvard Business Review,* September-October 1977, pp. 115-124; K. Weick, *The Social Psychology of Organizing* (Reading, Massachusetts: Addison-Wesley, 1979); B. Leavitt and J. G. March, "Organizational Learning," *Annual Review of Sociology* 14 (1988): 319-340; P. M. Senge, *The Fifth Discipline* (New York: Doubleday, 1990); and E. H. Schein, "How Can Organizations Learn Faster? The Challenge of Entering the Green Room," *Sloan Management Review,* Winter 1993, pp. 85-92.

2. C. K. Prahalad and G. Hamel, "The Core Competence of the Corporation," *Harvard Business Review,* May-June 1990, pp. 79-91.

3. J. Child and A. Kieser, "Development of Organizations Over Time," in N. C. Nystrom and W. H. Starbuck, eds., *Handbook of Organizational Design* (Oxford: Oxford University Press, 1981), pp. 28-64; and E. H. Schein, *Organizational Culture and Leadership* (San Francisco: Jossey-Bass, 1992).

4. J. Van Maanen and E. H. Schein, "Toward a Theory of Organizational Socialization," *Research in Organizational Behavior* 1 (1979): 1-37.

5. C. Argyris and D. A. Schön, *Organizational Learning: A Theory of Action Perspective* (Reading, Massachusetts: Addison-Wesley, 1978).

6. Senge (1990).

7. Huber identifies four constructs linked to organizational learning that he labels knowledge acquisition, information distribution, information interpretation, and organizational memory. Implicit in this formulation is that learning progresses through a series of stages. Our framework makes this sequence explicit and connects it to organizational action. Huber does not make this connection since to him learning alters the range of potential, rather than actual, behaviors. See: G. Huber, "Organizational Learning: The Contributing Processes and Literature, *Organization Science* 2 (1991): 88-115.

8. At Motorola, we observed and interviewed fifty senior managers, visited the paging products operations, and had access to about twenty-five internal documents. At Mutual Investment Corporation (a pseudonym for a large financial services company based in the United States), we observed and interviewed corporation employees in the investment funds group and the marketing groups. At Electricité de France, we observed and interviewed employees in the nuclear power operations. At Fiat, we observed and interviewed employees in the Direzione Technica (engineering division) in Torino, Italy.

9. A. Strauss, *Qualitative Analysis for Social Scientists* (Cambridge: Cambridge University Press, 1987).

10. For a discussion of "communities of practice" see J. S. Brown and P. Puguid, "Organizational Learning and Communities of Practice," *Organization Science* 2 (1991): 40-57.

11. Argyris and Schön (1978).

12. W. H. Schmidt and J. P. Finnegan, *The Race Without a Finish Line: America's Quest for Total Quality* (San Francisco: Jossey-Bass, 1992).

13. For the idea of the factory as a learning laboratory, see D. Leonard-Barton, "The Factory as a Learning Laboratory," *Sloan Management Review*, Fall 1992, pp. 39-52.

14. This skill has been referred to as "legitimate peripheral participation." See J. Lave and E. Wenger, *Situated Learning: Legitimate Peripheral Participation* (Palo Alto, California: Institute for Research on Learning, IRL Report 90-0013, 1990).

15. C. Argyris, *Strategy, Change, and Defensive Routines* (Boston: Putman, 1985).

16. See "Companies That Train Best," *Fortune*, 8 February 1993, pp. 44-48; and "Motorola: Training for the Millennium," *Business Week*, 28 March 1994, pp. 158-163.

17. T. Peters, *Liberation Management* (New York: Knopf, 1992).

18. Jay W. Forrester is considered to be the founder of the field of systems thinking.

19. S. Srivastra and D. L. Cooperrider and Associates, *Appreciative Management and Leadership* (San Francisco: Jossey-Bass, 1990).

20. E. Nevis, *Organizational Consulting: A Gestalt Approach* (Cleveland: Gestalt Institute of Cleveland Press, 1987).

21. W. R. Torbert, *Managing the Corporate Dream* (New York: Dow Jones-Irwin, 1987).

IMPLICATIONS FOR HUMAN RESOURCE DEVELOPMENT PROFESSIONALS

Although this article does not directly address the role of HRD professionals, there are nonetheless at least two implications for the field. First, the authors' work suggests that organizations must study their own learning orientation and capabilities to determine the most effective organizational learning strategies and tactics. If we conceive of HRD practitioners as learning/performance specialists who have expertise in the design, development, delivery/facilitation, and evaluation of educational experiences, it behooves those in the field to take the lead in fostering organizational learning; for it is HRD professionals whose specific training has focused on adult learning, effective instructional design, and organizational development practices and processes. If this group does not pick up the gauntlet, those in the field of HRD may be left behind.

The second implication relates to the need for HRD professionals to link their efforts to the organization's culture, mission, and strategic plan. No longer can the training function exist as a silo, isolated from the other systems within the organization. In times of downsizing, cost reduction, and a competitive global market, trainers must continually seek ways to determine how learning can best be facilitated at the individual, group, and organizational levels in ways that support the success of the organization and its employees.

IMPLICATIONS FOR RESEARCH DESIGN AND METHODOLOGY

The authors' "organizational learning inventory" and other surveys/ tools currently being developed provide rich opportunities for initiating applied organizational research. Using one of these tools in different companies and industries could contribute significantly to our understanding of the factors and competencies that influence organizational learning across work environments. Additional research using the model developed by Nevis, DiBella, and Gould (knowledge acquisition, knowledge sharing, and knowledge utilization) would also be instructive as a study involving multiple organizations. This cross-case, mixed-method research using a particular framework would provide us with greater depth of knowledge regarding the organizational learning construct and the degree to which the recommended processes and practices influence an organization's success.

IMPLICATIONS FOR FUTURE INQUIRY

Studies using the various learning assessment instruments currently being developed should also be undertaken. Comparative research using several of these tools in an organization and across organizations would help determine the construct validity of these instruments and identify which instruments are best used for diagnostic versus developmental purposes. Establishing the content and construct validity and recognizing the appropriate uses of these instruments would certainly further the development of organizational learning theory and practice.

At the end of the article, the authors suggested that organizations consider cultural factors in choosing and implementing any learning strategy. Research on what these cultural factors are and how they influence learning would be extremely valuable. Furthermore, research on organizational readiness warrants further study (e.g., Redding &

Catalanello, 1994). This research might address such questions as: How do we know when an organization is ready to "learn" more and differently? To what extent does it take a crisis or need for transformational change to create this readiness? How can researchers effectively assess the ways in which organizations learn? What are the most effective research designs and methods for such studies?

Finally, additional research must consider specific, concrete ways that organizational learning contributes to individual, team, and organizational performance. We must consider not only the financial outcomes of learning, if they can be determined, but also its effect on the more affective aspects of our work environment.

OTHER RESOURCES

Redding, J. C., & Catalanello, R. F. (1994). *Strategic readiness: The making of the learning organization.* San Francisco: Jossey-Bass.

Believing Is Seeing

Joint Ventures and Organization Learning

Andrew C. Inkpen
*Thunderbird, American Graduate School
of International Management, Arizona*

Mary M. Crossan
University of Western Ontario, Canada

THIS PAPER DEVELOPS A CONCEPTUAL FRAMEWORK FOR THE STUDY OF ORGANI-
*zation learning and applies it to learning in joint ventures (JVs). The
framework presents a multilevel view of the phenomenon, suggesting
that learning in organizations occurs at the individual, group and
organization levels. The framework integrates behavioral and cognitive
perspectives of organization learning and delineates both learning
processes and outcomes. Four key elements of organization learning
are addressed: the nature of managerial learning experiences, the
sharing and integration of managerial learning within an organization,
the institutionalization of learning, and the relationship between orga-*

Source: Inkpen, A. C., & Crossan, M. M. (1995). Believing is seeing: Joint ventures and
organization learning. *Journal of Management Studies, 32*(5), 595-618. Used by
permission.

Authors' Note: Research support was provided by the Centre for International Business
Studies, University of Western Ontario. We gratefully acknowledge the ideas and insights
contributed by Paul Beamish, Harry Lane, Peter Killing, Jim Rush, and Rod White. We
would also like to acknowledge the constructive comments from two anonymous *JMS*
reviewers. An earlier version of this paper was presented at the Annual Conference of the
Strategic Management Society, October 1992, London. Both authors contributed equally
to this paper.

nization learning and performance. In applying the framework to a study of learning and JVs, we observed firms with explicit learning objectives unable to put into place the appropriate mechanisms and systems to transfer knowledge from the JV to the parent. While individual managers in the JVs were often enthusiastic and positive about their learning experiences, integration of the learning experience at the parent firm level was problematic, limiting the institutionalized learning. The fundamental position in this paper is that a rigid set of managerial beliefs associated with an unwillingness to cast off or unlearn past practices can severely limit the effectiveness of organization learning.

Introduction

International joint ventures (JVs) and alliances are being formed in increasing numbers, leading to speculation that today's notion of global firms will be superseded by networks of alliances among large firms that span different industries and countries. As an important explanatory factor for the alliance trend, it has been argued that alliances and JVs provide a platform for organization learning, giving firms access to the skills and capabilities of their partners (Hamel, 1991; Kogut, 1988; Westney, 1988).

This paper presents a framework of organization learning and explores the conceptual ideas using data from a field study of JVs between North American and Japanese firms. As JVs continue to be widely used for both domestic and international corporate activity, an appreciation of the realities of JV-based learning strategies should be instructive. As a point of clarification, a JV is defined as a means of performing activities in combination with one or more firms instead of autonomously. A JV occurs when two or more distinct firms (the parents) pool a portion of their resources within a separate jointly owned organization. This definition excludes other forms of co-operative agreements such as licensing, distribution and supply agreements, research and development partnerships, or technical assistance and management contracts.

Building on previous research on organization learning, the conceptual framework in this paper integrates both behavioral and cognitive perspectives of organization learning. This framework provides the underpinnings for an important argument: that an existing set of managerial beliefs can constrain the learning process and hence the notion that "I'll see it when I believe it" rather than "I'll believe it when I see it."[1] The latter view is based on an information processing perspective of learning, while the former is based on an interpretive perspective. This distinction may be the primary reason that researchers underestimate the complexity of organization learning. It is often assumed that once managers are exposed to a new idea or technology, learning will occur. We observed firms with explicit learning objectives struggling to capitalize on their JV learning opportunities. While individual managers in the JVs were often enthusiastic and positive about their learning experiences, integration of the learning experience at the parent firm level was problematic. The fundamental position in this paper is that a rigid set of managerial beliefs associated with an unwillingness to cast off or unlearn past practices can severely limit the effectiveness of organization learning.

Background and Framework Development

A variety of strategic objectives have been suggested to explain firms' motives for the formation of JVs (Beamish & Banks, 1987; Contractor & Lorange, 1988; Hennart, 1988). The objectives include the reduction of risk, economies of scale, access to technology or markets, and the search for legitimacy. In much of the JV literature, the focus has been on firms' mutual desire to co-operate as the basis for JV formation. This focus emphasizes the performance of the JV task and the benefits of pooling resources and skills for co-operative results.

Viewing JVs as learning opportunities provides an alternative to mutual JV value creation. JVs can provide firms with access to the embedded knowledge of other organizations. This access creates the potential for firms to internalize partner skills and capabilities. Huber (1991) referred to this process as grafting, the process by which organizations increase their store of information by internalizing information not previously available within the organization. In a JV, two or more organizations are brought together because of their complementarity and their differences. The differences or discrepancies in partner competency areas are the fuel for learning. Whether or not the discrepancies are identified and resolved determines whether learning occurs.

While still rather small, there is a growing body of theoretical research (Kogut, 1988; Pucik, 1991; Westney, 1988) and empirical studies (Dodgson, 1993; Hamel, 1991; Simonin & Helleloid, 1993) addressing the issue of JVs and alliances as mechanisms for organization learning. This stream of research, and Hamel's (1991) work in particular, have begun to address some of the important questions associated with how organizations exploit JV learning opportunities. However, what is lacking in the existing literature is a clear linkage between organization learning concepts and learning through JVs. This paper develops a conceptual framework for the study of organization learning and applies it to learning in JVs.

A Learning Framework

Organization learning involves the basic elements and processes of organizational development and growth. Organizations can grow in the traditional sense of increased capital or revenues. From a learning perspective, organizations grow when there is an increase in shared understanding involving the organization, its environment and the relationship between the two. However, this understanding not only resides in individuals, but in the artifacts of the organization such as its systems and structures. Furthermore, organization learning involves an intimate relationship between understanding and action, as discussed below.

When an evolving and enhanced understanding is translated into action, organization learning is like the fountain of youth: it represents the organization's ability to undergo continual renewal, thereby prolonging the organization's life indefinitely. Unfortunately, understanding organization learning has been almost as elusive as locating the fountain of youth. In considering the lack of progress toward the development of a coherent theory of organization learning, Huber (1991) concluded that learning theorists were not building on the work of each other, let alone assessing other fields that provide insight into organization learning. According to Huber (1991, p. 107), "there is little in the way of substantiated theory concerning organizational learning and there is considerable need and opportunity to fill in the many gaps."

In our view, the major areas of disagreement among organization learning theorists are: (1) whether organization learning occurs at the individual, group, or organization level; (2) whether learning refers to cognitive and/or behavioral change and how the two are related; (3) whether learning refers to content or process; and (4) whether learning should be tied to performance.

The organization learning framework in Table 12.1 suggests that learning in organizations: (1) occurs over three levels—individual, group and organization; (2) involves both behavioral and cognitive change; (3) involves a process of change in cognition and behavior where the changes may be viewed as the outputs or content of learning; and (4) should not be tied directly to performance enhancement. After providing an overview of these four elements, we apply the framework to the JV study.

Levels of Learning: Individual, Group, Organization

Perhaps one of the weakest links in current theories of organization learning is their failure to take a multilevel perspective. Since learning occurs through individuals, it is necessary to have a grasp of individual learning before adding the complexity of the organization setting. As Cohen and Levinthal (1990) stated, the cognitive structures of individual managers provide the grounding for organization learning.

Although individual learning provides the foundation for understanding the organization learning process (Nonaka, 1994), organization

TABLE 12.1 Summary of Learning in Organizations

Level	Process	Outcome
Individual	Interpreting	Schema, cognitive map
Group	Integrating	Shared belief structures
Organization	Institutionalizing	Structure, systems, organization context

learning is different from the sum of individual learning. Nelson and Winter (1982), in their seminal work on organizational evolution, argued that reducing organizational memory to individual memories overlooked or undervalued the linking of those individual memories by shared experiences in the past. Furthermore, organizations represent patterns of interactions among individuals that endure even when individuals leave (Hedberg, 1981; Weick, 1979). Organizational artifacts and their social context play a role in organization learning.

We suggest that a concept of individual learning should be embedded in a concept of group learning, which in turn should be embedded in a concept of organization learning. At each level of learning, different learning processes are at work, as shown in Table 12.1. At the individual level, the critical process is interpreting; at the group level, integrating; and at the organization level, institutionalizing. This perspective of learning has similarities with Nonaka's (1994) notion of knowledge creation as an upward spiral process, starting at the individual level, moving up to the group level, and then to the organizational level. The outcome or product of the individual process of interpreting is a change in individual beliefs or schemas and individual behaviors. The manifestation of this product is individual behaviors. The product of the group process, manifested in co-ordinated group actions, is shared beliefs and concerted actions. The product of the organization process is the institutionalization of an organization schema reflected in the organizational systems and routines (March, 1991; Starbuck, 1983). The manifestation of institutionalization outcomes is organizational strategy as reflected by a coherent pattern of actions.

Organizational routines define a set of tasks that an organization is capable of doing in a reasonably coherent fashion (Nelson, 1991). Within a learning framework, the lessons of experience are accumulated in an organization's routines. New experiences may result in the encoding of new lessons into the organizational routines, and hence the organization learns. By definition, organizational routines are the persistent features of surviving organizations. Routines are embedded in the organization and are reflected in an organization's consistency in behavior.

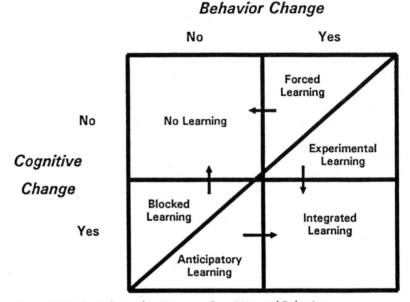

Figure 12.1. The Relationship Between Cognition and Behavior

The Relationship Between Cognition and Behavior

Discussions of individual learning generally refer to the product of the learning process as changes in beliefs (or cognition) and changes in behavior. The term "skill" is often used to describe behaviors for which an individual has developed a level of expertise or proficiency. While individual learning theorists continue to debate the relative merits of cognition over behavior (Mazur, 1990), we argue that cognition and behavior are so tightly intertwined that it is counter-productive to define learning as change in either one or the other. Rather than describing learning as a particular state of cognitive or behavioral change, different types of learning will depend on whether there is cognitive and/or behavioral change, as shown in Figure 12.1. Since individual learning is the foundation of organization learning, the learning states are introduced with reference to individuals. Subsequently, the individual learning states will be extended to the organization level.

Clearly, in cases of no cognitive or behavioral change, there is *no learning*. Conversely, when both changes occur, the outcome is *integrated learning*, as shown in Figure 12.1. This paper suggests that change in behavior without a corresponding change in cognition, or change in cognition without a corresponding change in behavior, are transitional states since they create a tension between one's beliefs and one's actions. The tension, however, is a cognitive tension between the interpretation of one's behaviors and other beliefs. This tension is synony-mous with the concept of cognitive dissonance. Festinger (1957, p. 4) supported the argument that the tension is transitional, stating that "the reduction of dissonance is a basic process in humans."

Changes in behavior without any change in cognition may be resolved in several ways. If the behavioral change arises from *forced learning* it will likely resolve itself into the no learning quadrant. Individuals will continue to interpret stimuli through their current belief systems, reinforcing existing beliefs. For example, individuals who feel forced to comply with governmental environmental standards may change their behaviors to comply with the standards. In doing so, they reinforce their views that government should not be intervening in their affairs. How-ever, if the learning is *experimental,* individuals may try new behaviors that result in cognitive change. There may then be a shift into the integrated learning quadrant. A key aspect of experimental learning is that individuals are willing to suspend their belief systems to try a new behavior, and in doing so are open to new and different interpretations of the results of the behavior.

Although a transitional state of behavioral change not accompanied by cognitive change may be resolved, a cautionary point should be raised. The model is designed to provide insight into the relationships between cognition and behavior, as opposed to a definitive statement about how and why the change occurs. As evidence of the complexity of the cognition-behavior debate, Schein (1971), for example, devoted an entire book to describing how and why American civilians held by the Chinese Communists between 1950 and 1956 changed or failed to change their beliefs as a result of the treatment they received.

A third transitional state occurs when individuals experience cogni-tive change without any behavioral change. In the simplest case, called *anticipatory learning,* a gap occurs between a change in cognition and the display of a change in behavior. For example, many years of medical education are required before a physician can attempt the first operation. None the less, it is the changes in cognition arising from the medical education which guide the surgeon in the behavior required to perform the operation.

The more difficult cases are those in which individuals have under-gone changes in cognition that are not reflected in their behavior and may likely never be reflected in their behavior. This situation is often associated with a physical skill such as playing golf or running. Although individuals may have experienced changes in cognition so that they "know" what they are supposed to do, they are not able to execute that know-how. In fact, they may not possess the physical resources to translate the know-how into action.

There are other cases where a change in cognition does not lead to a change in behavior. *Blocked learning* occurs when other beliefs override the situation. For example: I know the customer is always right, but I can't take this kind of abuse. To see the learning manifested in behavior, it is necessary to deal with the blocking element. For example, customer representatives might treat customers better if they did not have to deal with the extreme abuse they received from customers irate over shoddy products or service.

The debate in the psychology literature between learning as cognitive change and learning as behavioral change is also a point of contention for organization learning theorists. For example, Fiol and Lyles (1985) distinguished between cognitive change and behavioral change by suggesting that cognitive change is learning and behavioral change is adaptation. Firms in mature industries with stable environments were characterized as having low levels of cognitive or behavioral changes. These firms would be classified in the no learning quadrant in Figure 12.1. Fiol and Lyles suggested that organizations in crisis or undergoing rapid restructuring, perhaps through mergers, are characterized by a high level of behavioral change with a low level of cognitive change. By extending the previously discussed learning categories to an organization level, this type of transitional stage is similar to the forced learning and experimental learning situations shown in Figure 12.1. Friedlander (1984) supported the concept of forced learning, suggesting that mandated policy changes, for example, lead to changes in organization behavior but not to changes in organization cognition.

Researchers have also argued that learning is contingent upon the turbulence of the environment. Firms in industries experiencing structural change may be under pressure to learn new skills and capabilities (Kogut, 1988). Fiol and Lyles (1985) characterized organizations with a low level of behavioral change and a high level of cognitive change as being in a turbulent environment where too much change could cause the organization to lose its sense of direction. However, we suggest that it may be a matter of timing for the behavioral change, as opposed to overt resistance to change. The behavioral change may occur but only after a time-lag. Fiol and Lyles also suggested that a high level of cognitive and behavioral change is appropriate for organizations in a moderately turbulent environment. We suggest that this type of integrated learning will be a source of competitive advantage for organizations and therefore should be viewed as an ideal state.

The issue of whether organization learning encompasses cognitive change, behavioral change, or both is not a trivial matter. The definition which theorists adopt becomes the belief system that, in essence, guides their discoveries about the phenomenon of organization learning. Our position is that defining organization learning as involving either cognitive or behavioral change unnecessarily narrows the perspective of organization learning. Furthermore, in an effort to distinguish between the two types of change, theorists may fail to recognize and investigate the important linkages between the two. As Gioia and Manz (1985, p. 527) asserted, "although a great deal of energy has been spent debating the issue of cognition versus behavior, less effort has been devoted to the study of the more important issue of the connection between cognition and behavior."

Learning Process and Content

Underlying the learning framework in Table 12.1 is a set of assumptions about the process of learning. Changes in both cognition and behavior have been highlighted as the products or outcome of the learning process. Many theorists focus on these content aspects of learning without delving further into the process. We suggest that the process of organization learning should be conceived of as a dynamic interplay among beliefs, behaviors and stimuli from the environment, where beliefs are both an input and a product of the process as they undergo change.

At the core of learning is a process that involves: (1) the detection of a mismatch between one's beliefs and perceptions of stimuli, and (2) the modification of beliefs to resolve the mismatch. A mismatch, or discrepancy, may be experienced as a gap, for which the individual has no expectations of a particular stimulus, or as a conflict between expectations and actual experiences. Weick (1979) used the term enactment to define the stimulus encounter, describing it as "the bracketing of some portion of a stream of experience for further attention." A second process, selection, involves the interpretation of experiences, and retention refers to the storage of the interpretation as a guide for further applications.

While a primary reason for not processing stimuli is not noting them, a primary reason for not noting stimuli is a belief system that directs attention in a different direction.

> There is a dialectical contradiction between these two requirements: we cannot perceive unless we anticipate but we must not see only what we anticipate. . . . Although a perceiver always has at least some (more or less specific) anticipation before he begins to pick up information about a given object, they can be corrected as well as sharpened in the course of looking. . . . The upshot of the argument is that perception is directed by expectations but not controlled by them. (Neisser, 1976, p. 43)

Neisser's comments demonstrate how beliefs both guide and are a product of the learning process. Although beliefs guide what is enacted and interpreted, Neisser suggested that they do not control the process. Thus, there is the opportunity to interpret stimuli that may alter one's beliefs.

As an input to the process of learning, a highly developed belief system with many concepts and interrelationships enables an individual to make subtle distinctions and notice differences others may miss. Neisser (1976) used the example of a chess master to illustrate how the expert's ability to discriminate differed from that of the novice:

> The information that the master picks up from the chessboard determines not only where he will move his pieces but where he will move his eyes. Observations show that a good chess player's eye movements are closely related to the structure of the position on the board; he looks at crucial pieces and crucial squares. He quite literally sees the position differently—more adequately and comprehensively—than a novice or a nonplayer would. Of course, even the nonplayer sees a great deal: the chessmen are of carved ivory, the knight resembles a horse, the pieces are (perhaps) arrayed with a certain geometrical regularity. The differences among these perceivers are not matters of truth and error but of noticing more rather than less. The information that specifies the proper move is available in the light sampled by the baby as by the master, but only the master is equipped to pick it up. (Neisser, 1976, p. 181)

In summary, the debate on the relationship between cognitive change and behavioral change has tended to focus on the products of the learning process rather than on the process of learning. This paper suggests that the process of organization learning must be integrated with the learning product or outcome. As indicated earlier, the process involves three levels: interpreting, integrating and institutionalizing. Individual beliefs guide the process through the identification of gaps and conflicts, and are a product of the process as gaps and conflicts are resolved.

Learning and Performance

The relationship between organization learning and performance has generated a great deal of controversy in the field of management. Some theorists have equated learning with performance enhancement (Argyris & Schön, 1978; Fiol & Lyles, 1985; Gronhaug, 1977), while others have distinguished between the two. Our position is that organizations that learn more effectively will in the long run perform better than their competitors. However, while there should be a link between organization learning and performance, time-lags between the two make empirical observations very difficult. Additionally, just as with individuals, learning does not always lead to intelligent or improved behavior (Levitt & March, 1988). Organizations can incorrectly learn and they can correctly learn that which is incorrect (Huber, 1991).

March et al. (1991) addressed a similar issue in their discussion of reliable and valid learning. They suggested that in a reliable learning process, an organization develops common understandings of its experience and makes its interpretations public, stable and shared. In a valid learning process, an organization understands, predicts and controls its environment. As organizations engage in learning efforts, neither reliability nor validity is assured because different people and groups in an organization approach historical experience with different expectations and beliefs. As we found, shared understanding about the value of JV learning experiences was often obstructed by the variety and differences in managerial beliefs.

March (1991) also qualified the relationship between learning and performance. March argued that although learning is a major component in any effort to improve organizational performance and strengthen competitive advantage, the increased knowledge associated with a learning process may reduce the variability of performance rather than increase it. In that sense, learning makes performance more reliable. The risk associated with reduced variability is that the organization may become resistant to contradictory information.

Thus, performance provides important feedback about the efficiency and effectiveness of a learning process and, ultimately, an organization's strategy will come to reflect the accumulated learning (Mintzberg, 1990). However, to suggest that incremental learning should always lead to incremental performance improvements is misleading. Specific performance enhancements may result because of learning, but they also may be attributable to efforts of imitation, regeneration, or technological development. More important, learning and the learning benefits may be separated in time, or the benefits may be masked by intervening forces.

Summary

The three levels of learning presented in Table 12.1, and the associated processes and outcomes provide a framework with which to examine learning in organizations. For each element of the framework there is a potential tension that is either a supporting or limiting factor in an organization's ability to fully capitalize on learning opportunities. For example, at the individual level, how does an individual's schema affect the process of interpreting? What is the relationship between cognition and behavior? At the group level, what is the relationship between the learning process and the learning product? How is learning shared across group and organization boundaries? How does group learning become institutionalized into the organizational routines? What are the performance implications associated with the learning products at each of the three levels? Clearly, for an individual experience to become institutionalized in organizational systems and routines, there are many hurdles to overcome.

By delineating the different levels involved in the organization learning process, empirical research can be more focused and, hopefully, generate new insights. The framework presented in Table 12.1 can be used to highlight the factors that influence learning at the individual, group and organization levels. In the next section we use the organization learning framework as a lens to examine learning in JVs.

The Joint Venture Study

The study was designed to focus on American JV parents and their ability to exploit JV learning opportunities with their Japanese partners. The JVs studied were all North American-Japanese JVs located in North America[2] who were suppliers to automakers in North America. The automotive industry at the supplier level provided an interesting context for a study of learning. Ongoing structural changes in the industry have contributed to what could be referred to as a learning imperative for North American automotive suppliers. With the domestic automakers under pressure from Japanese firms, North American suppliers have found their traditional customer base shrinking. This situation, coupled with increasing foreign investment, has created increasingly difficult competitive conditions. The aggressiveness of foreign entrants in the industry and increasingly stringent customer demands suggested that this industry would be fertile ground for a study of organization learning. Many of the American partner firms in the study, struggling to compete in an industry in transition, saw their JVs as a point of leverage for the development of new skills and capabilities.

The primary data collection method for the study was field interviews with senior managers involved in JV management. Interviews were conducted with 58 managers associated with 40 JVs, which represented a response rate of 80% of qualifying ventures participating in the study. The majority of managers held positions such as JV president or JV general manager. Generally, the managers were either employed by the American partners or appointed by the American partners to senior management positions in the JVs. These managers were chosen as key informants for two main reasons: (1) as the managers at the interface between the parent and the JV partner, these managers have been found to be very familiar with partner relationships and a reliable source of data (Geringer & Hebert, 1991); (2) as the senior American managers in the JVs, these managers were knowledgeable about organizational processes and could assess the importance of processes from a strategic perspective.

The interviews followed a semistructured format based on an interview guide. There was both an open-ended sequence of questions and a focused set of questions designed to evaluate specific organizational attributes (see the Appendix for examples of the open-ended interview questions). With one exception, interviews were conducted in person in the informants' offices. Total interview time per scheduled interview ranged from one hour to more than four hours, with an average of two hours.

Data Analysis

For all interview data, data reduction began immediately following the interview, helping to bring the raw data into a manageable form. Within a 24-hour period, the detailed interview write-ups were completed. The interview write-ups summarized the interviews in a consistent and logical manner. The main objective of the write-ups was a "product intelligible to anyone, not just the fieldworker" (Miles & Huberman, 1984, p. 50). All write-ups were reviewed for omissions and clarity problems with follow-up data collected if necessary.

The write-ups were based on a classification scheme approximating the main analytic concepts, such as parent experience, parent-JV integration, JV performance, and organization learning mechanisms. The write-ups also incorporated information on company history, background of the informant, etc., and data from several other sources such as company documents (e.g. organization charts, promotional literature), business press articles, and annual reports. The write-up classification scheme was developed during a pre-test phase and was further refined over the course of the field work. As the classification scheme changed, revisions were made to earlier interview write-ups. By the end of the fieldwork, all the interviews were written up using a similar format. This consistency in format greatly simplified the cross-site analysis.

While doing the write-ups, any missing data were carefully noted for later follow-up. Given the semi-structured format of the interviews, there were occasions when questions were unintentionally omitted. Since the write-ups were based on a consistent format, missing or incomplete data could easily be detected. A follow-up telephone call was necessary for those cases with missing data.

An analysis activity that occurred throughout the research project was the development of analytic memoranda. This process, called "memoing" by Glaser (1978), involved the recording of conceptual and analytic impressions as they occurred. The impressions reflected several different themes including the preliminary identification of patterns, summaries of unique or surprising site attributes, and ideas on data analysis. Included in the interview write-ups was a separate section called "researcher's general impressions" (Bourgeois & Eisenhardt, 1988). In this section, emerging thoughts about the conceptual framework were summarized as they related to the particular interview site and also unique ideas about the site.

As the research progressed, the categorized data, write-ups and memos were examined for emerging patterns, themes, and processes that might account for the frequency and absence or presence of data categories. An objective of exploratory research is the discovery of new categories of data that emerge out of the data rather than having been decided prior to data collection and analysis (Patton, 1987). For example, a pattern that emerged early in the study was a relationship between JV performance and learning.

Joint Venture Characteristics

To limit inter-organizational complexity, only two partner JVs were included in the study. All JVs were suppliers to the automotive industry and only one had less than 50% of its sales to automotive customers. With two exceptions, the JVs were start-up or greenfield organizations. Most were direct suppliers to the automotive assemblers, that is, tier-one suppliers (see Table 12.2 for a summary of JV characteristics). Tier-one suppliers deal directly with the automotive manufacturers and often participate jointly in the design of new systems and parts. The first-tier suppliers co-ordinate the operations of many smaller second-tier suppliers.

The cases were classified according to the American partner's motive in forming the JV. In making this classification, it was recognized that JV parents often are motivated by multiple factors in forming JVs. Thus, the motive represents the American partner's *primary* motivating factor.

The primary motive for 29 American partners was access to the transplant market. All but five JVs were transplant suppliers and 11 supplied a single transplant (Table 12.2). Nine non-transplant access ventures were classified as technology-oriented because the American firms sought access to Japanese partner manufacturing or product technology. Of the remaining two cases, one American firm formed a JV to share the risk of developing a new product and one firm wanted a Japanese partner "because everyone else was doing it."

TABLE 12.2 Joint Venture Characteristics

Characteristics	Number of Cases	Percentage	Characteristics	Number of Cases	Percentage
American part-ner equity			Number of years operational		
20–30%	4	10.0	1	2	5.0
31–40%	5	12.5	2	5	12.5
41–48%	3	7.5	3	14	35.0
49%	3	7.5	4	12	30.0
50%	17	42.5	5	5	12.5
51%	4	10.0	6	2	5.0
60%	4	10.0			
Tiers supplied			JV customers		
Tier 1	33	82.5	Single transplant	11	27.5
Tier 2	4	10.0	Multiple transplants	13	32.5
Tier 1 and Tier 2	3	7.5	Domestic automakers and transplants	11	27.5
			Domestic automakers only	5	12.5

Broadly speaking, all of the JVs were formed to strengthen an existing business. With the size of existing domestic markets stable or declining, a JV could compensate the American partners by providing relatively quick access to a new customer or product market. The prevalent opinion of managers involved with transplant customers was that American firm access to the transplant market would have been difficult without a Japanese partner. Two factors contributed to the American firms' difficulty in penetrating the transplant market: (1) North American firms were faced with the perception, and perhaps reality, that Japanese suppliers produced higher quality products at lower prices (Cusumano & Takeishi, 1991):[3] (2) Japanese automotive suppliers operate within a network of supplier tiers that is difficult for outsider firms to penetrate (Inkpen, 1994). For American firms interested in supplying the transplants, a Japanese JV partner was seen as an effective and timely means of overcoming market entry barriers.

The Joint Venture Learning Opportunity

JVs provide companies with a window to their partners' capabilities (Hamel et al., 1989). For the American firms in this study, the window had two main sources of potential value. First, all but five JVs were transplants' suppliers and, generally, the products supplied to the transplants were similar to products manufactured by the Japanese partners in Japan. The Japanese partners were usually responsible for implementing the manufacturing process, installing the equipment, and supplying the product technology. Consequently, the JVs provided the American partners with a unique opportunity to study a new, state-of-the-art organization that would not have been possible without a collaborative relationship.

Second, the JVs were often the American partners' initial experience in supplying Japanese automakers. As a manager explained, Japanese automaker supplier-manufacturer relationships are radically different from those between domestic auto companies and their suppliers:

> The typical domestic automaker's relationship with its supplier is adversarial. With the transplants, the relationship is supportive if you can deliver the product. Transplants will work with their suppliers and help them when there is a problem. They also expect complete commitment. With our main transplant customer, if there is one problem, there is one phone call; we are expected to fix the problem immediately.

Informants tended to focus on three areas in which the transplants differed from the domestic auto companies in terms of supplier management. One area was pricing practices. The transplants expected that suppliers would meet target prices and that price reductions or costdowns would occur throughout the model life cycle. In their survey of supplier relationships in the automotive industry, Cusumano and Takeishi (1991) found that prices to the transplants typically decreased annually. In contrast, prices to domestic automakers rose approximately 1% annually. The second area of difference was quality management. The transplants expect that parts received from suppliers will be free of defects and, therefore, the burden of parts inspection is pushed down to the supplier level. The third area was the degree of involvement of transplants in supplier operations, as the previous quote indicates.

The JVs in this study created powerful learning opportunities and, accordingly, learning was an explicit objective for all but eight American partners. As indicated, the American partner usually gained the equivalent of unhindered access to the dedicated assets of their Japanese partners. Despite this access, learning often proved to be a difficult experience for American managers and their firms. Applying the learning framework to the data provides insight into the learning process. The discussion is organized into four sections. The first three relate to learning at each of the levels identified in Table 12.1: individual, group, and organization. Observations about the relationship between cognition and behavior, and learning as a process, are incorporated into the discussion of the learning levels. The fourth section addresses the relationship between learning and performance.

Individual Learning: Changes in Managerial Cognition and Behavior

The data suggest that at the managerial level in the American firms, existing sets of managerial beliefs severely constrained the learning process. American managers often failed to understand or appreciate their Japanese partner's areas of competency. A common expectation was that the knowledge associated with differences in skills between the Japanese and American partners would be visible and easily transferable. However, as Kogut and Zander (1992) pointed out, knowledge can be classified as information or know-how. Information implies knowing what something means and know-how is a description of knowing how to do something. Information is lower-level knowledge and far more accessible to outsiders. The American parent firms focused their learning efforts on visible information and differences rather than on partner know-how, an obstacle that has plagued General Motors in its joint venture with Toyota (Keller, 1989).

The notion of visible differences is analogous to Badaracco's (1991) description of migratory knowledge. Migratory knowledge was defined as knowledge that can be clearly and fully articulated and, therefore, is very mobile. Many American firms in this study expected to find migratory knowledge that could be transferred on a piecemeal basis. Instead, they encountered differences that were embedded in the know-how of their partners. Thus, the learning opportunities associated with the Japanese firms were generally not product or technology-specific but related to an overall philosophy of doing business. An executive described an American firm's learning situation:

> The American partner initially thought that access to the Japanese partner's manufacturing technology would be very important and that they would learn a lot about their partner's operation. However, the expectations were very general and were not in sharp focus. Once the JV relationship was formed and the American partner had the opportunity to see its partner's operation, they were subtly surprised by the simplicity of things. The key difference was improvement for improvement's sake and not sophisticated technology differences. The main differences were simple things like always paying your suppliers on time and shipping 7200 parts not 7201. . . . I was surprised by the simplicity of the differences between the two partners and so was the American partner CEO.

While the complexity of a manager's beliefs or schema could facilitate the identification of the subtle differences between Japanese and American operations, hands-on, original experience is usually the catalyst in knowledge creation (Nonaka, 1994). Hence, behavioral change often preceded cognitive change. The differences—such as 7200 parts not 7201 parts—were visible and easily recognized, but the deeper meaning associated with the differences required hands-on experience. American managers not involved in the JV management or its operation did not have the direct experience and, therefore, may not have appreciated the deeper meaning. These managers saw the flow of information concerning quality differences and delivery capabilities. However, information in the absence of the expertise and know-how behind the information is insufficient to effect cognitive change (Starbuck, 1992).

When there were clearly identified performance benefits managers were more willing to engage in experimental learning. In an experimental situation, managers try out new behaviors even though they may not have fully understood or agreed with them. In cases where performance benefits were not clearly identifiable, managers were reluctant to experiment. One manager suggested that North Americans tend to look for "home runs" before changes will be considered, consistent with the view that Western organizations learn in large, discrete steps (Hedlund & Nonaka, 1993). This proved problematic, since much of what was to be learned from the JVs was of an incremental nature. Those managers recognizing partner differences as incremental, managerial, and inextricably linked to their Japanese partner's business philosophy were usually more successful in their learning efforts.

In summary, we observed that the individual process of interpreting was affected by the complexity of managerial schemas, the managers' hands-on exposure to the activities of the Japanese partner, and managers' appreciation for the subtle differences that may not directly be tied to performance enhancement.

The Sharing and Integration of Managerial Learning

Individual knowledge and perspectives remain personal unless they are amplified and articulated through social interaction (Nonaka, 1994). The data suggest that the process of integrating individual learning into collective or shared learning was a major organizational challenge. Managers at the JV level were often frustrated by the apparent inability of the American parents to go beyond recognition of potential learning experiences to exploitation of the experiences. For example, a manager commented:

> The American parent should be learning through this experience. What good is the JV if the people and information in the JV do not go back to the parent? This information should not be limited to the partnership.

This study points toward three types of mechanisms that can promote individual to collective integration: (1) personal facilitation where a leader or influential individual guides the integration of the various schemas to develop a shared understanding; (2) shared facilitation where the individuals involved share enough common ground, or have enough trust and respect, to manage the integrating process themselves; and (3) artifactual facilitation where the organization's systems and structures act as integrating mechanisms. In the case of JVs, where managerial learning in the venture must migrate to a higher organizational level in order to impact the parent, integration through organizational artifacts can occur through various avenues, including: (1) the rotation of managers from the JV back to the parent; regular meetings between JV and parent management; (2) JV plant visits and tours by parent managers; (3) senior management involvement in JV activities; and (4) the sharing of information between the JV and the parent. Each of these avenues involves links between individuals that span boundaries.

The integration of individual learning across boundaries provides the basis for Brown and Duguid's (1991) concept of evolving communities of practice. Communities emerge not when the learners absorb abstract knowledge but when the learners become "insiders" and acquire the particular community's subjective viewpoint and learn to speak its language. In several cases, JV managers referred to parent managers as "transformed" because the parent and JV managers both saw the learning potential in the JVs. From Brown and Duguid's (1991) perspective, a community of practice had emerged.

While there may be organizational mechanisms in place that have the potential to facilitate integration, other factors inhibited the integrating process. We observed that some parent company managers were threatened by the learning occurring in the JV. This contributed to a situation of blocked learning, with managers discounting much of what was occurring in the JV. For example, the parents may have had difficulty accepting the JV child, a new organization with limited experience, as a legitimate "teacher." As a JV general manager explained:

> Yes, they [American parent management] know that there are differences [in the JV and originating with the Japanese partner] but it is

difficult for them to internalize the reasons for the differences. At a high level in the parent organization, people should be in a position to look at the JV and at the parent operations to see the differences and learn from the JV experience. But, you have to understand the people involved. It is very difficult for them to openly discuss the situation, particularly when it is the child that is outperforming its parent.

Managers in the American parents were often willing to concede that their partners were capable of producing a superior product. However, a focus on the key to the Japanese "mystique" was inevitably futile. A JV executive described the inability of the American partner to make sense of its JV:

> The American partner is in a different business than the Japanese partner. They are in the commodity business. Machines are run until they wear out. There is no capital reinvested. The Japanese partner is in a dynamic business in which capital must be reinvested to compete. There is always pressure to lower costs and to improve the product. It's hard for them [the American partner] to understand the JV business. They would have liked to get involved with the JV but they don't understand what the JV does.

This example illustrates a situation in which the parent managers, possibly because they did not experience the JV on a first-hand basis, seemed to lack the appropriate context for exploiting the learning opportunity. The JV manager was convinced of the validity of the learning opportunity. Unfortunately, the parent managers were unable to discard an existing belief system and recognize the learning and competitive implications associated with the JV. Consequently, integration into shared belief structures did not occur.

A related point, suggested by Hamel (1991), is that American firm reluctance to engage in experimental learning was associated with the perspective of the JV role. The JVs were often seen as stand-alone operations utilizing a set of complementary skills, rather than a bridge to the development of new skills in the parent. If JVs are viewed as a means of skills substitution rather than skills enhancement, learning will not be seen as a high priority. A focus on skills enhancement requires a willingness to suspend an existing belief system in favor of new behavior.

Finally, we found that in several cases, parent managers recognized the value of the learning opportunity when the degree of skill discrepancies between the JV partners became too great to ignore. An executive described the situation at the American parent after a skills gap was identified:

> Initially, we thought there was nothing to learn from our partner. We thought we were better than anybody. When we first went to Japan we thought our partners wanted a JV so they could learn from us. We were shocked at what we saw on that first visit. We were amazed that they were even close to us, let alone much better. We realized that our production capabilities were nothing [compared with the Japanese firm's]. We realized that we were not world class. Our partner was doing many things that we couldn't do.

In summary, our observations suggest a strong need for leader and artifactual facilitation to overcome the barriers to shared integration. Unfortunately, many companies were unwilling to incur the minimal expense of setting up learning-oriented systems, such as sending key parent managers to the JV on a regular basis to experience the JV firsthand. This type of action may have been seen as wasteful and not directly associated with successful JV management. However, as Nonaka (1990) suggested, allowing individuals to enter each others' areas of operation promotes the sharing and articulating of individual knowledge, which may lead to problem generation and knowledge creation. Nonaka referred to the outcome of this conscious overlapping of company information and business activities as redundancy of information. Our observations suggest that the Japanese parents frequently took the opportunity to send its Japan-based managers to visit the JV, probably because of a greater tolerance for redundancy and because in Japanese firms life-long learning is an explicit element in the career path of Japanese managers (Hedlund & Nonaka, 1993; Keys et al., 1994).

Learning at the Organization Level

The majority of JVs in the study had been operating for five to six years. While there was evidence of institutionalized learning, there was far less than one might expect given the potential for learning that existed. To explain the dearth of organizational level learning, we propose that as individual learning spirals its way to the organization level, dissipation in learning will occur. The rate of dissipation will be influenced by a variety of factors. Successful firms may become increasingly narrow in their perspective (Miller, 1993) and committed to a particular strategy. When confronted with learning opportunities, successful firms may see little need to change behavior and thus become trapped by their distinctive competence (Levinthal & March, 1993). The strength of a firm's learning intent will help determine the organizational resources committed to learning (Hamel, 1991). The type of institutional learning mechanisms plays a key role in how new knowledge is "managed" by JV parent firms (Hedlund and Nonaka, 1993). Finally, the nature of managerial belief systems permeates all levels of learning, and correspondingly contributes to learning dissipation.

As the learning process takes place and as the individual to group integration occurs (or does not occur), pieces of knowledge and information disappear. This dissipation means that in reality, new knowledge and ideas at the managerial level have a low probability of becoming institutionalized learning. The JV study showed that rather than using institutional mechanisms to transfer learning throughout the organization, learning was often transferred from group to group on an ad hoc and informal basis. Again, given the barriers to group and organization integration, dissipation of the learning was likely to occur.

Learning and Performance

The relationship between learning and performance at an organizational level was interesting. Managers in the American parent companies frequently pointed to the poor financial performance of the JVs as evidence that learning was not occurring, or could not occur. The Japanese parents, on the other hand, generally had longer time horizons and different expectations regarding JV performance. Informants indicated that the American JV partners were more likely than the Japanese to use profitability as a measure of both learning and JV success. A JV manager described a situation involving performance and learning:

> The American parent's emphasis on the profitability of the JV clouded their judgement. They just could not see past the startup period. The losses distorted the attitudes of the American parent. Learning was never allowed to surface. Their attitude became, they [the Japanese partner] don't know anything so how can we learn from these people?

More generally, a preoccupation with short-term issues was a common characteristic of the American partners. Although it is too simplistic to describe Japanese management as long-term oriented and American management as short-term oriented, the Japanese partner firms in this study appeared to focus on customer satisfaction and product quality rather than profit-based performance. Consistent with other studies (e.g., Abbeglen & Stalk, 1985; Doyle et al., 1992), the Japanese firms seemed less constrained by issues of share price and impatient boards of directors than their American counterparts. Because the American partners were heavily focused on financial performance issues, learning often became a secondary and less tangible concern. While North Americans focused on the bottom line, the Japanese focused on improving productivity, quality and delivery. For American managers, it was difficult to conceive that learning could be occurring in the face of poor performance. Consequently, there was a reluctance to commit to or even try out proposals generated at the JV level. This finding is consistent with Levinthal and March's (1993) argument that organization learning oversamples successes and undersamples failures. As a result, learning processes tend to eliminate failures and sustained experimentation becomes difficult.

The relationship between learning and JV performance posed a paradoxical challenge for JV general managers. On the one hand, general managers were charged with generating an adequate financial return for the American parents; on the other hand, they were expected to act as the conduit for the parent's learning initiative. A focus on one objective detracted from the other. More importantly, when either learning or performance were less than satisfactory, there were implications for the assessment of the other objective. Thus, while poor performance can act as a barrier to learning, unexploited learning opportunities may lead to perceptions of unsatisfactory JV performance.

Discussion

The framework of organization learning presented at the outset of this paper, in conjunction with data from the JV study, raises several important issues. Since organizations learn through their individual members, the individual aspects of organization learning, involving both cognitive and behavioral change, cannot be ignored. As stated previously, individuals learn by identifying gaps or conflicts between their experience and their beliefs, and by resolving identified discrepancies through changes in their beliefs and behaviors. It was suggested that changes in beliefs occur more readily in the face of gaps than in the face of conflicts. We observed that managers expected to find gaps in their knowledge but instead found subtle discrepancies that were not easily interpreted. Since the JV experience conflicted with established belief systems, discrepancies were not always seen.

The first ingredient of individual learning, the noticing of discrepancies, is more likely to arise when an individual has a complex belief system. Therefore, experts with more complex belief systems should notice more discrepancies than novices with less complex belief systems. Resolution, the second ingredient, is more likely to occur in individuals where the belief systems have some flexibility. We found that firms with a deteriorating competitive position often had managers with the most entrenched belief systems. The fact that these firms had competitive problems may be traced to an unwillingness to cast off or unlearn past practices.

The cognitive focus of the organization learning framework presented here differs in several respects from Hamel's (1991) model of JV learning. Hamel's inductively derived model of inter-partner learning consisted of three main concepts as determinants of learning: intent, transparency and receptivity. While this model helped in developing the foundation for this research, our framework and empirical observations suggest that to thoroughly develop these concepts, the importance of managerial beliefs and managerial interpretations must be recognized. Hamel's model treated the firm primarily as a processor of information; managerial belief structures as factors which aid or hinder learning are noticeably absent.[4]

According to Hamel (1991), transparency is the openness and willingness of the partner firm to share its embedded knowledge. In the JV context, transparency is clearly important, since without the opportunity to observe partner skill discrepancies there is no fuel for learning. However, even if a firm is open and accessible with its skills, individual managers must have the motivation and ability to notice the discrepancies. Thus, a key factor in a firm's ability to absorb new skills (i.e., its absorptiveness, using the concept suggested by Cohen and Levinthal, 1990) is a sufficiently complex managerial belief system with which to notice and appreciate firm differences.

Hamel defined receptivity as the learning firm's ability to absorb skills from its partner. Again, Hamel's focus at the firm level does not capture the complexity of receptivity. Receptivity can be analyzed at three levels: individual, group, and organization. At the individual level, receptivity is closely linked with individual interpretation and, therefore, transparency and receptivity overlap as learning determinants. Without the ability to interpret what is happening in the JV environment, the individual becomes an empty conduit of information for other members in the organization. An inability to absorb new information may be confused with low transparency. Managers may blame their lack of learning, and failure to notice differences, on their partner's unwillingness to share information. In fact, the problem may be that individuals are unable to perceive differences because the partner knowledge is context-bound. Therefore, as a prerequisite to learning through JVs, executives must overcome the uncertainty and ambiguity surrounding their assessment of partner capabilities.

While receptivity may exist at the individual level, its absence at the organization level may indicate that senior managers are not receptive to the JV stimuli, perhaps because they are not directly involved in JV management. Thus, even if individuals are able to share their learning through an integration process, without senior management receptivity, organization learning will not occur.

Perhaps the most salient observation from the JV study is the dynamic nature of learning and its determinants. Concepts such as intent, transparency, and receptivity should not be viewed as static. For a variety of reasons they may change over time. In several cases where the American firm did not have an initial learning intent, skill discrepancies became obvious and unavoidable. For example, an American firm that had prided itself on its high-quality product status found its quality lacking when it attempted to supply a Japanese transplant automaker:

> The American partner was considered a high-quality domestic supplier and had a Q1 [highest quality] rating from Ford. However, in the JV we quickly discovered that to deal with the Japanese you have to be world class; we were only American class. We initially had problems meeting our Japanese customers' quality standards.

Most of the American firms in this study formed their JVs with an objective of learning from their Japanese partners; their expectations often were to learn "what" the Japanese knew, rather than "how'"and "why" the Japanese firms knew what they knew. Again, this raises the notion of knowledge as information (the "what") and know-how (the "how" and "why"). Expectations about learning experiences typically revolved around clearly identifiable and visible activities. However, as General Motors discovered in its NUMMI venture, the most valuable learning experience was not associated with specific techniques but with an overall philosophy of organizing and competing. According to a JV vice president:

> The American firm was somewhat naive in their learning expectations; they knew little about the overall Japanese way of doing things. Learning could occur only if there was a complete acceptance of the philosophy since all its parts were interconnected.

The study also highlights how learning dissipates as it moves from individual interpretation to group integration and finally institutionalization at the organizational level. Many questions still remain about the interrelationships among the levels of learning, and in particular the feedback loops. Future research needs to address how institutionalized learning impacts new interpretation and integration, and how shared understanding in terms of integrated learning impacts the development of new and perhaps different insights. In addition to the cognitive-behavioral interface and its impact on the learning process, the study also highlights the complicated nature of the learning-performance relationship. This area should be investigated further, perhaps along the lines of Levinthal and March's (1993) concept of learning myopia.

Finally, the JV study raises the issue of learning how to learn as a competitive advantage. It has been suggested that Japanese firms are more adept than Western firms at maximizing learning opportunities (Hedlund & Nonaka, 1993). In a Japanese firm in Hamel's (1991) study, managers indicated they were not worried about disclosing what they had learned. These managers were so confident in their ability to learn that they knew they would always be one step ahead of their partner. In this regard, it is important to recognize that it is the *rate* of learning and not just the learning itself that is important. When the complexity associated with the rate of learning is added to the learning equation, it is clear that there are many further issues to address, since many of the companies we studied had difficulty recognizing learning opportunities, let alone exploiting them.

To conclude, this study used a broad framework of organization learning to explore the complexity of the phenomenon and illustrate that the important issues in organization learning span organization levels, which means the issues also span research boundaries. The limitation of this approach is acknowledged. A deeper level of analysis in areas such as schema complexity was not possible. However, the approach provides a platform to further investigate each of the areas in our framework and provides a point of integration for more specialized research. As well, the approach may help forge a better alignment between academic descriptions and prescriptions and the reality faced by managers.

APPENDIX
Interview Questions

The following are examples of the open-ended questions that provided structure to the interviews.

Questions for both parent managers and joint venture managers:

1. Describe the formation of the joint venture: why was it formed; how did the two partners get together; which partner initiated the joint venture?

Were the partners involved in prior relationships before the formation of the joint venture?

2. What were the Japanese partner's motives in forming the joint venture? How would you evaluate the contribution of the Japanese partner to the joint venture? Is the Japanese partner's managerial contribution critical to the success of the joint venture?

3. Was access to the Japanese partner's skills and knowledge an important consideration (for the American partner) in forming the joint venture?

4. Has the joint venture been a useful learning experience for the American parent? Why or why not?

5. Does the American parent aggressively try to acquire information from the Japanese partner?

6. What is different about the Japanese partner's operation? Can or should those differences be incorporated in the American parent's operations?

7. If the learning associated with this joint venture was limited, why do you think that this was not a good learning experience for the American parent?

8. What could have been done differently to maximize the learning?

Questions for joint venture managers only:

1. Do you think that you are making a superior product in the joint venture (i.e., superior to the parent)? Does your parent know? Agree? What has been their attitude towards your joint venture and its success?

2. Does the American parent encourage its joint venture managers to learn from the Japanese partner?

3. Do parent managers show an interest in the joint venture as a learning experience?

4. What effort does the American parent make to incorporate joint venture learning in its operations?

5. Will this joint venture affect the parent's strategy and operations?

Notes

1. Weick (1979) discussed "believing is seeing" and suggested that beliefs are cause maps that "people impose on the world after which they see what they have already imposed" (p. 135). This argument suggests that organization learning will be shaped and constrained by an existing set of managerial beliefs.

2. Although there were a few Canadian parent firms, for brevity we refer to North American parents as American.

3. Interestingly, Cusumano and Takeishi (1991) also found evidence that U.S. suppliers can work effectively with Japanese automakers if given the opportunity, suggesting that a lack of skills may not be a significant hurdle facing suppliers trying to gain access to the transplant market.

4. Hamel (1991) very briefly discusses the personal skills of receptors.

References

Abbeglen, J. C., & Stalk, G. (1985). *Kaisha: The Japanese Corporation.* New York: Basic Books.

Argyris, C., & Schon, D. A. (1978). *Organization learning: A theory of action perspective.* Reading, MA: Addison-Wesley.

Badaracco, J. L. (1991). *The knowledge link.* Boston, MA: Harvard Business School Press.

Beamish, P., & Banks, J. C. (1987, Summer). Equity JVs and the theory of the multinational enterprise. *Journal of International Business Studies, 18,* 1-16.

Bourgeois, L. J., & Eisenhardt, K. (1988). Strategic decision processes in high velocity environments. *Management Science, 34,* 816-835.

Brown, J. S., & Duguid, P. (1991). Organizational learning and communities of practice: Towards a unified view of working, learning, and organization. *Organization Science, 2,* 40-57.

Cohen, W. M., & Levinthal, D. A. (1990). Absorptive capacity: A new perspective on learning and innovation. *Administrative Science Quarterly, 35,* 128-152.

Contractor, F. J., & Lorange, P. (1988). Why should firms cooperate: The strategy and economics basis for cooperative ventures. In F. J. Contractor & P. Lorange (Eds), *Cooperative strategies in international business* (pp. 3-30). Toronto: Lexington Books.

Cusumano, M., & Takeishi, A. (1991). Supplier relations and management: A survey of Japanese-transplant and US auto plants. *Strategic Management Journal, 12,* 563-588.

Dodgson, M. (1993). Learning, trust, and technological collaboration. *Human Relations, 46,* 77-95.

Doyle, P., Saunders, J., & Wong, V. (1992). Competition in global markets: A case study of American and Japanese competition in the British market. *Journal of International Business Studies, 23,* 419-442.

Festinger, L. (1957). *A theory of cognitive dissonance.* Stanford, CA: Stanford University Press.

Fiol, C. M., & Lyles, M. A. (1985). Organizational learning. *Academy of Management Review, 10*(4), 803-813.

Friedlander, F. (1984). Patterns of individual and organization learning. In S. Srivastava & Associates (Eds.), *The executive mind* (pp. 193-220). San Francisco: Jossey-Bass.

Geringer, J. M., & Hebert, L. (1991). Measuring performance of international joint ventures. *Journal of International Business Studies, 22*(2), 253-267.

Gioia, D. A., & Manz, C. C. (1985). Linking cognition and behavior: A script processing interpretation of vicarious learning. *Academy of Management Review, 10*(3), 527-539.

Glaser, B. (1978). *Theoretical sensitivity.* Mill Valley, CA: Sociology Press.

Gronhaug, K. (1977). Water to Spain: An export decision analyzed in the context of organization learning. *Journal of Management Studies, 14,* 26-33.

Hamel, G. (1991). Competition for competence and inter-partner learning within international strategic alliances. *Strategic Management Journal, 12* (special issue), 83-104.

Hamel, G., Doz, Y. L., & Prahalad, C. K. (1989, January/February). Collaborate with your competitors and win. *Harvard Business Review, 67,* 133-139.

Hedberg, B. (1981). How organizations learn and unlearn. In P. C. Nystrom & W. H. Starbuck (Eds), *Handbook of organizational design* (pp. 8-27). London: Oxford University Press.

Hedlund, G., & Nonaka, I. (1993). Models of knowledge management in the West and Japan. In P. Lorange, B. Chakravarthy, J. Roos, & A. Van de Ven (Eds), *Implementing strategic processes: Change, learning, and co-operation* (pp. 117-144). Oxford: Basil Blackwell.

Hennart, J. F. (1988). A transactions costs theory of equity JVs. *Strategic Management Journal, 9,* 361-374.

Huber, G. P. (1991). Organizational learning: The contributing processes and a review of the literatures. *Organization Science, 2,* 88-117.

Inkpen, A. (1994). The Japanese corporate network transferred to North America: Implications for North American firms. *International Executive, 36,*(4), 411-433.

Keller, M. (1989). *Rude awakening: The rise, fall, and struggle for recovery of General Motors.* New York: William Morrow.

Keys, J. B., Denton, L. T., & Miller, T. R. (1994). The Japanese management theory jungle—revisited. *Journal of Management, 20,* 373-402.

Kogut, B. (1988). Joint ventures: Theoretical and empirical perspectives. *Strategic Management Journal, 9,* 319-322.

Kogut, B., & Zander, U. (1992). Knowledge of the firm, combinative capabilities, and the replication of technology. *Organization Science, 3,* 383-397.

Levinthal, D. A., & March, J. G. (1993). The myopia of learning. *Strategic Management Journal, 14,* 95-112.

Levitt, B., & March, J. G. (1988). Organizational learning. *Annual Review of Sociology, 14,* 319-340.

March, J. G. (1991). Exploration and exploitation in organizational learning. *Organization Science, 2,* 71-87.

March, J. G., Sproull, L. S., & Tamuz, M. (1991). Learning from samples of one or fewer. *Organization Science, 2,* 1-13.

Mazur, J. E. (1990). *Learning and behavior.* Englewood Cliffs, NJ: Prentice Hall.

Miles, M. B., & Huberman, A. M. (1984). *Qualitative data analysis: A sourcebook of new methods.* Newbury Park, CA: Sage.

Miller, D. (1993). The architecture of simplicity. *Academy of Management Review, 18,* 116-138.

Mintzberg, H. (1990). Strategy formation: Schools of thought. In J. W. Frederickson (Ed.), *Perspectives of strategic management* (pp. 105-235). New York: Harper Business.

Neisser, U. (1976). *Cognition and reality.* San Francisco: W. H. Freeman and Company.

Nelson, R. R. (1991, Winter). Why do firms differ, and how does it matter? *Strategic Management Journal, 12* (Special Issue), 61-74.

Nelson, R. R., & Winter, S. G. (1982). *An evolutionary theory of economic change.* Cambridge, MA: Harvard University Press.

Nonaka, I. (1990). Redundant, overlapping organizations: A Japanese approach to managing the innovation process. *California Management Review, 32*(3), 27-38.

Nonaka, I. (1994). A dynamic theory of organizational knowledge. *Organization Science, 5,* 14-37.

Patton, M. Q. (1987). *How to use qualitative methods in evaluation.* Newbury Park, CA: Sage.

Pucik, V. (1991). Technology transfer in strategic alliances: Competitive collaboration and organizational learning. In T. Agmon & M. A. Von Glinow (Eds.), *Technology transfer in international business* (pp. 121-138). New York: Oxford University Press.

Schein, E. H. (1971). *Coercive persuasion.* New York: W. H. Norton.

Simonin, B. L., & Helleloid, D. (1993). Do organizations learn? An empirical test of organizational learning in international strategic alliances. In D. Moore (Ed.), *Academy of Management Best Paper Proceedings 1993.*

Starbuck, W. H. (1983). Organizations as action creators. *American Sociological Review, 48,* 91-102.

Starbuck, W. H. (1992). Learning by knowledge intensive firms. *Journal of Management Studies, 29,* 713-740.

Weick, K. E. (1979). *The social psychology of organizing* (2nd ed.; 1st ed. 1969). Reading, MA: Addison-Wesley.

Westney, D. E. (1988). Domestic and foreign learning curves in managing international cooperative strategies. In F. J. Contractor & P. Lorange (Eds), *Cooperative strategies in international business* (pp. 339-346). Toronto: Lexington Books.

IMPLICATIONS FOR HUMAN RESOURCE DEVELOPMENT PROFESSIONALS

The finding that American firms are generally more preoccupied with financial performance and short-term results and that learning often takes a back seat to these interests challenges HRD professionals to find ways to link their efforts more effectively to organizational performance. The additional finding that firms in a "deteriorating competitive position often had managers with the most entrenched belief systems" (p. 322) and a strong resistance to unlearning past practices creates additional possibilities for HRD practitioners. One implication is the need to determine strategies that would be effective in increasing individuals' willingness to learn new ways of thinking and doing. If we in HRD are to make the transition from stand-up classroom trainers to "learning and performance consultants," we will have to find creative solutions to help the organization achieve its learning and performance goals.

IMPLICATIONS FOR RESEARCH DESIGN AND METHODOLOGY

The qualitative case study methodology used in this research reveals many aspects of the linkages between individual, group, and organizational learning. Future research might use a similar methodology but delve deeper into the constructs discussed by the authors. For example, the finding that the link between learning and performance was paradoxical and that learning is dynamic and changing suggests a need for studies that use a longitudinal research design. This type of design, integrating both qualitative and quantitative measures, would help us track the means and ways organizations learn and unlearn over time. By using a cross-sectional research design in conjunction with the longitudinal approach, researchers could also study certain variables during the intervention's implementation. Although it is often difficult for researchers to spend months or years studying an organization, we must be careful not to fall into the same short-term, quick-results trap that affected the learning of managers in this study.

IMPLICATIONS FOR FUTURE INQUIRY

Inkpen and Crossan have provided important evidence that the link between individual and organizational learning cannot be overlooked. They concluded that many questions remain concerning the interrelationships among learning levels (individual, group, organizational) and the feedback mechanisms used to support learning. They also highlighted the need for additional research that focuses on the nature of the learning-performance relationship and suggested that Levinthal and March's (1993) work on learning myopia be used to study this relationship further.

Further studies should be undertaken with regard to their findings that: (a) a strong leader is needed who can overcome barriers to shared learning (integration) and (b) few American companies are willing to spend the resources needed to establish learning-oriented systems. Questions regarding the relationship between the characteristics for a strong leader and one who understands the role of learning in achieving business goals should be considered by HRD researchers. It would be interesting to study how other American organizations have justified or lobbied for developing and implementing learning systems and determining what value (demonstrated in concrete, tangible ways) these systems have contributed to organizations' success. At the same time, additional studies of organizational learning in other countries could perhaps illuminate cultural variables that support or inhibit the implementation of learning systems. Finally, researchers should take into account the authors' point that we must also consider rate of learning in addition to the learning itself. Adding this variable to the learning equation creates additional questions for future study.

OTHER RESOURCES

Levinthal, D. A., & March, J. G. (1993). The myopia of learning. *Strategic Management Journal, 14,* 95-112.

The Relationship Between Organizational Transfer Climate and Positive Transfer of Training

Janice Z. Rouiller
General Research Corporation, Vienna, Virginia

Irwin L. Goldstein
University of Maryland

THIS STUDY DESCRIBES THE DEVELOPMENT AND INVESTIGATION OF THE CONCEPT of organizational transfer climate and discusses whether it influences the degree to which trainees transfer behaviors learned in a training program to their job situations. The study was conducted in a large franchise that owns and operates over one hundred fast-food restaurants in a large metropolitan area. Analyses indicated that when manager trainees were assigned to units that had a more positive organizational transfer climate, they were rated as better performers of the behaviors previously learned in training. As was predicted, it was also found that manager trainees who learned more in training performed better on the job. It was concluded that, in addition to how much trainees learn in training, the organizational transfer climate of the work situation affects the degree to which learned behavior will be transferred onto the actual job. This research suggests that organizational transfer climate is a tool that should be investigated as a potential

Source: Rouiller, J. Z., & Goldstein, I. L. (1993). The relationship between organizational transfer climate and positive transfer of training. *Human Resource Development Quarterly,* 4(4), 377-390. Used by permission.

Authors' Note: We wish to express our appreciation to the University of Maryland Computer Science Center for their financial support for the analyses of these data.

facilitator for enhancing positive transfer of training into the work environment.

In nearly all studies of training outcomes, the emphasis has been on identifying and examining the characteristics of training programs and individual learners and relating these factors to training and job performance. This focus ignores the characteristics of the job situation and the question of whether these characteristics help to determine transferability of training behavior onto the job. Specifically, this study asks whether an organizational transfer climate exists on the job that helps to determine if behavior learned in training actually gets put to use in the job situation.

Historically, Fleishman, Harris, and Burtt (1955) conducted the first study that suggested that a supportive climate is a factor in the transfer of learning to the job situation. They conducted a training program that resulted in managers being more considerate of their employees, but in a follow-up investigation, they found that the effects of the training had disappeared. To determine why this occurred, they conducted a series of interviews that suggested that the effects disappeared because the supervisors of the trained managers were not supportive of the goals of the training program. Over a number of years, other authors (Goldstein, 1986b; McGehee & Thayer, 1961; Marx, 1982; Michalak, 1981; Mosel, 1957) offered views suggesting the need for a supportive organizational climate in order for learning to transfer from the classroom to the job. Baumgartel and his colleagues (Baumgartel & Jeanpierre, 1972; Baumgartel, Reynolds, & Pathan, 1984) described some organizational characteristics that might influence whether training transferred into the organization. They studied managers who were being trained to promote the introduction of advantaged technology into their organization and found that according to the manager's self-reports, training transfer into the work organization was more likely to be supported in organizations that stimulated and approved of innovation.

In 1986, Goldstein analyzed this literature and suggested that a supportive organizational transfer climate is a critical component that should be examined as part of the needs-assessment process. His view was that unless trainees transfer into job situations that have a climate that supports the use of the behaviors learned in training, they will not be likely to use their learned skills. He argued for an expanded needs-assessment process to assess this concern. Goldstein also warned that a process that only focuses on identifying the skills required for job performance will often fail, because it does not recognize the organizational dynamics that affect the transfer process. Recently, with the development of cognitive instructional theory, interest has grown in the concept of positive transfer climate. Noe (1986) developed a model specifying some motivational factors as well as other attribute and attitude factors that might affect a trainee's success in the training program. Noe hypothesized that trainees assess their training environments to determine whether they are responsive to their efforts. One application of this view is that efforts to utilize learned behavior depend on the degree of perceived support. Ford and his colleagues (Ford, Quinnes, Sego, & Sorra, 1992) found that following four months of technical training, U.S. Air Force aviators had substantially different opportunities perform their trained tasks. These differences were related to supervisory attitudes and work-group support, further contributing to the idea that different transfer training climates exist in organizations. Unfortunately, with the exception of these few efforts, relatively few empirical efforts shed any light on these concerns. In extensive reviews of the entire training literature, Baldwin and Ford (1988) and Tannenbaum and Yukl (1992) noted the importance of this issue but found very few empirical efforts and virtually no understanding of what constitutes an organizational transfer climate.

The present study attempts to explore the issue of organizational transfer climate. Here, the term *climate* is used in a way similar to that used by Schneider (1975). He defines climate as the practices and procedures used in an organization that connote or signal to people what is important. Schneider suggests that organizations or work units can be characterized by a variety of climates, such as a climate for service or a climate for safety.

In this study, we describe the development and use of a measure of organizational transfer climate. As described in the Method section, our measure of organizational transfer climate consists of those situations and consequences that either inhibit or help to facilitate the transfer of what has been learned in training into the job situation. The predicted relationships are presented in Figure 13.1. Specifically, as shown in the figure by the line depicting a relationship between organizational transfer climate and training transfer behavior, it is hypothesized that the more positive the organizational transfer climate, the more likely it is that trainees will transfer key behaviors to the job that have previously been learned in training.

Testing of this issue assumes that people who learn more in training also perform better on the job. In other words, if no evidence exists that individuals who perform better in training also perform better on the job, there is no reason to test for the effects of the transfer climate. Therefore, it is also hypothesized that manager-trainees who receive higher exam scores and evaluation scores in training will also be more likely to transfer key training behavior onto the job. That relationship is shown in Figure 13.1 by the line between learning in training and training transfer

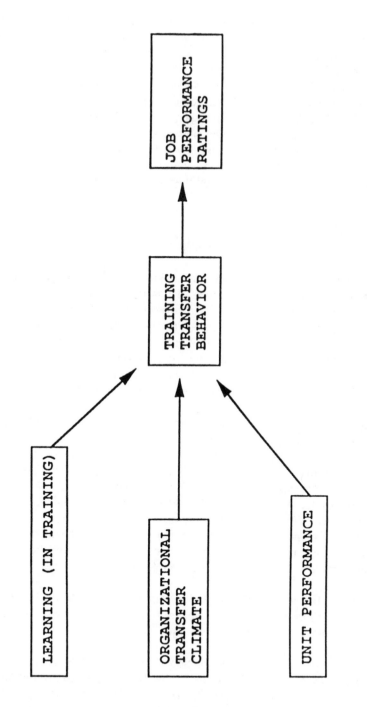

Figure 13.1. Relationship Between Learning in Training, Organizational Climate, and Trainee Performance in the Job Setting

behavior. A corollary to this hypothesis is that trainees who transfer more key training behavior onto the job will also receive higher job performance ratings. In other words, individuals who perform more of what they have learned in training on the job will also receive higher overall job performance ratings. That relationship is also shown in Figure 13.1. In addition, one more possible relationship is presented. It seems possible that if a trainee is assigned to an organizational unit where performance is already high, he or she might be influenced to perform at a higher level. This relationship is shown by the line between unit performance and training transfer behavior. The implications of this relationship for the testing of the other proposed hypotheses are presented in the Method section.

Method

Participants. A large, fast-food, franchised chain, hereafter known as ABC Foods, agreed to participate in this study. This franchise is the owner and operator of more than one hundred physically separate individual fast-food restaurants in a large metropolitan area. The structure in each restaurant consists of at least three managers and employees. Of these managers, one is the unit manager and the others are assistant managers. The participants in this study attended training as part of the process of being selected for the position of assistant manager.

Training Program. One of the programs offered by ABC Foods is a mandatory training program for individuals selected to be assistant managers. The program consists of nine weeks of intensive training; both classroom knowledge and hands-on performance are emphasized. Some of the topics included are learning administrative procedures for payroll development, appropriate food handling and preparation, shift management, and customer solicitation and service. The class size for this program is approximately ten assistant managers. One hundred and two assistant managers divided into eleven classes, completed the entire training program and were included in this study.

Measures. The measures collected in this study are outlined in Table 13.1; the proposed relationships between them are presented in Figure 13.1. Further information about the measures follows.

Climate Measure. At the completion of training, each trainee was randomly assigned to one of the 102 units that required an assistant managers. As noted in Table 13.1, two weeks before the arrival of any manager trainee at one of the 102 units, the researchers collected

TABLE 13.1. Explanation of Measures

Measure	Completed by	Timetable
Climate	Existing managers (n = 2 to 3 managers in each of 102 units)	Two weeks prior to arrival of new trainee manager
Learning	Training department (n = 102 trainees)	At end of training of new trainee manager
Transfer behavior	Existing managers, crew members (n = 6 to 24 managers, all members of unit)	First several weeks after arrival of new trainee manager
Job performance	Unit manager (n = 102 managers for 102 trainee managers)	Eight to twelve weeks after arrival of new trainee manager
Unit performance	Regional manager (n = 102 units)	Most recent rating prior to arrival of new trainee manager

responses to the organizational transfer climate scale from the managers who were already working in that unit. The following steps were followed in the development of the climate measure.

1. The training literature was reviewed and workshops were conducted with personnel officers to develop critical incidents describing job situations that were predicted to facilitate or inhibit the transfer of behavior learned in training onto the job (Goldstein, 1986a; Goldstein and Thayer, 1987). This initial activity resulted in the collection of 298 critical incidents.

2. Rouiller and Goldstein (1990) adapted a number of categories and definitions from a behavior-modification model (Luthans and Kreitner, 1985) that appeared useful to help cluster the critical incidents. The definitions of each of the categories and examples for each category are presented in Exhibit 13.1.

3. The 298 critical incidents were independently sorted by subject matter experts (SMEs) into the categories described in Exhibit 13.1. The SMEs were individuals who had a thorough understanding of the training literature. They were first required to sort the incidents into the major categories presented in Exhibit 13.1: situational cues or consequences. The SMEs then sorted the incidents into subcategories, such as goal cues and social cues. A critical incident was considered to be representative of the category if five of the six judges independently agreed on the initial placement of the item into the category of situational cues or consequences. The same criteria was employed for placement of the item into a subcategory, such as goal cues and task cues. These standards were met by 112 items.

1. *Situational Cues.* Cues that serve to remind trainees of their training or provide them with an opportunity to use their training once they return to their jobs. A number of different types of situational cues exist. Following are some definitions and examples:

   A. Goal cues. These cues serve to remind trainees to use their training when they return to their jobs; for example, existing managers set goals for new managers that encourage them to apply their training on the job.

   B. Social cues. These cues arise from group membership and include the behavior and influence processes exhibited by supervisors, peers and/or subordinates; for example, new managers who use their training supervise differently from the existing managers. (This is reverse-scored.)

   C. Task cues. These cues concern the design and nature of the job itself; for example, equipment is available in this unit that allows new managers to use the skills they gained in training.

   D. Self-control cues. These cues concern various self-control processes that permit trainees to use what has been learned; for example, "I was allowed to practice handling real and job-relevant problems."

2. *Consequences* As employees return to their jobs and begin applying their learned behavior, they will encounter consequences that will affect their further use of what they have learned. A number of different types of consequences cues exist. Following are some definitions and examples:

   A. Positive feedback. In this instance, the trainees are given positive information about their use of the trained behavior; for example, new managers who successfully use their training will receive a salary increase.

   B. Negative feedback. Here, trainees are informed of the negative consequences of not using their learned behavior; for example, area managers are made aware of new managers who are not following operating procedures.

   C. Punishment. Trainees are punished for using trained behaviors; for example, more experienced workers ridicule the use of techniques learned in training. (This is reverse-scored.)

   D. No feedback. No information is given to the trainees about the use or importance of the learned behavior; for example, existing managers are too busy to note whether trainees use learned behavior. (This is reverse-scored.)

Exhibit 13.1. Definitions and Illustration of Transfer Climate Items

4. A focus-group interview was then conducted with unit managers from ABC Foods to determine which of the items were relevant to the organization. Sixty-three items, consisting of forty-one items that had been categorized as situational cues and twenty-two considered to be consequences, were retained as relevant to the organization. These items represent the transfer climate measure used in this study.

As noted above, climate information was collected separately from two to three managers in each of the 102 units participating in the study two weeks before the arrival of the trainee. Each item, such as those presented in Exhibit 13.1, was rated on the degree to which it described the unit using a five-point Likert scale ranging from very infrequently (1) to very frequently (5). An exception was made for the self-control cues. In this instance, the trainees themselves rated the climate of the training organization in terms of the degree to which it permitted them to use what had been learned. For all of the other climate measures, a total of 273 surveys were collected that had been completed by the two or more managers in each of the 102 units. These data were aggregated separately for each unit based on the assumption that people generally agree about the climate of their work groups (Rousseau, 1988; Schneider & Reichers, 1983). In order to check on this assumption, inter-rater reliabilities were obtained for each scale within each unit, using the method developed by James, Demaree, and Wolf (1984).

Average within-group inter-rater reliabilities for each scale based on $r_{WG(J)}$ are as follows: goal cues = .79, social cues = .91, task cues = .85, positive feedback = .62, negative feedback = .53, punishment = .78, and no feedback = .83. The positive and negative feedback reliabilities are low but acceptable for research purposes.

Since these data were based upon a priori scales developed using a rational clustering procedure and were tested with only one sample, caution should be used in generalizing the results to all scales until more data are collected. In addition, the subscales within the situational cues were moderately to highly correlated, with an average correlation of .60. The same was true for the subscales within the consequences measure, with an average correlation of .66. The correlations between the subscales for the situational-cues measure and the consequences measure were somewhat lower, with an average correlation of .45. Given these data and the small number of items that constitute the various subscales, further analysis using the climate measure considered only two components, situational cues and consequences. Further research will be needed to determine whether the subscales within these two components are meaningful.

The development of the climate measure permitted testing of the first research question—that is, whether the organizational transfer climate (as measured by situational cues and consequences) is related to training transfer behavior. Specifically, as shown in Figure 13.1, the hypothesis is that the more positive the climate, the more likely it is that the assistant manager trainees will demonstrate key transfer behaviors.

Learning Measure. This measure consists of two components for each of the 102 trainees. The first component is a final examination score for each trainee on the knowledge gained from the various parts of the training program. Examples of some of the topics in the knowledge component are inventory procedures, use of daily cash reports, scheduling, shift management, and food and cost control. The second component of the learning measure is an evaluation score given by the training department for each trainee. This score is based upon trainee performance throughout the program on items such as completing daily sales tracking forms, properly completing orders, using flow charts to plan a work day, and completing interunit transfers. The two components were standardized and combined into one measure representing learning in the training program. Reliability for the measure was computed using a standardized-item alpha that was determined to be .89.

As presented in Figure 13.1, this measure was used to test hypothesis 2, which is that manager trainees who receive higher scores on the learning measure will be more likely to demonstrate key transfer behavior on the job.

Measure of Transfer Behavior. The transfer behaviors emphasized in the training program were identified by analyzing the training objectives and developing items that reflected the goals of the training program. The items were developed by a researcher who attended the training program and read the training material. All items were checked with the training department to ensure that they reflected the goals of the program. Examples of transfer behavior items are as follows: "Checks deliveries to make sure the product is in good condition," "Makes sure oldest products are used first," "Does not allow customers to empty their trash," "Makes sure trays are carried for customers who need assistance," and "Takes hourly readings from the cash registers." Ninety-two such items made up the transfer behavior measure.

The trainee assistant managers were evaluated during the first several weeks on the job by having managers and experienced crew members rate their transfer behavior. Each trainee was rated on the ninety-two-item measure by using a five-point Likert scale indicating how frequently the new managers had demonstrated the key behaviors; 919 surveys were collected. As with the climate surveys, the results of these surveys were aggregated within each of the 102 units. Inter-rater reliabilities were obtained using the James, Demaree, and Wolf (1984) method. An $r_{WG(92)}$ was obtained for each unit. The average $r_{WG(92)}$ is .93, with a range of .79 to .99 indicating high inter-rater agreement on the ninety-two items.

Measure of Job Performance. Hypotheses 1 and 2 predict the degree of positive organizational transfer climate (situational cues and consequences); the degree of learning in training will be related to the degree to which trainees exhibit transfer behavior on the job. As noted in Table 13.1, these transfer behaviors are assessed by managers and crew members within the first several weeks on the job. Approximately eight to twelve weeks after the arrival of the new trainee manager, the job performance of the new trainee is assessed by the head manager for the unit. This performance evaluation is conducted using a form developed by ABC Foods to evaluate the job performance of all assistant managers in areas such as quality, service, cleanliness, and financial management. In addition, an overall-summary evaluation rating is given; that measure was used in this study to assess the job performance of the manager trainees. As shown in Figure 13.1, hypothesis 3 states that the greater the exhibition of transfer behaviors on the job by the trainees, the higher will be their job performance appraisal ratings.

Unit Performance. In addition to the relationships already described, it is possible that the unit's general performance level can influence the extent to which transfer will occur. Thus, units that already achieve higher performance may also influence new trainees to perform better. If this is the case, this factor might explain performance differences in trainees across units and the fact that the situational cues and consequences that constitute the transfer climate measure do not add any additional predictive power. Thus, it is necessary to test the hypothesis that the higher a unit's performance score, the more likely it is that an assistant manager trainee will demonstrate key transfer behaviors. In order to assess this possibility, scores on a unit performance evaluation developed by ABC Foods were used. The evaluation consisted of averaged ratings of the entire unit done by regional supervisors and based on performance on factors such as quality, service, cleanliness, and financial management during the previous quarter. The overall unit performance rating was based upon the most recent rating, obtained prior to the arrival of the new trainee manager.

Results

Learning measures were obtained from the training course for 102 trainees attending a nine week assistant manager training program. After completion of the training program, the trainees were randomly assigned to one of the 102 physically separate units that participated in this study. Surveys of the organizational transfer climate were obtained from two to three managers in each unit just prior to the new trainee manager's arrival. Results from the climate surveys were aggregated within each of the 102 units. After the assistant manager had been on the job for several weeks, transfer behavior surveys were collected that rated the performance of the trainees on a form specifically designed to reflect training objectives. The forms were completed by the trainees' managers and experienced crew members. The results were aggregated within units and represent transfer of training behavior for each trainee. After eight to twelve weeks on the job, trainees were rated by the unit manager on the organization's standard performance appraisal form. This represents the measure of good performance. In addition, an overall unit performance rating based upon the most recent rating of the entire unit by the regional supervisor was obtained prior to the arrival of the new trainee manager.

Relationship of the Learning and Organizational Transfer Climate to Transfer Behavior. As described earlier, the major hypothesis of interest is that the organizational transfer climate (as measured by situational cues and consequences) is related to transfer of training—that is, the more positive the organizational transfer climate, the more the assistant manager trainee will demonstrate transfer behaviors. In order to test this hypothesis, a multiple-regression analysis was conducted with the transfer behavior measure as the dependent variable. As described in the Method section, the transfer behavior criterion was specifically designed as an on-the-job measure of the objectives of the training program.

In the multiple regression, the learning measure from training was entered as step 1, unit performance was entered as step 2, and the organizational transfer climate measure was entered as step 3. The logic used to determine the order of entry was that by entering learning and unit performance prior to organizational transfer climate, it was possible to determine how much variance the transfer climate would account for over and above these two variables. In other words, did the transfer climate measure account for any additional variance after the relationships between learning and transfer behavior and between unit performance and transfer behavior were determined? The order of entry for learning and unit performance is essentially an arbitrary choice.

The hypothesis that learning in training is significantly related to transfer behavior is supported (Inc $F_{(1,100)}$ = 8.26, $p < .01$). Learning accounts for 8 percent of the variance in transfer behavior. Thus, people who perform better on the learning measures from training also tend to

TABLE 13.2. Correlational Results Concerning the Relationships Between Learning in Training, Training Transfer Behavior, and Job Performance Ratings

	Transfer Behavior	Job Performance Ratings
Learning in training	.28*	.02
Transfer behavior		.52*

* $p < .01$.

perform better on the transfer behavior measure on the job. The alternate hypothesis, that previous unit performance is related to transfer behavior, is not supported (Inc $F_{(2,99)}$ = 3.58, $p > .05$). Thus, there is no evidence that trainees who are assigned to higher-performing units perform better. The main hypothesis is supported: after learning and unit performance are entered, organizational transfer climate is still significantly related to transfer behavior (Inc $F_{(10,91)}$ = 10.87, $p < .001$). Learning and organizational climate together account for 54 percent of the variance in transfer behavior. The effects of a possible interaction between organizational transfer climate and learning were also investigated. The result was not significant (Inc $F_{(11,90)}$ = .081, $p > .05$), indicating that the interaction did not add to the explained variance in transfer behavior.

Relationship Between Learning in Training, Transfer Behavior, and Ratings of Job Performance. In order to test whether learning, transfer behavior, and ratings of job performance are interrelated, a multiple-regression analysis was conducted with ratings of job performance as the dependent variable. As noted above, learning in training is significantly related to transfer of training behavior performance, but it is not significantly related to job performance ratings (Inc $F_{(1,100)}$ = .03, $p > .10$). The single-order correlations demonstrating these relationships are presented in Table 13.2.

In Table 13.2, the single-order correlation between learning in training and transfer behavior is .28; between transfer behavior and job performance ratings it is .52. Both zero-order correlations are statistically significant at $p < .01$. The regression analysis for learning and transfer was significant (Inc $F_{(1,100)}$ = 8.26, $p < .01$), as was the relationship between transfer and job performance (Inc $F_{(11,90)}$ = 7.75, $p < .01$). However, there is no relationship between learning in training and job performance ratings. Thus, a situation exists in which learning in training is related to transfer behavior on the job and transfer behavior on the job is then related to later ratings of job performance.

Exploration of Situational-Cues and Consequences Scales as Components of Training Transfer Climate. It was possible to examine whether the situational-cues measure and the consequences measure constituting the transfer climate scale contributed independently to the prediction of transfer behavior. A regression analysis indicated that even after learning was entered, the situational-cues measure yielded a significant effect (Inc $F_{(6,95)}$ = 11.32, p < .001); together, they accounted for 36 percent of the variance. When the consequence measure was entered, it also resulted in a significant effect (Inc $F_{(10,91)}$ = 7.95, p < .01). A final test of this hypothesis involved reversing the order of entry of situational cues and consequences. After learning was entered, the consequences scale yielded a significant effect (Inc $F_{(6,95)}$ = 8.83, p < .001), accounting for 30 percent of the variance in predicting transfer. The addition of situational cues also yielded a significant effect ($F_{(10,91)}$ = 11.48, p < .001). Thus, while further research is required, both pressures appear to add to the explained variance over and above the other.

Discussion

Positive Transfer Climate. This study provides support for the idea that, above and beyond learning, attributes of the setting (the organizational transfer climate) influence the transfer of training behavior onto the job. In addition, since the climate by learning interaction was not significant, both the degree of learning in training and the positive transfer climate appear to directly affect the degree of transfer behavior to the job situation. The finding is interesting, because this is one of the few empirical studies that establishes the importance of a positive organizational transfer climate in transferring training from the training program into the work organization. In this study, situational cues and consequences were each separately found to significantly add to the explained variance in the degree of transfer behavior and to independently contribute to transfer behavior. Further empirical research will be needed to address this question. Even more important, these data add to a growing belief that organizational transfer climate is a very important aspect in determining whether training will transfer into the organization. As noted earlier, Ford and his colleagues (Ford, Quinones, Sego, & Sorra, 1992) have actually found that four months after receiving technical training, U.S. Air Force aviators had substantially different opportunities to perform their trained tasks. Even more important, these differences in opportunities were related to differences in supervisory attitudes and work-group support. This suggests, as does the present study, that different transfer climates exist in organizations. The present study adds the idea that these differences in climate contribute to whether trainees transfer the behaviors they have learned in training onto the job. Other research is also proceeding, using some of the scales developed for this study. In one investigation, Tracey (1992) reports that organizational transfer climate, as well as a "continuous learning culture," was related to supervisory ratings of trainees in a supermarket chain.

Relationships Between Learning, Transfer, and Job Performance. The results (see Table 13.2) indicate that learning in training is related to transfer behavior on the job. In addition, transfer behavior is related to job performance ratings. Thus, as one might hope, learning in training is related to the performance of transfer behaviors on the job. These transfer behaviors are also related to job performance ratings collected at a later time. It should be noted that these types of relationships have not often been found, although they are usually assumed to exist. In this case, problems with methodological bias that might underlie such results were limited. Measures of learning in training were collected before the trainee entered the job situation and were also completed by different individuals. Similarly, measures of transfer behavior were collected prior to job performance ratings and were completed by different individuals than those who completed the job performance measure. These types of relationships deserve more systematic exploration.

In the present study, another result that is puzzling on the surface is that while learning in training relates to the measure of training transfer behavior on the job and the measure of transfer behavior relates to ratings of job performance, there is no direct relationship between learning in training and job performance ratings. A possible explanation for this is that the transfer behavior measure was systematically designed to examine only the objectives taught in the training program. However, the job performance measure examines many other facets of behavior besides what is taught in training. It does appear, however, that individuals who learned more in training and were able to transfer those behaviors also tended to learn on the job whatever else was necessary to perform better on the job performance measure. Perhaps another important point is that the results of training may not show up in overall job performance measures unless the measures are specifically designed to reflect the objectives that are achieved in the training program. This may also explain why no support was found for the hypothesis that units with higher performance ratings would also have higher transfer behavior performance by trainees: the units' high performance ratings were based on a variety of performance aspects and not necessarily on organizational support for trainees' use of the specific learned skills stemming from the training program. Another possibility stems from the fact that the unit performance measure (see Table 13.1) is the most recent rating by the regional manager before the trainee arrives. These ratings are given every several months and it is possible that the scores no longer reflect the performance of the unit by the time the trainee arrives.

Summary and Implications of the Study. The results of this study suggest several interesting research-related and practical implications. This study confirms that individuals who learn more in training also perform better in transferring those behaviors. However, it also adds the idea that a positive organizational transfer climate appears to be at least as important if transfer of training behavior is to occur. Further research is needed on the relationship of organizational climate to transfer behavior and job performance. If these relationships prove robust, organizational analysis assessing transfer climate should be a requirement in determining if the organization is ready to support its training program. It may also be the case that training members of the organization to provide a supportive organizational transfer climate is just as important as training the trainee in the skills needed for the job.

References

Baldwin, T. T., & Ford, J. K. (1988). Transfer of training: A review and directions for future research. *Personnel Psychology, 41,* 63-105.

Baumgartel, H., & Jeanpierre, F. (1972). Applying new knowledge in the back-home setting: A study of Indian managers' adoptive efforts. *Journal of Applied Behavioral Science, 8* (6), 674-694.

Baumgartel, H. J., Reynolds, M. J. I., & Pathan, R. Z. (1984). How personality and organizational climate variables moderate the effectiveness of management development programmes: A review and some recent research findings. *Management and Labour Studies, 9* (1), 1-16.

Fleishman, E. A., Harris, E. F., & Burtt, H. E. (1955). *Leadership and supervision in industry* (Report No. 33). Columbus: Bureau of Educational Research, Ohio State University.

Ford, J. K., Quinones, M. A., Sego, D. J., & Sorra, J. S. (1992). Factors affecting the opportunity to perform trained tasks on the job. *Personnel Psychology, 45,* 511-527.

Goldstein, I. L. (1986a, July). *Organizational analysis and needs assessment.* Paper presented at the meeting of the International Association of Applied Psychology, Jerusalem, Israel.

Goldstein, I. L. (1986b). *Training in organizations: Program development, needs assessment, and evaluation.* Pacific Grove, CA: Brooks/Cole.

Goldstein, I. L., & Thayer, P. W. (1987). *Panel discussion on facilitators and inhibitors of the training transfer process.* Presented at the Society for Industrial and Organizational Psychology, Atlanta.

James, L. R., Demaree, R. G., & Wolf, G. (1984). Estimating within-group interrater reliability with and without response bias. *Journal of Applied Psychology, 69* (1), 85-98.

Luthans, F., & Kreitner, R. (1985). *Organizational behavior modification and beyond.* Glenview, IL: Scott, Foresman.

McGehee, W., & Thayer, P. W. (1961). *Training in business and industry.* New York: Wiley.

Marx, R. D. (1982). Relapse prevention for managerial training: A model for maintenance of behavior change. *Academy of Management Review, 7* (3), 441-443.

Michalak, D. F. (1981, May). The neglected half of training. *Training & Development Journal,* pp. 22-28.

Mosel, J. N. (1957). Why training programs fail to carry over. *Personnel, 34,* 56-64.

Noe, R. A. (1986). Trainees' attributes and attitudes: Neglected influences on training effectiveness. *Academy of Management Review, 11* (4), 736-749.

Rouiller, J. Z., & Goldstein, I. L. (1990). *Determinants of the climate for transfer of training.* Paper presented at the meeting of the Society for Industrial and Organizational Psychology, St. Louis.

Rousseau, D. M. (1988). The construction of climate in organizational research. In C. L. Cooper & I. Robertson (Eds.), *International review of industrial and organizational psychology* (pp. 139-158). New York: Wiley.

Schneider, B. (1975). Organizational climates: An essay. *Personnel Psychology, 28,* 447-479.

Schneider, B., & Reichers, A. (1983). On the etiology of climates. *Personnel Psychology, 36,* 19-39.

Tannenbaum, S. I., & Yukl, G. (1992). Training and development in work organizations. In *Annual Review of Psychology.* Palo Alto, CA: Annual Reviews.

Tracey, J. B. (1992). *The effects of organizational climate and culture on the transfer of training.* Unpublished doctoral dissertation, State University of New York, Albany.

IMPLICATIONS FOR HUMAN RESOURCE DEVELOPMENT PROFESSIONALS

This study contains at least three major implications for HRD professionals. The authors briefly articulated two of them. First, HRD professionals need to make greater efforts to assess the organization's transfer climate. This means having not only the skills and knowledge to conduct needs assessment, organizational diagnoses, and program evaluations, but the capacity for negotiation, persuasion, political sensitivity, consultation, coaching, conflict resolution, and group process, to name a few. HRD professionals who continuously assess and monitor the organization's climate to determine the level of support for learning/training transfer will find themselves at the center of the organization, for this approach requires knowledge of the organization's culture, mission, vision, and business.

The second implication mentioned by Rouiller and Goldstein and related to the first implication concerns the training that employees will need to knowingly plan for and support the transfer of training. Employees at every level of the organization will have to learn specific ways they can support transfer—whether through coaching, feedback, or job redesign. Their understanding of the learning and transfer processes will be essential if the organization is to benefit from HRD's training efforts.

Finally, the authors' findings have implications for training program evaluation. We can no longer afford to evaluate programs according to models that fail to take into consideration the organizational context. Understanding how an organization's climate affects transfer is critical for trainers who hope to determine the effectiveness of their training programs. Although trainers may not be able to control all the organizational variables that affect training transfer, at the very least their evaluation methodology and approach can describe and interpret the organization's work environment (culture, resources, constraints) (Rothwell & Kazanas, 1994).

IMPLICATIONS FOR RESEARCH DESIGN AND METHODOLOGY

The authors have made several recommendations for further study related to the instruments they used to collect data for this research. Although their measures appear to have been developed using rigorous research methods, the quantitative data that resulted still left much to be learned. One of the "puzzlements" was why job performance ratings were not related to transfer. Rouiller and Goldstein postulated several different explanations, but in the end they could not answer this question. As we continue to experiment with the measures they used or with similar quantitative ones, it may be worthwhile to complement this research with more qualitatively oriented designs to peel back the onion and get beneath the layer of *what is* to *why it is.*

IMPLICATIONS FOR FUTURE INQUIRY

The Rouiller and Goldstein article lends further support to the critical role that organizational culture plays in supporting individual and organizational learning. As the authors indicated, further research on the relationship of organizational climate to the transfer of behavior and to job performance should be conducted. The authors have suggested that if future research supports their findings, then it would be incumbent upon trainers to assess the learning transfer climate before providing training to organization members so that trainers can be sure the culture will support the transfer.

Additional research might focus on what kinds of knowledge and skills from training are more or less affected by the organization's climate and culture. What are effective ways to measure this climate accurately? What aspects of the organization's culture contribute to or detract from positive transfer? What would training look like if it were specifically designed to support transfer? These are but a few of the questions the article stimulates.

OTHER RESOURCES

Rothwell, W., & Kazanas. (1994). *Mastering the instructional design process.* San Francisco: Jossey-Bass.

Organizational Learning

A Review of the Literature with Implications for HRD Professionals

Nancy M. Dixon
George Washington University, Washington, D.C.

ORGANIZATIONAL LEARNING REFERS TO LEARNING AT THE SYSTEM RATHER than individual level. The changing nature of work, global competitive challenges, and everpresent change require that human resource professionals focus on this higher level of learning. The literature on organizational learning can be classified into five areas: information acquisition, information distribution and interpretation, making meaning, organizational memory, and information retrieval. Each has special implications for the role of HRD professionals as learning facilitators.

Powerful forces demand a new way of thinking about learning in organizations. To meet the demands prompted by these forces, I propose adopting the concept of organizational learning for use in reframing learning within organizations. Organizational learning is complex and multifaceted. I review current literature on the topic and explore its implications for HRD professionals.

Forces Intensifying an Organizational Emphasis on Learning

Learning is the critical competency of the 1990s. Three powerful forces are working to intensify the emphasis organizations place on

Source: Dixon, N. (1990). Organizational learning: A review of the literature with implications for HRD professionals. *Human Resource Development Quarterly, 3*(1), 29-49. Used by permission.

learning. The first is the changing nature of work. Perelman (1984, p. xvii) notes, "By the beginning of the next century, three quarters of the jobs in the U.S. economy will involve creating and processing knowledge. Knowledge workers will find that continual learning is not only a prerequisite of employment but is a major form of work." Zuboff (1988) explains that information technology has altered basic assumptions about the relationship between work and learning. She says,

> The informated organization is a learning institution, and one of its principal purposes is the expansion of knowledge—not knowledge for its own sake (as in academic pursuit), but knowledge that comes to reside at the core of what it means to be productive. Learning is no longer a separate activity that occurs either before one enters the workplace or in remote classroom settings. Nor is it an activity preserved for a managerial group. The behaviors that define learning and the behaviors that define being productive are one and the same. Learning is not something that requires time out from being engaged in productive activity; learning is the heart of productive activity. To put it simply, learning is the new form of labor. (p. 395)

The second force increasing the organizational emphasis on learning is the competitive challenge posed by a global economy. In the short run, a company competes on the basis of the price and performance of its current products. In the long run, the competitive advantage lies with organizations that develop core competencies enabling them to create new products swiftly and thus adapt to rapidly changing opportunities. These core competencies represent the collective learning of the organization (Prahalad & Hamel, 1990). DeGeus (1988, p. 71), of Shell International, has noted that "the ability to learn faster than competitors may be the only sustainable competitive advantage."

A related response to the competitive challenge is the growing emphasis on quality. Training is an integral part of the quality movement, but a more central component is the continuous improvement process, which is fundamentally a learning process. As Reich (1987, p. 80) notes, "Competitive advantage today comes from continuous, incremental innovation and refinement of a variety of ideas that spread throughout the organization."

The third force encouraging organizational learning results from the increasing pace and unpredictable nature of the change experienced by organizations (Morgan, 1988; Peters, 1988; Vaill, 1989). Using a formula borrowed from ecology, $L \geq C$, Revans (1980) notes that in order to survive, an organism must be able to learn (L) at a rate that equals or exceeds the changes (C) that are occurring in its environment. It follows that organizations, as systems, must increase their capacity to learn if they are to function successfully in an environment characterized by continual mergers, rapid technological change, massive societal change, globalization, and increasing competition (Hedberg, 1981; Marsick, 1987; Morgan & Ramirez, 1983; Perelman, 1984).

HRD professionals have had the major responsibility for the learning that occurs within organizations. To date, most of that learning has taken place in classrooms and through on-the-job training. Both of these delivery systems focus on learning at the individual level. A learning response at the organizational level is, however, needed to respond to the forces I have summarized.

Organizational Learning as a Construct

Organizational learning has been discussed in the literature for over twenty years (Argyris & Schön, 1978; Bateson, 1971; Simon, 1969). Although a number of definitions have been proposed (Argyris & Schön, 1978; Fiol & Lyles, 1985; Hedberg, 1981; Normann, 1985), Duncan and Weiss's (1979, p. 84) definition is offered here: "Organizational learning is defined as the process by which knowledge about action outcome relationships between the organization and the environment is developed." I selected this definition because learning is viewed as a process, not an outcome (Levitt & March, 1988), and because learning focuses on the system (organization) rather than the individual.

Explaining the concept of organizational learning by contrasting it with individual learning provokes the question of whether an organization can, in fact, learn. Students of organizational learning acknowledge that all learning in an organization must necessarily occur through individuals, but also argue that organizational learning is more than the sum of the learning of individuals. Argyris and Schön (1978, p. 20) note, for example, that "there is no organizational learning without individual learning, and that individual learning is a necessary but insufficient condition for organizational learning."

Organizational learning may be most readily discerned when considering a performing organization such as an orchestra or basketball team (Yanow & Cook, 1990). The performance of a symphony or the winning of a game cannot be attributed to individuals alone or even to the sum of individuals' knowledge. There is a know-how in the collective that can be credited only to the group. This know-how is embedded in the shared understanding of the group. Daft and Weick (1984, p. 285) note that "individuals come and go, but organizations preserve knowledge, behaviors, mental maps, norms, and values over time. The distinctive feature of organizational level information activity is sharing." Schön (1979) provides a useful illustration of shared understanding by contrasting an individual craftsman with craftsmen who have banded together to produce a product. He delineates the orderly sequence of tasks in which the individual craftsman making wooden shovels would engage—for example, cutting down logs and shaping, storing, and selling the shovels. The band of craftsmen would divide such tasks among themselves. Schön notes, "They will do things in certain regular ways and sequences, and will make, detect, and correct errors. But they will, of necessity, communicate with one another concerning their interactive tasks. Each individual must generate an image of the cooperative system on which his or her own performance depends. . . . Intelligent action depends on a continuing mutual adjustment of individual behaviors, one to another. Their organizing depends, in turn, on each person's image of the larger system. In this sense, the organization exists in its members' heads" (p. 117).

Argyris and Schön (1978, p. 13) note, "It is individuals who decide and act, but they do these things *for* the collectivity by virtue of the rules for decision, delegation, and membership."

Organizations are created because a task is too large or complex for one individual. To accomplish this greater task, each individual within the organization must have a level of competence, but, likewise, the organization as a whole must have a competence. Organizations are not created with such organizational competence intact; the concept of organizational learning implies that organizations must learn in order to perform competently.

Although HRD professionals have developed substantial technology for increasing competence in individuals, they lack an equivalent technology for addressing organizational learning. The organizational learning literature is largely conceptual, but it nonetheless offers some categories and processes as a foundation for building such a technology.

Review of Research

Five major reviews of the literature on organizational learning have been conducted over the last ten years (Hedberg, 1981; Shrivastava, 1983; Fiol & Lyles, 1985; Levitt & March, 1988; Huber, 1991), each from a different perspective—for example, sociology, communication, or management. This review adds another perspective, that of HRD.

I organize the organizational learning literature into five major areas that modify and extend Huber's (1991) classification: (1) information acquisition, (2) information distribution and interpretation, (3) making meaning, (4) organization memory, and (5) retrieval of information. The implications outlined are intended to be illustrative rather than inclusive. But they will perhaps add weight to the argument that organizational learning is a concept that HRD professionals can use to reframe learning in organizations.

The five categories of organizational learning elements can be viewed as sequential; that is, information is first acquired, then distributed, given meaning, stored, and finally retrieved. However, such an interpretation would oversimplify current understanding of how organizations learn (Daft & Weick, 1984). Rather than being sequential, organizational learning elements appear to be continuous and to have an interaction effect upon each other. An illustration of the continuous, rather than sequential, nature of the elements is the distribution of information that occurs through multiple channels, each having differing time frames. Likewise, information within the organization is continually subjected to perceptual filters, not just initially as a sequential model might imply. Examples of the effects of interaction between categories include the effect of existing information on the way new information is interpreted and the retrieval of information, which is a process of reconstruction resulting in the retrieved version having a different meaning than the original. It is more accurate, then, to think of the elements of organizational learning as ongoing and interactive rather than sequential and independent.

Acquisition of Information. Organizations obtain information both from external sources and by generating information internally (see Figure 14.1). Organizations acquire knowledge externally by borrowing from other organizations, attending conferences, employing consultants, and availing themselves of print materials (Bedeian, 1986; deGeus, 1988; Hedberg, 1981); searching—that is, monitoring economic, social, and technological trends (Bennis & Nanus, 1985; Daft & Weick, 1984; deGeus, 1988; Hedberg, 1981; Lundberg, 1989; Meyer, 1982; Normann, 1985)—and systematically collecting data on customers, competitors, and other stakeholders (Bedeian, 1986; Bennis & Nanus, 1985; Daft & Weick, 1984; deGeus, 1988; Hedberg, 1981; Normann, 1985; Stata, 1989); grafting onto themselves new members or grafting on organizations through mergers or acquisitions (Badaracco, 1991; Pucik, 1988); and collaborating with other organizations, building alliances, and forming joint ventures (Jemison & Sitkin, 1986; Pucik, 1988).

Organizations generate information internally by relying on the prevailing technology and understanding of their founders (Huber, 1991); learning from experience (Levitt & March, 1988; March & Olsen, 1976); experimenting—that is, developing original innovations (Bedeian, 1986; Normann, 1985), inventing new processes to accomplish the

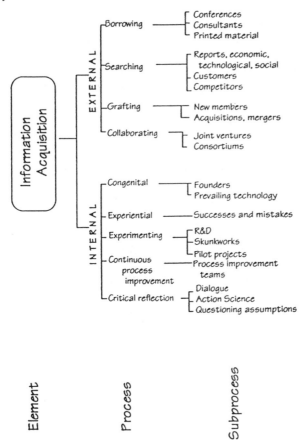

Figure 14.1. Information Acquisition

organization's tasks (Morgan & Ramirez, 1983), and deliberately creating experiments (Bedeian, 1986; Hedberg, 1981); implementing continuous process improvement (Hayes, Wheelwright, & Clark, 1988) and attending to feedback on incremental change (Bedeian, 1986); and critical reflection—that is, deliberately questioning organizational assumptions and norms (Argyris, 1990).

Hedberg (1981) notes that there is not a one-to-one correspondence between the real world and an organization's map of the world. Information, whether it is acquired from an external source or generated internally, is subjected to perceptual filters, made up of the organization's norms, procedures, and beliefs, that influence what information the organization attends to and ultimately accepts. Daft and Weick (1984, p. 287) identify two key dimensions that affect how an organization relates to its environment: "(1) management's beliefs about the analyzability of the external environment, and (2) the extent to which the organization intrudes into the environment to understand it." They also describe four interpretive modes based on the two dimensions of analyzability and intrusiveness: *enacting,* in which the organization intrudes into the environment to create information in what is presumed to be an unanalyzable environment; *discovering,* in which the organization is equally active but assumes the environment is analyzable and therefore employs formal search processes to identify correct answers; *undirected viewing,* in which the environment is assumed to be unanalyzable and the organization takes a passive stance, relying on informal data such as hunches and chance opportunities to provide needed information; and *conditioned viewing,* in which the environment is assumed to be analyzable, and the organization uses routine, formal data generated by information systems that have developed over the years.

The process of acquiring information is not unidirectional; the organization may have an impact on the environment and vice versa. Daft and Weick (1984, p. 287) note that search processes "may shape the environment more than the environment shapes the interpretation." Botkin, Elmandjra, and Malitza (1979, p. 48) maintain, "While all other creatures are forced to permanently adapt themselves genetically to the changing environment, humanity has begun to adapt the outside world to its own needs."

Acquiring and generating information is not always intentional. Much information is obtained as a by-product of an organizational action that is taken for some other purpose. For example, Pucik (1988) notes that strategic alliances, which may be developed for the purpose of reducing capital investment or lowering risks associated with entry into new markets, can be a major source of learning for the organization. Pucik advocates that rather than accepting such learning as fortuitous, the organization regard it as a deliberate and strategic part of such endeavors.

Human resource professionals can assist the organization by identifying for management the learning consequences of strategic decisions that may increase or diminish opportunities to acquire information. As Pucik (1988) has noted, this may be of particular relevance for strategic decisions the organization makes related to alliances and joint ventures. He has identified a number of human resource strategies that he considers critical to maximizing learning in such situations:

1. Human resources should get involved in the early planning stages of the strategic alliance.
2. Learning should be built into the partnership agreement, with responsibilities for learning specified.
3. The venture should be staffed to facilitate learning.

4. The organization should not give away to the partner the control of the human resource function. There is a temptation to give up control, particularly when the venture is in the partner's territory.

5. The learning strategies of the partner need to be monitored to gain understanding about their direction.

6. The organization needs to reward learning activities by transferring expatriates into critical positions.

Badaracco (1991, p. 14) has said, "Strategic decisions are not only choices about the allocation of resources, but also about what a company will learn, what core skills it will build, and the extent to which it will do so on its own or through alliances." Human resource professionals can provide this perspective.

HRD professionals can also assist the organization with information acquisition by assessing the use the organization makes of the many external and internal sources of information available to it. It is helpful to identify which sources the organization focuses on and which it neglects. Daft and Weick (1984) provide a useful framework for that assessment.

Distribution and Interpretation of Information. Daft and Huber (1987) summarized two prevailing views of organizational learning, the systems-structural perspective and the interpretive perspective (see Figure 14.2).

Systems-Structural Perspective. The systems-structural perspective of organizational learning views information as messages and is therefore concerned with amount, frequency, and distribution. Information is distributed within organizations in order to decide what actions to take, to relay those decisions, to impart implementation information, and to convey progress and results (Huber, 1982). Huber (1991) suggests that wide distribution of information within an organization leads to more broadly based organizational learning. Cantley (1980, p. 21) goes so far as to say, "Where the information flows, so does the potential for learning."

There are, however, factors that limit the distribution of information. One factor that has an obvious impact on the extent of distribution is cost. A second factor is the cognitive capacity of the receiving unit, which, if limits are exceeded, will result in information overload. Two processes are used to manage the problem of information overload, message routing and message summarizing (Daft & Huber, 1987). Message routing is the selective distribution of information. Message summarizing is the reduction of message size without changing the meaning; for example, reducing large sets of numbers to averages.

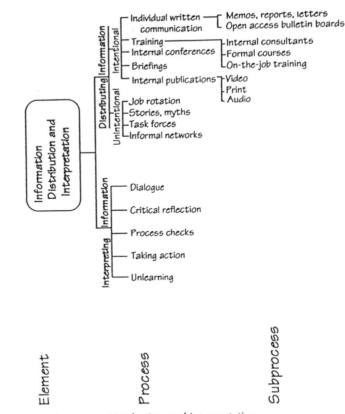

Figure 14.2. Information Distribution and Interpretation

Two additional processes that affect information distribution are message delay and message modification. Message delay may occur because of the priorities of the sending unit, or for other reasons that do not necessarily carry a negative implication. Message modification is the distortion of meaning, which might occur intentionally or unintentionally. These four processes affect the availability, form, accuracy, and meaning of information in the organization. They have been the subject of considerable empirical study and are well documented in the organizational communication literature (Huber, 1982). However, most of the studies have been at the individual level; thus their impact on organizational learning is, for the most part, determined by analogy rather than investigation.

Interpretive Perspective. The interpretive perspective of organizational learning emphasizes the equivocality of information. This view is well articulated by Weick (1979), who holds that meaning is created, not interpreted: "The manager literally wades into the swarm of 'events' that surround him and actively tries to unrandomize them and impose some order" (p. 148). Thus, a given event may be interpreted in numerous different ways by organizational participants. From the interpretive perspective, the resulting ambiguity precipitates an exchange of views rather than the collection of additional data. "The essence of organizational learning is reduction of equivocality, not data gathering" (Daft & Huber, 1987, p. 9).

Daft and Huber (1987) suggest that the medium through which information is effectively managed differs in terms of the equivocality of the message. If the message is unequivocal, one-way mediums such as letters, reports, and regulations are effective. If, however, the message is subject to interpretation, then a richer medium, such as face-to-face communication, is more appropriate. "Rich media enable managers to construct a joint cognitive map and to resolve equivocality through discussion and rapid feedback that would be impossible if communication channels consisted only of letters, electronic mail, or other written or numeric documents" (p. 15). Thus Daft and Huber suggest organizations need two information systems, a logistical system to handle the distribution of information and an interpretive system that enables the parts of the system to come to agreement on the interpretation of information.

Based on the amount and the equivocality of the information, Daft and Huber (1987) construct four organizational learning modes (see Figure 14.3). In *self-designing organizations,* which have high equivocality and low information content, the learning emphasis is on assumption sharing, an interpretive approach. *Experimenting organizations* have high equivocality and high information content, creating the most demanding learning situation. Their learning emphasis is adaptive because they try to both define the environment and gather data about it. The *extended bureaucracy* has low equivocality and high information content. The learning emphasis is on developing an internal knowledge base that can guide action. The *traditional bureaucracy* has low equivocality and low information content. The learning emphasis is on institutionalized experience, a reliance on rules and records.

Increasingly, technology makes the wider distribution of information less costly and potentially more relevant to the specific needs of the end user (Zuboff, 1988). Computer conferencing capabilities provide a medium that is potentially rich enough to facilitate shared interpretation.

Tushman and Scanlan (1981) note that specialization within organizations increases the efficiency of information processing within a unit. But they see specialization as a double-edged sword because it also blocks information processing across unit boundaries. Idiosyncratic language and local conceptual frameworks work against the distribution of information across specializations—and thus the need for boundary-

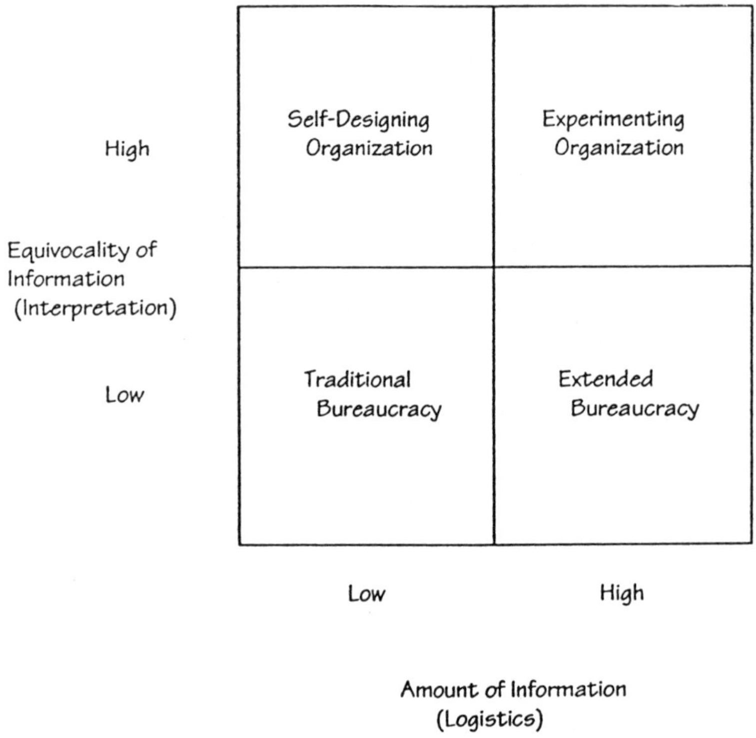

	Low	High
High	Self-Designing Organization	Experimenting Organization
Low	Traditional Bureaucracy	Extended Bureaucracy

Equivocality of
Information
(Interpretation)

Low   High

Amount of Information
(Logistics)

Figure 14.3. Model of Organizational Learning Modes
SOURCE: Adapted from Daft and Huber, 1987.

spanning individuals who are able to understand and translate the information and facilitate shared understanding across organizational boundaries.

This boundary-spanning role is one that human resource professionals often play in organizations by virtue of their cross-functional focus. It may be useful for human resource professionals to expand their role as translators and interpreters intentionally in order to facilitate information distribution in organizations.

Equally important could be HRD's role in acknowledging and helping to reduce the equivocality of information. It has long been accepted that cross-functional dialogue, which is highly valued by participants, occurs unplanned during training programs. HRD professionals could take responsibility for creating forums where fuzzy or conflicting issues might be discussed and equivocality reduced. Such forums would acknowledge the viability of varying viewpoints and make dialogue deliberate and legitimate.

Taking the systems-structural view, human resource professionals may want to analyze the distribution of information more thoroughly than a consideration of who gets what information would allow. Daft and Huber's (1987) concepts of message delay and message modification, as well as message routing and message summarizing, may provide a more comprehensive picture of what happens to knowledge within the organization. If Cantley (1980) is correct that the potential for learning follows the information flow, then an understanding of the distribution of information would be essential to implementing organizational learning.

Finally, Daft and Huber's (1987) construct of four organizational learning modes may be a useful framework that HRD professionals can use to examine the information distribution needs that are involved when an organization is attempting a change effort.

Making Meaning

In order to use information an organization must give meaning to it. The two perspectives described in the section on information distribution and interpretation, the systems-structural and interpretive perspectives, also lend insight into how organizations assign meaning to information. In the systems-structural view the organization attempts to understand the environment sufficiently to determine appropriate action, while the interpretive perspective holds that action itself leads to understanding (see Figure 14.4).

Systems-Structural Perspective. The systems-structural view uses the tools of rational analysis and extrapolation from past events to give meaning to information. March and Olsen (1976) provide a model that represents the systems-structural view. In their model, individuals take action, which precipitates an organizational action, which in turn creates an environmental response. The environmental response reinforces or alters the individual's beliefs, which in turn influence the individual's actions (see Figure 14.5). March and Olsen propose four situations in which the learning cycle is incomplete. The first situation is when learning is role constrained: "In this situation, everything proceeds in the same manner as in the complete cycle except that individual learning has little or no effect on individual behavior. The circle is broken by the constraints of role definition and standard operating procedures" (p. 57). The second is superstitious experiential learning: "The critical feature is that the connection between organizational action and environmental response is severed. Learning proceeds. Inferences are made and action is changed. Organization behavior is modified as a result of an interpretation of the consequences, but the behavior does not affect the consequences significantly" (p. 58). The third situation is audience

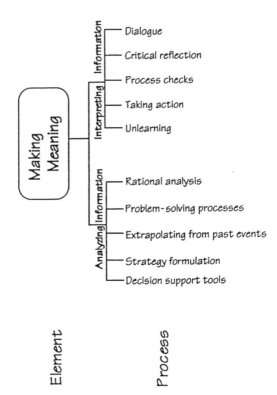

Figure 14.4. Making Meaning

experiential learning: "In this situation the connection between individual action and organizational action becomes problematic. The individual no longer affects (at least in an unambiguous way) organizational action. What he learns cannot affect subsequent behavior by the organization. . . . Much of our understanding of learning within politics or research falls within this situation" (p. 58). The fourth is ambiguity: "In this situation it is not clear what happened or why it happened. The individual tries to learn and to modify his behavior on the basis of his learning. In the simple situation, he affects organizational action and the action affects the environment; but subsequent events are seen only dimly, and causal connections among events have to be inferred" (p. 58).

The belief that an organization can learn from its experience is intuitively compelling. Evidence from the manufacturing literature indicates that as organizations gain experience in producing a product, cost and production time decrease. This concept of a learning or experience curve has been applied extensively within manufacturing organizations, and in the last ten years has been applied to such areas as accident

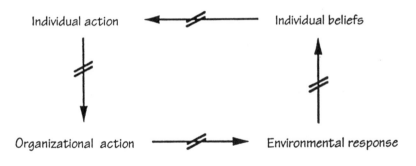

Figure 14.5. Organizational Learning Model
SOURCE: Adapted from March and Olsen, 1976.

reporting and warranty maintenance (Yelle, 1990). Its applicability to a more comprehensive theory of organizational learning has yet to be established.

Miles and Randolph (1980) note that while there is evidence that organizational learning occurs as a result of failure, there is less evidence that organizations learn from their successes. Cangelosi and Dill (1965, p. 196) concluded from their business simulation research that "failure . . . leads to change. The consequences of success . . . are less clear."

Taking the two views of making meaning, interpretive and analytical, it is clear that most HRD tools have focused on analyzing information. This, however, appears to be changing. Human resource professionals are introducing organizations to processes such as action learning, action science, and critical thinking (Dixon, 1990) to help them interpret their experiences.

From the analytical perspective, the model proposed by March and Olsen (1976) could be a useful conceptual framework for human resource professionals examining where organizational learning is incomplete. For example, is superstitious learning occurring? Does behavior have little impact on consequences?

HRD professionals may be uniquely situated to help the organization make meaning by facilitating learning from both successes and failures. Without the line responsibility that can bias honest reflection, human resource professionals may be able to gain a picture of what happened related to a critical decision or action and also uncover the supporting rationale.

Human resource professionals may themselves need to develop the tools of critical reflection if they are to assist others in this task. Argyris (1986) takes human resource professionals to task for reinforcing organizational defensive routines rather than helping organizations overcome unproductive assumptions.

Interpretive Perspective. From the interpretive perspective the meaning of organizational information is invented rather than discovered. A consequence of invented interpretations is that each individual arrives at his or her own unique interpretation, resulting in multiple explanations of a given phenomenon within the organization. "The thread of coherence that characterizes organizational interpretations is made possible by sharing of interpretations. Thus through this process of sharing, the organizational interpretation system in part transcends the individual level" (Walsh & Ungson, 1991, p. 61).

For equivocal information the sharing of interpretations is critical (Daft & Weick, 1984). Such sharing acts to reduce equivocality and thus leads to organizational learning.

Senge (1990) uses the term *mental models* to represent deeply held interpretations of information. Mental models are generalizations that have been inferred from past experience. They are reflected in the interpretation of current experience, and through that interpretation they influence the choice of actions. However, mental models that have become entrenched in the organization may prevent new learning and hinder constructive change. Janis's (1983) concept of "groupthink" describes the phenomenon of shared mental models that block the effectiveness of the group.

As Senge (1990) acknowledges, his conceptualization of mental models is based on Argyris and Schön's (1978) organizational theories of action. Argyris (1990) describes two kinds of theories of action that exist within organizations: espoused theories, which the organization is able to articulate and disseminate; and theories-in-use that organizational members cannot readily articulate, but which can be inferred from the actions individuals within the organization take. Both theories-in-use and espoused theories are collectively held among organizational members, but theories-in-use are held tacitly rather than consciously, making them unavailable for examination and challenge.

Argyris describes two levels of learning that occur in organizations: single loop and double loop. Single-loop learning results from the organization reflecting on the consequences of its actions when those consequences do not match the desired outcome. This mismatch leads the organization to modify the actions it takes. When an organization engages in double-loop learning, its reaction to a mismatch is to examine and perhaps alter the theories-in-use upon which the action was based. Argyris notes that most learning in organizations is single loop, but that double-loop learning is pivotal. Double-loop learning allows the organization not only to improve its performance but to improve its capacity to learn.

Weick (1979) uses the term *enactment* to indicate the reciprocal influence between organizations and their environment. In part, the

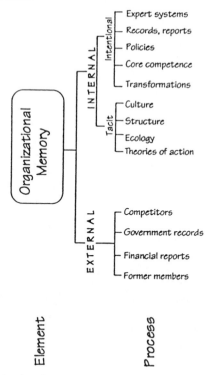

Figure 14.6. Organizational Memory

concept of enactment implies a self-fulfilling prophecy; that is, the perceiver tends to see what is anticipated. But the concept of enactment also suggests that the organization implants meaning and thereby creates the environment.

Organizational Memory

Walsh and Ungson (1991, p. 61) define organizational memory as the "stored information from an organization's history that can be brought to bear on present decisions." They identify five storage bins in which organizational memory resides: individuals, culture, transformations, structures, and ecology (see Figure 14.6). *Individuals* have their own memories about what has transpired—retained, for example, as knowledge, assumptions, beliefs, and cause maps. In addition, individuals maintain written records and files that aid their memories. *Culture* is a learned way of perceiving, thinking, and feeling about problems that is transmitted to members of the organization both purposefully and unintentionally. Culture is embedded in the myths, stories, language, and symbols of the organization. *Transformations* are the processes of the organization, ranging from the design of work itself to the budgeting process. Transformations are "the logic that guides the transformation of an input . . . to an output" (p. 65). *Structures* refer to organizational roles that differentiate tasks and control. Structures also refer to the design of the organization itself. *Ecology* is the actual physical structure of the work environment. Walsh and Ungson note that in addition to the five bins of organizational memory, organizational information is also stored externally in former members, government reports, and competitors' records.

Positive Impact. Organizational memory may have both a positive and a negative impact on organizational learning. A positive impact occurs because the retrieved learning of the organization can be brought to bear on new situations. Organizational memory can guide making sense of the overwhelming mass of information that occurs in any new situation by first, identifying what is important and second, reducing the number of possible explanations to a manageable size. Organizational memory provides a history of what has and has not worked and thus carries the potential for preventing the organization from making the same mistakes again and for providing tested solutions. In this sense organizational memory works as a sorting device for identifying successful practice.

Negative Impact. Organizational memory may affect organizational learning negatively to the extent that it predisposes how a situation will be viewed, automatically eliminating alternative explanations that might be more useful (Nystrom & Starbuck, 1984). Levitt and March (1988, p. 320) note that "the experiential lessons of history are captured by routines in a way that makes the lessons, but not the history, accessible to organizations and organizational members who have not themselves experienced the history." In so doing, the rules become inflexible and unchangeable because the information that could have determined the merit of the change is not available. Levitt and March also note that "a competency trap can occur when favorable performance with an inferior procedure leads an organization to accumulate more experience with it, thus keeping experience with a superior procedure too low to make it rewarding to use." Hedberg (1981) advocates unlearning as a necessary component of organizational learning. Unlearning is the intentional process through which the organization discards obsolete or misleading information.

The tools of critical reflection referenced earlier in relation to making meaning—that is, action science (Argyris, 1990), critical thinking (Brookfield, 1987), and uncovering organizational assumptions (Schein, 1985) —are equally pertinent to organizational memory. The purpose of such tools for organizational memory is to raise tacit knowledge to a level where it can be examined, challenged, and, if necessary, discarded.

If the concept of unlearning is taken seriously, HRD professionals who facilitate critical reflection that leads to unlearning may be as essential to organizational learning as those who design the process to acquire new information.

Human resource professionals may take on the responsibility of creating systems to collect the "lessons learned" of the organization. Such information could be placed in sophisticated relational data bases that allow full exploration of related issues. The design of such storage mechanisms is as critical a task for HRD as are the more human processes through which the lessons learned might be uncovered.

Retrieving Information

The retrieval of information may be either controlled or automatic (see Figure 14.7). Some measure of automatic retrieval is necessary to the smooth functioning of both individuals and organizations. That is, for an organization to function efficiently, much of what is learned must be so well learned that its retrieval is automatic, freeing the cognitive capacity of the organization for new learning. There remains, however, the major liability that automatically retrieved information is tacit and therefore unavailable for reflection or challenge (Argyris, 1990). Although necessary for efficient functioning, automatic retrieval can lead to errors of which the organization is unaware.

Walsh and Ungson (1991) note that retrieval differs for each of the five storage bins. The controlled retrieval from the memory and records of individuals may occur either through a single individual or through a collection of individuals who prompt each others' memories. Collective memories produce a more comprehensive picture even when the individuals involved have conflicting memories of the decision and consequences. Automatic retrieval of collective information occurs when situations trigger mental models (Senge, 1990), scripts (Gioia & Poole, 1984), and theories-in-use (Argyris, 1990). The retrieval of information from the culture bin is primarily automatic. It is, in fact, difficult for individuals who are themselves influenced by a culture to purposefully retrieve information from it. Schein (1985) suggests that an external perspective is needed to examine and challenge cultural information. The retrieval of information from transformations, structures, and ecology is also more likely to be automatic than controlled. Walsh and Ungson (1991) note that controlled retrieval from these bins tends to change the content of what is stored.

Weick (1979) cautions that the storage house image of organizational memory should not be taken literally. Concrete items are put into

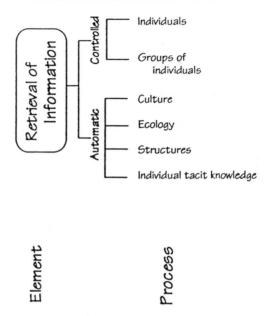

Figure 14.7. Retrieval of Information

a storage house with the intent to retrieve them at some later date, at which time they are assumed to be in approximately the same condition as when they were placed there. Information, however, does not function that way. In order to retain information, whether in an individual's memory, in records, or in one of the other bins such as culture or transformations, the information must be translated into symbols; that is, it must be changed. When information is retrieved, it is reconstructed from symbols and through this reconstruction is again changed. Thus, through the transformational nature of the storage and retrieval process, the normal disintegration of human memory, the impact of perceptual filters, and the loss of supporting rationales, information that is retrieved from organizational memory may bear little resemblance to what was originally stored. Weick (1979) suggests that decision makers should "treat memory as a pest" (p. 221) and attempt to discredit it. This skeptical attitude toward memory would cause managers to work to establish the predictive validity of retrieved information.

Given the extensive amount of information that faces all professionals, a critical need for organizations is to have knowledgeable people who can identify where specific organizational memories are located. For example, who knows about a particular issue or process? Who has been through it before? How does this situation compare to the one five years ago? HRD can play a role in identifying and tracking the location of pertinent information. Human resource professionals can also fill a second critical organizational need by designing processes to ensure that the retrieval of information occurs collectively so that a comprehensive picture is gained.

Summary

Organizational learning is a conceptual framework that holds considerable promise for improving organizational effectiveness in the 1990s. Over twenty years of literature on the topic have provided a rich theoretical foundation composed of five major elements: information acquisition, information distribution and interpretation, making meaning, organizational memory, and information retrieval. Each element can be further partitioned into processes and subprocesses, many of which have been identified in the literature.

HRD professionals are uniquely positioned to facilitate organizational learning because they are the recognized learning specialists. To succeed, however, they must design new learning processes rather than simply expand old methods. The literature on organizational learning can be extrapolated to suggest some of these needed processes. The key for human resource professionals is to reframe learning in order to meet the new challenges.

References

Argyris, C. (1986). Reinforcing organizational defensive routines: An unintended human resources activity. *Human Resource Management, 25*(4), 541-555.

Argyris, C. (1990). *Overcoming organizational defenses: Facilitating organizational learning.* Needham Heights, MA: Allyn & Bacon.

Argyris, C., & Schön, D. A. (1978). *Organizational learning: A theory of action perspective.* Reading, MA: Addison-Wesley.

Badaracco, J. L. (1991). *The knowledge link.* Boston: Harvard Business School Press.

Bateson, G. (1971). *Steps to an ecology of mind.* New York: Ballantine Books.

Bedeian, A. G. (1986). Contemporary challenges in the study of organizations. *Journal of Management, 12*(2), 185-201.

Bennis, W., & Nanus, B. (1985). *Leaders: Strategies for taking charge.* New York: Harper-Collins.

Botkin, J., Elmandjra, M., & Malitza, M. (1979). *No limits to learning.* Elmsford, NY: Pergamon Press.

Brookfield, S. D. (1987). *Developing critical thinkers: Challenging adults to explore alternative ways of thinking and acting.* San Francisco: Jossey-Bass.

Cangelosi, V. E., & Dill, W. R. (1965). Organizational learning: Observations toward a theory. *Administrative Science Quarterly, 10,* 175-203.

Cantley, M. R. (1980). *Who learns what? A conceptual description of capability and learning in technological systems.* Laxenburg, Austria: International Institute for Applied Systems Analysis.

Daft, R. L., & Huber, G. P. (1987). How organizations learn: A communication framework. *Research in the Sociology of Organizations, 5,* 1-36.

Daft, R. L., & Weick, K. E. (1984). Toward a model of organizations as interpretation systems. *Academy of Management Review, 9*(2), 284-295.

deGeus, S. P. (1988, March/April). Planning as learning. *Harvard Business Review*, pp. 70-74.

Dixon, N. M. (1990). Action learning, action science and learning new skills. *Industrial and Commercial Training, 22*(3), 10-16.

Duncan, R., & Weiss, A. (1979). Organizational learning: Implications for organizational design. *Research in Organizational Behavior, 1,* 75-123.

Fiol, C. M., & Lyles, M. A. (1985). Organizational learning. *Academy of Management Review, 10*(4), 803-813.

Gioia, D. A., & Poole, P. P. (1984). Scripts in organizational behavior. *Academy of Management Review, 9*(3), 449-459.

Hayes, R. H., Wheelwright, S. C., & Clark, K. B. (1988). *Dynamic manufacturing: Creating the learning organization.* New York: Free Press.

Hedberg, B. (1981). How organizations learn and unlearn. In P. C. Nystrom & W. H. Starbuck (Eds.), *Handbook of organizational design* (pp. 8-27). London: Oxford University Press.

Huber, G. (1982). Organizational information systems: Determinants of their performance and behavior. *Management Science, 28*(2), 138-155.

Huber, G. (1991). Organizational learning: The contributing processes and the literatures. *Organizational Science, 2*(1), 88-115.

Janis, I. L. (1983). *Groupthink: Psychological studies of policy decisions and fiascoes* (2nd ed., rev.). Boston: Houghton Mifflin.

Jemison, D., & Sitkin, S. (1986). Corporate acquisitions: A process perspective. *Academy of Management Review, 11*(1), 145-163.

Levitt, B., & March, J. G. (1988). Organizational learning. *Annual Review of Sociology, 14,* 319-340.

Lundberg, C. C. (1989). On organizational learning: Implications and opportunities for expanding organizational development. *Research in Organizational Change and Development, 3,* 612-682.

March, J. G., & Olsen, H. P. (1976). *Ambiguity and choice in organizations.* Oslo, Norway: Universitetsforlaget.

Marsick, V. (Ed.). (1987). *Learning in the workplace.* New York: Croom Helm.

Meyer, A. D. (1982). Adapting to environmental jolts. *Administrative Science Quarterly, 27,* 515-537.

Miles, R. H., & Randolph, W. A. (1980). Influence of organizational learning styles on early development. In J. R. Kimberly & R. H. Miles (Eds.), *The organizational life cycle: Issues in the creation, transformation, and decline of organizations* (pp. 44-82). San Francisco: Jossey-Bass.

Morgan, G. (1988). *Riding the waves of change: Developing managerial competencies for a turbulent world.* San Francisco: Jossey-Bass.

Morgan, G., & Ramirez, R. (1983). Action learning: A holographic metaphor for guiding social change. *Human Relations, 37*(1), 1-28.

Normann, R. (1985). Developing capabilities for organizational learning. In J. M. Pennings & Associates (Eds.), *Organizational strategy and change: New views on formulating and implementing strategic decisions* (pp. 217-248). San Francisco: Jossey-Bass.

Nystrom, P. C., & Starbuck, W. H. (1984, Spring). To avoid organizational crises, unlearn. *Organizational Dynamics*, pp. 53-65.

Perelman, L. (1984). *The learning enterprise: Adult learning, human capital and economic development.* Washington, DC: Council of State Planning Agencies.

Peters, T. (1988). *Thriving on chaos.* New York: Knopf.

Prahalad, C. K., & Hamel, G. (1990, May/June). The core competence of the corporation. *Harvard Business Review*, pp. 79-91.

Pucik, V. (1988). Strategic alliances, organizational learning, and competitive advantage: The HRD agenda. *Human Resource Management, 27*(1), 77-93.

Reich, R. (1987, May/June). Entrepreneurship reconsidered: The team as hero. *Harvard Business Review,* pp. 77-83.

Revans, R. W. (1980). *Action learning: New techniques for management.* London: Blond & Briggs.

Schein, E. H. (1985). *Organizational culture and leadership: A dynamic view.* San Francisco: Jossey-Bass.

Schön, D. A. (1979). Organizational learning. In G. Morgan (Ed.), *Beyond method: Strategies for social research* (pp. 114-127). Newbury Park, CA: Sage.

Senge, P. (1990). *The fifth discipline: The art and practice of the learning organization.* New York: Doubleday.

Shrivastava, P. (1983). A typology of organizational learning systems. *Journal of Management Studies, 20*(1), 8-28.

Simon, H. A. (1969). *The sciences of the artificial.* Cambridge, MA: MIT Press.

Stata, R. (1989, Spring). Organizational learning—The key to management innovation. *Sloan Management Review,* pp. 63-74.

Tushman, M. L., & Scanlan, T. J. (1981). Boundary spanning individuals: Their role in information transfer and their antecedents. *Academy of Management Journal, 24*(2), 289-305.

Vaill, P. (1989). *Managing as a performing art: New ideas for a world of chaotic change.* San Francisco: Jossey-Bass.

Walsh, J. P., & Ungson, G. R. (1991). Organizational memory. *Academy of Management Review, 16*(1), 57-91.

Weick, K. E. (1979). *The social psychology of organizing.* New York: Random House.

Yanow, D., & Cook, S. (1990). *What does it mean for a culture to learn? Organizational learning from a cultural perspective.* Paper presented at the Theory Workshop, American Society for Public Administration Conference, Los Angeles.

Yelle, L. E. (1990). The learning curve: Historical review and comprehensive survey. *Decision Sciences, 10,* 302-328.

Zuboff, S. (1988). *In the age of the smart machine.* New York: Basic Books.

IMPLICATIONS

Implications for HRD research, practice, and future inquiry regarding this article are discussed after Chapter 15.

Building the
Learning Organization

A New Role for
Human Resource Developers

Karen E. Watkins
University of Texas at Austin

Victoria J. Marsick
Columbia University

CHANGING WORKPLACE DEMANDS NOW CHALLENGE HUMAN RESOURCE
*developers to extend the scope of their practice from predominantly
one of training individuals, to one of facilitating learning of individuals,
teams, and organizations. In our work, we suggest that human resource
developers need an equally broad vision of the field in order to
embrace this broader scope. One such compelling vision which we
believe may drive a redefinition of the field is that of the learning
organization. The learning organization is defined both in terms of the
outcomes by which we assess whether or not the organization has
learned, and by the process by which the organization must change to
embed learning. A model of how the organization learns is given along
with design principles for human resource developers who would
create a learning organization.*

As we have conceptualized the field of human resource development,
we have explored the need for a shift from a reliance on behaviorism to

Source: Watkins, K. E., & Marsick, V. (1992). Building the learning organization: a new
role for human resource developers. *Studies in Continuing Education, 14*(2), 115-129.
Used by permission.

a broader, more transformative conception of learning (Marsick & Watkins, 1990a, 1990b), the need for a broader definition of the field of human resource development (Watkins, 1989), and differences and demands brought about by learning in the workplace which call for greater inclusion of informal and incidental learning strategies by human re- source developers (Marsick & Watkins, 1990a). In this paper we briefly revisit these ideas about the field of human resource development and then turn to a discussion of why we believe that the learning organization is an integrating vision for the field of human resource development. Our view of the learning organization and the consequent implications for the practice of human resource development will be presented.

Broadening the Conception
of Human Resource Development

It is clear from all of our work that we aim to open the paradigm of practice in the field of human resource development. This aim is in direct conflict with that of Nadler (1983) who hopes to clarify the field by rigorously defining it and categorizing what it is and what it is not; or the American Society for Training and Development through the McLagan (1989) competency study which defines the field by identifying eleven human resource roles and then limiting human resource development to three of them, which then further delimits the field through lists of competencies and skills of practitioners. Although we agree that such efforts to define a field are healthy and needed in an emerging field, these approaches have been informed by a behavioristic view of practice and a reductionistic bias (Watkins & Willis, 1991). Practitioners may special- ize in one or more areas of practice, but many, if not most human resource developers, do not find that their work falls neatly into one or more of eleven roles. Indeed, more often than not, a senior practitioner may have had job experiences in all eleven roles. Skills under these conditions must be broad. What is more important is a practice-based definition which may also provide a vision for the field. A definition which captures such a vision for the field of human resource development is found in Watkins (1989):

> Human resource development is the field of study and practice responsible for the fostering of a long term, work-related learning capacity at the individual, group, and organizational levels. As such, it includes—but is not limited to—training, career development, and organizational development. (p. 427)

This means that human resource developers are involved in facilitating or monitoring all types of learning in the workplace including formal, informal, and incidental learning. While the learner or client will vary from individuals to groups or departments to the entire organization, the professional mission of embedding an enhanced learning capacity or a learning-how-to-learn capacity will not. From the perspective afforded by this definition, the range of activities that human resource developers might engage in is vast.

This definition leads quite logically to the idea that human resource developers have a role as developers of the organization's learning system. A senior trainer for a multi-million dollar service industry described his role as "internal marketer." He said his role was to "sell" the organization's mission to the employees, to interpret and help to operationalize the chief operating officer's visions and dreams, and to embed the norms and values that characterize his organization's unique culture. He developed a video sharing the organizational saga—the critical turning points in its history, the vision of the founding fathers, and the current heroes who now carry the torch that was lit the day the organization was founded. He worked with top level staff to develop corporate vision and mission statements. His primary training function was new employee orientation.

In many training departments, new employee orientation is often viewed as a distasteful task which is relegated to new trainers. This trainer saw that new employee orientation was the pressure point for embedding the organizational culture. Done well, it could produce employees who know from the start what the organization stands for and how they can be a contributor to the mission. It can give them a sense of being part of something larger than themselves that is worthwhile, something worthy of their loyalty. It can also allow them to make an informed choice about whether or not this organization is one to which they want to make a long-term commitment. In this organization, new employee orientation became not just a means to share rules and procedures, but rather a means to enhance the long-term learning capacity of the organization by producing employees who know how to focus their learning and work on organizational needs and, potentially, by reducing turnover so that the wisdom accumulated by these employees stays in the organization allowing the organization to grow as they do. This is the kind of thinking about one's task which we think characterizes effective human resource developers and which is consistent with this definition of the field.

Human resource developers have either moved in this direction or become, as Knowles (1986) predicted, logistics arrangers; scheduling conferences, handling outside consultants who can do these things, or managing resources like film libraries or packaged courses. We would not expect that training would be immune to the paradigm shift attendant on a society as a whole moving into an information age. Human resource developers may find that they must either become expert at nonprogrammable learning strategies, or they will design or manage preprogrammed, technologically-delivered learning strategies.

In Watkins's definition, it is the outcome of one's efforts as a human resource developer that is stressed rather than the processes used to get there. Many means are possible, and in fact desirable. This definition asks human resource developers to increase individual learning as well as the overall learning capacity of the organization by enabling individuals to be more effective continuous learners, groups to identify and overcome barriers to collective learning, and organizations to create structures and a culture for continuous learning.

In this instance, the role of the human resource developer is really more of enacting a vision. This requires continual reshaping and creativity. Results can be measured in terms of the enhanced learning effectiveness of individuals, groups, and organizations. It is precisely because our vision of human resource development is both broad and yet goal-focused that we see the learning organization as a natural evolution of the field. Human resource developers who are systematically and developmentally increasing the learning capacity of the organization are creating learning organizations.

Theories of organizational change and development, the contributions of developmental stage theory and career development theory add to the knowledge base of the human resource developer. It is when human resource developers attempt to integrate learning strategies, particularly informal and continuous learning strategies, with a larger organizational change objective such as total quality management, that this merger of educational and organizational development roles becomes operational.

One reason this vision of the field is more vision than practice is that human resource development is seldom strategically positioned to influence the organization as a whole. Carnevale, Gainer, and Villet (1990) believe that training should already be at the corporate planning table but note that it seldom is.

> Ideally, the ascension of training to the upper regions of the organizational planning process results when top decision makers elevate and actively integrate it into the decision-making process, or when training is a vital thread in the institutional infrastructure, so that its omission from strategic management discussions would be unthinkable. In most U.S. organizations, however, neither of these ideal situations exist. . . . Therefore, trainers can either take action to move training into the strategic realm or accept the reality of continual service as a fire fighter. (p. 216)

We agree and believe that a broader conceptualization of the field will enable human resource developers to take action to create this strategic alignment.

Toward the Learning Organization

In the field of human resource development, we have long sought to define who we are in order to clarify what it is that we do that is unique. Ours is an applied field and therefore one that necessarily draws on many disciplines. Gradually, scholars are beginning to claim a niche that is distinctive. We think that the concept of a learning organization is one such niche for human resource developers as it brings together the two primary foci for this field: learning and the workplace context in which it occurs. Figure 15.1 illustrates the type of knowledge that we think human resource developers should seek in research and practice.

The learning organization is an evolutionary stage of thinking about workplace education in the United States. Early efforts to systematize training after World War II focused on simple procedures for developing behavioral skills for several reasons. Work procedures were standardized in an industrial economy, allowing for little deviation from desired routines. The workforce was not highly educated, so people could not easily be asked to use independent judgment or to perform complex operations. Training became skill-oriented and systematic to meet these needs. But the workplace has changed dramatically, while learning approaches have not kept pace. The information age demands judgment, autonomy, and complex thinking from the shop floor to the manager. While there is a large group of functional illiterate workers, the workforce on average is more highly educated and able to perform complex operations. The learning organization provides a home for new thinking about old educational needs, but it goes beyond that as well because it links individual learning with organizational learning. In many ways, organizational learning is a metaphor for understanding how systems change. Organizations do learn through individuals, but only when that learning is socially constructed, shared, and used to make a difference in larger social units or subdivisions of the organization, or more typically in the entire organization. In fact, learning organizations are characterized by total employee involvement in a process of collaboratively initiated, collaboratively conducted, collectively accountable change directed toward shared values or principles. Individuals work together to learn how to become a new entity.

The idea of the learning organization is one that has captured the interest of scholars for some time. We here review those scholars whose work informs ours in order to determine the nature of the learning

WORKPLACE	LEARNING
• How do you create a learning culture in an organization?	• What is different about learning in the workplace?
• What is it about the organization that enhances or thwarts learning?	• How is learning enhanced in the workplace?
• How do we systematically develop an organization over time as a learning system?	• How do we systematically design learning for maximum personal, career, and organizational learning and development?

Figure 15.1. Conceptualizing HRD: The Nexus Is the Learning Organization

organization and implications for this field. Those who write about the learning organization or about organizational learning emphasise either a conception of learning as process or product. The sections which follow classify various theories of the learning organization along these two dimensions. We begin with the metaphor of organizational learning.

Organizational Learning as Product

In a product definition of learning, we define learning by its outcomes. Learning has therefore occurred when a learner has changed either by acquiring new knowledge, skill, or attitudes. In a product model of organizational learning, the organization has learned when it has developed better systems for error detection and correction; changed the mental models of its members to a new way of doing business; changed its organizational memory by changing some part of how we encode memory (the management information system, the budget, policies and procedures, etc.); unlearned old ways of thinking; or has learned how to capture and encode knowledge latent in experience. Each of these types of learning are described below.

Learning as Error Detection and Correction. Argyris and Schön (1978) define organizational learning as that which occurs when "members of the organization act as learning agents for the organization, responding to changes in the internal and external environments of the organization by detecting and correcting errors in organizational theories-in-use, and embedding the results of their inquiry in private images and shared maps of organization" (p. 29).

The approach to organizational learning advocated by Argyris and Schön is action science. The intellectual roots of action science can be traced both to Dewey's ideas of reflective thinking and learning from experience and problem solving and to Kurt Lewin's approach to uniting theory and practice, that is, action research, which is based on the scientific method.

Argyris and Schön (1978) are interested in improving practice over the long term by enhancing the organization's ability to detect and correct unconscious error. They believe that no one ever sets out to deliberately create error, but despite their best efforts, errors occur and often recur persistently. Argyris and Schön suggest that a gap occurs between the formulation of plans and their implementation, a gap of which individuals are often unaware and which they therefore cannot eliminate even when they try. They describe this gap as the difference between espoused theories and theories-in-use. Simply put, espoused theories are what individuals or organizations say or think they do, while theories-in-use are what they actually do. One reason for the difficulty in correcting errors is that individuals and organizations do not dig deeply enough into the underlying values governing actions. This kind of deeper analysis is difficult because governing values are often taken-for-granted.

Argyris and Schön borrow the notion of single-loop and double-loop learning to explain the difference between surface causes and governing variables. Single-loop learning works well in most ordinary situations where assumptions about cause and effect are correct. Double-loop learning is needed when expected results are not achieved. At the organizational level, double loop learning involves a challenging of the assumptions, values, even the vision and mission of the organization.

Argyris and his colleagues attempt to create a learning organization by first working with key individuals, typically top management, to examine tacit theories-in-use which prevent learning in the organization. They alone among scholars of the learning organization have a transformative learning theory which calls for a change in the fundamental way in which individuals relate—from a unilateral, control-oriented manner, to one in which mutual, collaborative learning is the dominant value. Argyris and Schön have developed a model of organizational learning which involves a systematic set of tools to change people's embedded defensive routines which now prevent substantive change. Unfortunately, Argyris and Schön do not believe that they have yet created or observed what they would call a learning organization.

Defensive routines are stubborn, in people and in organizations. Perhaps the severity of this model, its all or nothing depiction of an organization as either Model I (closed) or Model II (open), makes it almost impossible to achieve when human nature so readily slips into Model I behavior. Consider the following cliches:

"There's many a slip twixt cup and lip."
"The road to hell is paved with good intentions."

"He talks the talk, but doesn't walk the walk."
"Do as I say, not as I do."

This gap between thoughts and actions is found in cliches because it is a fundamental problem of human nature. Argyris and Schön's (1978) approach is particularly useful for detecting error and for helping people change their mental models of how the organization should function. It is certainly the best approach we have found for detecting and attacking the root problems which impede learning at the organizational level. Their approach may not be sufficiently robust to help the organization correct the learning system, but it launches organizations into the most important change arena—the mental models of organizational members.

Changing Mental Models. DeGeuss (1988) said that "institutional learning begins with the calibration of existing mental models" (p.74). The only competitive advantage organizations of the future will have is their manager's ability to learn faster, to continually revise their mental models of the world. For example, DeGeuss defines "institutional learning, which is the process whereby management teams change their shared mental models of their company, their markets, and their competitors" (p. 70).

One way in which planners helped Shell Oil Company prepare for changes in oil prices in 1984 was through creatively "playing" with Shell's possible responses to different oil price scenarios. Planners used games to involve managers in creating and playing with various models. Consultants interviewed people, came back to management with a model of what they found, and used that model as a springboard to play with ideas, sometimes using computers. Computer models had several advantages. They allowed people to play with a few key variables at a time, to see how effects could be caused by events that took place much earlier than people would imagine, and to find out what information is relevant in a particular situation. The models helped people make their tacit thinking explicit: "When people play with models this way, they are actually creating a new language among themselves that expresses the knowledge they have acquired" (p. 74). Changing mental models is a significant component in the design of a learning organization.

To Shrivastava (1983), mental models are usually embodied in some way in the organization's management information system or its decision support system. According to Shrivastava, attempts to enhance the learning characteristics of organizations have traditionally advocated design and development of management information systems which he calls designed learning systems. By contrast, his research led to the conclusion that evolutionary learning systems and socio-cultural learning norms may explain the frequent *failure* of designed learning systems. To the extent that organizations have embedded norms which suppress learning, designed learning systems are often less effective.

Technology has certainly made possible extraordinary new ways for people to work together, to handle information, and to learn. Technologically-based strategies are not likely to work if there is a flaw in the ability and willingness of the organization to adapt and respond to the information generated by technology. A learning organization changes people's thinking and uses technology to create alternative futures, to connect people throughout the organization at all levels and in all places, to make information available at the point of action, and to make systemic problem solving viable.

Capturing Knowledge From Experience: Organizational Learning as a Change in Organizational Memory and Capacity. An emphasis on capturing knowledge gained from experience is central to the work of James March (March & Olsen, 1975; Levitt & March, 1988). Organizations learn by encoding inferences from history into routines that guide behavior. These routines are both formal (forms, rules, procedures, policies, strategies, technologies or work processes) and informal (culture, beliefs, paradigms). Changes in these routines constitute a measure of the learning of the organization. Some might argue that a policy and procedure manual in a learning organization is the kind of thing that one might want on an electronic bulletin board—readily changeable and accessible to all. What is routine is the process of changing policies and procedures, rather than the procedures themselves.

March and his colleagues find that the ambiguity of learning from experience leaves what is learned highly influenced by the limits of individuals. Individuals have differing patterns of interaction, degrees of trust, degrees of integration, and orientations to events which influence what is learned. Theories of learning which focus on changing belief structures need to incorporate individuals' tendency toward logical inconsistency and unpredictability. What has been learned in the organization can be determined by examining formal and informal routines, but changing what has been learned is a trickier business since people tend to be irrational.

March and Olsen further define the limits of individual and organizational rationality which impede organizational learning. They suggest that a theory of organizational learning must take into account information exposure, memory and retrieval; learning incentives, belief structures and their micro development in organizations. In other words, organizations, like people, learn only if information becomes sufficiently salient or relevant for them to become aware of it. Like people, they are limited in their capacity to store and retrieve information, and subject to biases which may lead to storing inaccurate information. Experience may or may not lead to learning. A learning organization has to create systems which help managers test the accuracy of their assumptions about the lessons of experience. Finding ways to both surface and capture the knowledge latent in experience is an important feature of a model of a learning organization.

The product conception of organizational learning allows us to operationalize and ultimately to measure an organization's movement toward different types and levels of organizational learning. Those interested in the process of designing an organization that can learn take a process perspective.

The Process of Designing a Learning Organization

Some organizational scholars focus on learning as a continuous process which is highly unlikely to be achievable in any sustained or transformative fashion. In their view, there are no learning organizations, but only organizations in the process of becoming learning organizations. The emphasis in these scholars' work is on the learning process, on creating a culture that supports continuous learning as opposed to the more outcome-oriented or summative depiction of learning at the organizational level implicit in the concepts presented of organizational learning. One such scholar of the learning organization is Peter Senge.

The Fifth Discipline (1990), by Peter Senge, Director of the Systems Thinking and Organizational Learning program at the Massachusetts Institute of Technology Sloan School of Management, outlines five disciplines that lead to an organization with not simply an adaptive capacity but with generativity—the ability to both adapt and also to create alternative futures. Senge envisions an organization characterized by continuous learning and the ability to "run experiments in the margin." He suggests that the total quality movement in Japan has been the first wave in building learning organizations.

Systemic thinking is critical to generative thinking. Systems thinking is the fifth discipline; it is the glue that holds the others together. The other four disciplines are: developing personal mastery with an emphasis on clarifying a personal vision, having mental models which distinguish data from assumptions and which test assumptions, building shared visions, and understanding the power of team learning. The problems we now face come from our early training to analyze and dissect and therefore both fragment our world and distance ourselves from the consequences of our actions. We lose our intrinsic sense of connection to a larger whole. He would destroy the illusion that the world is made up of separate unrelated forces in order that we may build learning organizations "where people continually expand their capacity to create the results they truly desire, where new and expansive patterns of thinking are nurtured, where collective aspiration is set free, and where people are continually learning how to learn together" (p. 3).

Senge, like Argyris and Schön, emphasizes metanoic learning, learning which is really a shift of mind. When you ask most people to describe their most significant learning experience, they will usually describe what some call "real learning." Real learning occurs less and less in schools. It is characterized by a kind of aha! and a congruence of intention, action, and affect. There is a leap, a sense of having experienced something "real"—not "dead" or book learning—something that transforms who we are and changes how we act. It is this type of learning which Senge believes is at the heart of a learning organization.

Senge's vision of a learning organization closely parallels ours. Unlike Senge, however, we focus our attention on the nature of continuous learning at the individual, team, and organizational levels, on building organizational capacity to adapt and change, and we are deeply interested in the implications of the learning organization for changing the nature of practice in human resource development, while Senge focuses exclusively on the role of managers and leaders.

Another model of the learning company which is also quite compatible with ours is that developed by Pedler, Boydell, and Burgoyne (1988). These authors define the learning company as "an organization which facilitates the learning of all of its members and continuously transforms itself in order to meet its strategic goals" (p. 92). The authors emphasize that this requires a major emphasis on training but not training as we now understand it. Rather, training is developmentally conceived to enhance the generic problem-solving capacity of the organization through individual and organizational self-development. Learning is viewed as the key developable and tradeable commodity of an organization. Work tasks are the primary learning vehicle.

> The Learning Company is one in which learning and working are synonymous; is peopled by colleagues and companions rather than bosses, subordinates and workers; where both inside and outside are continuously searched and examined for newness—new ideas, new problems, new opportunities for learning. (p. 94)

When we look at the differing views which scholars have presented of how organizations learn, we have been struck by how few really depict the learning process and how unclear it is what will be different in a learning organization. One model which appears to us to both define how the organization learns *and* to characterise the outcomes of this learning process is that developed by Alan Meyer (1982).

Building Organizational Capacity to Learn

Meyer developed a model of the learning organization based on his study of hospitals in northern California. He had completed field observations of each hospitals' corporate strategies when the doctors went on strike. A malpractice insurer dropped 4,000 California doctors and offered to reinsure them as individuals at a 384% increase and surgeons and referral physicians supported the strike. Nothing like this had ever happened before. It was clear that organizations would have to learn new ways of responding to the "jolt." Since Meyer had collected a great deal of information about each hospital's strategy, it seemed likely that he would be able to predict how they would respond.

Based on earlier work by Argyris and Schön (1978) and others on the nature of organizational learning, Meyer developed a model of the organizations' responses to the jolt as depicted in Figure 15.2. In it, a jolt or surprise triggers a learning cycle. This is interpreted through the organization's theory of action. The theory of action is a combination of strategy (the organizations' overall approach to its environment) and its ideology (the beliefs, mission, and values which drive action). Strategy and ideology determine cues in the situation to which the organization will pay attention and determine the warp and woof of its response. The response is influenced by structure, that is, the system of relationships in the organization; and slack, that is, the available human, financial, and technological resources to use in responding to the shock. While ideology and strategy shape action, slack and structure constrain the possible options.

In his research, Meyer found two kinds of outcomes to a learning event—the organization would either absorb the impact of the jolt without changing in any fundamental way, or it would retain new practices or information gained during the change experience: Further, he learned that strategy and slack help organizations absorb the shock of jolts, but lead to change which occurs only incrementally and within the same framework (first order change or single loop learning). Slack gives the organization the cushion it needs to absorb the impact while strategy tends to lead organizations to a consistent way of framing problems. Meyer termed the outcomes of the organizations' responses as either resilience (the shock was absorbed and the organization returned to its old ways of functioning) or retention (the organization used the lessons learned in the strike to change the way it selected and interpreted information and therefore how it would act in the future).

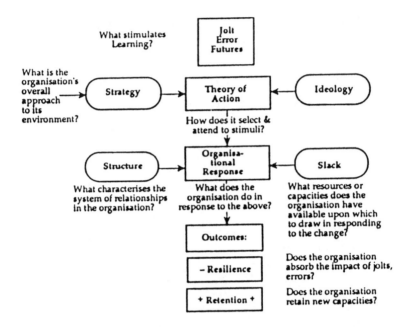

Figure 15.2. A Conceptual Framework for the Learning Organization

Retention responses were driven by ideology and structure. Occupancy, employment, and revenue declined least in those hospitals whose ideologies:

- encouraged surveillance of the environment
- fostered strategic reorientations
- embraced organizational changes
- valued members' capabilities
- encouraged participation

Entrepreneurial strategies and adaptive, participative ideologies therefore enhanced learning, while formalized, complex structures retarded learning. Structures which decentralize decision making therefore enhance learning. Slack contributed less to learning, though Meyer (1982) found that organizations which invested in people and technology learned more than those who invested in capital reserves or control systems. Jolts or crises "infuse organizations with energy, legitimize unorthodox acts, and destabilize power structures" (p. 533).

Meyer's findings help explain why continuous learning strategies alone are not sufficient to create a learning organization. If people are learning continuously, the overall skill threshold of the organization improves, and a greater degree of slack is created in the learning system. As a result, the capability of the organization to respond to change and to act more skillfully (with total quality) improves. Yet, the organization as a whole is only doing "as before, but more." The organization must also be able to change itself fundamentally, which it can only do by changing the beliefs or mental models of its members. It is through ideology and structure that the organization is able to see new relationships and to change the framework through which the organization works. Ideology shapes the responses of the organization and structure constrains its responses. By changing the ideology and/or the structure, you can transform the organization.

A jolt or a surprise triggered the learning cycle in Meyer's research. Other scholars have suggested that a learning cycle is triggered in the organization by new experiences (March & Olson, 1988), by the detection of error or a mismatch between what was intended and what was produced (Argyris & Schön, 1978), by the gap between current reality and one's vision (Senge, 1990), and by designing future scenarios. It is the gap between current reality and vision that is the source of the creative tension which produces learning. At the organizational level, we would expect to see the gap between the organization's goals and their enactment as a source of tension which produces learning. Argyris, Putnam, and Smith (1985) suggest that the gap between what the organization says it believes (its values), and its actions suppresses learning and escalates the use of control strategies which then makes the gap undiscussable. Inconsistency may disorient, unfreeze, or destabilize a situation and stimulate learning, but it may also stimulate defensive maneuvers such as face-saving and cover up strategies which prevent or deter learning.

On the other hand, the current rate of change may be so great that organizations are in a constant state of inconsistency. In this scenario, learning how to absorb impacts, how to stay afloat in a sea of changes, to choose changes to retain, and to become expert at a consistent overall strategy may be equally valuable skills. Learning when to change, when not to; how to stabilize the organization in turbulent times; and how to create a clear direction and aim toward it amidst a typhoon are as important as learning how to become a different organization in order to respond to different times.

We conclude that organizations learn when they retain new skills or information, i.e., when they actually change. They increase their capacity to learn by making changes in the four systems which influence learning:

strategy, structure, slack, and ideology. All organizations learn. A learning organization is one which has an enhanced capacity to learn.

At the organizational level, the capacity of the organization to learn is enhanced through workplace literacy initiatives which change the threshold of skill in the organization. System-wide skills assessments and training strategically targeted to skill gaps are strategies which hold promise in enhancing the capacity of the organization to learn. Organizations which have a wide range of options for both recognizing and rewarding achievement, options for linking pay with individual and team needs and performance, as well as for funding learning, motivate continuous learning. Work redesign and experiments with self-directed or self-managed teams also may create the motivation to learn by making work challenging. Empowerment and employee involvement are also essential to change the structures which now prevent learning. Structures which encourage dependency lead to learned helplessness. Under these conditions, people do not try new things.

More collaborative structures enhance the organization's ability to learn. Boundary spanning in the form of building networks and collaborative endeavors rather than, as now, building one way communication, enhance learning. Slack is another key to whether an organization either has the capacity to learn or to change. An organization that has neither financial, technological, nor human reserves has no spare resources to learn or to try new things. One computer corporation we know of has had a philosophy group, a kind of internal think tank which continuously evaluated and rethought the mission of the organization. Market downturns have led to a questioning of the survival of this group. If it is eliminated, the capacity of this organization to transform itself will be diminished. Cuts in training threaten the body of new knowledge available in the organization. On the other hand, quality action teams with their technologies for problem solving greatly influence the available know-how in the organization for solving critical problems.

Lewin (in Argyris, 1952) wrote that learning is goal-directed behavior which requires "space of free movement." Education becomes a process of making space. Whether one is challenging existing prejudices, therefore making room for new beliefs; increasing an individual's ability to think abstractly or conceptually, thereby making space for theories and ideas which are broader, more able to "hold" and order large bodies of concrete, factual information; or teaching new skills, the net effect is that the individual has more room—"space of free movement"—to act and to think.

The ability to articulate and pursue a personal vision functions to trigger organizational learning. In total quality management, a cornerstone is "management by fact." Putting accurate data in the hands of everyone about current functioning along with a standard or benchmark of what is ideal (e.g., zero defects) creates a goal that can trigger learning. Space of free movement at the organizational level might be accomplished by learning to work collaboratively because it extends the organizations' capacity to achieve unified action on common goals/ problems. Learning to think systemically may also ensure greater space of free movement because this allows more individuals in the organization to have an accurate picture of the interdependence of the parts of the organization, the people, and the actions taken. Finally, the approaches with the greatest potential to enhance the space of free movement in the organization are those which empower all members of the organization. Autonomy is having the power to act on one's own initiative. Rigid structures constrain autonomy and collaboration, but so does the tacit belief system of the organization when it is control-oriented and philosophically authoritarian. A more democratic workplace could achieve this balance of collaboration and autonomy.

In short, the challenge and the excitement presented by the idea of the learning organization is that it calls on organizations to make good the promises of the past. Literature abounds calling for more open systems, for democratic workplaces, and for more participative, less authoritarian leadership. Despite numerous attempts to change organizations in these directions, the fundamental dynamic in the organization has changed little. A focus on learning necessarily challenges this. Learning occurs developmentally from the making of mistakes; to awkward hit and miss, trial and error achievement; to high performance. A zero defect culture where mistakes are high risk is highly unlikely to encourage learning. A climate of public humiliation and an atmosphere of criticism and punitive, subjective performance appraisal are also deadly for learning. Learning dies or is squelched in the little incidental moments when a quality team, for example, mentions a project tentatively and a top manager says that "it's already been done." Or, when a team suggests that one way to make managers more interpersonally sensitive is to "reward up" by letting employees nominate their managers for recognition awards, other management members of the team immediately say that this suggestion is outside of the scope of authority of the team. In each of these cases, learning is threatened.

Learning is opportunistic. Those who develop the sense of when they are in a "teachable moment" and when others have "shut down," make effective teachers. Those who know what the learner needs to know next or what words the learner must hear to comprehend in order to move along the developmental continuum are effective teachers/ coaches. What does this look like at the organizational level? Experiments in teaching managers to be facilitators, coaches, interpreters and guides hold promise. Strategies which empower, which enable bottom up movement and communication again make sense here since they create

Designers of learning organizations will need to:
- Focus on the essential elements:
  - Increase the overall learning threshold: Assess and enhance current capacity
  - Create an ongoing adaptive capacity: Embed holistic, systemic linkages between needs, work, and rewards
  - Build autonomy and empowerment: "space of free movement"

This means that human resource developers will be called on to
- Break the training frame
- Embed continuous learning strategies (learning groups, reading and study groups, learning labs with self learning materials available, on-line learning resources, desk top learning, etc.)
- Teach people how to learn from experience, to think systemically, to bend and to break frames
- Conceptualize and plan individual development as long term, multi-career, and as preparatory for multiple organizational futures
- Monitor and upgrade the overall knowledge/skill set of the whole organization
- Help people enact more participative, democratic workplaces and more autonomous environments
- Lead the organization's development toward a learning organization (and be able to measure its progress)
- Craft policies which make learning continuous, self-regulated, and autonomously funded

Figure 15.3. Design Principles for Learning Organizations

the possibility for everyone to become both teacher and learner. But most especially, what this looks like is a long term process of evolution. Strict, tightly controlled environments do not break free overnight. Figure 15.3 summarizes these strategies for building a learning organization.

Conclusion

In fact, organizations learn all of the time. Aren't they therefore learning organizations? What is it that this idea offers that has captured so many of our hearts and minds? We think that the idea of the learning organization brings together the fields of training, career development and organizational development into a single vision of the role of the human resource developer. It offers human resource developers the chance to invite the organization to embrace the deeper, more long term learning programs which we have always known were needed to effect any change in behavior that will create the organizational results desired. We think, in other words, that this idea has captured human resource developers because it may create the kind of leverage in the organization they have needed in order to be effective. Human resource developers have the opportunity to enter the board room, to help the organization see the way in which learning is intrinsic and essential to the achievement of organizational goals.

What then, finally, is a learning organization? A learning organization is one that has embedded a continuous learning process and has an enhanced capacity to change or transform. This means that learning is a continuous, strategically-used process—integrated with, and running parallel to, work—that yields changes in perceptions, thinking, behaviors, attitudes, values, beliefs, mental models, systems, strategies, policies and procedures. Learning is sought by individuals and shared among employees at various levels, functions, or units. As a result, learning is embedded in an organization's memory of past wisdom, current repertoire of beliefs and actions, and future thinking processes.

Learning can either be incremental, that is, focused on refinements to current strategy, or transformational, that is focused on re-creating strategy because people understand the organization or its work in new, fundamentally different ways. Learning that is incremental allows the organization to be more resilient to changes or jolts while learning that is transformative leads to retention of new responses. The learning organization is an exciting concept for human resource developers because it has the potential to expand their role to include not only changing the threshold of skills in the organization, but also to become partners in the transformation of the entire organization.

References

Argyris, C. (1952). An *introduction to field theory and interaction theory*. New Haven, CT: Yale University Labor and Management Centre.

Argyris, C., Putnam, R., & Smith, D. (1985). *Action science*. San Francisco: Jossey-Bass.

Argyris, C., & Schön, D. (1978). *Organizational learning: A theory of action perspective*. Reading, MA: Addison-Wesley.

Carnevale, A., Gainer, L., & Villet, J. (1990). *Training in America.: The organization and strategic role of training*. San Francisco: Jossey-Bass.

DeGeuss, A. (1988). Planning as learning. *Harvard Business Review, 66* (2), 70-74.

Fiol, C. M., & Lyles, M. A. (1985). Organizational learning. *Academy of Management Review, 10* (4), 803-813.

Heider, F. (1958). *The psychology of interpersonal relations*. New York: Wiley & Sons.

Levitt, B., & March, J. G. (1988). Organizational learning. *Annual Review of Sociology, 14,* 319-340.

March, J. G., & Olsen, J. P. (1975). The uncertainty of the past: Organisational learning under ambiguity. *European Journal of Political Research, 3,* 147-171.

Marsick, V. J., & Watkins, K. (1990a). *Informal and incidental learning in the workplace*. London & New York: Routledge.

Marsick, V. J., & Watkins, K. (1990b). Facilitating critical reflection. In M. Galbraith (Ed.), *Facilitating adult learning*. Malabar, FL: Krieger.

McLagan, P. (1989). *Models for HRD practice*. Alexandria, VA: ASTD Press.

Meyer, A. (1982). Adapting to environmental jolts. *Administrative Science Quarterly, 27* (12), 515-537.

Nadler, L., & Nadler, Z. (1989). *Developing human resources* (3rd ed.). San Francisco: Jossey-Bass.

Pedler, M., Boydell, T., & Burgoyne, J. (1989). The learning company. *Studies in Continuing Education,* 11 (2), 91-101.

Senge, P. (1990). *The fifth discipline: The art and practice of the learning organization.* New York: Random House

Shrivastava, P. (1983). A typology of organizational learning systems. *Journal of Management Studies,* 20 (1), 8-28.

Watkins, K. (1989). Business and industry. In S. Merriam & P. Cunningham (Eds.), *Handbook of adult and continuing education* (pp. 422-435). San Francisco: Jossey-Bass.

Watkins, K., & Willis, V. (1991). A critique of the *models for HRD practice*. In N. Dixon, & J. Henkelman (Eds.), *Models for practice: The academic guide.* Alexandria, VA: ASTD Press.

IMPLICATIONS FOR HUMAN RESOURCE DEVELOPMENT PROFESSIONALS

As Kramlinger (1992) stated, "In a learning organization, the role of training is to support the forces and methods that favor widespread, spontaneous learning. This means that the training function needs to be redefined" (p. 49). The articles by Dixon (Chapter 14) and by Watkins and Marsick strongly recommend that HRD professionals consider how their role might be reframed to address more broadly the learning and performance issues of the organization. For example, Dixon suggests that human resources professionals create systems to collect and disseminate the "lessons learned" of the organization. Much of what we read today about the future of training in the workplace predicts that classroom training will no longer be the primary delivery method. Instead we will see an increasing use of technologies and small group or on-the-job teaching/training strategies to foster individual, group, and organizational learning (*Training & Development*, 1994).

RESEARCH DESIGN AND METHODOLOGY

Although one might argue for experimental field studies to further the examination of HRD's role in organizational learning and its effects, there are other options that might prove even more fruitful in our quest to understand and reposition HRD within learning organizations. Dixon

(1991) described these as interventionist, historical, and case studies. Interventionist research would require that we study the organizations in which we are employed by following the form of action research or action science, where we are the "interventionist," observer, and recorder. By conducting historical research, we can learn more about how different organizations have succeeded or failed in implementing learning systems and what the role of HRD was in these processes. Case studies offer us the opportunity to study "the particularity and complexity of a single case, coming to understand its activity within important circumstances" (Stake, 1995). By conducting several case studies across organizations, we can begin extrapolating findings that fit across cases and inform us of the relative effectiveness and outcomes of various learning strategies.

Carefully constructed and thorough literature reviews, such as the one conducted by Dixon and the one included in this book, should also be pursued by HRD researchers and scholars. Because HRD's roots are interdisciplinary, the field would benefit greatly from literature reviews across disciplines on important HRD topics. As we continue to mature and evolve as a field, these reviews will help us both reflect on what we know and identify what we still don't know.

IMPLICATIONS FOR FUTURE INQUIRY

Both the Dixon and the Watkins and Marsick articles in this part create several research possibilities for HRD scholars. One area of research could focus on the effect of the different roles HRD professionals perform. How does the role of a "trainer" differ from that of a "learning and performance consultant"? What are the differential effects of these roles? Another area of research might focus specifically on the skills needed for "learning and performance consultants" versus the traditionally trained HRD practitioner. Dixon (1991) suggested that research should specifically investigate the processes that facilitate organizational learning, how these processes differ from other types of learning (e.g., social processes, technological information, values), the processes that increase the learning capacity of organizations, and the criteria for determining whether an organization has learned. All of these questions can and should be addressed by HRD researchers and scholars.

OTHER RESOURCES

Chawla, S., & Renesch, J. (1995). *Learning organizations: Developing cultures for tomorrow's workplace*. Portland, OR: Productivity Press.

Daft, R. L., & Huber, G. P. (1987). How organizations learn: A communication framework. *Research in the Sociology of Organizations, 5*, 1-36.

Dixon, N. (1991). Organizational learning. In R. Jacobs (Ed.), *Organizational issues and human resource development research questions* (pp. 23-31). Columbus, OH: University Council for Research in Human Resource Development, ED 334349.

Fiol, C. M., & Lyles, M. A. (1985). Organizational learning. *Academy of Management Review, 10*(4), 803-813.

Garvin, D. A. (1993, July-August). Building a learning organization. *Harvard Business Review*, 78-91.

Kim, D. H. (1993, Fall). The link between individual and organizational learning. *Sloan Management Review*, pp. 37-50.

Kramlinger, T. (1992). Training's role in a learning organization. *Training, 29*(7), 46-51.

Pedler, M., Burgoyne, J., & Boydell, T. (1991). *The learning company: A strategy for sustainable development*. London: McGraw-Hill.

Preskill, H. (1994). Evaluation's role in enhancing organizational learning: A model for practice. *Evaluation and Program Planning, 17*(2), 291-297.

Stake, R. E. (1995). *The art of case study research*. Thousand Oaks, CA: Sage.

Watkins, K. E., & Marsick, V. J. (1992). Towards a theory of informal and incidental learning in organizations. *International Journal of Lifelong Education, 11*(4), 287-300.

Watkins, K. E., & Marsick, V. J. (1994). *Sculpting the learning organization: Lessons in the art and science of systemic change*. San Francisco: Jossey-Bass.

CONCLUSION

Why Bother With Research?

They still cling stubbornly to the idea that the only good answer is a yes answer. . . . If they say, "Is the number between 5,000 and 10,000?" and I say yes, they cheer; if I say no, they groan, even though they get exactly the same amount of information in either case. —John Holt, *How Children Fail*

It is the peculiar and perpetual error of the human understanding to be more moved and excited by affirmatives than negatives. —Francis Bacon, *Novum organum*

Testimonials and success stories are extremely powerful. They give us evidence that something exists or that something works. Such testimonials are a *necessary* condition if the listener or the reader is to have some confidence in the truth of the statement. However, we should not be overly impressed, because such testimonials only suggest that something may be true. The problem is that such responses are not sufficient evidence of truth.

Gilovich (1991) pointed out that humans find it easier to deal with positive information. For example, rain preceded by cloud seeding provides a positive example of the effectiveness of cloud seeding. In contrast, rain preceded by no cloud seeding seems to yield little information. We view that second situation as only indirectly relevant to any argument about the use of cloud seeding to produce rain. In fact, such nonconfirming evidence provides a baseline against which to measure the effectiveness of cloud seeding. A third situation of no rain preceded by cloud seeding seems to provide another negative example and could be viewed as problematic. In fact, this last situation may yield evidence of some limitations to cloud seeding, or more specifically, of conditions in which cloud seeding may not prove effective.

The problem is that when we rely on positive instances only, we may see relationships that do not really exist. Lee (1980) describes examples of that predilection even among those considered "researchers." As one example, we can look at the famous Hawthorne studies. The standard version appears in piecemeal fashion in various textbooks, journals, and lay accounts.

According to that version, six relay assemblers from the Hawthorne plant of Western Electric Company were selected from the 100 employees in the main relay assembly department and placed in a separate experimental room. The researchers investigated the effect on productivity of a variety of changes in work scheduling such as rest pauses, lunch breaks, and overall hours per day and week. The research was divided into different experimental periods. The first period provided a baseline and consisted of the two-week period in the main room prior to selection. During this period, the assemblers produced about 2,400 relays per person per week. The second period provided another baseline, with the assemblers in the experimental room but without any other changes. This output remained about the same. In the third through the eleventh periods, various conditions involving money, rest periods, or hot snacks were introduced. In the last period, the assemblers returned to the original conditions. With each new condition, the researchers reportedly found increasing or stable output. Indeed, when the assemblers returned to the original, main room, they produced an all-time high of 3,000 relays per week per operator. The researchers explained that such increases could only result from the psychological and sociological climate changes resulting from social factors and friendly supervision. (See Mayo, 1960; Roethlisberger & Dickson, 1939; and Homans, 1941 for original accounts and Chase, 1941; Lindgren & Byrne, 1961; and Longnecker, 1973 for more popular versions.)

Omitted from most of the accounts of the experiment were several variables that could have had an important effect on the results. These included longer production runs, better set-up coverage, easier-to-assemble relay models, fewer differing models of relays to assemble, and relief from housekeeping activities. Indeed, in reanalyzing the data from the Hawthorne studies, Franke and Kaul (1978) concluded that most of the variance in output could be explained by such variables as managerial discipline (56 percent of the variance), work hours per week (24 percent of the variance), the Great Depression of 1929 (8 percent of the variance), rest time (8 percent of the variance), and the small group incentive (1 percent of the variance).

Reading the original text of the research helps to identify any potentially confounding variables or flaws that might exist. The research on accelerated learning that appears in this book provides one example. In this case, the original "research" consisted of reports of positive instances. The Swets and Bjork review of such reports led to some questioning of the effectiveness of the method. The Bretz and Thompsett comparison of the accelerated learning method with the lecture method confirmed that the accelerated learning method yielded little advantage. Thus the reason for investing in research is to provide more than success stories and testimonials. Well-designed and well-conducted research leads us to more complete answers to questions and to the generation of more questions.

Why Bother With HRD and With HRD Research in Particular?

The preindustrial economy valued human and animal labor as required components for economic success. During the industrial revolution, physical assets took on great importance for an organization. In the postindustrial information economy, human intellect, creativity, and innovation provide the basis for a successful organization. As a result, executives must manage this human capital to improve organizational performance through the development and delivery of needed products and services.

According to Quinn, Anderson, and Finkelstein (1996), this human capital, or the professional intellect of an organization, exists at four levels: (a) cognitive knowledge or the basic mastery of a discipline, (b) advanced skills or the ability to solve real-world problems, (c) systems understanding or the ability to solve complex problems and to anticipate unintended consequences, and (d) self-motivated creativity. All four levels exist within individuals but the first three levels can also reside in an organization's systems, databases, and technologies. Only the fourth level, that of self-motivated creativity, can be developed solely within individuals and in the organization's culture.

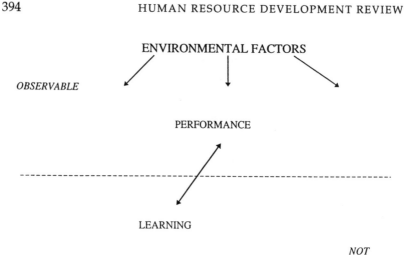

Figure 16.1. Relationship Between Learning and Performance

The HRD professional, as the "Chief Knowledge Officer" or CKO, or the "Chief Learning Officer" or CLO, can provide the tools and methods for managing the organization's human capital. However, to do so, this HRD professional must be aware of the relationships among individual learning and performance, team learning and performance, and organizational learning and performance.

What Are These Relationships?

Figures 16.1, 16.2, and 16.3 present an expanding model of these relationships. Figure 16.1 begins by showing that learning affects and is affected by performance. Those effects occur through feedback.

Torres (1994) suggested the importance of feedback for both learning and performance. Research articles in each part of this book point out the importance of feedback. For example, the improved generalization for those viewing the positive and negative video models, as described in the Baldwin study (Chapter 1), may result from the differential feedback resulting from those models. Similarly, the success of mental practice, as discussed in Swets and Bjork (Chapter 2), may result from feedback to the human system, even in the absence of specific physical movement. Driskell and Salas (Chapter 8) showed that using or not using feedback led to different team outcomes. Campion, Medsker, and Higgs (Chapter 6) found that workload sharing, communication, and cooperation within the group (all of which can be viewed

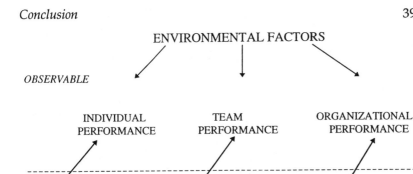

Figure 16.2. Feedback Between Performance and Learning in Individuals, Teams, and Organizations

as forms of feedback) were positively correlated with work group productivity. Dixon (Chapter 14) pointed out the critical role of feedback for organizational learning and performance: "Individuals take action, which precipitates an organizational action, which in turn creates an environmental response. The environmental response reinforces or alters the individual's beliefs, which in turn influence the individual's actions" (p. 359).

Figure 16.2 shows this model applied to the individual, the team, and the organization—a model that has been assumed in each of the parts of this book. Thus, individual learning directly affects and is affected by performance, with both effects occurring through feedback mechanisms; team learning directly affects and is affected by performance through feedback; and organizational learning directly affects and is affected by performance, again through feedback. All of these relationships are influenced by internal and external environmental factors, such as economic conditions, regulations and standards, and management practices and attitudes. The model implies that learning, whether individual, team, or organizational, cannot be observed; what can be observed is performance. In addition, the model shows that learning precedes performance initially, but performance can affect later learning.

Figure 16.3 expands this model to show the relationships among individual, team, and organizational learning and among individual, team, and organizational performance. According to this model, individual learning directly affects and is affected by team and organiza-

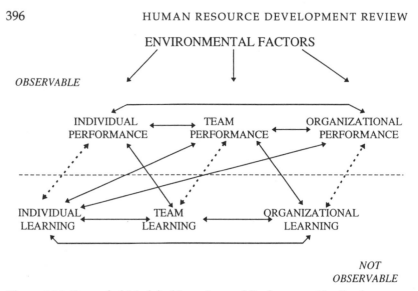

Figure 16.3. Expanded Model of Learning and Performance Feedback

tional learning, in addition to individual, team, and organizational performance. Similarly, team learning directly affects and is affected by individual and organizational learning and by individual, team, and organizational performance. Finally, organizational learning directly affects and is affected by individual and team learning, in addition to individual, team, and organizational performance.

We can use this last model as the basis for examining the relationships among the various research articles and themes presented in this book. The following brief paragraphs, rather than provide exhaustive analysis of these relationships and themes, offer suggestions for how individual, team, and organizational learning and performance interact and affect one another. Certainly, there is much here to provoke further study and analysis.

In Part I, we see that Baldwin (Chapter 1) provides positive evidence of some tools that affect individual learning and performance (in this case, the use of variability in behavioral models). Such tools might also prove useful in achieving team and organizational learning and performance. Similarly, the Rowe and Cooke article (Chapter 4) on mental models focuses on individual learning and performance. Perhaps we need to create and use such mental models to support both team and organizational learning and performance. Sternberg, Wagner, Williams and Horvath's (Chapter 5) notion of tacit knowledge could also be applied to teams and to organizations. Perhaps it is this tacit knowledge at all levels that distinguishes high-performing organizations.

The Driskell and Salas article (Chapter 8) from Part II shows that team learning and performance are dependent on individual learning and performance. Those individuals who learned to work collaboratively were able to work with others who had learned such collaboration and thus achieved superior performance. Presumably, the team learning and performance that followed would also affect organizational learning and performance. From Brooks (Chapter 7), we see that individual power (an environmental factor) affects team learning and performance; furthermore, the article by Campion et al. (Chapter 6) shows that the process characteristics of the team were most highly correlated with measures of team productivity. By extension, we can assume that individual power and process variables also influence individual and organizational learning and performance.

In Part III, the Nevis, DiBella, and Gould article (Chapter 11) demonstrates the importance of knowledge acquisition, knowledge sharing, and knowledge utilization for organizational learning. These same variables are critical for individual and team learning and performance. The Rouiller and Goldstein article (Chapter 13) shows the importance of the organizational transfer climate (an environmental factor). Such environmental factors affect learning and performance at the individual, team, and organizational levels.

We need a cautionary note here. Successful interventions at the individual and team level may or may not translate into improved organizational performance; structures and processes may facilitate or inhibit change from one level to the next. According to Druckman and Bjork (1994), "to date, methods have not been developed to follow changes through a system—from individual to group to organization" (p. 120). For example, the enhanced cohesion resulting from team-building activities may increase conflict between teams within an organization. These comments lead us to suggest the importance of examining these relationships over time. Only by following individuals, teams, and organizations over time can we identify and clarify the dynamics from a systems perspective.

What Are Some Next Steps for Practitioners and Researchers?

We encourage practitioners to use the research highlighted in this book to enhance their work. Many of the implications described in the material following each article can be applied immediately. As suggested in the introduction, the criteria listed on pages xvi and xvii and the questions listed on page 55 provide tools for reviewing and evaluating future research articles.

We hope that researchers consider further investigation into issues raised by these research studies. Such research will enhance both HRD practice and theoretical knowledge.

Finally, we recommend that the research and practitioner communities explore ways to promote the ongoing critical review of HRD research literature on a regular basis. Whether such reviews take the form of a traditional literature review or use a meta-analytic approach is not of great importance. What is important is the assembling of applicable research, a critique of the methodological strengths and weaknesses, suggestions for immediate application, and recommendations for future research. Such reviews will facilitate the advancement of both HRD practice and theory.

References

Bacon, F. (1960). Novum organum. In F. H. Anderson (Ed.), *The new organon and related writings*. New York: Liberal Arts. (Original work published 1620)

Chase, S. (1941, February). What makes workers like to work. *Reader's Digest*, pp. 15-20.

Druckman, D., & Bjork, R. A. (Eds.). (1994). *Learning, remembering, believing: Enhancing human performance*. Washington, DC: National Academy Press.

Franke, R. H., & Kaul, J. D. (1978). The Hawthorne experiments: First statistical interpretation. *American Sociological Review, 43*, 623-643.

Gilovich, T. (1991). *How we know what isn't so: The fallibility of human reason in everyday life*. New York: Free Press.

Holt, J. (1964). *How children fail*. New York: Pitman.

Holt, J. (1982). *How children fail* (Rev. ed.). New York: Delacorte.

Homans, G. C. (1941). *Fatigue of workers*. New York: Reinhold.

Lee, J. A. (1980). *The gold and the garbage in management theories and prescriptions*. Athens, OH: Ohio University Press.

Lindgren, H. C., & Byrne, D. (1961). *Psychology: An introduction to the study of human behavior*. New York: Wiley.

Longnecker, J. G. (1973). *Principles of management and organizational behavior*. Columbus, OH: Charles E. Merrill.

Mayo, E. (1960). *The human problems of an industrial civilization*. New York: Macmillan. New York: The Viking Press. (Original work published 1933)

Quinn, J. B., Anderson, P., & Finkelstein, S. (1996, March-April). Making the most of the best. *Harvard Business Review*, pp. 71-80.

Roethlisberger, F. J., & Dickson, W. J. (1939). *Management and the worker*. Cambridge, MA: Harvard University Press.

Torres, R. (1994). Linking individual and organizational learning. *Evaluation and Program Planning, 17*(3), 327-337.

AUTHOR INDEX

SUBJECT INDEX

ABOUT THE AUTHORS

DARLENE RUSS-EFT, Ph.D., is Division Director, Research Services at Zenger Miller, an international consulting, training, and education company headquartered in San Jose, California.

She is responsible for overall management of the research function at Zenger Miller, which includes services in research and evaluation and needs assessment. She has ongoing responsibility for consulting with clients about methods for measuring the effectiveness of consulting, training, or other interventions, management audits, and climate surveys. She also has responsibility for all corporate market and product research activities.

Prior to joining Zenger Miller, Dr. Russ-Eft was a Senior Research Scientist at the American Institutes for Research in Palo Alto, California. In that role, she was the principal investigator or project director on a variety of research projects. Before that, she was a Research Fellow at the Human Performance Center of the Department of Psychology, University of Michigan.

Dr. Russ-Eft is currently Adjunct Faculty Instructor at the University of Santa Clara, UC Berkeley, and UC Santa Cruz. She holds Ph.D. and M.A. degrees from the Department of Psychology at the University of Michigan, and a B.A. from the Department of Psychology at the College of Wooster.

An active member of numerous professional organizations, she is the author or coauthor of many articles and essays about research issues that have appeared in major journals. She is a speaker at both regional and national psychology and training association meetings. She is immediate past chair of the Research Advisory Committee of the American Society for Training and Development, a member of the Research Committee of the Instructional Systems Association, and a recently elected member of the board of the American Evaluation Association.

Zenger Miller, part of the Times Mirror Company, a Los Angeles-based media and information company, works with over 3,000 public and private sector client organizations worldwide.

HALLIE PRESKILL, Ph.D., is Associate Professor in the Organizational Learning and Instructional Technologies graduate program at the University of New Mexico, where she primarily teaches courses in Progam Evaluation and Instructional Systems Design.

Her consulting and research interests include program evaluation theory and methods, organizational learning and culture, and the transfer of learning. She has written several articles on the relationship between organizational culture and evaluation, the role of evaluation in HRD, and has recently coauthored (with Torres and Piontek) the book *Evaluation Strategies for Communication and Reporting: Enhancing Learning in Organizations* (Sage, 1996).

CATHERINE M. SLEEZER, Ph.D., works with organizations to address their specific employee training and performance needs. The many projects that she has successfully completed range from analyzing training needs for state judges to helping decision makers in manufacturing plants implement performance improvement systems to evaluating human performance needs related to new services and technology. As an assistant professor at Oklahoma State University, she conducts research and teaches courses in human resource development (HRD). Her presentations and published works focus on using HRD research and theory to improve the practice of workplace learning and performance.

LIST OF
CONTRIBUTORS

Timothy Baldwin, Indiana University

Robert A. Bjork, University of California, Los Angeles

Robert D. Bretz, Jr., Cornell University

Ann K. Brooks, University of Texas, Austin

Michael A. Campion, Purdue University

Nancy J. Cooke, New Mexico State University, Las Cruces

Elizabeth Cooley, Far West Laboratory for Educational Research and Development

Mary M. Crossan, University of Western Ontario, Canada

Anthony J. DiBella, Boston College

Nancy M. Dixon, George Washington University, Washington, DC

James E. Driskell, Florida Maxima Corporation, Winter Park, Florida

Irwin L. Goldstein, University of Maryland

Janet M. Gould, Organizational Learning Center

A. Catherine Higgs, Allstate Research and Planning Center

Joseph A. Horvath, Yale University